Federal Resume Guidebook

Strategies for Writing a Winning Federal Resume

FIFTH EDITION

Kathryn Kraemer Troutman

America's Career Publisher®

Federal Resume Guidebook, Fourth Edition

© 2011 by Kathryn Kraemer Troutman

Published by JIST Works, an imprint of JIST Publishing
7321 Shadeland Station, Suite 200
Indianapolis, IN 46256-3923
Phone: 800-648-JIST   Fax: 877-454-7839   E-mail: info@jist.com

Visit our Web site at **www.jist.com** for information on JIST, free job search tips, tables of contents, sample pages, and ordering instructions for our many products!

Quantity discounts are available for JIST books. Please call our Sales Department at 800-648-5478 for a free catalog and more information.

See the back of this book for information on ordering this book's resume samples on CD.

Trade Product Manager: Lori Cates Hand
Contributing Editor: Heather Stith
Cover Designer: Alan Evans
Interior Designer and Page Layout: Aleata Halbig
Proofreaders: Charles Hutchinson, Jeanne Clark
Indexers: Pilar Wyman, Jeanne Clark

Printed in the United States of America
16 15 14 13 12 11   9 8 7 6 5 4 3 2 1

Library of Congress Cataloging-in-Publication Data

Troutman, Kathryn K.
  Federal resume guidebook : strategies for writing a winning federal
resume / Kathryn Kraemer Troutman. -- 5th ed.
     p. cm.
  Includes index.
  ISBN 978-1-59357-850-3 (alk. paper)
  1. Civil service positions--United States. 2. Résumés
(Employment)--United States. I. Title.
  JK716.T73 2011
  650.14'2--dc22
                          2011010512

ISBN: 978-1-59357-850-3

Contents

Index of Resume Samples

Foreword

One of the advantages associated with the four decades I've spent working on federal workforce issues is that it becomes easier to put new developments into perspective. That's why I'm actually quite impressed with where the federal government is right now in its ongoing quest to create an effective, modern, and applicant-friendly approach to hiring. It's not that the government has yet achieved that goal—it hasn't—but it has made improving the hiring process a top priority and real progress is being made! This is good news for the American public. The daunting challenges facing our nation make attracting and hiring a highly talented workforce an absolute imperative for the federal government, and improving the federal hiring process will certainly help in that regard.

The news for potential applicants for federal jobs, however, is mixed. The good news is that it is slowly becoming easier to find and apply for a federal job. Further, with more than 80,000 federal employees retiring or otherwise leaving the federal government each year, there are many jobs that need to be filled. The less positive news for potential applicants, however, is that there will still be stiff competition for most of those jobs. And while the quantity of information that must be submitted to apply for a federal job is less than in previous years, the quality of that information may need to be higher in order to be successful. And that's where this fifth edition of Kathryn Troutman's *Federal Resume Guidebook* comes in.

Let me elaborate just a bit. To be sure, there have been other substantial changes in the federal hiring process over the last 40 years. For example, in the '70s almost all job candidates submitted their applications to the U.S. Civil Service Commission (which became the U.S. Office of Personnel Management in 1978) under a centralized approach to screening job applicants. Today, recruiting and examining is almost totally decentralized. Each federal department and agency has been delegated authority to recruit and assess job applicants for their positions. However, almost all of the changes that occurred prior to this time focused on the needs and administrative process requirements of the agencies. What is different now is that the focus has shifted to take into account the impact of the hiring process on the applicant. This shift is driven by an understanding that some of the best potential candidates for any job will simply not bother to apply if the process is too onerous, time-consuming, or lacking in transparency.

A memo dated May 11, 2010, from the President of the United States directed the heads of each federal department and agency to make substantial changes to their hiring process by November 1, 2010. The memo made it clear that those changes were to also make the process more applicant-friendly. For example, among the directed changes was the elimination of any requirement that applicants start the process by writing essay-style answers to questions about their relative knowledge, skills, and abilities (KSAs). Further, individuals must now be able to apply for a federal job by submitting a resume and cover letter or by completing a "simple, plain-language" application.

This is great for applicants, but it has created a challenge for at least some federal agencies. Those agencies that have been relying heavily on the information provided in the KSA essays to help guide their selections now need to find alternative ways to get the information they need. This means that the savvy job applicant has to find ways to make it as easy as possible for those federal agencies to find out everything they should know about their personal qualifications and their "fit" for the job. But they have to do that in a very concise format.

So—what's the savvy job applicant to do? Clearly, they will need to do their homework and pay close attention to the relevant details about the job and the application process contained in the announcement for each federal job in which they are interested. Simply submitting the same boilerplate resume and cover letter to every job one sees is not going to be nearly as successful as a carefully tailored response that speaks to the specifics of each job.

Finally, another action the savvy job applicant can take is to seek out those who have spent considerable time and effort in studying the federal hiring system and who have some helpful advice to offer. The really good news in this last regard is that if you are reading this foreword, you already hold in your hands (or are looking at on your screen) some really good advice on how to enhance your chances of being hired for a federal job. Kathryn Troutman has literally made a career out of understanding and tracking the evolution of the federal hiring system and translating that understanding into practical advice for the job seeker. The federal government and the public it serves have a vested interest in ensuring that federal jobs are carried out by highly talented, motivated employees. If you have the talent and an active interest in being one of those employees—I commend this book to your attention!

—John M. Palguta, Vice President for Policy, Partnership for Public Service

Acknowledgments

I am thankful for our clients, who teach us with every federal resume request how to write the best federal resume targeted toward a USAJOBS announcement in 3,000 characters. Your career challenges are our federal resume writing challenges. We do our best to follow every rule in this book to make sure the resume matches the announcement and stands out as Best Qualified!

The sample federal resumes in this book were contributed by real federal job seekers who were translating their skills into the USAJOBS federal resume. Thank you so much to Phyllis Day, Tim Shea, Angella Greaves, Greg Hall, Sonia Neblett, Louise Rubin, Lisa Casillas, Anlecta L. Kenney, Chris Troutman, David Raikow, and Harrell Watkins.

Thank you, RP writing team! The Resume Place Certified Federal Resume Writers are magicians and miracle workers with our career-change federal resumes. They are expert analysts, listeners, coaches, writers, and editors. They created the outstanding federal resumes in this book, which resulted in new federal careers for our clients.

Thank you to my government training coordinators who trusted me to teach their employees federal resume writing and ECQ writing. This book was used as a text in most of these federal resume and KSA writing and ECQ writing workshops throughout the U.S. and Europe. Special thanks to Joan Guidinas from HQ AFPC/DPIFDA, Randolph AFB; Glovinia Harris from USN CNREURAFSWA, Naples; Ron Rothberg from NAVSEA Workforce Development Branch; Kari Hurlburt, 19FSS/FSFR Section Chief, Little Rock AFB; Saundra R. Nichols, DAF, Airman, Family & Community Operations Branch, Directorate of Personnel Services, Headquarters Air Force Personnel Center; Kenneth Elstein, Organizational Change and Communications Specialist, U.S. Environmental Protection Agency, Office of Research and Development/ OARS; Dominique Mitchell, Government-wide Internship Programs, Department of Interior University; Scott L. Cromwell, Chief, DHS/FEMA, Distribution Center Frederick, Frederick, MD; Brigitte Keels, WASO Learning and Development, Washington, DC; Teresa Shipman, Army Community Service, Employment Readiness Branch Manager, Ft. Hood, TX; Lenora Challenger, NSWC PHD, Port Hueneme, CA; Venis V. Mathews, Training Coordinator, VA Health Eligibility Center, Atlanta, GA; Tamika Beverly, Patent and Trademark Office, Equal Employment Office, Alexandria, VA; Loretta Gladden, USDA–AMS, Washington, DC; and Sandra Smith from the BRAC Center, Arlington County, VA.

Thank you, CFJST Ten Step Trainers from Navy, AF, USCG, USMC, ANG, universities, and veteran's centers for believing in the curriculum for your customers! The Certified Federal Job Search Trainers and *Ten Steps to a Federal Job* trainers are my colleagues and help me follow all of the hiring reforms, hiring programs, and veteran/spouse challenges.

Thank you to my trusted federal human resources advisors, who answer my technical HR questions and support my research and development of the latest federal resume formats. Thank you to Ligaya Fernandez, John Palguta, Sandy Keppley, Susan Custard, Faith Skordinski, Phyllis Day, and CJ Johnson.

I want to thank The Resume Place, Inc.'s, Certified Federal Resume Writers, for their outstanding federal resume samples and bios. Also thank you to the RP client services and administrative team, including Bonny Day, Sally London, Zoey Troutman, and Chris Troutman, for taking excellent care of our federal job seekers and analyzing hundreds of federal resumes for clients. Thank you for your interpretation and caring about their job searches.

Thank you to my family for patience with the time it took to rewrite this book. My mother, Bonita Kraemer, who is 90 years old and still works part-time at The Resume Place, hopes that this will be my last book. Probably not.

Thank you to Lori Cates Hand and Heather Stith from JIST, who had amazing patience to edit and organize this complicated guide with dozens of samples, charts, keywords, and references. Thank you for your detailed and expert professional editorial help!

This book is dedicated to the current and future federal civil servants who provide safety and excellent services for the American public every day. Your accomplishments do make a difference to Americans!

About the Contributors

Author **Kathryn Troutman** is a federal resume expert and career consultant and government human resources career trainer with more than 30 years of experience in the specialized federal job market. She is founder and president of The Resume Place, a leading resume writing service in Baltimore that originated in 1971. A sought-after trainer of federal job seekers and HR professionals, Troutman has written ten career books and produces www.resume-place.com.

Marcie Barnard, IT Specialist Writer, Federal Resumes. Technical writer, document manager, and member of the publications staff of Sperry Corporation, she received a solid foundation in dealing with these military specifications. Marcie directed the work of 18 technical writers and editors and managed large commercial, government, and military projects. Marcie received a B.S. in early childhood education from the University of Maryland at College Park and an M.S. in health education and business administration from Towson University.

Sarah Blazucki is a chapter editor, sample designer, federal resume and private-industry resume writer, and Certified Federal Resume Writer. Ten years of experience in federal job analysis and career-change writing for mid-career and senior-level job seekers. Sarah served as a development editor and contributor to *Ten Steps to a Federal Job,* Second Edition; editor and proofreader for *The Student's Federal Career Guide, Federal Resume Guidebook* (Third Edition), and *Ten Steps to a Federal Job;* and resume sample developer and editor for *The Military to Federal Career Guide* and *Resumes For Dummies,* Fifth and Sixth editions. Sarah received her B.A. from Towson State University in mass communications, with a concentration in journalism. In addition to her work with The Resume Place, Sarah is also the editor of a Philadelphia newspaper.

Diane Hudson Burns is a career management strategist and career coach focusing on job-search-proofing. An international conference speaker and train-the-trainer coach on career-related topics, Diane specializes in composing quality career-change, military transition, private-industry, and federal resumes from mid-management (GS-12) to Senior Executive Service. She is an expert in writing SES and ECQ packages and in coaching clients to define their strengths, "tell their leadership stories" according the ECQ leadership competencies/requirements, and target ROI for employers. She has co-trained SES Development Leadership program candidates at the Naval Ship Yard at Capitol Hill, and Air Force Leadership, with Kathryn. Her resumes, cover letters, and case studies are published in more than 45 books and periodicals; she is a chapter author in *Federal Resume Guidebook,* Third and Fourth editions; case study author for *Ten Steps to a Federal Job,* Second Edition; and multiple case studies author for *Creating Your High School Resume,* Third Edition. She holds a bachelor's degree in journalism from California State Polytechnic University and a number of industry credentials: Certified Leadership and Talent Management Coach (CLTMC); Certified Professional Career Coach (CPCC); Certified Professional Resume Writer (CPRW); Certified Employment Interview Professional (CEIP); Certified Career Management Coach (CCMC); Certified Federal Resume Writer and Coach (CFRWC); Credentialed Career Master (CCM); and Job and Career Transition Coach (JCTC).

Rita Chambers is a Senior Executive Service Advisor and Certified Federal Resume Writer and Coach with more than 15 years of technical writing expertise. She is currently an active IT Project Manager in government and has extensive knowledge of project management and defense contracting. In her work for The Resume Place, Rita combines her technical background with outstanding writing skills. She is a master of the KSA and federal resume, and as a contributing writer, she addressed KSAs for *Federal Resume Guidebook.* As a hiring manager in commercial industry and federally related institutions, Rita has often been on the other side of the hiring process. As a result, she has a solid understanding of what managers are looking for. Rita has a Master of Science in Computer Science from Iona College in New Rochelle, NY, and a bachelor's degree from Agnes Scott College in Decatur, GA, with a double major in Philosophy and Education.

Jessica Coffey is a senior Resume Place writer, interview coach, Certified Federal Resume Writer and Coach (CFRWC), Certified Professional Resume Writer (CPRW), and Certified Employment Interview Professional (CEIP) with more than 15 years of experience providing career management strategies to all levels of government and private-sector employees. She established a formal interview coaching service that provides one-on-one interview training with clients and can include a mock interview. Jessica has been a contributing author and editor for three of Kathryn Troutman's books, *The Student's Federal Career Guide,* 2004; *Federal Resume Guidebook,* Third Edition, 2004; and *Ten Steps to a Federal Job,* 2002; and Joyce Lain Kennedy's *Resumes For Dummies,* Fifth Edition. Jessica received a B.S. in Business Management and a M.Ed. in College Student Personnel Administration (with an emphasis in Career Services) from Virginia Tech.

Amy Connelly is a seasoned professional with more than 14 years of providing resume writing services, and has progressive experience working in the pharmaceutical educational association, higher education, health care, federal government, and private-sector contracting environments. Amy has exceptional human resources, career expertise, and outplacement experience. She worked with IRS, DOI, and BPD employees providing career development and outplacement services, such as determining best-suited career choices and instructing employees on job application details and submission. As head of human resources for an association, Amy directed all facets of HR, including interviewing, selecting, and placing the best-qualified staff. Amy obtained her B.S. in Psychology from George Mason University and her MAIS degree—combining Business Management, Industrial/Organizational Psychology, and Employee Assistance Counseling—from GMU as well.

Jim Dalton is a former U.S. Navy Chief Petty Officer. Retired after 22 years of service, he went on to a 20+-year career working for well-known defense contractors, where he served as a systems integration and test engineer, technical writer and senior analyst. In his government career, Jim was responsible for gathering, drafting, updating, and finalizing documentation on voluminous training materials and program manuals. He successfully authored and edited several editions of the Mission Performance Report (MPR)—a highly technical, engineering-oriented document for a diverse client base, sent to more than 75 national and defense commands worldwide—and was recognized by his clients for the high quality and timeliness of his work. Jim has a master's degree in information technology from the University of Colorado and a bachelor's degree in business management from the University of Maryland.

Dottie Hendricks, trained and certified in federal human resources recruitment and selection, has written professionally for more than 30 years. She joined The Resume Place as a full-time writer and career consultant in early 2008 and has trained numerous job seekers in writing strategies. She also serves as a professional mentor and has written hundreds of federal and private resumes. Her real-world executive experience with a wide array of industries, associations, and government agencies has given Dottie a broad base of knowledge across many fields. Applying her 30 years of experience in high-level customer service, training, sales, and marketing in private industry allows her to utilize her keen skill in providing persuasive and easy-to-understand writing. Her private-industry experience includes business plans, budget and forecast justifications, operational and training manuals, customer and industry communications, and more. Dottie is a contributor to Kathryn Troutman's *Ten Steps to a Federal Job,* Second Edition, providing case studies of successful applicants.

Rod Jussim joined The Resume Place after about 20 years of work in TV network news. Rod was most recently a writer and producer for ABC News in New York. He previously worked for CNN Headline News, CNN International, MSNBC, and CNBC. He is a member of the Writers Guild of America and brings to The Resume Place a TV newsman's sense of how to use his writing to grab attention and keep it. Rod has a B.A. in Latin American Studies from The University of California Santa Cruz and an M.A. in Corporate and Organizational Communications. He has lived and studied in Mexico, the United Kingdom, and Israel. He is married and has four children.

Sandy Keppley comes to The Resume Place as a human resources professional with more than 25 years of solid experience as a manager, supervisor, team leader, and technical professional in the field of human capital management. Sandy began her federal career in the clerical field at one of the lowest levels, GS-2. Through years of diligence, self-improvement, and hard work, she recently retired as Director, Labor Employee Relations, at the Department of Labor, Washington, DC, at the GS-15 level. Her career spans various federal environments such as the Department of the Navy; Department of the Army (Fort George G. Meade, MD Garrison); Army Materiel Command (Army Research and Development); U.S. Army Corps of Engineers (Baltimore District and Corps of Engineers Headquarters in Washington, DC); and Department of Labor (Director of Labor Management Relations). Sandy is also a Certified Federal Job Search Trainer and teaches all facets of training offered by The Resume Place, to include Department of Defense training both domestically and internationally.

Lex Levin is a Certified Federal Resume Writer and uses his superior skills in research, writing, and analysis to help his clients succeed in the federal job search process. Lex is a confident analyst and editor and knows how to present his clients in the best possible light, thanks to his strong communication and interpersonal skills. Prior to joining The Resume Place, Lex worked as a private-sector consultant and public relations specialist in the foreign policy and medical/pharmaceutical fields, where he introduced and advocated complex policy and technological issues to a mass audience. Lex is also an experienced trainer and helps Kathryn Troutman teach her popular monthly "Ten Steps to a Federal Job" workshop. Lex has contributed sample resumes to the second edition of *Military to Federal Career Guide* (2010) and to *Federal Resume Guidebook,* Fifth Edition (2011). He earned a bachelor's degree in political science and a master's degree in international relations.

Nicole Schultheis serves as 2010–2012 President of the Maryland Writers' Association. She is an AV-rated attorney and former appellate clerk and trial lawyer with state and federal trial and appellate experience. She is a West author, having contributed a chapter on document discovery to a major litigation treatise. Nicole is also an experienced science writer, newsletter editor, and journalist with federal agency experience. Her articles have been published in *The Maryland Daily Record, Maryland Bar Journal, Maryland Journal of Contemporary Legal Issues,* and other professional and lay publications. Nicole holds a B.S. in Biology from the Massachusetts Institute of Technology and a J.D. from Boston University School of Law. She is a member of the Maryland bar.

Karen Silberstein is an experienced federal resume and KSA writer and coach. She came to The Resume Place with more than 12 years of professional writing experience and more than five years in educational publishing, designing and implementing training, education, and professional development programs. She also has experience in outreach and communications on Capitol Hill. Using her skills in writing, research, and analysis, Karen helps clients identify strengths and accomplishments to create competitive, successful resumes and present polished applications with superlative materials. Karen holds a Ph.D. from Columbia University in French literature. Prior to working for The Resume Place, Karen taught French language and humanities classes for more than 10 years to college students in New York City.

Carla Waskiewicz is an experienced Resume Place writer and has created federal application packages for federal and private-sector employees with a wide variety of occupational backgrounds and career interests. Carla has been a contributing writer for a number of Resume Place publications. She wrote the chapter on administrative positions for the *Federal Resume Guidebook.* Her administrative resumes are among the examples on the CD-ROM for this book. Her presentation format for administrative resumes is very popular, and it is used all over the country. Her resumes appear in two of Kathryn Troutman's latest books: *Creating Your High School Resume,* Second Edition, published by JIST, and *Ten Steps to a Federal Job,* Second Edition. A number of her private-sector resumes were selected for inclusion in the 2006 edition of *Resumes For Dummies* by Joyce Lain Kennedy. Carla is recognized by the Professional Association of Resume Writers and Career Coaches as a Certified Professional Resume Writer (CPRW) and has also earned the professional designation of Certified Federal Resume Writer and Coach (CFRWC). She earned her B.A. in Communications from Penn State University, and she has completed postgraduate work in business management at the University of Baltimore.

Brian Wolak is a seasoned technical writer with experience in marketing, communications, and management in his career with T. Rowe Price. As a communications and marketing specialist, Brian wrote on a variety of topics, including tax implications, investments, and legal matters. As a supervisor, he managed the work of up to 15 employees per department, working with various departments within the company. Brian has invaluable experience in the hiring process. He is a skilled interviewer from the perspective of a technical writer interviewing subject-matter specialists and of a supervisor interviewing potential employees. At T. Rowe Price, he developed a new and consistent approach to interviewing and hiring employees, created a guide for interviewers, and developed a packet for prospective employees to provide information on job qualifications and job expectations. Brian received his B.S. in English and Philosophy from Towson University and his M.A. in English from the College of Notre Dame of Maryland.

Introduction

The fifth edition of the *Federal Resume Guidebook* has three objectives: first, to teach you how to target your resume content toward a specific position; second, how to add accomplishments so your resume will stand out and hopefully get referred to a supervisor; and third, to help you format your content for the best readability for the USAJOBS resume builder.

President Obama's Hiring Reform—enacted on November 4, 2010—was exciting and resulted in a number of changes in this book toward the last minute.

Part 1 is all about successful writing strategies for the federal resume. Chapter 1 has a sample of a USAJOBS resume and a paper federal resume. Chapter 2, about what happens to your resume, is all new and was added because of Category Rating and Hiring Reform. Federal job seekers want to know how applications are scored and what happens to their federal resume. Chapter 3 introduces the highly successful Outline Format resume, which could be one of the most important things in the book. The federal human resources specialists really like this format because it is so easy to read and see the top skills they need for their jobs. Because of Hiring Reform, the KSAs are now proven in the resume with accomplishments. The federal resume samples in this book include KSA Accomplishments in the resume. The matching strategies and KSA accomplishments added into the federal resume can help you get Best Qualified and Referred. The keyword chapter is better and shorter than ever. Nowadays we are looking for 10 keywords for each announcement and resume. This entire section is a *must read* for anyone who wants a federal job.

Part 2 will help you write your federal resume with the best possible language. Being concise, positive, professional, and interesting is important in getting your federal resume read by both federal human resources specialists and supervisors. Chapter 8, "Researching the Agency's Core Competencies," is becoming more critical than ever. HR specialists and supervisors are looking for basic core competencies in their new hires, including customer services, creative thinking, and interpersonal skills. These competencies are important and should be included in your federal resume.

Part 3 is about the second part of the federal application. This section covers Knowledge, Skills, and Abilities narratives. Yes, the KSAs are supposed to be eliminated, but they are still written on the vacancy announcements, covered in the questionnaires, and even sometimes included in required narratives. KSA Accomplishments are critical to the success of your resume. In almost all cases, the total federal application should include the federal resume and a questionnaire. The questionnaire is a multiple-choice self-assessment of your skills. And with Hiring Reform, now cover letters are accepted along with your resume, questionnaire, and other documents. The cover letter needs to be persuasive, informative, and impressive.

Part 4 covers how to apply for federal jobs. We look at the language and instructions in the vacancy announcements and questionnaires. It's all about the details and following the directions. The federal resume is the critical application, but if you do not submit your transcripts, or submit them on time, you will lose consideration for the job. This chapter reviews the USAJOBS resume builder so that you know the character limits and what to expect.

Part 5 is written to inspire job applicants in certain occupational series. Each of the series we selected for the book has a certain challenge for writing. Scientists are challenged to write a resume that the human resources specialist *and* the expert hiring manager can understand. IT specialists do not think of projects or competencies. Contract specialists don't remember that they are negotiators and business representatives, and manage customer services. Administrative assistants don't give themselves enough credit. Management analysts analyze, give briefings, create Excel reports, write, and analyze programs for managers; this is a very popular job series in government. Engineers need help with describing specific projects and core competencies. Human resources specialists need to know that the Engineering series is technical and specific—and they are hiring!

Part 6 covers special applications for Senior Executive Service, DOD Priority Placement Program employees, military personnel who are seeking federal careers, and military spouses who would like to begin a stable federal career while accompanying their spouse around the world. And this edition includes a new chapter for federal job seekers with disabilities; this part gives excellent insight into using Schedule A to find positions with special accommodations that are targeted for people with disabilities. Each of the chapters in Part 6 includes an excellent sample federal resume to help job seekers see the writing strategies discussed.

Part 7 covers the all-important behavior-based interview. It is an amazing opportunity to be invited to the federal job interview. It is imperative that you get prepared and practice for the interview. The interview is a test and you will be scored. This requires practice. Chapter 27 gives you practice questions and ideas for the best answers.

Overall, this federal career text is dedicated to federal job seekers who are persevering, determined, and deserving of an outstanding career. Good luck with your applications and follow the directions! Thank you for purchasing this book and following the samples in it. The HR specialists will appreciate your effort when they are reviewing resumes.

—Kathryn K. Troutman, author, kathryn@resume-place.com

Part 1

Writing a USAJOBS Resume and Other Electronic Federal Resumes

CHAPTER 1

Successful Writing Strategies for Your Federal Resume

After the Federal Hiring Reforms, your federal resume will be more important than ever. The following memorandum from President Obama sets the stage for a revolution in federal resume writing.

Presidential Memorandum

The White House | May 11, 2010

Improving the Federal Recruitment and Hiring Process

Section 1. Directions to Agencies. Agency heads shall take the following actions no later than November 1, 2010:

(a) consistent with merit system principles and other requirements of title 5, United States Code, and subject to guidance to be issued by the Office of Personnel Management (OPM), adopt hiring procedures that:

(1) **eliminate any requirement that applicants respond to essay-style questions** when submitting their initial application materials for any Federal job;

(2) allow individuals to apply for Federal employment by **submitting resumes and cover letters** or completing simple, plain language applications, and **assess applicants using valid, reliable tools;** and

(3) provide for selection from among a larger number of qualified applicants by using the **"category rating" approach** (as authorized by section 3319 of title 5, United States Code), rather than the "rule of 3" approach, under which managers may only select from among the three highest scoring applicants.

Figure 1.1: The presidential memorandum on Hiring Reform.

What Is a Federal Resume?

A federal resume is the most important federal career document you can write. This resume is written to apply for a job with the federal government. The federal resume is usually three to five pages in length, which is longer than a typical business resume. The federal resume is a career document that must include certain information in order for you to be rated as Best Qualified for a position. Each generalized and specialized skill that you have developed in your career has to be written into the document.

A federal resume is not

- A functional resume
- A curriculum vitae
- A Transition Assistance Program private-industry resume
- A private-industry resume

Your Federal Resume Is Your Federal Application and Examination (and Sometimes the Interview, Too)

The federal resume is your application for a federal job. The federal resume is also an examination. Your federal resume will be assessed for your qualifications and skills, and possibly will be graded by the human resources specialist to determine the level of your qualifications. The federal resume could even be your job interview. On some occasions, supervisors make hiring decisions based only on the resume.

Now KSAs Are in the Resume

Now that the separate written narratives—KSAs, or Knowledge, Skills, and Abilities statements— will be eliminated, you will need to include them in the text of the federal resume. The KSA narratives formerly were Part 2 of the federal application (Part 1 is the Federal Resume). But now, the shorter-version accomplishments or "mini-KSAs" will be added right into the text of the resume.

The vacancy announcement instructions will stress the importance of adding accomplishments into the content of your resume.

We will show you many samples of how to cover the KSAs in the resume in later chapters.

Your Federal Resume Should Be Super-Specialized to Compete

Competition is growing for the federal jobs. In today's job market, hundreds and thousands of job seekers are sending resumes for federal positions. It's well publicized in the media that the federal jobs pay better, and benefits and retirement are better than in private industry. To stand out from among more competition, your federal resume has to be super-specialized for each position.

Here's how your federal resume can become a super-specialized federal resume:

- **Read the Occupational Groups and Families description of your target job.** Target your resume toward one occupational series at a time (or two at the most). But be careful to include the specialized experience and skills for each series in your federal resume.

- **Add your KSAs into the resume.** Because the separate narratives will be eliminated, now applications will ask you to demonstrate your KSAs in your resume. The KSAs to be added into your resume will be different for each vacancy announcement even if you are applying for generally the same types of jobs. Make your resume super-specialized by adding these KSAs right into the text of your resume in the Work Experience section to get the best score.

- **Highlight your Specialized Experience.** Human resources specialists are overwhelmed with resumes. Because they have so many resumes to review, they are looking for quick ways to eliminate you from consideration. You will want the initial human resources reviewer to see your specialized experience quickly. He or she will give you more consideration because your resume clearly demonstrates your qualifications. This could result in a better score on your federal resume (best scores are 90+).

- **Add keywords from the Specialized Experience section.** Change at least 10 to 20 keywords and phrases in your federal resume for each announcement so that the resume clearly hits the Specialized Experience. Find the keywords in the Mission, Duties, and Qualifications sections of the vacancy announcements.

- **Give examples to *prove* that you have the Specialized Experience.** Vacancy announcements will request examples, so you should include them in your federal resume. These examples are your Accomplishment Record; they use your past performance to prove that your future performance will be good.

- **If possible, add your Specialized Experience to the first page of your resume.** The most valuable real estate in your federal resume is the first page. If your last job or current job is your most relevant, list this one first.

- **Readability counts—add the Specialized Experience in the Outline Format.** Use all caps and spacing to help the HR specialist find this important specialized experience. If it's easy for busy HR specialists to read, that can help you get a better score and get referred.

Are You Qualified or Best Qualified?

Prove it in your federal resume. Your resume will be reviewed by the human resources specialist to see whether you have the qualifications for the position and a certain grade level. See Chapter 3, "Work Experience and the Outline Format," for what the HR specialist will be looking at when determining which candidates are Best Qualified. The time, research, writing, and editing you put into your federal resume should demonstrate your qualifications in a way that makes the human resources specialist rate your resume Qualified or Best Qualified.

The Difference Between Federal Resumes and Private-Industry Resumes

One of the biggest differences between a private-industry resume and a federal resume is the length. The federal resume includes longer and more detailed descriptions of your work experience so that the human resources specialist can ensure that you have performed work at the specific level of the job you are seeking. Table 1.1 is a comparison of the two resume types.

Table 1.1: Federal Resume to Private-Industry Resume Comparison

Private Industry	Federal Resume
One to two pages	Three to four pages
No specific description	Include specific qualifications for certain jobs and salary levels
Concise	Concise, but detailed and descriptive
Industry language	Announcement keywords and skills
Few acronyms	Fewer acronyms (for military or current federal employees)
Targeted toward corporate mission	Targeted toward agency mission
Profit focused	Budget focused
Striving to increase sales	Efficient service or program within a budget
Corporate mission driven	Agency, office, legislative, congressional, regulation, compliance, and rule driven
Compliant with corporate policies	Compliant with federal regulations, policies, and procedures
Performance analysis and quantitative	Also performance driven, with extensive qualitative analysis
Business analysis	Program and management analysis
Presentations	Briefings
Writing	Same
Technical details	Same
Customer focused	Same
Project based	Same
Recommendations and solutions	Same
IT database, systems management	Same
Communications skills	Same
Teamwork, team leader	Same

The four biggest differences between federal and private-industry resumes are outlined in the following sections.

Length and Readability

The biggest difference is the length of the resume. The federal resume is usually two times longer than the average private-industry resume. The reason for this difference is that the federal human resources specialists must see your skills, abilities, and experience written on paper. And now with the job market, unemployment numbers, and veterans applying for federal jobs, there are hundreds of federal resumes for each application. Our Outline Format is easy to read; it's fast with all-cap keywords.

April 1997 to Present   **Electronics Technician**
                                   Naval Surface Warfare Center Port Hueneme Louisville
                                   Detachment
                                   160 Rochester Drive   Louisville, Kentucky

Maintain and support electronic and computer systems and workload forecasting for the Electronic/Engineering Laboratory.

COMPUTER CUSTOMER SUPPORT: Configure portable personal computers, performed installation of four peripheral component interconnect (PCI) circuit cards, two synchro, and two Naval Tactical Data System (NTDS) Type E Low Level Serial (LLS) and Type A Fast Parallel in each. Perform installation and configuration of Windows XP Operating System on each portable personal computer.

ELECTRONIC TECHNICIAN: Support the acquisition and engineering efforts within the Mark 34 Gun Weapons System (GWS) Division. Plan, organize, and execute projects in development. Independently accomplish work assignments on systems and subsystems requiring solutions of both design and operational discrepancies. Coordinate with other technical personnel both within and outside the immediate work group to resolve difficult problems and to be a resource for the task group. Hazmat coordinator.

RESOLVED CONTROVERSIAL OR NOVEL PROBLEMS: Extensive knowledge of the MK 160 Gun Computer System (GCS) and MK 46 Optical Sight System. Valuable technical source for operational, maintenance, system integration, and engineering lab support. Resolved controversial or novel problems. High-level understanding of state-of-the-art hardware and software applications. Defined systems actions, security principles, methods and procedures for documenting resolutions. Updated problem-resolution databases. Performed troubleshooting and data analysis. Used communicative methods and techniques in order to receive, respond to, and ensure complete resolution of any inquiry. Documented actions taken and gave needed guidance or training to customers to prevent recurrences. Resolved complex problems.

Figure 1.2: Outline Format resume example.

Writing Style

The second biggest difference is the way you write a federal resume. The federal resume includes more details about your experience. See the difference between the following two resume sections, one from a private-industry resume and one from a federal resume, for MSW Social Worker, GS 11.

Private-industry sentence that does not give the federal HR specialist enough information:

Provide direct social services to over 400 homeless families within the San Antonio area. Assess students' and families' needs and assist them in accessing educational, medical, and other support services within the community. Provide counseling and crisis intervention for students and families. Monitor and track students' attendance and educational progress. Facilitate inter-district and out-of-district transportation services for over 200 students. Coordinate services with other campus inter-disciplinary teams to develop service plans. Advocate for students in order to meet their educational needs. Responsible in maintaining accurate and complete student records. Attend homeless conferences, advisory council meetings, and network with various districts and community agencies.

The federal resume sentence includes more details and descriptions of specialized experience.

Social Worker, February 2003 to Present
Southside Independent School District – Everyone Caring Program, San Antonio, Texas; Hours per week: 40; Supervisor: Marta Garcia 210 555-5555; May Contact: Yes

PROVIDE DIRECT SOCIAL SERVICES to a variety of individuals from various socioeconomic, cultural, ethnic, and educational backgrounds. Work under FEDERAL GRANT from McKinney Vento Homeless Education Assistance Act to serve over 400 homeless families per year, totaling 2,800 homeless families in the San Antonio area.

INDEPENDENTLY ASSESS STUDENT'S AND FAMILY'S NEEDS by addressing their physical, mental, social, and educational situation. Identify student and family problems, strengths, weaknesses, coping skills, and types of assistance needed. Formulate and implement treatment plan. Provide counseling and crisis intervention for students and families.

- Approximately 15 percent of my clients are homeless veterans and their families. I assessed emergency needs for a homeless single father and his two children who were living in their car. First I met with the father and evaluated the family's situation. I referred them to the transitional housing resources and to the San Antonio Housing Authority so that they could obtain more permanent housing. I contacted the school administrator and facilitated transportation with two different school districts in order to get the children back and forth to school. As a result of my ability to evaluate and assess their needs in the emergency situation, this father and his children were able to obtain temporary housing and apply for more permanent housing. The children's education was not disrupted, and they were provided transportation to and from school.

PROVIDE OUTREACH, ASSESSMENT, REFERRALS, AND CASE MANAGEMENT, demonstrating knowledge of the principles and theoretical concepts of social work. Assist students and families in accessing educational, medical, and other support services within the community. Make appropriate referrals to community and other agencies and coordinate services.

COMMUNICATE EFFECTIVELY AND PROVIDE PYSCHOSOCIAL TREATMENT TO PEOPLE FROM VARIED BACKGROUNDS, including people from the Philippines, Czech Republic, Germany, Guam, and Mexico. Obtain translators and coordinate other services for non-English-speaking clients.

MONITOR AND TRACK STUDENTS' ATTENDANCE AND EDUCATIONAL PROGRESS. Facilitate inter-district and out-of-district transportation services for over 1,400 students. Coordinate services with other campus interdisciplinary teams to develop service plans.

ADVOCATE FOR STUDENTS IN ORDER TO MEET THEIR EDUCATIONAL NEEDS. Responsible in maintaining accurate and complete student records. Attend homeless conferences and advisory council meetings, and network with various districts and community agencies.

ESTABLISH AND MAINTAIN EFFECTIVE WORKING RELATIONSHIPS with clients, staff, and representatives of community agencies. Educate staff and others in the community about available program services. Participate in weekly professional peer-review case conferences.

SERVED AS A FIELD INSTRUCTOR FOR SOCIAL WORK GRADUATE STUDENT (2006). Provided orientation and coaching. Demonstrated independent judgment and skill in utilizing supportive problem solving and providing guidance on crisis-intervention techniques.

Accomplishments:
- Developed highly effective homeless transportation database.
- Received consistently excellent evaluations for the past 7 years.

Figure 1.3: Federal resume sentences with more details and descriptions of specialized experience.

Keywords

The third biggest difference is the federal language and detailed descriptions of a skill or duty. You can read more about how to find and analyze keywords in Chapter 6. The keywords from the announcement and KSAs are in all caps here in the Outline Format.

AGRICULTURAL MARKETING SPECIALIST, GS1146 -12, Step 2   11/2004 – Present
United States Department of Agriculture   40 hours/week
1400 Independence Avenue, SW, S. Bldg.   Salary: $77,368/year
Room 3119, Stop 1030, Washington, D.C. 20250-1030
Supervisor: Bernie Kenneth (202) 555-5555, Contact me first

REVIEW, ADMINISTER, AND CLOSE FOOD AID AGREEMENTS
Demonstrate knowledge of Federal Acquisition Regulations and contract laws to perform reviews of agreement language and Logistics and Monetization (LOGMON) reports submitted by Private Voluntary Organizations (PVO) for the Office of Capacity Building and Development (OCBD) food assistance programs, including Food for Progress and Food for Education. Review budgets; compare reports to determine success of program.

• My role is combating world hunger. As an Agricultural Marketing Specialist, I helped enable the USDA to implement a $2.9 million food processing agreement with Zambia. I read the agreement language, closed the deal, reviewed report logs, and checked audits. I ensured proper shipping costs and fair prices. Despite logistical challenges and potential fraud, my awareness of details and procedures ensured that there were no major commodity losses.
• RESULT: The USDA food program successfully functioned in areas frequently plagued by hunger.

ANALYZE CONTRACT PRICE / COST DATA AND PROCUREMENT ACTIONS
As the lead for government-to-government food aid agreements, analyze data submitted by the governments of specific countries and Private Voluntary Organizations (PVOs) designated by the program. Review agreements for completeness and accuracy in keeping with the program's closure regulations. In addition, review tax certifications, lists of equipment valued at more than $50,000 purchased in host countries, and how assets will be disposed.

• I helped desperately poor people in the Third World. I supervised multiple agreements that funded micro- and mini-entrepreneurs through FINCA (Foundation for International Community Assistance). I negotiated and implemented deals to help fund family farms that needed to boost agricultural production. Funds also went to HIV patients, including many women who were primary breadwinners and caring for infants.

REPRESENT THE AGENCY AFTER ANALYZING ACQUISITION PLANS
Monitor and evaluate data to ensure that all objectives and criteria for measuring progress have been met, including amounts sold, distributed, bartered, lost or destroyed; budget, audit, reporting, and tax requirements; along with the results of the program. Provide success stories – written and pictures – to Public Affairs of unexpected outcomes for a program. The information is forwarded to Congress for a yearly report and snippets are posted on the FAS's website.

ANALYZE POST-AWARD PROCUREMENT ACTIONS
Determine cost-effectiveness and compliance with legal and regulatory requirements. Review compliance with Federal Acquisition Regulations for post-award compliance and administration.

REVIEW DOCUMENTS FOR CONTRACT COMPLIANCE
Evaluate documents and proposals for compliance with specifications and purchase descriptions. Review applicable clauses in contracting document notes provided by third party

---

Figure 1.4: Federal resume in Outline Format with all-caps keywords.

Accomplishments Will Represent Mini-KSAs

Since the separate written narratives will be eliminated, the short accomplishments (or mini-KSAs) should be added to the resume to demonstrate your knowledge, skills, and abilities.

FINANCIAL CONSULTANT & PROJECT MANAGER, 6/2005 to Present
CV Partners, Inc., Kreuzberger Assoc., and Ajilon Finance
San Francisco, CA
Annual Salary: $58.00-$65.00 per hour; Hours per week: 40-50
Supervisor: (name, phone, contact, y/n)

FINANCIAL / ACCOUNTING CONSULTANT to public, private, and nonprofit organizations for resolving complex business process, financial, and accounting issues. Lead and support projects to optimize performance; improve efficiency; enhance accountability and transparency; and strengthen financial and accounting process, procedures, and regulatory compliance. Recruited to projects through financial consultancy and staffing companies in San Francisco area.

SELECTED PROJECTS:

SENIOR ACCOUNTANT, Genentech, Division of Roche, 12/2009-Present: Preparing month-end-close journal entries and inventory reports analyzing write-offs and royalty-bearing stock. Providing audit support, including work papers and reconciliations, management reporting, documentation preparation, and integration-related tasks such as data review, SAP function testing, and account mapping for a Roche integration GL project.

SENIOR SEC REPORTING ANALYST, Autodesk, 1/2009-3/2009 & 10/2006-9/2007:
UTILIZED GAAP AND KNOWLEDGE OF FEDERAL SECURITIES LAWS AND ACTS to prepare financial statements and work papers for Forms 10-K and 10-Q and executive compensation disclosures for the annual proxy statement. Produced work papers substantiating disclosures for external auditors, SEC staff, and client review of stock-option-granting practices. Produced external financial reports for earnings releases.

- PROVIDED ASSISTANCE AND TECHNICAL ADVICE on SEC filings. Resolved accounting and disclosure issues. Assisted in interpretation and application of financial statement requirements.
- FACILITATED COMMUNICATION with management, staff, and external auditors. Worked collaboratively with SEC attorneys, HR, and payroll personnel to ensure compliance with expanded SEC rules and regulations and meet filing deadlines.
- RESULT: The review of stock-option-granting practice was approved. Filings were completed on time and in full compliance, and were error-free. Established detailed work papers for future use by staff.

Figure 1.5: Accomplishments in the resume.

OF-510 Federal Resume Chart: What to Include in Your Federal Resume

Job Information

- Announcement number, title, and grade(s) of the job you are applying for

Personal Information

- Full name, mailing address (with ZIP code), and day and evening phone numbers (with area codes)
- Social Security number
- Country of citizenship (most federal jobs require United States citizenship)
- Veterans' preference
- Reinstatement eligibility (if requested, attach SF-50 proof of your career or career-conditional status)
- Highest federal civilian grade held (also give job series and dates held)

Education

- Colleges or universities
- Name, city, and state (ZIP code if known)
- Majors
- Type and year of any degrees received (if no degree, show total credits earned and indicate whether semester or quarter hours)
- Copy of your college transcript (only if the job vacancy announcement requests it)

Work Experience

Give the following information for your paid and nonpaid work experience related to the job you are applying for (do not send job descriptions):

- Job title (include series and grade if it was a federal job)
- Duties and accomplishments
- Employer's name and address
- Supervisor's name and phone number
- Starting and ending dates (month and year)
- Hours per week
- Salary
- Indicate whether it's okay to contact your current supervisor

Other Qualifications

- Job-related training courses (title and year)
- Job-related skills; for example, other languages, computer software/hardware, tools, machinery, and typing speed
- Job-related certificates and licenses (current only)
- Job-related honors, awards, and special accomplishments; for example, publications, memberships in professional or honor societies, leadership activities, public speaking, and performance awards (give dates but do not send documents unless requested)

Federal Resume Formats

There are two federal resume formats: Outline Format and paper with formatting (see the sample formats at the end of this chapter).

The Outline Format Federal Resume

One focused Outline Format federal resume basically works for all of the resume builders on the agency websites. Look for the agency's resume builder character count instructions and copy and paste the resume into all of the resume builders.

You will learn how to write a basic Outline Format federal resume that you can copy and paste into all of the agency resume builders. The builders may have different character and page length requirements, but you can adjust your content to fit their directions.

This chapter introduces you to the various resume builders and their official names so that you can begin to recognize different formats and systems. Some of the names you will see are USAJOBS, QuickHire, Resumix, and Avue Central. These licensed names are owned by companies that work with federal agencies to help manage recruitment. These systems post vacancy announcements, collect resumes, and help manage the assessment process for the best-qualified candidates. No matter how many names the agencies use for their resume builders and job sites, you can still copy and paste your Outline Format federal resume into their system as your application.

The USAJOBS Resume Builder

The USAJOBS resume has a distinctive look, which is pretty good and is becoming popular among job seekers and agency human resources recruiters. Eventually, most or all agencies will use the USAJOBS resume builder for resume collection. Now, however, only approximately 50 percent of all agencies are using it.

The chapters and samples in this book will teach you how to write a successful, focused USAJOBS resume. You will submit your USAJOBS resume to the USAJOBS website, which is the federal government's official one-stop source for federal jobs and employment information.

USAJOBS is the number-one resume builder. USAJOBS is operated by the Office of Personnel Management (OPM) and provides job vacancy information, employment fact sheets, job applications/forms, and online resume development. Job seekers can create a My USAJOBS account, where they can create up to five resumes. These resumes are stored in one location, where they can be updated, saved, or sent at any time. The five resumes can be focused toward different federal job titles. This is an excellent feature of the USAJOBS resume builder.

 Tip: Each resume can be five pages, and each job block in your work experience section can be 3,000 characters long.

Department of the Army Resumix

The Resumix is a keyword resume format written for the Department of the Army. (See Chapter 6 for more about keywords.) The Resumix is challenging for many job seekers who have not spent time searching for the most prominent skills for their target position. The Human Resources Specialist searches Resumix resumes for the Best Qualified people with keywords.

 Tip: The good news about your Outline Format federal resume is this: You need one good three- to four-page Outline Format federal resume to apply to most federal jobs. Most resume builders will accept this length and content.

The "Paper" Federal Resume

Some agencies still request a paper resume, which can be submitted by mail, by e-mail as an attached file, by fax, or in person. This is the formatted "paper" resume that is impressive for human resources managers and supervisors.

You can upload your paper resume into USAJOBS now. But beware of the USAJOBS resume upload feature. It might not forward to all of the other agencies' automated application systems. It's better to submit your resume to the builder than to use the Upload feature with your "paper" resume. You will see in Chapter 13, "USAJOBS and Other Federal Resume Builders," that there are several builders, not just the USAJOBS builder.

 Caution: Beware of the USAJOBS Resume Upload Feature. The resume might not include all of the required information, and it might not be forwarded to all of the other automated resume systems.

Federal Resume Case Study

Following are samples of federal resumes presented in the Outline Format for USAJOBS:

- Outline Format federal resume
- Four-page paper federal resume format for e-mailing, networking, or uploading into the online application systems
- Two-page private-industry resume
- Cover letter for one applicant

Double Occupational Series Objective

Target Job: Management and Program Analyst, GS-0343-13/14, and Human Capital Management/ Human Resources.
Resume Format: KSAs in the Resume.
Private industry to federal resume.
Targeted, written, and designed by Carla Waskiewicz, Certified Professional Resume Writer (CPRW), Certified Federal Resume Writer (CFRW).

MANAGEMENT AND PROGRAM ANALYST, GS-0343-13/14

Emphasis on Human Resources, USDA, Dept. of Management, Office of HR Management

Specialized Experience:

GS-13 includes <u>one year of specialized experience</u> comparable to GS-12 which is directly related to the work of this position and which has equipped the applicant with the knowledge, skills, and abilities to perform successfully the duties of the position. For this position, specialized experience is experience **analyzing processes and systems related to human capital planning and accountability.**

GS-14 includes <u>one year of specialized experience</u> comparable to GS-13 which is directly related to the work of this position and which has equipped the applicant with the knowledge, skills, and abilities to perform successfully the duties of the position. For this position, specialized experience is experience **conducting substantive studies to address human capital planning and accountability challenges** including **increasing the effectiveness and efficiency of HR operations and improving customer service.**

KSAs: (to be included in the resume)

1. Ability to assess the impact of new programs and legislative changes on existing HR programs, processes and resources.

2. Skill in the **research and analysis** of a wide range of organizational and agency level issues pertaining to **strategic management of human capital.**

3. Skill in **developing, monitoring, and tracking an agency's execution and reporting of information** in response to the Office of Personnel Management and Office of Management and Budget under the **human capital initiative** of the President's Management Initiative.

4. Ability to **represent USDA in meetings with high level Federal officials within and outside of the Department, vendors,** and members of external organizations on topics related to **human capital planning policy initiatives**.

MARY T. JONES
333 Third St.
Blacksburg, VA 2222
Day Phone: 999-999-9999
Email: marytjones@yahoo.com

WORK EXPERIENCE   **Thompson Associates**   **5/2004 - Present**
                       Blacksburg, VA US

                                                        Salary: $158,000 USD Per Year
                                                        Hours per week: 40

Senior Human Resources Manager

SENIOR HUMAN RESOURCES (HR) MANAGER FOR PROGRAM IMPACTING 10,000 EMPLOYEES: Selected to lead HR operations team in North America for this global management and consulting firm. Oversaw planning, design, coordination, and implementation of the full range of HR programs, policies, and services within the organization. Accountable for organizational structure planning, employee on-boarding and off-boarding, domestic relocation, international transfers, customer service, and HR vendor management. Managed a $3.5M operating budget and five direct reports.

3. HUMAN CAPITAL (HC) PLANNING & ACCOUNTABILITY: Analyzed and assessed the impact of new programs, legislative changes, and organizational issues impacting the strategic movement of HC and the impact of change on existing HR programs and resources. Designed and implemented process improvements, aligned with organizational goals, which positively impacted the full employee lifecycle.

5. • CONDUCTED STUDIES TO IMPLEMENT CHANGE that positively impacted design of the employee Call Center, employee on-boarding/off-boarding processes, and background check review. Analyzed and updated domestic and international relocation processes.

1. • RESEARCH AND ANALYSIS--INTRODUCED SIX SIGMA GREEN BELT LEAN TRAINING program for the HR Operations Team, increasing the effectiveness and efficiency of HR
4. operations.

3. DEVELOPED AND IMPLEMENTED COMPREHENSIVE HUMAN CAPITAL MANAGEMENT (HCM) STRATEGY to accurately measure and improve human productivity at the macro and micro levels. Provided HCM planning leadership that enabled the organization to build and shape what it wanted to become and how it would effectively deliver services in a global economy.

6. FOSTERED COLLABORATION ACROSS DEPARTMENTAL LINES TO DEVELOP strategic HR and HC program plans to optimize utilization of resources and productivity, improve efficiency, and leverage technology. Resolved program problems and tracked compliance.

2. DEVELOPED AND MONITORED THE EXECUTION AND REPORTING OF PERFORMANCE DATA for strategic HC and HR projects and initiatives. Applied knowledge of analytical tools and techniques to analyze and evaluate effectiveness; recommended improvements.

2. • US I-9 COMPLIANCE AND AUDIT: Spearheaded automation of I-9 Employment Verification form through E-Verify, which streamlined the process and ensured compliance with federal regulations and contract requirements.

+++MORE DUTIES AND ACCOMPLISHMENTS ... CONTINUED IN ADDITIONAL INFORMATION... (Contact Supervisor: Yes, Supervisor's Name: James Thompson, Chief Human Resources Officer, Supervisor's Phone: (410) 999-9999)

(continued)

Figure 1.6: Outline Format federal resume.

KEYWORDS FOR THE OUTLINE FORMAT RESUME

1. **Research and analysis** of processes and systems
2. **Conducting studies**
3. **Human capital planning** and accountability
4. **Increasing the effectiveness and efficiency of HR operations**

5. **Improving customer service**
6. **Internal/external liaison** (represent USDA in meetings with high-level federal officials within and outside of the department, vendors)

(continued)

Thompson Associates
Blacksburg, VA US
      7/2001 - 5/2004

Salary: 158,000 USD Per Year
Hours per week: 40

Director, Human Resources Administration

3. PLANNED, MANAGED, AND DIRECTED HR ADMINISTRATION: Recruited to provide strategic planning and HR leadership to support company growth and ensure HR programs and procedures were aligned with the company's mission, vision and goals. Created, directed, and oversaw complex HR projects and project teams for high-profile initiatives to strengthen, streamline, and improve HR programs, processes, and resources.

3. • HR TRANSFORMATION: Advisor on Transformation Team that led company's separation from JPGG. Identified best practices and processes for ensuring a smooth, efficient, and positive employee transition. Led review of current workflow processes. Identified and documented country-specific, global HR policy and procedure.

3. • HRST INTEGRATION: Directed HR Service Team (HRST) during a successful PeopleSoft System migration. Transitioned all international HR data to the HRST. Redesigned key reporting tools, improving data consistency and reporting of workforce analytics. Through centralization, reduced headcount while increasing volume output. Initiated a cross-training program for team members that increased flexibility in

3. addressing future human capital planning needs.

MANAGED THREE STAFF: Oversaw the expansion of the HR staff. Created job descriptions and outlined areas of responsibility. Approving authority on final staff selection. Mentored and motivated staff, conducted performance reviews, recommended promotions and salary, and counseled and advised staff on developmental training opportunities.

1. ANALYZED ORGANIZATIONAL NEEDS AND PLANNED AND IMPLEMENTED HR POLICY AND PROGRAMS: Spearheaded HR policy administration. Designed, implemented, and monitored a wide range of HR programs and oversaw the rollout of policy. Provided expert advice to staff at all levels of the organization on HR issues, regulations, policy, and procedures.

5. • VENDOR/CONTRACT MANAGEMENT: Named HR Relationship Manager to oversee external vendor selection for transition plan implementation. Developed and refined major processes. Teamed with Legal Dept. to develop contract language.

5. • GLOBAL MOBILITY OUTSOURCING: On team that interviewed and selected vendors, successfully negotiated revised fee structures, and resolved all unpaid invoices owed to JPGG. Hired new manager with strong immigration and taxation background.

1. • PROCESS IMPROVEMENT: Improved efficiency of the employee orientation program and reduced cost by $1.6M annually by implementing webcasting. (Contact Supervisor: Yes, Supervisor's Name: James Thompson, Chief Human Resources Officer, Supervisor's Phone: (410) 999-9999)

JPPG LLP
Lima, Ohio US
      2/1998 - 7/2001

Hours per week: 40

Director, HR Administration

3. HR ADMINISTRATOR/MANAGER: Promoted to HR Director in 1998 and transferred from Pennsylvania to Ohio to provide HR leadership for performance optimization, Human Capital analysis and management, career development, and formulation of HR policy and strategy. Engaged in proactive communications and led weekly meetings with HR Director to resolve programmatic issues and problems.

1. RESEARCHED AND ANALYZED HR PROGRAMS AND PROCESSES. Developed and executed complex studies to assess HR programs. Gathered and compiled data, identified issues, and recommended techniques and approaches to support company goals and objectives.
• ADMINISTERED NEW-HIRE ASSIMILATION PROGRAM: Partnered with internal team to roll out on-boarding orientation program in three major U.S. cities.

2. • PROGRAM ANALYST: Successfully championed advancement of a centralized HR

2. — service center. Researched and presented metrics on outsourcing versus providing of HR services in house. Provided data to senior management essential to forming an independent organization.

2. — • DESIGNED, IMPLEMENTED, AND MANAGED CAREER DEVELOPMENT, PERFORMANCE MANAGEMENT, AND PROCESS IMPROVEMENT PROGRAMS that positively impacted HR operations organization-wide. Developed benchmarking studies and researched best practices and industry trends for HR services. Developed reports, metrics, quarterly activity, and quality analysis reports for the HR Managing Director and leadership team.

4. — • SALARY REVIEW PROCESS IMPROVEMENT TEAM LEAD: Project Manager/cross-functional team lead for the design and implementation of a web-based salary review tool in the U.S. and overseas.

JPGG LLP   **2/1974 - 9/1998**
Lima, OH US

                                               Hours per week: 40

Various, Human Resources
Advanced through human resources positions of increasing responsibility: Personnel Assistant, Supervisor of Personnel Services, and HR Sr. Business Consultant. Directed new-hire orientation and on-boarding, oversight of benefits administration, performance management, salary administration/review, career counseling, and employee relations. Contributed to the evolution of the HR function from standalone teams to a regional centralized program.

EDUCATION

Albany State College
Albany, NY US
Bachelor's Degree - 6/1995
Major: Liberal Arts

JOB RELATED TRAINING

COURSES, LICENSES, AND CERTIFICATIONS
Six Sigma Green/Lean Belt, Certification, 2006

PROFESSIONAL TRAINING
Executive Leadership Program, Harvard University, 2008
Leadership Skills II Workshop & Project Management Skills, AMA, 2009

MEMBERSHIPS & AFFILIATIONS
Society for Human Resource Management (SHRM)
HRA-NCA SHRM Chapter member

ADDITIONAL INFORMATION

WORK EXPERIENCE CONTINUED ...

DIRECTOR, HUMAN RESOURCES ADMINISTRATION, 10/2007 to present
Thompson Associates

(continued)

(continued)

6. HR REPRESENTATIVE AT HIGH-LEVEL MEETINGS WITH A VARIETY OF INTERNAL AND EXTERNAL STAKEHOLDERS in order to provide information, champion for new approaches, and respond to a range of questions. Prepared and presented briefings, training, presentations, and reports to a variety of audiences.

5. ACTING CONTRACT REPRESENTATIVE (COR) FOR HR AND HCM INITIATIVES. Reviewed and selected vendors; managed outsourced relationships. Reviewed language in Service Level Agreements (SLAs); and ensured deliverables exceeded expectations. Managed change throughout the contract lifecycle.
• RENEGOTIATED VENDOR CONTRACTS. Restructured scope that resulted in a cost reduction of $500K.

++++++++++++++

PROFESSIONAL PROFILE
• Highly motivated, results-oriented and decisive Human Resources Administrator and Human Capital leader with a focused approach to developing and integrating strategies to steer and achieve organizational objectives.
• Verifiable record of success defining and driving process improvements in all areas of HR operations to include human capital planning, HR policy, and procedures.
• Expertise in HR vendor and contract management, program analysis and reporting, project management, organizational design and development, and policy analysis.
• Experienced in leading functional teams and managing change to achieve quantifiable results. Skilled trainer, mentor, coach, and staff supervisor.
• Outstanding oral and written communication skills. Able to build trust and rapport quickly with both management and associates.
• Recognized throughout career for integrity, honesty, flexibility, resilience, decisiveness, and outstanding problem-solving competencies.

3. SUMMARY OF HR EXPERTISE: HR Operations, Human Capital Planning & Accountability, Vendor Management & Outsourcing, Core Employee Process Design, Project Management, Human Resource Information Systems (HRIS), Performance Management Systems, Quality & Performance Improvement, New Hire Orientation, Recruitment & Selection, and Negotiation & Mediation. Six Sigma Green Belt Certified.

COMPUTER SKILLS: Microsoft Office (Excel, PowerPoint, Outlook, Word). Human Resource Systems: PeopleSoft

Mary T. Jones

333 Third St.
Blacksburg, Virginia 22222
Home: 999-999-9999 • Cell: 999-999-9999
Email: maryTJones@yahoo.com

SSN: xxx-xx-xxxx • United States Citizen • No Veterans' Preference

HUMAN RESOURCES MANAGER
HR Administration / Human Capital Planning / Program Management

3. — • Highly motivated, results-oriented, and decisive Human Resources Administrator and Human Capital leader with a focused approach to developing and integrating strategies to steer and achieve organizational objectives.

4. — • Verifiable record of success defining and driving process improvements in all areas of HR operations to include human capital planning, HR policy, and procedures.

2. — • Expertise in HR vendor and contract management, program analysis and reporting, project management, organizational design and development, and policy analysis.

1. — • Experienced in leading functional teams and managing change to achieve quantifiable results. Skilled trainer, mentor, coach, and staff supervisor.

6. — • Outstanding oral and written communication skills. Able to build trust and rapport quickly with both management and associates.

• Recognized throughout career for integrity, honesty, flexibility, resilience, decisiveness, and outstanding problem-solving competencies.

AREAS OF EXPERTISE INCLUDE:

- HR Operations
- Human Capital Planning & Accountability
- Vendor Management & Outsourcing
- Core Employee Process Design
- Project Management
- Human Resource Information Systems

- Performance Management Systems
- Quality & Performance Improvement
- New Hire Orientation
- Recruitment & Selection
- Negotiation & Mediation.
- Six Sigma Green Belt Certified

PROFESSIONAL EXPERIENCE

Senior Human Resources Manager   X/20XX–X/20XX
Thompson Associates   Annual Salary: $158,500
102 Cross Street, Blacksburg, VA 22222   Hours per week: 40+
Supervisor: James Thompson, Human Resources Officer, 999-999-9999, permission to contact

3. — **Senior Human Resources (HR) Manager for program impacting 10,000 Employees:** Selected to lead HR operations team in North America for this global management and consulting firm. Oversaw planning, design, coordination, and implementation of the full range of HR programs, policies, and services within the organization. Accountable for organizational structure planning, employee on-boarding and off-boarding, domestic relocation, international transfers, and HR vendor management. Managed a $3.5M operating budget and five direct reports.

(continued)

Figure 1.7: Four-page paper federal resume.

KEYWORDS FOR THE OUTLINE FORMAT RESUME

1. **Research and analysis** of processes and systems
2. **Conducting studies**
3. **Human capital planning** and accountability
4. **Increasing the effectiveness and efficiency of HR operations**

5. **Improving customer service**
6. **Internal/external liaison** (represent USDA in meetings with high-level federal officials within and outside of the department, vendors)

(continued)

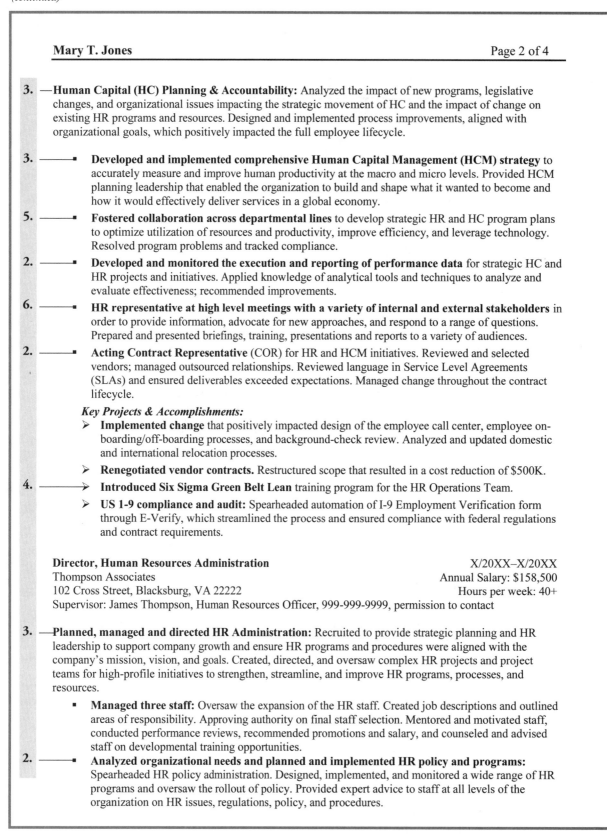

3. —**Human Capital (HC) Planning & Accountability:** Analyzed the impact of new programs, legislative changes, and organizational issues impacting the strategic movement of HC and the impact of change on existing HR programs and resources. Designed and implemented process improvements, aligned with organizational goals, which positively impacted the full employee lifecycle.

3. ——■ **Developed and implemented comprehensive Human Capital Management (HCM) strategy** to accurately measure and improve human productivity at the macro and micro levels. Provided HCM planning leadership that enabled the organization to build and shape what it wanted to become and how it would effectively deliver services in a global economy.

5. ——■ **Fostered collaboration across departmental lines** to develop strategic HR and HC program plans to optimize utilization of resources and productivity, improve efficiency, and leverage technology. Resolved program problems and tracked compliance.

2. ——■ **Developed and monitored the execution and reporting of performance data** for strategic HC and HR projects and initiatives. Applied knowledge of analytical tools and techniques to analyze and evaluate effectiveness; recommended improvements.

6. ——■ **HR representative at high level meetings with a variety of internal and external stakeholders** in order to provide information, advocate for new approaches, and respond to a range of questions. Prepared and presented briefings, training, presentations and reports to a variety of audiences.

2. ——■ **Acting Contract Representative** (COR) for HR and HCM initiatives. Reviewed and selected vendors; managed outsourced relationships. Reviewed language in Service Level Agreements (SLAs) and ensured deliverables exceeded expectations. Managed change throughout the contract lifecycle.

   Key Projects & Accomplishments:
   ➤ **Implemented change** that positively impacted design of the employee call center, employee on-boarding/off-boarding processes, and background-check review. Analyzed and updated domestic and international relocation processes.
   ➤ **Renegotiated vendor contracts.** Restructured scope that resulted in a cost reduction of $500K.

4. ——➤ **Introduced Six Sigma Green Belt Lean** training program for the HR Operations Team.
   ➤ **US 1-9 compliance and audit:** Spearheaded automation of I-9 Employment Verification form through E-Verify, which streamlined the process and ensured compliance with federal regulations and contract requirements.

Director, Human Resources Administration   X/20XX–X/20XX
Thompson Associates   Annual Salary: $158,500
102 Cross Street, Blacksburg, VA 22222   Hours per week: 40+
Supervisor: James Thompson, Human Resources Officer, 999-999-9999, permission to contact

3. —**Planned, managed and directed HR Administration:** Recruited to provide strategic planning and HR leadership to support company growth and ensure HR programs and procedures were aligned with the company's mission, vision, and goals. Created, directed, and oversaw complex HR projects and project teams for high-profile initiatives to strengthen, streamline, and improve HR programs, processes, and resources.

   ■ **Managed three staff:** Oversaw the expansion of the HR staff. Created job descriptions and outlined areas of responsibility. Approving authority on final staff selection. Mentored and motivated staff, conducted performance reviews, recommended promotions and salary, and counseled and advised staff on developmental training opportunities.

2. ——■ **Analyzed organizational needs and planned and implemented HR policy and programs:** Spearheaded HR policy administration. Designed, implemented, and monitored a wide range of HR programs and oversaw the rollout of policy. Provided expert advice to staff at all levels of the organization on HR issues, regulations, policy, and procedures.

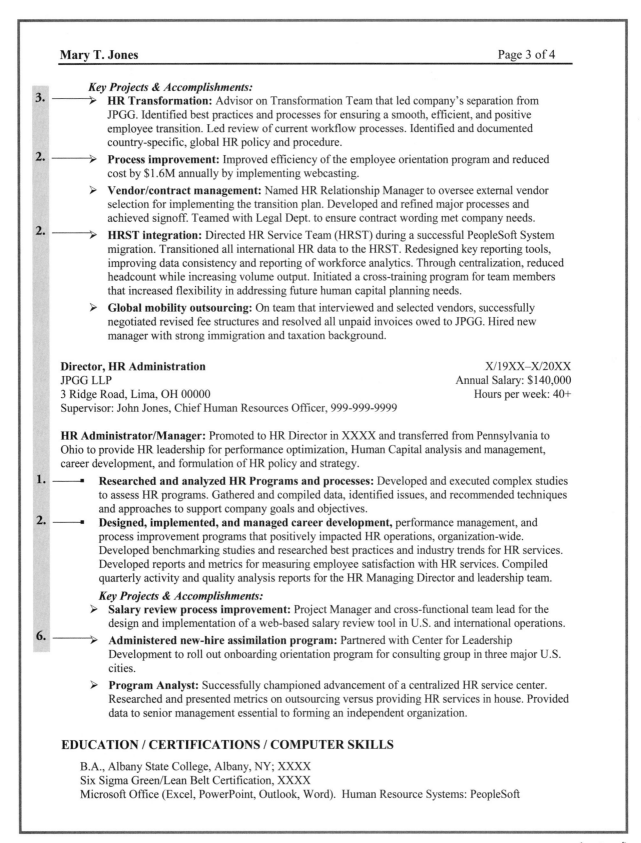

Key Projects & Accomplishments:

3. ➤ **HR Transformation:** Advisor on Transformation Team that led company's separation from JPGG. Identified best practices and processes for ensuring a smooth, efficient, and positive employee transition. Led review of current workflow processes. Identified and documented country-specific, global HR policy and procedure.

2. ➤ **Process improvement:** Improved efficiency of the employee orientation program and reduced cost by $1.6M annually by implementing webcasting.

➤ **Vendor/contract management:** Named HR Relationship Manager to oversee external vendor selection for implementing the transition plan. Developed and refined major processes and achieved signoff. Teamed with Legal Dept. to ensure contract wording met company needs.

2. ➤ **HRST integration:** Directed HR Service Team (HRST) during a successful PeopleSoft System migration. Transitioned all international HR data to the HRST. Redesigned key reporting tools, improving data consistency and reporting of workforce analytics. Through centralization, reduced headcount while increasing volume output. Initiated a cross-training program for team members that increased flexibility in addressing future human capital planning needs.

➤ **Global mobility outsourcing:** On team that interviewed and selected vendors, successfully negotiated revised fee structures and resolved all unpaid invoices owed to JPGG. Hired new manager with strong immigration and taxation background.

Director, HR Administration   X/19XX–X/20XX
JPGG LLP   Annual Salary: $140,000
3 Ridge Road, Lima, OH 00000   Hours per week: 40+
Supervisor: John Jones, Chief Human Resources Officer, 999-999-9999

HR Administrator/Manager: Promoted to HR Director in XXXX and transferred from Pennsylvania to Ohio to provide HR leadership for performance optimization, Human Capital analysis and management, career development, and formulation of HR policy and strategy.

1. ▪ **Researched and analyzed HR Programs and processes:** Developed and executed complex studies to assess HR programs. Gathered and compiled data, identified issues, and recommended techniques and approaches to support company goals and objectives.

2. ▪ **Designed, implemented, and managed career development,** performance management, and process improvement programs that positively impacted HR operations, organization-wide. Developed benchmarking studies and researched best practices and industry trends for HR services. Developed reports and metrics for measuring employee satisfaction with HR services. Compiled quarterly activity and quality analysis reports for the HR Managing Director and leadership team.

Key Projects & Accomplishments:

➤ **Salary review process improvement:** Project Manager and cross-functional team lead for the design and implementation of a web-based salary review tool in U.S. and international operations.

6. ➤ **Administered new-hire assimilation program:** Partnered with Center for Leadership Development to roll out onboarding orientation program for consulting group in three major U.S. cities.

➤ **Program Analyst:** Successfully championed advancement of a centralized HR service center. Researched and presented metrics on outsourcing versus providing HR services in house. Provided data to senior management essential to forming an independent organization.

EDUCATION / CERTIFICATIONS / COMPUTER SKILLS

B.A., Albany State College, Albany, NY; XXXX
Six Sigma Green/Lean Belt Certification, XXXX
Microsoft Office (Excel, PowerPoint, Outlook, Word). Human Resource Systems: PeopleSoft

(continued)

(continued)

Mary T. Jones	Page 4 of 4

PROFESSIONAL TRAINING
Executive Leadership Program, Harvard University, XXXX
Leadership Skills II Workshop & Project Management Skills, AMA; XXXX

MEMBERSHIPS & AFFILIATIONS
Society for Human Resource Management (SHRM)
HRA-NCA SHRM chapter member

MARY T. JONES
333 Third St., Blacksburg, VA 22222
Home: 999-999-9999 / Cell: 999-999-9999
maryTJones@yahoo.com

HUMAN RESOURCES MANAGER
HR Administration / Human Capital Planning / Organizational Development

- Results-oriented and decisive Human Resources Administrator and Human Capital leader with a focused approach to developing and integrating strategies to steer and achieve organizational objectives.
3. • Verifiable record of success defining and driving process improvements in all areas of HR operations to include human capital planning, HR policy, and procedures.
4. • Extensive experience in HR vendor and contract management, program analysis and reporting, project management, organizational design and development, and policy analysis.
2. • Experienced in leading functional teams and managing change to achieve quantifiable results. Skilled trainer, mentor, coach, and staff supervisor.

Areas of Expertise Include

- HR Operations
- Human Capital Planning & Accountability
- Vendor Management & Outsourcing
- Core Employee Process Design
- Project Management
- Human Resource Information Systems

- Performance Management Systems
- Quality & Performance Improvement
- New Hire Orientation
- Recruitment & Selection
- Negotiation & Mediation
- Six Sigma Green Belt Certified

PROFESSIONAL EXPERIENCE

Thompson Associates, Blacksburg, VA   20XX–20XX

Senior Human Resources Manager (20XX–20XX)

3. Selected to lead HR operations team in North America for this global management and consulting firm with 10,000 employees. Oversaw planning, design, coordination, and implementation of the full range of HR programs, policies, and services within the organization. Accountable for organizational structure planning, employee on-boarding and off-boarding, domestic relocation, international transfers, customer service, and HR vendor management. Contract representative for HR and Human Capital Planning initiatives. Managed a $3.5M operating budget and five direct reports.

1. *Designed and implemented process improvements, aligned with organizational goals, which positively impacted the full employee lifecycle.*
- Reorganized and improved the employee call center, employee on-boarding/off-boarding processes, and background check review. Updated domestic and international relocation processes.
- Introduced Six Sigma Green Belt Lean training program for the HR Operations Team.
- Spearheaded automation of U.S. I-9 Employment Verification form through E-Verify, which streamlined the process and ensured compliance with federal regulations and contract requirements.
- Renegotiated vendor contracts. Restructured scope that resulted in a cost reduction of $500K.

Director, Human Resources Administration (20XX–20XX)

Recruited to provide strategic planning and HR leadership to support company growth. Created, directed, and oversaw complex HR projects teams for high-profile initiatives to strengthen, streamline, and improve HR programs, processes, and resources.
4. • Improved efficiency of the employee orientation program and reduced cost by $1.6M annually by implementing webcasting.

(continued)

Figure 1.8: Two-page private-industry resume.

KEYWORDS FOR THE OUTLINE FORMAT RESUME

1. **Research and analysis** of processes and systems
2. **Conducting studies**
3. **Human capital planning** and accountability
4. **Increasing the effectiveness and efficiency of HR operations**
5. **Improving customer service**
6. **Internal/external liaison** (represent USDA in meetings with high-level federal officials within and outside of the department, vendors)

(continued)

| Mary T. Jones | mTJones@yahoo.com | *Page Two* |

Director, Human Resources Administration, *continued*

3. • On Transformation Team that led company's separation from JPGG. Identified best practices and processes for ensuring a smooth, efficient, and positive employee transition. Led review of current workflow processes. Identified and documented country-specific, global HR policy and procedure.

5. • Directed HR Service Team (HRST) during a successful PeopleSoft System migration. Redesigned key reporting tools, improving data consistency and reporting of workforce analytics. Through centralization, reduced headcount while increasing volume output.

• Initiated a cross-training program for team members that increased flexibility in addressing future human capital planning needs.

Director, HR Administration   20XX–20XX
JPGG LLP, Lima, OH

6. Promoted to HR Director in 20XX and transferred from Pennsylvania to Ohio to provide HR leadership for performance optimization, Human Capital analysis and management, career development, and formulation of HR policy and strategy. Engaged in proactive communications and led weekly meetings with HR Director to resolve programmatic issues and problems.

• Administered new-hire assimilation program: Partnered with internal team to roll out on-boarding orientation program in three major U.S. cities.

4. • Successfully championed advancement of a centralized HR service center. Researched and presented metrics on outsourcing versus providing HR services in house.

• Salary Review Process Improvement Team Lead. Served as Project Manager and cross-functional team lead for the design and implementation of a web-based salary review tool in U.S. and overseas.

EDUCATION, PROFESSIONAL TRAINING & CERTIFICATIONS

B.A., Liberal Arts, Albany State College, Albany, NY, XXXX
Six Sigma Green/Lean Belt Certification, XXXX
Executive Leadership Program, Harvard University, XXXX

AFFILIATIONS

Society for Human Resource Management (SHRM)
HRA-NCA SHRM chapter member

COMPUTER SKILLS

Microsoft Office (Excel, PowerPoint, Outlook, Word). Human Resource Systems: PeopleSoft

Summary

One impressive, keyword-filled, Outline Format resume with accomplishments will get you started with your federal job search campaign. It is best if you edit the resume slightly for each announcement so that you can pick up the keywords from the announcement. The next resume writing chapters give you more strategies for writing an outstanding federal resume in the USAJOBS resume builder that will result in your being Best Qualified and landing an interview and ultimately a job offer and a career opportunity with the U.S. government.

The History of the Federal Resume

In 1995, then Vice President Al Gore initiated Reinvention Government, which called for the simplification of forms and language in government procedures. One of the best recommendations from this initiative was to eliminate the SF-171, which had gotten out of control. Federal employees were writing "Life History 171" forms that were up to 50 pages long and were placed into three-ring binders with indexes and tabs and mailed in large Jiffy bags with return receipts.

CHAPTER 2

What Happens to Your Resume and Other Application Materials

Before you begin to develop a federal resume, you need to understand what happens to your resume (and any other required application materials requested in the vacancy announcement) after you submit it. This will help you highlight the most important things in your application package.

Many applicants feel that their applications go into a mysterious black hole. This chapter explains the simple steps of application processing, review, and Veterans' Preference. It explains how agencies generally process applications so that you will understand why the various information required in your federal resume is so important.

Five basic steps are required to process each application received for a federal position. Agencies receiving applications must process and adjudicate each application individually—which can explain, in part, the sometimes-lengthy processing times for federal jobs.

 Note: Some of the material in this chapter is an interpretation of OPM's delegated examining guide, *Office of Personnel Management Delegated Examining Operations Handbook, 2007.*

Each application is reviewed as described in the following list. This process is commonly referred to as "rating and ranking." These are the basic steps in the rating and ranking process:

- **Step 1:** Determine minimum qualifications.
- **Step 2:** Identify and apply selective factors and quality ranking factors (if applicable).
- **Step 3:** For applicants who meet minimum qualifications and selective factors requirements, apply the assessment tool to determine the applicants' numerical score/rating.
- **Step 4:** Adjudicate Veterans' Preference.
- **Step 5:** Rank eligibles in the order of their rating adjusted for Veterans' Preference.

These five basic steps are explained in detail in the rest of this chapter.

Step 1: Determine Minimum Qualifications

Certain items are required, at a minimum, for hiring or promoting an individual into a job under the competitive process. They are typically expressed in terms of job-related years of job-related experience or job-related education (for example, course credit hours) or a combination of the two. They may also be expressed as proficiency levels on a competency-based assessment.

Minimum qualification requirements always include the qualification standards that OPM validates and sets for occupations in the federal government. Such qualification standards usually apply government-wide, but occasionally some are established as agency-specific standards. In addition, minimum qualification requirements may also include any selective factors an agency establishes and applies for its positions. These general occupational qualification standards and selective factors are discussed further later in this chapter. The minimum qualifications must be stated in the vacancy announcement.

Applicants are first screened to determine whether they meet the minimum qualification requirements. This is called an "in" or "out" decision, or a "screen out." Applicants who pass this initial screening continue on in the assessment process.

The Role of Minimum Requirements in the Assessment Process

Minimum requirements are intended to reduce the processing of unqualified applicants by screening out those who are unlikely to succeed in the job. The qualification standards OPM issues are *not* designed to rank applicants, identify the Best Qualified candidates for particular positions, or otherwise substitute for a comprehensive assessment of job qualifications.

Applicants who satisfy minimum requirements are not automatically entitled to a qualifying score of 70 or more points (out of 100) in an assessment process that uses a numerical rating procedure (see "Rating and Ranking Procedures: Category Ranking," later in this chapter). Minimum qualifications screening and subsequent assessment are two separate steps in the examining process. Screening for minimum qualifications is usually the first hurdle in the selection process. The first step is to sort applicants into two groups: ineligible and eligible. Applicants who do not meet the minimum qualification requirements are ineligible and thus are "screened out."

When the examining process uses numerical rating procedures, applicants meeting minimum requirements are eligible for assessment of their relative qualifications on a scale of 100. Only those who pass both the initial minimum qualifications screen and the assessment phase are eligible for appointment.

Occupational Qualification Standards

The minimum qualification requirements for any occupation are stated in the vacancy announcement and are established by the Office of Personnel Management (OPM). OPM has the responsibility to develop, validate, and publish the occupational qualification standards that must be used when examining applicants for appointment to the competitive service. Together with any applicable selective factors, which are discussed below, these occupational qualification standards make up the minimum qualification requirements.

The current government-wide minimum qualification standards including most agency-specific standards are published on OPM's website.

For General Schedule (white-collar) positions, the minimum qualification standards are located in the *Operating Manual for Qualification Standards for General Schedule Positions* at www.opm.gov/fedclass/html/gsseries.asp.

For Wage Grade positions (blue-collar jobs), the minimum qualification standards are located in the *Job Qualification System for Trades and Labor Occupations Handbook* at www.opm.gov/qualifications/x-118c/index.htm.

Step 2: Identify and Apply Selective Factors and Quality Ranking Factors

In addition to the component of the minimum qualification requirements that is expressed as occupational qualification standards, selective factors identify any qualifications that are also important for the job. These are already required when the person starts the job. A selective factor must be stated in the vacancy announcement.

Characteristics of a Selective Factor

Characteristics of a selective factor include the following:

- Extensive training or experience to develop
- Essential for successful performance on the job (in other words, if individuals do not have the selective factor, they cannot perform the job)
- Almost always geared toward a specific technical competency/KSA
- Cannot be learned on the job in a reasonable amount of time

When using selective factors, agencies will specify the required proficiency level. Based on their characteristics, selective factors can be used as a "screen out"—that is, if an applicant does not meet a selective factor, he or she is ineligible for further consideration.

Example of a Selective Factor

A commonly applied selective factor is a special language requirement. Learning a language involves several years of training; and for certain positions, a person cannot perform successfully unless he or she can communicate in a second language. In addition, applicants cannot compensate for a lower language proficiency level with higher levels of proficiency on other competencies. In these types of situations, it is appropriate to apply a special language requirement as a selective factor. Because selective factors are used as "screen outs," read them carefully. This factor is a screen out. Do not apply if you do not have this selective factor skill.

Rating and Ranking Procedures: Category Rating

With the Presidential Executive Order directing hiring reform (see Chapter 1), candidate assessment has been streamlined to use category rating procedures. Category rating is a ranking and selection procedure authorized under the Chief Human Capital Officers Act of 2002 (Title XIII of the Homeland Security Act of 2002) and codified at 5 U.S.C. § 3319. Category rating is part of the competitive examining process. Under category rating, applicants who meet basic minimum qualification requirements established for the position, and whose job-related competencies or KSAs have been assessed, are ranked by being placed in one of two or more predefined quality categories instead of being ranked in numeric score order. Preference eligibles are listed ahead of nonpreference eligibles within each quality category. Veterans' Preference is absolute within each quality category.

Under 5 CFR part 337, subpart C, agencies are required to describe each quality category in job announcements. They must use the "Basis of Rating" section to communicate to applicants that category rating procedures will be used to rank and select eligible candidates. Agencies are not expected to disclose crediting plans or rating schedules with scoring keys. Quality category descriptions can be as simple as naming the categories, such as "Highly Qualified and Qualified" or "Highly Qualified, Well-Qualified, and Qualified." In addition, agencies must clearly describe how Veterans' Preference is applied under category rating procedures.

Defining Quality Categories

In category rating, agencies must establish and define a minimum of two quality categories. Quality categories should be written to reflect the requirements to perform the job successfully and to distinguish differences in the quality of candidates' job-related competencies/KSAs. Each quality category will have eligible candidates who have demonstrated, through an assessment tool(s), similar levels of proficiency on the critical job-related competencies/KSAs.

Quality categories must be established and defined by the employing agency prior to announcing the job. Some factors agencies may consider when defining quality categories may include

- Breadth and scope of competencies/KSAs
- Increased levels of difficulty or complexity of competencies/KSAs
- Successful performance on the job
- Level of the job

Table 2.1: Examples of Quality Categories

Example 1	Example 2	Example 3
Highly Qualified	Gold	Highly Qualified
Qualified	Silver	Well Qualified
Qualified	Platinum	

Examples

Following is an example using two quality categories:

Human Resources (HR) Specialist (Staffing), GS-201-14, position in an agency headquarters policy office.

- **Highly qualified:** Senior HR Specialist in an agency headquarters office with experience writing regulations or agency policy or providing guidance on staffing, downsizing, realignments, classification, or compensation.
- **Qualified:** Senior HR Specialist with operations experience in staffing, downsizing, realignments, classification, or compensation.

The next example illustrates one way quality categories can be used. This illustration shows quality categories for an Accountant, series 510, at the 12 grade level.

Step 1: Use the job analysis process to identify job-related competencies/KSAs.

The following three competencies/KSAs were identified through the job analysis process to be job-related; for example:

1. Oral Communication
2. Technical Knowledge
3. Project Management

Step 2: Identify the indicators of proficiency for each of the competencies/KSAs identified in Step 1.

1. Oral Communication
   - Makes presentations
   - Answers technical questions
2. Technical Knowledge
   - Financial analysis
   - Accounting
3. Project Management
   - Reviews budget cycles
   - Uses project-management software

Step 3: Identify level of proficiency required by the level of the position.

Based on *demonstrating possession only* of the competencies (applicant's specific level of proficiency does not matter); or based on *specific level of proficiency* for each competency (applicant's specific level of proficiency in each competency does matter).

Example (Possession Only): Accountant, Series 510, Grade 12

Categories	Required Competencies/KSAs
Highly Qualified	Oral Communication Technical Knowledge Project Management
Well Qualified	Oral Communication Technical Knowledge
Qualified	Technical Knowledge

Step 3: Apply the Assessment Tool to Determine the Applicants' Numerical Score/Rating

Applicants who meet the basic minimum qualification requirements established for the position (i.e., OPM-established occupational standards, plus any selective factors) *and* whose job-related competencies have been assessed are ranked by being placed in one of the predefined quality categories instead of being ranked in numeric score order. Names of eligible candidates may be listed in any order (for example, alphabetical order), subject to the requirement, described below, that preference eligibles must be listed ahead of nonpreference eligibles.

Here are two examples of how the human resources specialists will score your total application:

Example 1: How You Will Be Evaluated

You will be evaluated on the quality and extent of your experience, education, and training relevant to the duties of this position. The evaluation will be based on information you provide in your online resume, your answers to the job-specific self-assessment questions for this announcement, and a review of the documents that are requested as part of this announcement. Qualified candidates are assigned a score between 70 and 100.

Example 2

Eligible candidates will be placed for selection consideration into three categories:

1. **Qualified:** Applicants who have a "Q" score between 70 and 84.99 meet the specialized experience outlined in the Minimum Qualification Requirements section of this announcement.

2. **Well Qualified:** Applicants who have a "WQ" score between 85 and 94.99 exceed the Minimum Qualification Requirements based on review of resume and vacancy-specific questions.

3. **Best Qualified:** Applicants who have a "BQ" score between 95 and 100 Outstanding level based on review of resume and vacancy-specific questions.

Do not overstate or understate your level of experience and capability. You should be aware that your ratings are subject to evaluation and verification.

Step 4: Adjudicate Veterans' Preference

Since the time of the Civil War, veterans of the Armed Forces have been given some degree of preference in appointments to federal jobs. Recognizing their sacrifice, Congress enacted laws to prevent veterans seeking federal employment from being penalized for their time in military service. Veterans' Preference recognizes the economic loss suffered by citizens who have served their country in uniform, restores veterans to a favorable competitive position for government employment, and acknowledges the larger obligation owed to disabled veterans.

Veterans' Preference in its present form comes from the Veterans' Preference Act of 1944, as amended, and is now codified in various provisions of title 5, United States Code. By law, veterans who are disabled or who served on active duty in the Armed Forces during certain specified time periods or in military campaigns are entitled to preference over others in hiring from competitive lists of eligibles and also in retention during reductions in force.

In addition to receiving preference in competitive appointments, veterans may be considered for special noncompetitive appointments for which only they are eligible. (See Chapter 4.)

The Office of Personnel Management (OPM) administers entitlement to Veterans' Preference in employment under title 5, United States Code, and oversees other statutory employment requirements in titles 5 and 38. (Title 38 also governs veterans' entitlement to benefits administered by the Department of Veterans Affairs.)

Both title 5 and title 38 use many of the same terms, but in different ways. For example, service during a "war" is used to determine entitlement to Veterans' Preference and service credit under title 5. OPM has always interpreted this to mean a war declared by Congress. But title 38 defines "period of war" to include many nondeclared wars, including Korea, Vietnam, and the Persian Gulf. Such conflicts entitle a veteran to VA benefits under title 38, but not necessarily to preference or service credit under title 5. Thus, it is critically important to use the correct definitions in determining eligibility for specific rights and benefits in employment.

For additional information, including the complete text of the laws and regulations on veterans' rights, consult Feds Hire Vets (www.fedshirevets.gov/job/vetpref/index.aspx).

When Preference Applies

Preference in hiring applies to permanent and temporary positions in the competitive and excepted services of the executive branch. Preference does not apply to positions in the Senior Executive Service or to executive branch positions for which Senate confirmation is required. The legislative and judicial branches of the federal government also are exempt from the Veterans' Preference Act unless the positions are in the competitive service (Government Printing Office, for example) or have been made subject to the act by another law.

Preference applies in hiring from civil service examinations conducted by the Office of Personnel Management (OPM) and agencies under delegated examining authority, for most excepted service jobs including Veterans Recruitment Appointments (VRA), and when agencies make temporary, term, and overseas limited appointments. Veterans' Preference does not apply to promotion, reassignment, change to lower grade, transfer, or reinstatement.

Veterans' Preference does not require an agency to use any particular appointment process. Agencies have broad authority under law to hire from any appropriate source of eligibles, including special appointing authorities. An agency may consider candidates already in the civil service from an agency-developed merit promotion list; or it may reassign a current employee, transfer an employee from another agency, or reinstate a former federal employee. In addition, agencies are required to give priority to displaced employees before using civil service examinations and similar hiring methods.

Types of Preference

To receive preference, a veteran must have been discharged or released from active duty in the Armed Forces under honorable conditions (with an honorable or general discharge). As defined in 5 U.S.C. § 2101(2), "Armed Forces" means the Army, Navy, Air Force, Marine Corps, and Coast Guard. The veteran must also be eligible under one of the preference categories in this section (also shown on the Standard Form (SF) 50, "Notification of Personnel Action").

Military retirees at the rank of major, lieutenant commander, or higher are not eligible for preference in appointment unless they are disabled veterans. (This does not apply to reservists, who will not begin drawing military retired pay until age 60.)

For nondisabled users, active duty for training by National Guard or Reserve soldiers does not qualify as "active duty" for preference. For disabled veterans, active duty includes training service in the Reserves or National Guard, per the Merit Systems Protection Board decision in *Hesse v. Department of the Army,* 104 M.S.P.R.647 (2007).

For purposes of this chapter and 5 U.S.C. § 2108, "war" means only those armed conflicts declared by Congress as war and includes World War II, which covers the period from December 7, 1941, to April 28, 1952.

When applying for federal jobs, eligible veterans should claim preference on their application or resume. Applicants claiming 10-point preference must complete Standard Form (SF) 15, "Application for 10-Point Veteran Preference," and submit the requested documentation.

The following preference categories and points are based on 5 U.S.C. § 2108 and 3309 as modified by a length of service requirement in 38 U.S.C. § 5303A(d). (The letters following each category, for example, "TP," are a shorthand reference OPM uses in competitive examinations.)

5-Point Preference (TP)

Five points are added to the passing examination score or rating of a veteran who served

- During a war; or
- During the period April 28, 1952, through July 1, 1955; or
- For more than 180 consecutive days, other than for training, any part of which occurred after January 31, 1955, and before October 15, 1976; or
- During the Gulf War from August 2, 1990, through January 2, 1992; or
- For more than 180 consecutive days, other than for training, any part of which occurred during the period beginning September 11, 2001, and ending on the date prescribed by Presidential proclamation or by law as the last day of Operation Iraqi Freedom; or
- In a campaign or expedition for which a campaign medal has been authorized. Any Armed Forces Expeditionary medal or campaign badge, including El Salvador, Lebanon, Grenada, Panama, Southwest Asia, Somalia, and Haiti, qualifies for preference.

A campaign medal holder or Gulf War veteran who originally enlisted after September 7, 1980 (or began active duty on or after October 14, 1982, and has not previously completed 24 months of continuous active duty), must have served continuously for 24 months or the full period called or ordered to active duty. The 24-month service requirement does not apply to 10-point preference eligibles separated for disability incurred or aggravated in the line of duty, or to veterans separated for hardship or other reasons under 10 U.S.C. § 1171 or 1173.

A Word About Gulf War Preference

The Defense Authorization Act of Fiscal Year 1998 (Public Law 105-85) of November 18, 1997, contains a provision (section 1102 of Title XI) which accords Veterans' Preference to everyone who served on active duty during the period beginning August 2, 1990, and ending January 2, 1992—provided, of course, the veteran is otherwise eligible.

This means that anyone who served on active duty during the Gulf War, regardless of where or for how long, is entitled to preference if otherwise eligible (in other words, was separated under honorable conditions and served continuously for a minimum of 24 months or the full period for which called or ordered to active duty). This applies not only to candidates seeking employment, but to federal employees who may be affected by reduction in force, as well.

10-Point Compensable Disability Preference (CP)

Ten points are added to the passing examination score or rating of a veteran who served at any time and who has a compensable service-connected disability rating of at least 10 percent but less than 30 percent.

10-Point 30 Percent Compensable Disability Preference (CPS)

Ten points are added to the passing examination score or rating of a veteran who served at any time and who has a compensable service-connected disability rating of 30 percent or more.

10-Point Disability Preference (XP)

Ten points are added to the passing examination score or rating of

- A veteran who served at any time and has a present service-connected disability or is receiving compensation, disability retirement benefits, or pension from the military or the Department of Veterans Affairs but does not qualify as a CP or CPS; or

- A veteran who received a Purple Heart.

10-Point Derived Preference (XP)

Ten points are added to the passing examination score or rating of spouses, widows, widowers, or mothers of veterans as described in this section. This type of preference is usually referred to as "derived preference" because it is based on service of a veteran who is not able to use the preference.

Both a mother and a spouse (including widow or widower) may be entitled to preference on the basis of the same veteran's service if they both meet the requirements. However, neither may receive preference if the veteran is living and is qualified for federal employment.

SPOUSE

Ten points are added to the passing examination score or rating of the spouse of a disabled veteran who is disqualified for a federal position along the general lines of his or her usual occupation because of a service-connected disability. Such a disqualification may be presumed when the veteran is unemployed and

- Is rated by appropriate military or Department of Veterans Affairs authorities to be 100 percent disabled and/or unemployable; or
- Has retired, been separated, or resigned from a civil service position on the basis of a disability that is service-connected in origin; or
- Has attempted to obtain a civil service position or other position along the lines of his or her usual occupation and has failed to qualify because of a service-connected disability.

Preference may be allowed in other circumstances, but anything less than the above warrants a more careful analysis.

 Note: Veterans' Preference for spouses is different than the preference the Department of Defense is required by law to extend to spouses of active-duty members in filling its civilian positions. For more information on that program, contact the Department of Defense.

WIDOW OR WIDOWER

Ten points are added to the passing examination score or rating of the widow or widower of a veteran who was not divorced from the veteran, has not remarried, or the remarriage was annulled, and the veteran either

- Served during a war or during the period April 28, 1952, through July 1, 1955, or in a campaign or expedition for which a campaign medal has been authorized; or
- Died while on active duty that included service described immediately above under conditions that would not have been the basis for other than an honorable or general discharge.

MOTHER OF A DECEASED VETERAN

Ten points are added to the passing examination score or rating of the mother of a veteran who died under honorable conditions while on active duty during a war or during the period April 28, 1952, through July 1, 1955, or in a campaign or expedition for which a campaign medal has been authorized; and

- She is or was married to the father of the veteran; and
- She lives with her totally and permanently disabled husband (either the veteran's father or her husband through remarriage); or
- She is widowed, divorced, or separated from the veteran's father and has not remarried; or
- She remarried but is widowed, divorced, or legally separated from her husband when she claims preference.

MOTHER OF A DISABLED VETERAN

Ten points are added to the passing examination score or rating of a mother of a living disabled veteran if the veteran was separated with an honorable or general discharge from active duty, including training service in the Reserves or National Guard, performed at any time, and is permanently and totally disabled from a service-connected injury or illness; and the mother

- Is or was married to the father of the veteran; and
- Lives with her totally and permanently disabled husband (either the veteran's father or her husband through remarriage); or
- Is widowed, divorced, or separated from the veteran's father and has not remarried; or
- Remarried but is widowed, divorced, or legally separated from her husband when she claims preference.

Adjudication of Veterans' Preference Claims

Agencies are responsible for adjudicating all preference claims, except claims for preference based on common-law marriage, which should be sent to the Office of Personnel Management (OPM), Office of the General Counsel, 1900 E St. NW, Washington, DC, 20415

Applying Veterans' Preference in Category Ranking

The qualified candidates assigned to a category are not given numeric ratings (scores); therefore, preference eligibles *do not* receive points, as prescribed by 5 U.S.C. § 3309.

Agencies will identify the qualified preference eligibles and then apply Veterans' Preference by listing preference eligibles ahead of nonpreference eligibles within the same quality category in which they were assigned based on the job-related assessment tools(s).

No points are assigned under category rating. Qualified preference eligibles with a compensable service-connected disability of 30 percent or more (CPS) and those with a compensable service-connected disability of at least 10 percent but less than 30 percent (CP) move from the category in which they would otherwise be placed to the top of the highest quality category (except for scientific or professional positions at the GS-9 level or higher). A selecting official may not pass over a preference eligible to select a nonpreference eligible unless there are grounds for passing over the preference eligible and the agency has complied with the pass-over procedures at 5 U.S.C. § 3318.

For most jobs and grade levels under category rating, the Certificate of Eligibles (selection list) or equivalent certifies eligibles in the following order:

1. Interagency Career Transition Assistance Program (ICTAP) eligibles
2. Eligibles who lost consideration due to erroneous certification
3. Eligibles in highest quality category
4. Eligibles in the next lower quality categories, as needed

Names Referred to Selecting Official

Agencies may list the names of eligible candidates on the Certificate of Eligibles in any order (for example, alphabetical order) as long as preference eligibles are listed ahead of nonpreference eligibles. The "rule of three" procedures do not apply under category rating.

When providing the Certificate of Eligibles to the selecting official, agencies must certify all eligible candidates in the highest quality category; or if there are fewer than three eligible candidates in the highest quality category and the agency decides to merge the highest quality category with the next lower category, it must certify all eligible candidates in the newly merged category because it becomes the highest quality category.

Step 5: Rank Eligibles in the Order of Their Rating Adjusted for Veterans' Preference

In ranking eligibles, the agency establishes at least two categories. Individuals are assigned to a category based on their qualifications. All candidates in the highest category are referred for selection. Candidates with Veterans' Preference are placed ahead of those without preference. CPS and CP candidates move to the top of the highest category. The agency can hire anyone in the top category. It must justify passing over a preference eligible.

Summary

Your application will go through a minimum of three to five steps to determine your qualifications and whether you are among those in the highest category to be referred to the selecting manager. In general, you won't be contacted during the application process; HR professionals generally do not contact applicants for missing information. The determination of your status within the applicant pool will rely, at this point in the process, only on the strength of your federal resume. So move to Chapter 3 to get started on it!

 Note: The material in this chapter provides a brief overview of the selection process and how applications are processed in the federal HR environment. Agencies will have specific instructions that may vary from the information in this chapter.

Work Experience and the Outline Format: How to Stand Out and Get Referred

President Obama's Memorandum to Agency Heads states that essay-style questions (or KSAs) will be eliminated and individuals will be able to apply for federal employment by submitting resumes and cover letters. What this really means to the federal resume writer is that the resume will now need to cover the Knowledge, Skills, and Abilities, along with accomplishments, in a shorter version of the federal resume.

Since the last edition of this book, the average federal resume length has grown to five to seven pages. But with the larger number of applicants (100 to 1,000 for each job), and the Human Resources specialists becoming unable to read longer resumes because of time management and the desire to "get through" reading the resumes, they are scanning for the education, experience, and specialized experience they are seeking. So we are now recommending a more concise federal resume, with keywords from the announcement and more accomplishments.

Quick Checklists for Writing Your Federal Resume

A federal resume will prove you have the qualifications; specialized experience; and Knowledge, Skills, and Abilities to do the job. It will also prove this knowledge and expertise with accomplishments from the last 10 years of experience (up to 15 years is also acceptable).

The outstanding federal resume could get you Best Qualified; hopefully Best Qualified and Referred to a Supervisor; and Interviewed for a federal job; and hopefully will result in a job offer.

Critical Content in Work Experience

Your Work Experience section is the *most* important section in your entire federal resume. Here are some key facts to know as you prepare to write your resume:

- Focus on relevant work experience that demonstrates your One Year Specialized Experience (or more) from the announcement.
- Include keywords from the announcement.
- Include accomplishment examples that support the KSAs in the announcement.
- Include education, certification, and training that is relevant to the position.

Time Management Strategies

Allow enough time to prepare your resume:

- Thirty minutes to one hour to analyze the target job announcement for your list of keywords and to study the Duties and Specialized Experience
- One hour to find versions of resumes, accomplishments, and other documents
- One hour to set up your account/profile in USAJOBS
- Four to five hours to write, edit, and proofread the federal resume

Typical Length

The typical length of a federal resume is

- Four to six pages in the USAJOBS format
- Five pages in Microsoft Word with one-inch margins

Methods for Writing

Here are some top writing tips for your federal resume:

- Create the Outline Format with all-cap headings using keywords and KSA language.
- Cover the specialized experience from the announcement.
- Focus on the last 10 years of dates and employers.
- Summarize or write short paragraphs for positions for the prior 10 years.
- Maximum length of paragraphs should be between 5 and 10 lines.
- Do not include positions from 20 years ago unless they are very short descriptions.
- Eliminate positions that are short-term or irrelevant.
- Write well, edit well, and proofread it.
- Include at least one interesting, quantified accomplishment on page one of the federal resume to grab the HR specialist's or supervisor's attention.

The Outline Format in the USAJOBS Builder

You can copy and paste your Outline Format resume into the USAJOBS resume builder. It should match the announcement easily with all-cap keywords, read easily, and impress with a few accomplishments that prove you are a great candidate for this job (see Figure 3.1).

EXPERIENCE:
04-1997 to present; 40 hours per week; Electronics Technician; NT-0856-04/00;
Last Promoted 04-1997; Temporary Employee No; Temporary Promotion No; NSWC
PHD Detachment Louisville; 160 Rochester Drive; Michael Corum; (502) 364-5132; Contact supervisor? Yes.

I perform the duties of an electronic technician in support of the acquisition and engineering efforts within the Mark 34 Gun Weapons System (GWS) Division. I have extensive knowledge of Gun Computer Systems (GCS) and Electro-Optic Systems. I provide technical support in the installation, alignment, operation, maintenance, and system integration test site performance. I perform modifications on the AN-UYK-44 (V) Data Processing Set Enhanced Processor Open System Module (DPS-EP/OSM), modifications involve the installation of Electro-Magnetic Protection Interface Panels which consists of the Recommended Standard-232 (RS-232), Ethernet, Small Computer System Interface (SCSI), Low Level Serial (LLS), and Fiber Data Distributed Interface (FDDI). I perform wire wrapping for the internal memory Versa Module EuroCard (VME) Cage that specifies Power PC Circuit Card Assembly (CCA) locations and identifies land-based sites and ship hull numbers (i.e.; Wallops Island and DDG-51). I perform integrations of the OF-174 Expansion Adapter Group (EAG) with the AN-UYK-44 for added communication and input/output channels, testing circuit card assemblies (CCAs) such as Enhanced Processor/Versa Module Euro Card (EP/VME), Input/Output Controllers (IOCs), Power PCs, FDDIs, ScramNet, and Programmable Maintenance Processors (PMPs).

Figure 3.1: The federal resume in Outline Format with keywords and accomplishments.

Target Job: USDA Forest Service Training Technician, USDA Forest Service, Forest Service Job Corps Civilian Conservation Center, GS-1702-07.
Resume Format: Federal Resume in USAJOBS resume builder.

Allen Christopher Troutman
1010 Edmondson Ave.
Catonsville, MD 23228
Day Phone: 444-44-4444
Email: actrout@gmail.com

WORK EXPERIENCE   Baltimore County Public School System   12/2008 - Present
Baltimore, Maryland US

Salary: 120.00 USD Per Day
Hours per week: 40

1.
3.

Substitute Secondary Education Teacher
INSTRUCTOR IN MULTIPLE DISCIPLINES AND ALL GRADE LEVELS at diverse Baltimore County schools. Assess student individual learning needs. Master and apply established educational evaluations, models, rules, and guidelines to establish individual goals for students; establish a safe, stable learning environment; and exhibit positive behavioral models for students to follow.

5.
+ ACCOMPLISHMENT: Commended by school teachers and administrators for succeeding with this class for the first time in two school years. SERVED AS LONG-TERM SUBSTITUTE in Windsor Mill Middle School, Lansdowne High School, and Winfield Elementary School.

+ Successfully taught highly challenging 5th-grade class of 8 Special Needs minority students for 5 months after their two prior teachers quit. Ensured all students matriculated to 6th grade and improved their behavior and academic achievement.

6.
DEVELOP AND FOLLOW SPECIFIC CURRICULA FOR HISTORY, SOCIAL STUDIES, AND GEOGRAPHY CLASSES. Engage students with text and class exercises and research activities, and lead discussions about modern U.S. history in relation to historical events. Engage students in active dialogue to foster interest, awareness, and class participation.

2.
LESSON PLAN DESIGN: Prepare lessons, activities, and projects to meet class learning objectives, using available resources to augment education resources for the classroom. Develop activities and lessons to demonstrate American history and world history and geographic lessons.

COMMUNICATE SUCCESSFULLY orally and in writing with parents, guardians, and school administrators to monitor progress and help students overcome obstacles and achieve personal goals.

5.
GUIDANCE TO DIVERSE STUDENT AUDIENCES, including emotionally disturbed students; students suffering from ADD, ADHD, and various other psychological disorders; and low-income, minority, and recent-immigrant students with poor prior academic achievement. Prepare students for required benchmark examinations and provide testing accommodations for Special Needs students. (Contact Supervisor: Yes, Supervisor's Name: Susan Thomas, Supervisor's Phone: 444-444-4444)

US Census Bureau   2/2010 - 4/2010
Catonsville, MD US

Salary: 16.00 USD Per Hour
Hours per week: 20

(continued)

KEYWORDS

1. Guidance and instruction to new Job Corps Students
2. Vocational exploration
3. Assess new students' needs
4. Career development and training achievement system implementation
5. Advice to students on goal-setting
6. Mentoring students toward career success
7. Work-based learning opportunity

(continued)

Census Enumerator
Interviewed individuals in Baltimore County to update Census Reports. Managed a schedule and updated data on hundreds of local area residents. Met deadlines. Skilled in interviewing, gaining confidence of the American public for important census-taking for 2010. (Contact Supervisor: Yes, Supervisor's Name: John Smith, Supervisor's Phone: 443-444-4444)

Tweeter   12/2005 - 12/2008
Owings Mills, Maryland US

                                               Salary: $800- $1,500 USD Per
                                               Week
                                               Hours per week: 40

Sales Manager/Mentor
EXPERT IN MEETING AND GREETING VISITORS, building rapport with strangers, and managing a rush of customers with unique needs. Seven years of experience in retail sales and business development. Skilled in interpreting needs of customers and providing demonstrations throughout the day and in a complex technology environment. Listened to clients and responded in narrative format with relevant and engaging information.

4./5. ────────── COACHED, TRAINED, AND MOTIVATED SALES TEAM OF 11 PROFESSIONALS IN MEET-AND-GREET TECHNIQUES, product interpretations and demonstrations, soft skills, customer service, rapport building, conflict resolution, and negotiations. Led sales team to consistently achieve personal and company benchmarks.

ENSURED 100% client satisfaction with scope and quality of work performed. Educated customers in setting realistic and reasonable expectations. Delivered innovative solutions and exceeded customer goals.

4. ────────── AS PROJECT MANAGER FOR INSTALLATION CONTRACTS, researched, evaluated, managed, scheduled, and served as point of contact for up to five professional installers.

NEGOTIATED PRE- AND POST-AWARD CONTRACT FUNCTIONS, and procurement and delivery of goods and services with multiple installers. Oversaw and monitored contractor performance. Maintained procurement records. Developed contacts and maintained information on attendees. Collected funds, prepared invoices, and handled retail sales and reports. Performed and supervised opening and closing procedures for store. (Contact Supervisor: Yes, Supervisor's Name: Greg Hans, Supervisor's Phone: 443-444-4444)

EDUCATION   UNIVERSITY OF MARYLAND, BALTIMORE COUNTY

Baltimore, Maryland US
Bachelor's Degree - 5/2008
120 Semester Hours
Major: Psychology
Relevant Coursework, Licensures and Certifications:
Advanced Coursework:
PSYC215 EDUCATIONAL PSYCHOLOGY
SOCY335 SOCIOLOGY OF VIOLENCE
PSYC304 ADOLESCENT PSYCHOLOGY
PSYC335 PHYSIOLOGICAL PSYCHOLOGY
PSYC380 PERSONALITY
PSYC340 SOCIAL PSYCHOLOGY
PSYC370 SENSATION AND PERCEPTION
PSYC407 ADV CHILD PSYCHOLOGY
PSYC331 and 332 EXPERIMENTAL PSYCH I and II
PSYC485 SEMINAR ON BEHAVIOR - PATHOLOGY/ADDICTION

Related Coursework GPA: 3.71

Related Coursework:
ECON201 MACRO ECONOMICS
POLS131 POLITICAL SCIENCE COMPARATIVE GOVERNMENT
PHIL150 CONTEMPORARY MORAL ISSUES
PHIL399 PHILOSPHY OF CITIZENSHIP
HIST361 THE FRENCH REVOLUTION
HIST407 FOUNDING OF AMERICAN NATION
HIST459 JAPAN SINCE 1800

UNIVERSITY OF MARYLAND, BALTIMORE COUNTY
Baltimore, MD US
Master's Degree
15 semester hours. Expect to graduate May 2011
Major: Education
Relevant Coursework, Licensures, and Certifications:
Working toward Secondary Teacher's Certificate with Master's in Education.

5. **ADDITIONAL INFORMATION**

PROFESSIONAL PROFILE

COMMUNICATIONS: Skilled instructor, group leader, speaker, and motivator. Experienced Communications Professional with exceptional interpersonal skills and proven track record of providing excellent customer service, communicating clearly and effectively, meeting and greeting customers/clients, and providing frontline information and support services to diverse audiences.

HISTORICAL INTERESTS: Very strong personal and family interest in history, and proven professional success as a Baltimore-area history teacher. As a Baltimore County and City teacher, communicate effectively and appropriately with individuals and groups to design, achieve, and promote a healthy learning environment, including history curricula.

RELEVANT SKILLS

+ Keyboard skills: 60 wpm; proficient with MS Office and online software.

5. + Excellent oral communication skills; track record of inspiring and motivating others.

+ Proven success in interacting successfully with wide range of individuals in diverse settings, including adults and children with special needs.

+ Strong problem solving skills, especially in social/conflict resolution.

+ Effective leadership and multitasking skills, including leading large-scale projects with multiple players.

+ Strong and demonstrated personal, family, and professional interest in history.

+ Completed Bachelor's degree, including coursework in American history.

The easier the federal resume is to read with the keywords from the announcement, the more likely the HR specialist and supervisor will determine that your resume is Best Qualified. If your resume includes accomplishments, the HR specialist and supervisor will be impressed and hopefully interview you about your projects and accomplishments and what you can offer their agency or office.

Four Ways to Achieve Federal Resume Success

Your federal resume can be successful in four ways:

- By getting your resume scored as Best Qualified
- By getting you referred to the supervisor
- By getting you selected by the supervisor for an interview
- By getting you a job offer

Before and After: Five Ways to Not Write Your Work Experience Section—and Solutions

This section shows you a few of the most prevalent ways not to write your federal resume. The "before" resumes are difficult to read, not focused, and unimpressive, and they do not demonstrate the specialized experience from an announcement. The "after" formats show you how to improve the readability with writing strategies that will impress the HR specialist and the supervisor. The objective is to get Best Qualified, referred to the supervisor, selected by the supervisor for an interview, and hired.

Table 3.1: The Most Common Resume Problems

Resume Writing Problem	Federal Resume Writing Solutions
The big block	Outline with small paragraphs
Laundry list	Outline with accomplishments
Generic with semicolons	Special projects featured
Too short	Specialized experience featured
Filled with acronyms	Plain language; active voice

Example 1

Before: Big Block, Too Many *I*s and Acronyms

EXPERIENCE:
04-1997 to present; 40 hours per week; Electronics Technician; NT-0856-04/00;
Last Promoted 04-1997; Temporary Employee No; Temporary Promotion No; NSWC
PHD Detachment Louisville; 160 Rochester Drive; Michael Corum; (502) 364-5132; Contact supervisor? Yes.

I perform the duties of an electronic technician in support of the acquisition and engineering efforts within the Mark 34 Gun Weapons System (GWS) Division. I have extensive knowledge of Gun Computer Systems (GCS) and Electro-Optic Systems. I provide technical support in the installation, alignment, operation, maintenance, and system integration test site performance. I perform modifications on the AN-UYK-44 (V) Data Processing Set Enhanced Processor Open System Module (DPS-EP/OSM), modifications involve the installation of Electro-Magnetic Protection Interface Panels which consists of the Recommended Standard-232 (RS-232), Ethernet, Small Computer System Interface (SCSI), Low Level Serial (LLS), and Fiber Data Distributed Interface (FDDI). I perform wire wrapping for the internal memory Versa Module EuroCard (VME) Cage that specifies Power PC Circuit Card Assembly (CCA) locations and identifies land-based sites and ship hull numbers (i.e.; Wallops Island and DDG-51). I perform integrations of the OF-174 Expansion Adapter Group (EAG) with the AN-UYK-44 for added communication and input/output channels, testing circuit card assemblies (CCAs) such as Enhanced Processor/Versa Module Euro Card (EP/VME), Input/Output Controllers (IOCs), Power PCs, FDDIs, ScramNet, and Programmable Maintenance Processors (PMPs).

After: Outline Format with Keywords

April 1997 to Present   **Electronics Technician**
                                         Naval Surface Warfare Center Port Hueneme Louisville
                                         Detachment, Louisville, KY

COMPUTER CUSTOMER SUPPORT: Maintain and support electronic and computer systems and workload forecasting for the Electronic/Engineering Laboratory. Configure portable personal computers, performed installation of four peripheral component interconnect (PCI) circuit cards, two synchro, and two Naval Tactical Data System (NTDS) Type E Low Level Serial (LLS) and Type A Fast Parallel in each.

ELECTRONIC TECHNICIAN: Support the acquisition and engineering efforts within the Mark 34 Gun Weapons System (GWS) Division. Plan, organize, and execute projects in development. Independently accomplish work assignments on systems and subsystems requiring solutions of both design and operational discrepancies.

RESOLVED CONTROVERSIAL OR NOVEL PROBLEMS: Extensive knowledge of the MK 160 Gun Computer System (GCS) and MK 46 Optical Sight System. Valuable technical source for operational, maintenance, system integration, and engineering lab support. Resolved controversial or novel problems.

KEY ACCOMPLISHMENTS:
- Rework of Velocimeter resulted in significant cost savings for the Navy and in developing a procedure to test units following repair.
- Developed watertight integrity procedures to protect against water intrusion aboard navy vessels for the Mark 5 Velocimeter.
- Recognized by management for the rapid completion of antenna repacking efforts at Tobyhanna, which made a positive difference in theater due to lack of antennas.

Example 2

Before: Too Short

Northside Independent School District — Connections Program, San Antonio, Texas

Social Worker, February 2003–Present

Provide direct social services to over 400 homeless families within the San Antonio area. Assess student's and family's needs and assist them in accessing educational, medical, and other support services within the community. Provide counseling and crisis intervention for students and families. Monitor and track students' attendance and educational progress. Facilitate inter-district and out-of-district transportation services for over 200 students. Coordinate services with other campus interdisciplinary teams to develop service plans. Advocate for students in order to meet their educational needs. Responsible in maintaining accurate and complete student records. Attend homeless conferences, advisory council meetings, and network with various districts and community agencies.

After: Outline Format with Clear Skills

Social Worker, February 2003 to Present
Northside Independent School District—Connections Program, San Antonio, Texas; Hours per week: 40; Supervisor: Marta Martinez 210 397 0530; May Contact: Yes
PROVIDE DIRECT SOCIAL SERVICES to a variety of individuals from various socioeconomic, cultural, ethnic, and educational backgrounds. Work under FEDERAL GRANT from McKinney Vento Homeless Education Assistance Act to serve over 400 homeless families per year, totaling 2,800 homeless families within the San Antonio area.

INDEPENDENTLY ASSESS STUDENT'S AND FAMILY'S NEEDS by addressing their physical, mental, social, and educational situation. Identify student and family problems, strengths, weaknesses, coping skills, and types of assistance needed. Formulate and implement treatment plan. Provide counseling and crisis intervention for students and families.

PROVIDE OUTREACH, ASSESSMENT, REFERRALS, AND CASE MANAGEMENT demonstrating knowledge of the principles and theoretical concepts of social work. Assist students and families in accessing educational, medical, and other support services within the community. Make appropriate referrals to community and other agencies and coordinate services.

ESTABLISH AND MAINTAIN EFFECTIVE WORKING RELATIONSHIPS with clients, staff, and representatives of community agencies. Educate staff and others in the community about available program services. Participate in weekly professional peer-review case conferences.

Accomplishments:
- Developed highly effective homeless transportation database.
- Received consistently excellent evaluations for the past 7 years.

Example 3

Before: Laundry List

Implementation Project Manager DISA-COCOM—Defense Information Systems Agency
07/2002 to present
Job Description:
Direct project staff in executing a wide range of DISA IT program plans and objectives.

- Lead numerous IT professionals with responsibilities in operating systems and customer support to ensure mission-related activities are effectively planned, coordinated, and executed.
- Communicate to team the overall organizational mission, specific details of assignments, work product requirements, project work plans, individual and team project deadlines.
- Provide advice and guidance on technical problems and issues.
- Responsible for the overall management of multiple special projects within the Defense Agencies Branch, Programs and Implementation Division, including Federal Electronic Business System (FEDeBIZ), Defense Personal Property System (DPS), Global Combat Support System (GCSS), and Real Property Unique Identifier Registry System (RPSUID).
- Coordinate and lead project meetings involving civilian and contractor personnel during weekly teleconference calls.

After: Outline Format with KSAs in the Resume

Implementation Project Manager DISA-COCOM—Defense Information Systems Agency
07/2002 to present

PROJECT STAFF SUPERVISION
Direct project staff in executing a wide range of DISA IT program plans and objectives. Lead numerous IT professionals with responsibilities in operating systems and customer support to ensure mission-related activities are effectively planned, coordinated, and executed. Communicate to team the overall organizational mission, specific details of assignments, work product requirements, project work plans, and individual and team project deadlines. Provide advice and guidance on technical problems and issues.

MANAGED MULTIPLE PROJECTS FOR MAJOR CUSTOMERS
Managed multiple special projects within the Defense Agencies Branch, Programs and Implementation Division, including: Federal Electronic Business System (FEDeBIZ), Defense Personal Property System (DPS), Global Combat Support System (GCSS), and Real Property Unique Identifier Registry System (RPSUID). Coordinate and lead project meetings involving civilian and contractor personnel during weekly teleconference calls.

- The tasking involved implementation of hosting hardware and software application within DISA's DECCs. As Implementation Manager, led the successful completion of the customer's (SRF) Service Request Form. Led the implementation team to include Customer Account Reps (CARs), engineers, and a host of team members in the successful completion of Service Request Forms (SRFs) and delivery to GS-426 Business Office for pricing, ultimately delivering a Letter Estimate (LE) to customer base.

RECOGNIZED EXPERT IN CONFIGURATION MANAGEMENT:
Recognized expert in configuration management, software services capabilities, and operations. Serve as Subject Matter Expert (SME), providing in-depth briefings at high-level DISA meetings. Assemble, research, analyze, and report on information to improve IT systems, indicating specific recommendations for enhancement of IT systems.

Example 4

Before: Big Block and No Accomplishments

General Services Administration	3/2009 to present
Ft. Worth, TX US	Grade Level: GS07
Realty Technician, 1101	Salary: $41,002 USD Per Year; Hours per week: 40

Individually perform all close-out administration procedures for lease contracts and provide procurement support throughout the process. Prepare and analyze contract data from various automated procurement systems to create and maintain aging contract termination list. Consolidated and archived completed contract files. Prepare new lease files and serve as the control point for new project requirements. Prepare award letters to Contracting Officer Representative, Lessor, Agency, and Federal Protective Service. Individually assist senior Realty Specialist in drafting and editing standard contracts, other legal documents, and correspondence. Research and respond to rent inquiries from Lessors and Customers to determine necessary action. Use Rent Bill Management Communication Tool (RBM) to create building numbers, modify building information, terminate leases, and change lease information. Individually draft Supplemental Lease Agreements. Use various types of software to process different types of documents. Individually perform Realty Transaction Surveys on accepted contracts. Individually perform quality-control procedures on all new contracts. At the Real Estate Division conference, I individually presented on the subject of contract close-out and procedures. Individually train other Realty Technicians on contract close-out procedures. (Contact Supervisor: Yes, Supervisor's Name: Kathleen Manors 444-444-4444)

After: Outline Format with KSAs in the Resume

Realty Technician, 3/2009–Present
General Services Administration

CONTRACT MANAGEMENT: Work with a broad and diverse range of government agencies to perform contract management, close outs, and terminations, including: Social Security Administration, U.S. Customs and Border Protection, Agricultural Marketing Services, Animal and Plant Health Inspection Service, Internal Revenue Service, Bureau of Indian Affairs, and Fish and Wildlife Service.

- Slashed processing time of close out procedures from months to hours. Suggested and helped implement personnel realignment so that key individuals now communicate critical steps, information, and updates. Devised inspection criteria to reduce processing time; errors are now spotted in minutes and missing information is easy to procure.

CONTRACT ADMINISTRATION: Support 15 contracting officers, 30 project managers, and more than 300 projects. Manage paperwork, organize files, and provide general support while performing daily responsibilities. Knowledgeable of contractor and vendor performance parameters, and the need for clear, concise performance-based statements and measurements.

- Created new procedures that reduced contract processing time and enabled the swift identification of key documents among thousands to be reviewed. Drafted checklists to aid in the review process.

CONTRACT CLOSE OUTS: Process seven to ten contract close outs per month. Perform notification procedures to building service centers over the phone and in writing. Partner with contract officer. Correct documents as necessary. Create new agreements. Quality check documents to bill out correctly. Ensure that all paperwork, terms, steps, and procedures are complete so that contract is completed with absolute accuracy and integrity.

Example 5

Before: Position Description in Big Block

Procurement Technician, GS-1106-5, 4/9/2001 to Present, Work 40 hrs/wk
Defense Logistics Agency, DCSO-H, 8725 John J. Kingman Rd., Fort Belvoir, VA 22060
Supervisor: Michael Rogers; Telephone: (703) 777-7777

Coordinate administrative work for Contract Division by handling multiple projects simultaneously. Interact with members of staff, organization, and individuals outside our agency ranging from government agencies to the public. Research and contact contractors and customers; then type forms in automated contracting system, SPS, to close out contracts for division. Work with finance sections to de-obligate funds from closed-out contracts. Develop statistical and narrative data into an electronic format using office-automation equipment for report writing and statistical charts in spreadsheets for management. Execute a wide variety of special project requests by Director or team leads. Independently respond to requests for information by performing detailed fact-finding searches and providing technical assistance when warranted. Research precedent studies to determine past issues; collect/evaluate a variety of data and formulate recommendations. Collect, edit, and analyze all input from selected experts. Clarify information and instructions, exchange information, and refer inquires to appropriate resources. Operate office auto equipment and electronic media using high-level software and printers. Possess expert knowledge in Windows operating system and use of office automated software. Analyze automated database management systems to isolate problems, such as logic loops. Possess superb oral and written communication skills evident in speaking with customers and writing correspondence for director. Plan, manage, and participate in major studies or related efforts connected with the development of policies, goals, and new objectives on administrative support procedures, processes, practices. Wrote operating procedures for contract close outs, acceptances for Military Interdepartmental Purchase Requests (MIPR), tracking sheets, and DD 350s. Wrote position description for my job and verified information with compensation and classification policies. Wrote peer award in which two colleagues won cash awards.

After: Outline Format with KSAs in the Resume

PROCUREMENT TECHNICIAN, GS-1106-5, step 10   04/2001 - Present
Defense Logistics Agency, DLA Contracting Services Office, Fort Belvoir, VA

PERFORM AND MONITOR ADMINISTRATIVE ACTIVITIES associated with project support, acquisition, and the budget. Modify and close out approximately 120 contracts per year; clear, sort, and maintain files with more than 30,000 contracts.

IDENTIFY, ANALYZE, AND RECOMMEND SOLUTIONS to problems in organizational structure, staffing, position management, work processes, and workload distribution.
- Gather two-year data on Military Interdepartmental Purchase Requests (MIPRs) to assist finance office and business offices. Collect and analyze input from experts.
- Modify and close out contracts, which saved agency more than $3 million per year.

ANALYZE PROBLEMS TO IDENTIFY SIGNIFICANT FACTORS, GATHER PERTINENT DATA. Compile, maintain, review, interpret, analyze, and evaluate data relevant to specific procurement program funding, contractor performance, and contract payments.
- Use fact-finding and investigative techniques to determine discrepancies in payments, analyze records, and coordinate with the Defense Finance and Accounting System agency to resolve problems.

DEVELOP FINDINGS AND RECOMMENDATIONS BASED ON ANALYSIS AND WORK OBSERVATIONS; verify invoices on government purchase cards to ensure amounts are accurate and in compliance with the corresponding contracts. Review program materials for consistency with established policies, procedures, regulations, and legislation when preparing contracts for closeout.
- Exceptional teaching ability with software programs to help incoming personnel excel in using Excel, PowerPoint, PD2, EBS, and Access Online.

Building Your Outline Format Federal Resume: A Match Between You and Your Target Job

Federal HR specialists like the Outline Format because it is easy to read. The all-new, popular Outline approach is based on the concept of "how many hats do you wear at work?" The "hats" you wear at work can actually match the critical skills needed in your target job. These critical skills are included in the vacancy announcement. It's a matter of matching your resume to the announcement and making it readable.

The Writing Concept: How Many Hats Do You Wear at Work?

The Outline Format was created at a meeting I had with a management consultant in 1999. In order to advise me in my business management, he asked me what I did at work. At first I was overwhelmed with the question (and realized why writing a resume was overwhelming) and didn't know where to start with the answer. Then I thought of a quick way to answer the question just by giving him the "hats I wear at work." I answered him simply with this list. I am a

- Webmaster
- Author/publisher
- Small-business owner
- Career counselor
- Trainer

Building your Outline Format resume can be as easy as asking yourself that question and then building the resume into four to six small paragraphs that describe each hat. The hats are simply the critical skills that the HR specialist and the supervisor are looking for. If the announcement states in the duties and qualifications that "the incumbent will supervise, train, and lead teams," obviously, one of the hats you should write about should be "supervisor, team lead, and trainer."

Your objective is to mirror the skill set desired in the announcement with your own skills while keeping it very simple and easy to read. The hats here are also keywords from the announcement. And the hats should be typed in all caps so that they stand out in the resume.

- Supervisor
- Trainer/Facilitator
- Project Manager
- Team Leader
- Planner and Coordinator
- Problem-solver
- Customer Service Representative
- Liaison
- Advisor
- Briefer
- Writer/Editor
- Analyst
- Researcher
- Program Manager
- Subject-Matter Expert
- Engineer

Example: Supervisory Transportation Security Inspector (Aviation), SV-1801-J

Target Job: Supervisory Transportation Security Inspector (Aviation), SV-1801-J.
Resume Format: Federal resume with KSA accomplishments in the resume—seeking promotion.
Targeted, written, and designed by Julie Jasper, Certified Professional Resume Writer (CPRW), Certified Federal Resume Writer (CFRW)

Job Announcement Analysis and Keyword List

Job Title: Supervisory Transportation Security Inspector (Aviation) SV-1801-J

Department: Department of Homeland Security

Sub Agency: DHS-Transportation Security Administration

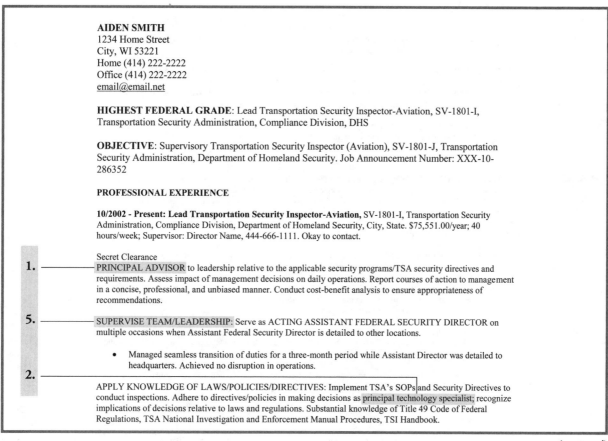

AIDEN SMITH
1234 Home Street
City, WI 53221
Home (414) 222-2222
Office (414) 222-2222
email@email.net

HIGHEST FEDERAL GRADE: Lead Transportation Security Inspector-Aviation, SV-1801-I, Transportation Security Administration, Compliance Division, DHS

OBJECTIVE: Supervisory Transportation Security Inspector (Aviation), SV-1801-J, Transportation Security Administration, Department of Homeland Security. Job Announcement Number: XXX-10-286352

PROFESSIONAL EXPERIENCE

10/2002 - Present: Lead Transportation Security Inspector-Aviation, SV-1801-I, Transportation Security Administration, Compliance Division, Department of Homeland Security, City, State. $75,551.00/year; 40 hours/week; Supervisor: Director Name, 444-666-1111. Okay to contact.

Secret Clearance

1. PRINCIPAL ADVISOR to leadership relative to the applicable security programs/TSA security directives and requirements. Assess impact of management decisions on daily operations. Report courses of action to management in a concise, professional, and unbiased manner. Conduct cost-benefit analysis to ensure appropriateness of recommendations.

5. SUPERVISE TEAM/LEADERSHIP: Serve as ACTING ASSISTANT FEDERAL SECURITY DIRECTOR on multiple occasions when Assistant Federal Security Director is detailed to other locations.

- Managed seamless transition of duties for a three-month period while Assistant Director was detailed to headquarters. Achieved no disruption in operations.

2. APPLY KNOWLEDGE OF LAWS/POLICIES/DIRECTIVES: Implement TSA's SOPs and Security Directives to conduct inspections. Adhere to directives/policies in making decisions as principal technology specialist; recognize implications of decisions relative to laws and regulations. Substantial knowledge of Title 49 Code of Federal Regulations, TSA National Investigation and Enforcement Manual Procedures, TSI Handbook.

(continued)

KEYWORDS

1. **Principal Advisor**
2. **Principal Technology Specialist**
3. **Administer Compliance Performance Programs**
4. **Plan and Organize Work**

5. **Supervise Team**
6. **Solve Complex Security Problems**
7. **Independently Conduct Inspection and Compliance Assessments**

(continued)

7. ─── INSPECT AND CONDUCT VULNERABILITY ASSESSMENTS: Independently conduct inspection and compliance assessments. Investigate security concerns; establish preventative methods/procedures. Conduct vulnerability assessments to test effectiveness of airports' current security systems/procedures.

6. ─── • Support safe execution of large public events, including Championship tournament, which brought a large number of visitors/high-profile VIPs to the local county airport. Execute SPECIAL EMPHASIS INSPECTION (SEI) as directed by Headquarters. Extensively use PARIS for input of inspections, investigations, and outreach.

6. ─── • Inspected and subsequently identified security shortfalls identified at the county airport, which led to the county seeking and obtaining a grant for the purchase of new security measures.

6. ─── SOLVE COMPLEX SECURITY PROBLEMS: Apply experience/comprehensive technical knowledge and understanding of new technologies/methodologies. Evaluate mission-critical programs and operational requirements. Identify /evaluate underlying causes of issues; distinguish relevant from irrelevant information; weigh alternative solutions in advance of deadlines with limited guidance. CONDUCT RISK ANALYSIS AND DEVELOP SPECIFIC CONTINGENCY PLANS to overcome them.

   • Used ingenuity to develop a solution to carrier's gateway security violations. Fostered buy-in from carrier, which became committed to a reasonable security improvement measure as opposed to paying violation fines. Carrier has not had security violations after implementation of security solution.

3. ─── ADMINISTER COMPLIANCE PERFORMANCE PROGRAMS: Identify actions that affect the efficiency and performance of work unit. Evaluate performance-improvement actions; ensure compliance with laws and regulations. LEADER/PROGRAM MANAGER for Ronald Reagan Washington National Airport (DCA) Access Security Program (DASSP) to support new designation of local airport as a Gateway Airport.

   • Encouraged and gained cooperation among local corporate flight departments and the local fixed-base operator to ensure completion of broad organizational objective.
   • Due to successful program management, local airport achieved gateway approval in early June 2006 and held the inaugural flight in late June; Received Time Off Award for superlative work.

5. ─── LEAD TEAMS/SUPERVISE STAFF as Team Lead for Aviation Inspectors. Role model and peer-to-peer coach. Consistently volunteer services, on short notice, to meet unexpected challenges, circumstances, and/or situations. Track all assignments, training, airport strikes and special assignments to ensure that all work is equally/fairly distributed among team; verify completion of all tasks. Engage team and subordinates in project planning and tasking; gain project buy-in through involvement. Ensure understanding of mission and objectives; troubleshoot problems to develop solutions.

4. ─── • Ensured tasks were equitably dispersed among team members and resolved conflicts among team members. Inclusive environment motivated staff and specifically delineated tasks and schedules helped to keep project on schedule. Received positive feedback from team members regarding team approach to conducting inspections. Overall abilities of staff improved due to rotation of inspections.
   • Manage issue of team member's intransigence in performing work. Provided mentoring to support performance improvements of faltering team member.

5. ─── PROVIDE TRAINING to new inspectors. Developed the Transportation Security Inspector On-the-Job Training Program. CREATED REPORT WRITING CLASS for all local Supervisory Transportation Security Officers and Transportation Security Officers.

   • Successfully completed development of training program within one month despite original timeline of nine months so Assistant Federal Security Director could reveal the program at a statewide TSA Conference and later at the National Assistant Federal Security Director's Conference in 2006.
   • Training program was submitted to Compliance Division and posted nationally on the TSA Employee Web Board.

2/1992 - 10/2002: **Police Officer, City Police Department,** City, State. $48,800 per year; 40 hours per week; Supervisor: Sergeant Name, 111-222-3333 Permission to contact.

5. ─── PROVIDED DIRECTION/LEADERSHIP to district police officers as Acting Desk Sergeant. Supervised 39 of the district's sworn and civilian office personnel. Enforced local, state, and federal laws. Conducted arrests and processed suspects who violated laws.

3. ─── ADMINISTERED OPERATIONS: Ensured that personnel performed duties according to laws/regulations/SOPs. Accounted for currency taken in by all shifts; filed appropriate reports. MANAGED EVIDENCE INVENTORY, ensuring proper storage. Monitored booking procedures of all prisoners coming into the district for processing.

   • Elevated to acting desk sergeant in recognition of performance and capabilities despite freeze on promotions.

COMMUNICATED ORALLY, providing courtroom testimony in both criminal and civil court.

TOOK DECISIVE ACTION to include making sound, though sometimes unpopular, decisions in situations of greater than normal pressure, adverse circumstances, and heightened complexity. Based decisions on analysis of facts/data with minimal or no supervision.

- Made sound and quick decisions in response to suicide attempt. Followed standard procedures yet relied on experience and knowledge to react effectively under pressure. The subject was rescued without harm.

EDUCATION
Associate degree, Police Science, Minor: Psychology, Milwaukee Area Technical College (MATC), Milwaukee, WI, 1991
GPA: 3.818, Major GPA: 3.895. 66 total credits.
Honors Standing: Received Certificate for Scholastic Achievement by MATC and Phi Theta Kappa Honorary Society for maintaining an Honors Standing.

SPECIALIZED TRAINING
Chemical-terrorism Vulnerability Information, one-day course, DHS Office of Infrastructure Protection, 2008
Introduction to the Incident Command System (ICS-100), one-day course, FEMA, 2008
ICS-200 for Single Resources and Initial Action Incidents, one-day course, FEMA, 2008
ICS-300, two-day course, Waukesha County Technical College, 2008
Behavior Recognition Training, Transportation Security Administration, 2008
Planning Considerations for Terrorism Response, two-day course, St. Petersburg College, 2007
Evaluating Truthfulness, The Ekman Group, two-day course, 2007
Introduction to Railroads Course, Transportation Technology Center, 2007
Reid Technique of Interviewing and Interrogation, two-day course, John Reid and Associates, 2006
Perimeter Security, one-week course, Lockmasters Security Institute, 2006
State and Local Anti-Terrorism Training, Train-the-Trainer two-day workshop, U.S. Bureau of Justice Assistance, 2005
Airport Security Coordinator Certification, two days, American Association of Airport Executives, 2005
Transportation Security Inspector Basic Core Training, four weeks, 2004
Police Training Bureau, 20 weeks, Law Enforcement Officer Certification, 1992

ADDITIONAL INFORMATION:

2. PROFILE

Experienced TSA Lead Inspector with extensive knowledge of laws, policies, and regulations and ability to lead security programs to support specific and immediate security objectives as well as DHS's overall security mission. Advise leadership as a technical specialist using sound judgment and consistently displaying decisiveness, based on research and experience, to promote operational enhancements and procedural efficiencies. Plan and set priorities of subordinates' work effort using team approach, maintaining accountability of actions. Excellent record of solving complex issues by fostering innovation

6. and cooperation of team and coordinating actions with stakeholders. Communicate security procedures and requirements to team in easily understood terms. Maintain composure under difficult, pressure-filled circumstances. Outstanding role model displaying integrity, consistently volunteering for special projects, and completing projects under tight and restricted deadlines.

COMPUTER PROFICIENCIES
Microsoft Office Suite, PARIS, ASAP database, Ishare

PUBLIC SPEAKING
Report Writing: Provided training to all Transportation Security Officers, 2006
Report Writing: Created and presented class instruction to 250 local STSOs and TSOs. Presentation was reviewed prior to presentation by North Central Region's Legal Counsel, who in return asked if they could use my presentation to present to airports in our region.

(continued)

(continued)

PUBLICATION
Name, *Aviation Security Inspector,* 2006
Name, *On The Job Training Evaluation Checklist,* 2006. Document was prepared for TSI and, due to its valuable content, was subsequently provided to the Compliance Division and posted nationally on the TSA Employee Web Board.

HONORS AND RECOGNITIONS
Dependability/Reliability Award from DHS/TSA, 2006
Chief of Police Superior Achievement Award: Awarded Merit Citation for calm and quick thinking in preventing a suicide attempt of a subject attempting to jump from a viaduct, 1995.
Certificate for Scholastic Achievement by MATC and PHI THETA KAPPA Honorary Society for maintaining an Honors Standing, 1991

 Note: The nouns/keywords are the "hats" this Lead Screener wears in his job every day. They are also the critical keywords and skills needed to apply for this promotion at TSA.

Summary

It takes time and research for keywords and inspiration to write the most important section of your federal resume: Work Experience. Your extra effort in writing the accomplishments that prove your specialized skills and knowledge can help you stand out and get Best Qualified. Think about the examples that demonstrate your past performance. This could give the supervisor the information he or she needs to interview you for the position. If the human resources specialist receives 200 resumes, your resume must demonstrate that you have the experience for the position, using the language from the announcement.

CHAPTER 4

Matching Strategies: KSAs in the Resume, Keywords, Qualifications, Accomplishments, and Specialized Experience

Matching your resume to the federal vacancy announcement is critical whether you are changing your career, seeking a promotion, or hoping to move to a lateral position. There are seven ways to match your resume toward your next position:

- **Include KSAs in the resume.** KSAs in the resume will be important for the human resources specialist to determine whether you have the experience for the position. Add a mini-KSA to your Outline Format for each of the specialized experience areas in the announcement.

- **Add a keyword list.** Analyze the keywords from the announcement and add them into your federal resume in the Outline Format. Summarize your career in a Profile narrative that will serve as your "elevator speech" and present a total picture of your relevant career experience.

- **Feature One Year Specialized Experience.** This is described in each USAJOBS vacancy announcement under the Qualifications section. Make sure that it matches the announcement and that it stands out. You might have eight top skills, but only five of them are relevant to your target position. You need to feature the five that are relevant.

- **Add accomplishments.** Add accomplishments to demonstrate your knowledge, skills, and abilities that are mentioned in the announcement. You may have two or three outstanding accomplishments that you want to make sure the HR specialist and the supervisor read. These accomplishments could result in an interview.

- **Highlight specialized experience.** The announcement might ask for specialized experience and examples that demonstrate this specialized experience. You can add these very clear examples to your focusing section. In the USAJOBS resume builder, the focusing section is called "Additional Information."

- **Highlight the most important positions.** Emphasize the most important positions; deemphasize or delete positions that are not important or not job-related or recent. You may have two or three outstanding accomplishments that you want to make sure the HR specialist and the supervisor read. These accomplishments could result in an interview.

- **Add summary information.** Add a Profile statement, Summary of Qualifications, or Critical Skills List at the top of the resume (in a paper application) or in Additional Information field in the USAJOBS builder. You may have two or three outstanding accomplishments that you want to make sure the HR specialist and the supervisor read. These accomplishments could result in an interview.

Overview of the Seven Matching Strategies

Here is a brief description of each of the seven matching strategies that can help your federal resume to become Best Qualified. You can choose to use one or all of these matching techniques.

Include KSA Accomplishments in the Resume

Many of the vacancy announcements will not ask for separate KSAs on sheets of paper. You will find the knowledge, skills, and abilities required for the position listed in the Specialized Experience or the questionnaire. Wherever the KSA language is in the announcement, you will need to add this experience and a mini-KSA accomplishment into the federal resume.

Here are some sample KSAs:

- Specialized experience must have provided a knowledge of **contract administration, laws, regulations,** and **methods of contracting**; knowledge of the principles, concepts, and techniques of **procurement**.
- Knowledge of **basic acquisition procedures to include close-out procedures.** Carry out development assignments involving use of standard procedures and techniques.

Here are federal resume paragraphs that match the preceding KSAs:

CONTRACT ADMINISTRATION: Support 15 contracting officers, 30 project managers, and more than 300 projects. Manage paperwork, organize files, and provide general support while performing daily responsibilities. Knowledgeable of contractor and vendor performance parameters, and the need for clear, concise performance-based statements and measurements.

- Created new procedures that reduced contract processing time and enabled the swift identification of key documents among thousands to be reviewed. Drafted checklists to aid in the review process.

CONTRACT CLOSE OUTS: Process seven to ten contract close outs per month. Perform notification procedures to building service centers over the phone and in writing. Partner with contract officer. Correct documents as necessary. Create new agreements. Quality check documents to bill out correctly. Ensure that all paperwork, terms, steps, and procedures are complete so that the contract is completed with absolute accuracy and integrity.

- Slashed processing time of close-out procedures from months to hours. Suggested and helped implement personnel realignment so that key individuals now communicate critical steps, information, and updates. Devised inspection criteria to reduce processing time; errors are now spotted in minutes, and missing information is easy to procure.

Add a Keyword List

The samples in this book will give you methods for analyzing announcements for keywords for your federal resume. The keywords are critical whether the application is automated or a federal human resources specialist will read your federal resume. We always strive to find 5 to 10 keywords or phrases that are critical to match a federal resume to an announcement. Following is a sample keywords list:

KEYWORDS

CONTRACT MANAGEMENT

CONTRACT ADMINISTRATION

CONTRACT TERMINATIONS AND CLOSE OUTS

KNOWLEDGE OF CONTRACT LAWS, REGULATIONS, AND POLICIES

CUSTOMER SERVICE AND INTERPERSONAL SKILLS

ACQUISITION PROCEDURES

APPLY PROCEDURES AND TECHNIQUES TO CARRY OUT DEVELOPMENT ASSIGNMENTS

APPLICATION OF LAWS AND REGULATIONS GOVERNING ACQUISITIONS

COMPARE PRICES, DISCOUNTS, DELIVERY DATES, AND HANDLING CHARGES

INTERPRET PROCUREMENT REGULATIONS AND TECHNICAL MATERIAL

Feature One Year Specialized Experience

The announcement will state that the agency wants One Year Specialized Experience equal to the position being advertised. This information is critical for showing the human resources specialist that you have the knowledge and experience for the position.

Following is a sample One Year Specialized Experience statement from a job announcement:

SPECIALIZED EXPERIENCE FOR GS-9

To qualify for the GS-9, you must have one year of specialized experience equivalent to at least the GS-7 grade level; OR two years of progressively higher-level graduate education OR masters OR equivalent graduate degree or LL.B. or J.D. Specialized experience is described as demonstrated experience: (1) reviewing contracting or procurement actions to determine that **proper specifications/purchase descriptions** are included in **solicitation documents,** and (2) **evaluating bids** or **proposals** for **compliance** with **specifications/purchase descriptions** and applicable clauses; OR comparable experience.

Add Accomplishments

It's time to brag a little. If you are excellent in your field of work, give specific examples. In the federal human resources world, the accomplishments will demonstrate your past performance. HR wants you to prove that you have certain experiences that demonstrate that you have the knowledge, skills, and abilities needed for this position. So, think about three to five accomplishments that prove you have the experience to perform the position. The accomplishments will help you get Best Qualified and referred to a supervisor.

Highlight Specialized Experience

Do you have specialized experience that will prove your expertise for this job? Be sure to feature your specialized experience in the federal resume. If the agency wants One Year Specialized Experience in database maintenance or customer services, be sure to emphasize the position that shows this experience the most clearly. If your most relevant experience is your second or your third position, that can be okay. Hopefully that One Year Specialized Experience is within the last 10 years.

Highlight the Most Important Positions

Look at your work experiences and decide which positions are the most relevant for this position. Emphasize those positions and deemphasize the least-important positions. Delete positions that are short or not related to your target position. Count the number of your positions. It's best if you have five to eight jobs in your Work Experience section. You do not need to add every position to your Work Experience section. If you have short positions or nonrelevant positions, you can leave them out. Emphasize the last 10 years and most relevant positions.

The sample federal resume in this section is for an applicant who is seeking a Contract Specialist, GS-9 position. His first position is relevant for the Contract Specialist resume. But if he had taken a position in retail sales at Nordstrom, for instance, for a year, because his contractor position ended, we would include the Nordstrom position with only about two sentences of description. We would not write a full Outline Format description with keywords and accomplishments for the Nordstrom position because it is not relevant to the Contract Specialist position. By keeping the Nordstrom position short, we can lead the human resources specialist's eye to the next position at CACI, which is relevant and does demonstrate the One Year Specialized Experience.

Many federal job seekers have held various short-term positions that may not be relevant to the total application. These short-term positions can be left off the federal resume. The human resources specialist is looking for recent and relevant positions. Recent in a federal resume is 10 years, or the last 5 years. The human resources specialist will be most interested in the positions within the last 10 years.

The former SF-171 federal application required that every job, every change of address, and every supervisor be included as a "job block." Now with the federal resume, the human resources specialists want to see the positions that are Recent and Relevant.

Add a Critical Skills List or Profile Statement

A Critical Skills list is easier to write than a Profile statement. This is a list of skills that you have that are also in the vacancy announcement. This simple list of skills should be easy to read. The Critical Skills section is especially useful for technical positions where certain skills are mandatory. Do you have specific expertise that is required for your desired position? Make a list and copy and paste this into the Additional Information field in the USAJOBS resume builder.

Private-industry resumes almost always include a Profile statement to introduce the reader to the applicant's qualifications, competencies, and background. This section can save the human resource professional's time. Do you want the reader to be interested in you and keep reading your resume? Then you need a Profile statement on your resume. You can write your Profile statement in your Additional Information field in the USAJOBS resume builder.

Following is an example of a Profile statement and a Critical Skills list. You can choose which works best for your situation.

PROFILE: Analytical, expert professional with contract, real estate, and appraising experience. Constantly seeking ways to improve processes and optimize efficiencies. Take charge of initiatives with minimal guidance and complete all assignments ahead of schedule while exceeding expectations. Continually seeking new opportunities to broaden skills and knowledge while devoting maximum effort to all assigned tasks. Deconstruct complex activities into simpler, more manageable components. Able to perceive the larger picture while recommending and helping implement departmental or procedural alignments to reduce labor/time while ensuring accuracy. MSW Seeking VA Position

CRITICAL SKILLS

COMMITTED, PROFESSIONAL LICENSED MASTER SOCIAL WORKER with ten years of experience providing direct social services, conducting needs assessments, developing treatment plans, performing case management, and coordinating services and referrals.

EXPERT KNOWLEDGE OF PRINCIPLES AND THEORIES OF SOCIAL WORK to provide outreach assessment referrals and case management. In-depth knowledge of human development and human behavior. Extensive knowledge of community resources.

HIGHLY EFFECTIVE COMMUNICATOR. Extensive experience successfully working with individuals from a wide range of socioeconomic, cultural, ethnic, educational, and other diversified backgrounds.

Completed 2½ years of clinical supervision, where I was supervised by a Licensed Clinical Social Worker. Clinical Social Worker Licensure pending.

Skilled in the use of computer software applications for drafting documents, data management, and tracking.

Matching Your Resume to Each Announcement

You should match your resume to each announcement you apply to by changing your Profile statement. It takes only about an hour or so to customize your federal resume for each vacancy announcement.

Reading, understanding, and valuing the information in the announcement are important when you are focusing your resume. Read and analyze the Duties and Responsibilities section of the announcement. Read between the lines, too!

If you don't understand the position description, go to the agency's website and find out the agency's functions and programs. Think about the agency's and the hiring manager's needs. You will be the person who will perform this job. Whatever problems or special situations exist in this office, you will be the person who will solve them. Chapter 11 reviews how to analyze the announcement in more detail.

Federal Resume Samples That Match an Announcement

The applicants in the resume case studies that follow focused their resumes toward a specific position by using the Profile statement, Critical Skills list, Specialized Experience list, or Accomplishments list.

Case Study 1: KSA Accomplishments in the Resume

Correspondence Analyst / Management Analyst, GS-9

The KSAs and accomplishments in this Work Experience section are

- Coordination of Administrative Functions
- Office Automation Software
- Oral and Written Communication
- Communicating with Widely Divergent Populations

CORRESPONDENCE ANALYST/MANAGEMENT ANALYST, GS-9   05/2007 - present
U.S. Department of Homeland Security (DHS), Office of the Secretary
Washington, DC 20528
40 + hours/ week, $46,000 Salary/year

COORDINATED AND MONITORED ADMINISTRATIVE FUNCTIONS AND ACTIVITIES in the Office of the Secretary, as a federal employee from 09/2007 to present, and as a contractor from 05/2007 to 09/2007.

- Manage time and attendance and payroll records of more than 50 staff within the 4 divisions. Acted as point of contact with DHS mailroom staff.
- Received, reviewed, and prioritized more than 2,500 items of mail per day for the Secretary and DHS senior leaders.
- Primary point of contact for purchasing of supplies supporting 45 professional and admin staff. Managed contracts for custodial, repairs, and maintenance. Monitored contracts and reviewed costs and services. Improved quality assurance through direct communication with vendors and service providers.
- Coordinated a multi-facility carpet-cleaning project.

DEMONSTRATED SKILL IN USE OF OFFICE AUTOMATION SOFTWARE

- Proficient with Microsoft Office suite, database system, Intranet Quorum (IQ) to maintain complex tracking of individual items of written correspondence.
- Used WEBTA Time and Attendance software to track and account for payroll among more than 50 staff.

UTILIZED SKILL IN ORAL AND WRITTEN COMMUNICATION to obtain and provide information, guidance, instructions; prepare correspondence, reports, and other documents. Coordinated the creation, clearance, and distribution of written communication and responses on behalf of the former DHS Secretary and other senior leaders.

- Handled complex correspondence for 6 months concerning the Underwear Bomber from multiple law-enforcement agencies. Prioritized critical actions.

COMMUNICATED WITH INDIVIDUALS AND GROUPS REPRESENTING WIDELY DIVERGENT BACKGROUNDS, interests, and points of view.

- Professionally collaborated with individuals in 11 divisions of DHS. Maintained ongoing interaction with multiple governmental and nongovernmental vendors.
- Developed solid working relationships with colleagues, maintenance, custodial, building engineers, and emergency management personnel.

SET GOALS, PLANNED STRATEGIES, scheduled and coordinated work, and integrated planning efforts to meet organizational goals.

- Assisted in launching "DHScovery," the online, professional, educational development program for staff throughout DHS.
- Served as Content/Training Manager; assisted in coordinating the preservation and records management of Professional Development accomplishments for a staff of 50.
- Supported Congressional testimony by the Secretary that could impact changes to governing statutes, regulations, policies, and guidance on a variety of subjects affecting the administration and substance of critical departmental programs.

Case Study 2: Profile with Certifications, Core Competencies, and Technical Skills

IT Specialist in private industry targeting an IT Specialist government position, GS-2210-12

Additional Information

Enter job-related honors, awards, leadership activities, skills (such as computer software proficiency or typing speed) or any other information requested by a specific job announcement. Need more space? Click here to expand this field.

> PROFILE
> Results-oriented information technology professional with a proven track record in providing effective customer service, desktop management, network administration, and systems analysis demonstrated
> through more than five years in help desk support and systems administration. Qualifications include the following:
> ~~Highly skilled in providing excellent customer service to all levels~~

(You have 18114 characters remaining for your description...)

ADDITIONAL INFORMATION

PROFILE

Results-oriented information technology professional with a proven track record in providing effective customer service, desktop management, network administration, and systems analysis demonstrated through more than five years in help desk support and systems administration. Qualifications include the following:

= Highly skilled in providing excellent customer service to all levels of users.
= Proficient in mastering sophisticated software and tools while regularly identifying and implementing the latest industry innovations.
= Success at reviewing, analyzing, testing, and maintaining computer and network systems.
= Demonstrated experience preserving system integrity utilizing a variety of proactive backup and recovery strategies.
= Proven abilities in administering security to protect data and access to company network.

CERTIFICATIONS

Microsoft Certified Systems Engineer (MCSE), Windows Server 2000/2003, Received 2003
Microsoft Certified Systems Administrator (MCSA), Windows Server 2003, Received 2003

CORE COMPETENCIES
Network Administration
User Support and Training
Managing Security to Network
Business Systems Administration
Proactive Data Recovery and Management
Software Configuration, Installation, and Upgrade

TECHNICAL SKILLS

Maufacturers: 3COM; Cisco; Compaq; Dell; Gateway; Hewlett-Packard; Intel

Environments: CITRIX Mainframe XP; Windows 9x/NT/2000/XP

Software: Active Directory; Adobe Acrobat; Filemaker Pro; McAfee (Netshield, VirusScan ASAP); Microsoft Office Suite 9x/XP/2003; Norton (Antivirus & Ghost 5x/7x); Veritas Backup Exec

Databases: SQL Server 7.0/2000/2005

Mail Programs: Exchange 5.5/2000/2003

Networking DHCP; DNS; firewalls; hubs; routers; switches; TCP/IP; WINS

Applications: ADP, Business Objects; GIFTS; Great Plains; HRIS; ULTIMUS

Peripherals: Blackberry; Palm; Treo

Case Study 3: Profile with Certifications, Expertise, and Significant Accomplishments

IT Specialist, Team Coordinator, GS-2210/14, seeking new IT Systems Specialist position, GS-2210/14

Additional Information

Enter job-related honors, awards, leadership activities, skills (such as computer software proficiency or typing speed) or any other information requested by a specific job announcement. Need more space? Click <u>here</u> to expand this field.

> PROFILE
> SENIOR IT SPECIALIST with an outstanding record of success delivering cost-effective and efficient Information Technology infrastructures and processes tightly aligned with agency business requirements. Apply extensive experience translating user and management automation needs to the proactive management of outsourced IT services. LEADS MULTI-DISCIPLINED PROJECT TEAMS through the full life cycle of IT modernization efforts, from

(You have 17710 characters remaining for your description...)

ADDITIONAL INFORMATION

PROFILE

SENIOR IT SPECIALIST with an outstanding record of success delivering cost-effective and efficient Information Technology infrastructures and processes tightly aligned with agency business requirements. Apply extensive experience translating user and management automation needs to the proactive management of outsourced IT services.

LEADS MULTI-DISCIPLINED PROJECT TEAMS through the full life cycle of IT modernization efforts, from requirements capture, through design, implementation, and ongoing administration. Apply innovation and persistence to consistently deliver project objectives on time and within budget. Self-motivated and goal-oriented, with a demonstrated ability to handle complex responsibilities in a demanding work environment.

CERTIFICATIONS

Information Security Officer (ISO) Certification, National Defense University, 2005
Chief Information Officer (CIO) Certification, National Defense University, 2004

EXPERTISE

IT Operations: Direct enterprise data, computing, and networking operations to support critical business functions.

Technical and Project Management: Provide technical direction and oversight to IT Operations and modernization projects.

User Support: Provide customer service, technical assistance, and training on all aspects of software applications, systems, and network infrastructure.

IT Consultation: Recommend industry best practices in the implementation of new technologies.

SIGNIFICANT ACCOMPLISHMENTS

EPA SERVER OPERATIONS MOVE: Project Manager to relocate EPA Server Operations following facility damage in the aftermath of Hurricane Katrina. Targeted for completion in Month, 200x, this move has required detailed planning for a fully renovated network, server, and office infrastructure.

EPA ENTERPRISE IT OPERATIONS: Manage all IT services for multiple EPA buildings and facilities in the Washington, D.C., area, including the Ronald Reagan Building. Coordinate network, telecommunications, systems, and user services for over 2,000 users in a high-paced and demanding work environment.

EMERGENCY OPERATIONS CENTER (EOC): Led the design, implementation, management, and oversight of the computing infrastructure for a state-of-the-art Emergency Operations Center for the EPA (2005).

Case Study 4: Profile with Specialized Functional Skills Targeted Toward New Position

Contractor Operations Specialist seeking Logistics Management, Systems Analyst positions, GS-11/12-level

Additional Information

Enter job-related honors, awards, leadership activities, skills (such as computer software proficiency or typing speed) or any other information requested by a specific job announcement. Need more space? Click here to expand this field.

CAREER
PROFILE
OPERATIONS SPECIALIST, Halliburton, Iraq, seeking Federal Civil Service
position utilizing Logistics Management, Systems Analyst, and Training Instructor experience.
Top performing, results-focused Operations Specialist, Computer
Systems

(You have 17599 characters remaining for your description...)

ADDITIONAL INFORMATION

CAREER PROFILE

OPERATIONS SPECIALIST, Halliburton, Iraq, seeking Federal Civil Service position utilizing Logistics Management, Systems Analyst, and Training Instructor experience.

Top performing, results-focused Operations Specialist, Computer Systems Analyst, and Training Instructor with over 20 years of multidimensional private-sector and U.S. military experience.

Highly successful supervisor with cross-functional expertise in Operations Analysis, Project Management, Information Technology, Education/Training, Personnel Administration, and Organizational Development. Experience managing, mentoring, evaluating, and coordinating the work of up to 90 employees.

Successful working with and across multiple functions, countries, and cultures to achieve goals. Flexible in dynamic, challenging, and multicultural business environments. M.S., Education. Education/Instructional Design Doctoral candidate.

INFORMATION TECHNOLOGY: Over three years of experience as a Computer Analyst supervising help desk operations and providing customer service support for computer operations. Record of success designing computer information systems to improve production and work flow. Skilled in network troubleshooting and support. Expertise planning, developing, implementing, and maintaining programs, polices, and procedures to protect the integrity and confidentiality of systems, networks, and data. A+ Network Certification.

TRAINING & INSTRUCTIONAL TECHNOLOGY & DESIGN: Experience developing and implementing college-level training and instructional programs. Excel in curriculum design, program evaluation, and instructor coordination. Comprehensive knowledge of technology-based e-learning, adult learning techniques, needs assessments, learning technologies, and performance improvement systems.

OPERATIONS MANAGEMENT/PROJECT MANAGEMENT: Proven ability to plan, manage, and coordinate resources and large-scale infrastructure, services, facilities maintenance, and operational support projects. Expertise in quality assurance, best practices, project lifecycle monitoring, and facilities process development.

COMPUTER/TECHNICAL EXPERTISE: A+ Certified. Proficient in MS Office, HTML, JAVA, ActionX.

SECURITY CLEARANCE: Top Secret (SCI) (Expired)

PERSONAL INTERESTS: Physical fitness training

TRAVEL / RELOCATE: Willing to travel and relocate. Flexible.

Case Study 5: Qualifications Summary Featuring Specialized Experience in Contracting

Contract Attorney focusing on contracting and procurement experience seeking Contractor Specialist positions, GS-12/13

Additional Information

Enter job-related honors, awards, leadership activities, skills (such as computer software proficiency or typing speed) or any other information requested by a specific job announcement. Need more space? Click here to expand this field.

QUALIFICATIONS SUMMARY
Senior supervisory legal assistance attorney and Contract Attorney with 15+ years of progressive, professional experience in private industry, government, and the U.S. military. Licensed to practice law in 4 state and in the District of Columbia. Successful track record as advisor and legal counsel to government agencies, military organizations, and administrative boards. Direct and decisive. Skilled in all aspects of contract negotiations. Strong oral and written

(You have 18375 characters remaining for your description...)

ADDITIONAL INFORMATION

QUALIFICATIONS SUMMARY
Senior supervisory legal assistance attorney and Contract Attorney with 15+ years of progressive, professional experience in private industry, government, and the U.S. military. Licensed to practice law in 4 state and in the District of Columbia. Successful track record as advisor and legal counsel to government agencies, military organizations, and administrative boards. Direct and decisive. Skilled in all aspects of contract negotiations. Strong oral and written communications skills. Excellent organizational, analytical, and research capabilities. PC proficient.

CONTRACT PROCUREMENT: Currently administering over $1 million in contracts for five U.S. military installations. Juris Doctorate and Master of Law degrees. Outstanding record of performance in contract administration and procurements. Including four years of experience as Judge Advocate General for the U.S. Air Force, Strategic Air Command (SAC). Expert knowledge of federal contracting laws, regulations, policies, and procedures, including Government Procurement Procedures and Federal Acquisition Regulations (FARs). Demonstrated ability to manage and administer all facets of the contract process from pre-award to post-award including acquistion strategy, acquistion planning, procurement package input and validation, solicitation, negotiation, contract award, administration, and closeout/termination. Experienced in all contracting/procurement methods and types. Strong skills in working with logistics managers, product quality managers, engineers, and other subject-matter experts and stakeholders.

Case Study 6: Profile for an Administrative Professional

Administrative Assistant summarizing top-level administrative skills and competencies, seeking GS-9 positions

Additional Information

Enter job-related honors, awards, leadership activities, skills (such as computer software proficiency or typing speed) or any other information requested by a specific job announcement. Need more space? Click here to expand this field.

PROFILE:
Administrative professional with over 6 years of developing background information for analytical studies, researching official documents, and updating databases and creating spreadsheets to manage information. Possess skill and experience in summarizing and analyzing information for incorporation into final reports and supporting analysts with research, data compilation, project coordination, and tracking. I am an

(You have 19361 characters remaining for your description...)

ADDITIONAL INFORMATION	PROFILE: Administrative professional with over 6 years of developing background information for analytical studies, researching official documents, and updating databases and creating spreadsheets to manage information. Possess skill and experience in summarizing and analyzing information for incorporation into final reports and supporting analysts with research, data compilation, project coordination, and tracking. I am an experienced professional administrator with outstanding skills in identifying and resolving problems. Strong analytical and communications skills; expertise in multitasking, working under pressure, and teamwork.

Case Study 7: Relevant Skills for a Biologist

Biologist summarizing top-level field, clinical, and research skills, seeking GS-7/8 positions

Additional Information

Enter job-related honors, awards, leadership activities, skills (such as computer software proficiency or typing speed) or any other information requested by a specific job announcement. Need more space? Click here to expand this field.

RELEVANT SKILLS:
1. FIELD SAMPLING AND INVESTIGATION: Underwater scientific data collection Survey, taxonomic identification and sampling of Atlantic/Caribbean corals, reef fish, invertebrates, and macroalgae; coral reef monitoring and restoration; water quality testing using field/laboratory equipment (Hobos, pH meter, dissolved oxygen meter, etc.); Use of radio telemetry to monitor terrestrial wildlife.
2. DOCUMENTATION AND DATA MANAGEMENT: Perform

(You have 17409 characters remaining for your description...)

<table>
<tr>
<td valign="top">ADDITIONAL INFORMATION</td>
<td>

RELEVANT SKILLS:

1. FIELD SAMPLING AND INVESTIGATION: Underwater scientific data collection Survey, taxonomic identification and sampling of Atlantic/Caribbean corals, reef fish, invertebrates, and macroalgae; coral reef monitoring and restoration; water quality testing using field/laboratory equipment (Hobos, pH meter, dissolved oxygen meter, etc.); Use of radio telemetry to monitor terrestrial wildlife.

2. DOCUMENTATION AND DATA MANAGEMENT: Perform underwater photography and videography, using transect and quadrat methods. Skilled in using image processing and enhancement software (Adobe Photoshop, Jasc Paint Shop Pro). Use MS Excel and Statistica to manage and maintain data. Make field notes, record observations, and take size measurements. Prepare and classify collected samples.

3. STATISTICAL ANALYSIS AND REPORTING: Substantial experience analyzing tissues for signs of disease, stress, reproduction, and other factors; draw conclusions of environmental impact. Perform field analysis to determine next steps. Utilize computer programs such as MS Word to draft project reports and perform data manipulations. Statistical programs (Statistica, MS Excel, SAS). Statistical data analysis (e.g. ANOVA, Regression, t-test, non-parametric statistics, etc.). Coral reef assessment (Coral Point Count with Excel extensions 3.4) and mapping software (ArcGIS, ENVI).

4. WRITING AND PUBLIC SPEAKING: Design and present informative audiovisual presentations at scientific meetings using MS PowerPoint; lecture to undergraduate students and lead discussions regarding animal and plant biology/ecology/taxonomy; lead educational outreach tours and field trips regarding resource management issues. Write and edit project reports. Good experience with abstracts.

HONORS:
-- Fellowship, Summer Undergraduate Research Fellowship in Oceanography, Graduate School of Oceanography, University of Rhode Island, 2001.
-- Golden Key National Honor Society, University of Missouri, 2000-2001.
-- Allen Greenberg Biology Scholarship, University of Missouri, 1999, 2000.
-- University Scholar Scholarship, University of Missouri, 1998, 1999, 2000.
-- Dean's List, all semesters, University of Missouri, 1998-2001.

VOLUNTEER COMMUNITY SERVICE:
-- Florida Keys National Marine Sanctuary, Reef Medics Program, volunteer since July 2005. Perform bleaching, disease, and small-scale damage assessments within the sanctuary.
-- Reef Environmental Education Foundation, member since January 2005. Perform reef fish surveys via SCUBA in South Florida/Florida Keys.

</td>
</tr>
</table>

Summary

Congratulations! You have just finished focusing your resume toward the position with KSAs in the resume, accomplishments, keywords, specialized experience, and a profile. The human resources specialist will see that you have made the effort to match your resume toward the announcement and this will help you get Best Qualified and referred to a supervisor.

CHAPTER 5

Education, Job Related Training, and Additional Information

Your educational background is an important part of your federal resume. The amount of information you provide, the way you present the information, and the organization of this section can impress HR professionals and hiring managers. HR professionals are looking for specific degrees, majors, courses, and specialized training to determine whether you are qualified for the position.

This chapter looks at the Education, Job Related Training, and Additional Information sections of the federal resume and gives tips on optimizing the information you include in them.

Education

Some federal jobs require degrees; other federal positions will accept specialized or generalized experience in place of college degrees. The federal job announcement is clear about the qualifications for the position. Read the Specialized or Generalized Qualifications section of the vacancy announcement to see whether you have the necessary educational qualifications for the position. If the qualifications require that you have 25 credits in accounting for a Staff Accountant position, you *must* have these credits. List them in your resume and add up the credits.

Here is the education information that *must* be on your federal resume, according to OPM brochure OF-510:

> Colleges or universities (name and address, majors, type of degree); if no degree, show total credits earned and whether semester or quarter hours

Considerations for Organizing Your Educational Background

The Education section gives you space for college degrees, majors, universities, and dates. Dates are not mandatory in USAJOBS. In order to add your relevant course list, course descriptions, significant papers, team projects, and activities, you might have to write this information in the Additional Information section toward the end of the builder.

If you are qualifying for a position with your education, most announcements require you to upload copies of your transcripts. You can describe specific courses in the USAJOBS resume builder if you feel that your courses are significant in showing your qualifications and performance for a particular federal job.

Education Section Samples

These two education samples are from a paper-formatted resume. You can copy and paste your resume information into the builder. These examples give you ideas of the types of information you can add to your Education section, including course descriptions, papers, presentations, and projects.

 Tip: If you graduated from college or university within the last 20 years, go ahead and add the dates. Otherwise, you could leave the dates off the USAJOBS federal resume.

Sample 1: Education section for Accounting Specialist, GS-0525-07/09

EDUCATION

Masters of Business Administration—August 20XX
Completed 39 credit hours in graduate study
Elon University, Elon, NC 27244
Relevant Courses:
Enhancing Leadership Effectiveness—The development of skills and behaviors in communications that are required for successful leadership.
Managerial Accounting—The use of accounting information in management decision-making.
Financial Management—A study of the management from the financial perspective.
International Business—International trade mechanisms and operations of facilities abroad are analyzed.
Advanced Finance Strategies—Selected topics in corporate finance are examined through case and seminar approach.
Quantitative Decision—Statistical analyses and mathematical techniques frequently used as aids in managerial decision-making.
Strategic Implementation—Focusing on the implementation of organizational strategies used to position products or services in the competitive marketplace.

Bachelor of Science—May 19XX

Completed 138 credit hours in undergraduate study

Elon University, Elon, NC 27244
Major: Leisure Sports Management
Minor: Business Administration and Mathematics

Sample 2: Education, Specialized Courses, College Projects.
New BSEE graduate seeking Mechanical Engineering position, GS-7.

EDUCATION:

B.S. IN MECHANICAL ENGINEERING HONORS PROGRAM, 20XX

University of Maryland, College Park, MD

Diploma, Centennial High School, Ellicott City, MD, Class of 19XX

B.S. IN MECHANICAL ENGINEERING HONORS PROGRAM

University of Maryland, College Park, MD

Expected July 20XX   Overall GPA: 3.6/4.0   Engineering GPA: 3.7/4.0

RELATED COURSEWORK
Calculus, physics, chemistry, differential equations, statistics, dynamics, thermodynamics, introduction to matlab, fluid mechanics, electronics and instrumentation, engineering materials and manufacturing processes, statistical methods of product development, transfer processes, vibration controls and optimization, product engineering and manufacturing, automotive design, manufacturing automation, technical writing, human resource management, introduction to transportation in supply chain management.

Team Semester Projects:
REDESIGN OF THE DEWALT TRADESMAN DRILL using the nine-step product development process. Directed the testing and building of a prototype cordless/corded drill. Compared results to necessary specifications to determine effectiveness of the design. Gave PowerPoint presentations on project results. Utilized analytical tools such as the House of Quality, Weighted Decision Matrix, Morphological Chart, and Functional Decomposition to redesign drill. 20XX

DESIGN OF HYBRID SUV FOR FUTURETRUCK COMPETITION. In charge of testing the performance of the electric motor. Analyzed complex schematics to determine connector specifications and location. Negotiated donation of connectors for the high-voltage system. Researched torque curves for the stock engine and the replacement engine. 20XX–20XX

DESIGN OF MATLAB CODE TO MODEL AIRBORNE CONCENTRATIONS OF DUST IN TURBULENT WINDS. Modeled winds with force vectors. Displayed results in multiple plots corresponding to different wind conditions. Experimented with different mesh densities to determine the degree of computing power necessary for accurate results. 20XX

OTHER PROJECTS HAVE INCLUDED:

Design of portable water pump
Statistical analysis of campus traffic flow
Evaluation of scale wind tunnel testing of a high-rise building
Analysis of stress, bending, and failure in a lug wrench

(continued)

(continued)

ADDITIONAL INFORMATION:

AS TEAM LEADER for more than 10 significant projects, developed skill in analyzing projects, delegating tasks, and establishing timelines. Also developed the following engineering and project management skills:
-Draft project details.
-Devise and recommend alternative methods of standardized analysis as a basis for solving problems.
-Recommend and devise deviations to details.
-Assist in reviews of engineering changes.
-Review compliance to contract during design, development, and production.
-Evaluate control of baseline products.
-Manage and/or witness tests.
-Evaluate quality assurance activities.
-Conduct cost and schedule analysis and estimations.
-*Manage engineering data collection and analysis.*

Additional Information

Outside your 9-to-5 position, you might have another life. That's what the Additional Information section is about: the experience and qualifications you've gathered outside of work experience, formal education, and training. Among the many possibilities to include here are specialized skills, other languages, honors and awards, accomplishments, publications, professional memberships, community involvement or leadership, and public speaking. HR professionals might be impressed or interested in what you do above your job description.

Be sure to notice, however, the number of times the phrase "job-related" is repeated in government requirements. Your federal resume should emphasize recent and job-related information. Federal HR professionals are looking for skills, accomplishments, and professional involvement that qualify you for a specific federal position.

A federal vacancy announcement will ask for additional information in the following sections of the USAJOBS resume builder:

* Additional Language Skills
* Affiliations
* Professional Publications
* Additional Information, which can include job-related honors, awards, leadership activities, skills (such as computer software proficiency or typing speed), or any other information requested by a specific job announcement

Work Experience Continuations

If you need more than 3,000 characters for each of your Work Experience sections, you can continue those descriptions in the Additional Information section.

Job-Related Honors, Awards, or Special Accomplishments

Your honors, awards, and special accomplishments might be important in qualifying you for certain positions. This section on your resume can include such items as publications, memberships in professional or honor societies, leadership activities, public speaking, and performance awards, as well as the dates you received them. Here is an overview of the items you might list and describe in this section on your federal resume:

- **Honors and awards** demonstrate career or educational excellence and recognition.
- **Affiliations** demonstrate involvement, motivation to learn about specific industries, and knowledge of state-of-the-art industry information through reading newsletters and attending conferences and meetings.
- **Public speaking and presentations** show communications skills before groups and the ability to write and present information orally.
- **Publication lists or written works** illustrate your ability to research, write, edit, use computers, and study a specific topic area.
- **Collateral duties and details** in your federal job can be listed in this section. These additional responsibilities might lead to new careers and positions. The responsibilities you carry out 5 to 20 hours per week can provide the skills you need to make a career change.
- **Community or civic activities** demonstrate personal interest, dedication, and time committed to helping others. Involvement in community activities might give you valuable responsibilities such as leading groups; planning, promoting, and coordinating events; managing budgets; negotiating contracts; directing volunteers; and achieving organizational goals.

Sports, Activities, and Special Interests

You might wonder why this information should go on your federal resume. This information will demonstrate competencies that are important for your federal job performance. If they are seeking a good listener, team player, problem solver, and someone who works well under pressure, they might like an athlete, actor, or semi-professional singer.

Public Speaking

If you've been quoted in a newspaper, spoken before a class or association on your area of expertise, been interviewed on the radio, or presented an impressive briefing, write it in your resume and prove your skills with your KSA accomplishments.

Job Related Training

Add recent and relevant training and continuing education to this section. You can see that you can add training courses organized by type of training, classroom hours, and impressive training information. The training can result in the human resources specialist adding points to your application score.

Sample 3: Job-Related Training–Specialized Training Sections for three candidates: Visual Information Specialist, IT Specialist, and TSA Lead Screener.

JOB RELATED TRAINING

INSTRUCTION AND TRAINING:
• ColorNet Printing & Graphics, Sterling, VA; 20XX–Present; Host classes and give seminars to diverse groups of technical and nontechnical staff and customers. Discuss proper use of graphics and print production techniques to effectively communicate ideas.
• ColorNet Printing & Graphics, Sterling, VA; 20XX–Present; Present classes to educate individuals on the properties and usage of multiple print substrates and papers.
• September 20XX; ColorNet Printing/Rockville Printing & Graphics Print Show and Open House. Attend as a consultant to promote and educate attendees on the usage of various on-demand print options. Specifically, my focus will be the HP Indigo digital press and variable data usage.

TRAINING/COURSES:
Orcal Professional Wrapping Academy, June 20XX.
New Horizons Desktop Publishing, Graphics and Microsoft Office Courses, 19XX.

LICENSES AND CERTIFICATES:
• FAA-issued Private Pilot License #333333, 20XX.
• HP Indigo Digital Press Operation, 2010.
• HP Indigo Digital Press SmartStream Designer Front End, 20XX.
• HP Indigo Digital Press Shared Maintenance, 20XX.

JOB RELATED TRAINING	Information Assurance Awareness (April 20XX)
	Fiber Optic Maintenance Technician Course, January 20XX (five-day course)
	JCREW 2.1 FSR Training, August 20XX (four-day course)
	AN/UYQ-70 Maintenance Course (M-32), 6/19XX, at Combat Systems Engineering Development Site (CSEDS)
	Hazardous Materials Coordinator (HAZMAT)
	LightTech Fiber Optic FOT-SHIP-4 MIL-STD-2042A Certified, 19XX

SPECIALIZED TRAINING

Chemical-terrorism Vulnerability Information, one-day course, DHS Office of Infrastructure Protection, 20XX
Introduction to the Incident Command System (ICS-100), one-day course, FEMA, 20XX
ICS-200 for Single Resources and Initial Action Incidents, one-day course, FEMA, 20XX
ICS-300, two-day course, Waukesha County Technical College, 20XX
Behavior Recognition Training, Transportation Security Administration, 20XX
Planning Considerations for Terrorism Response, two-day course, St. Petersburg College, 20XX
Evaluating Truthfulness, The Ekman Group, two-day course, 20XX
Introduction to Railroads Course, Transportation Technology Center, 20XX

Summary

Your Education, Job Related Training, and Additional Information (including Awards, Professional Memberships, Publications and Public Speaking, Volunteer Activities, and Work Experience continuation) sections will support your qualifications for the federal jobs you are applying for. The total picture of your education and qualifications will help you get Best Qualified and referred for a federal position.

CHAPTER 6

Keywords for Federal Jobs

What are the top 6 to 10 keywords for the federal position you seek?

Federal resume writers, Resumix resume writers, and private-industry writers all know that the keywords and skills included for a certain job are critical for the resume's success. They are especially critical to busy federal human resources specialists who have hundreds of resumes to review from USAJOBS.gov.

The Department of Defense automated resume system is called Resumix™, and it is known as a keyword system. The supervisor and HR specialist decide on five to eight keywords/skills that are most important for the position. They search the database of all of the candidates for resumes that contain all of the keywords. If the resume does not contain the keywords for the position, the resume might not be selected in the system. Therefore, the applicant will not be referred to a supervisor for consideration for an interview.

A Professional Indexer Selects Keywords

I asked professional indexer Pilar Wyman (www.wymanindexing.com) to do a keyword analysis for the Logistics Management Specialist position. She said the following about the keyword analysis and selection process:

I put the keywords into a table, pulled out the junk, and then sorted them alphabetically. I also eliminated place names (which could be innumerable) and Defense Department agencies, and some that were just gobbledygook, incomplete terms. You'll see that some don't necessarily occur in the job announcement, but are clearly related. "Teaching," for example, isn't in the job announcement, although "training" is, and both are covered, if only conceptually. What's left is indeed relevant to logistics management and to these announcements—more than 25 percent, I believe. You can see a variety of forms for some concepts, and many terms are very specific: WPM, communication, military experience, library experience, logistics, equipment management, creative writing, MIS, crime prevention, conflict resolution, teamwork, customer support, damage analysis, textiles, and so on.

 Note: Many job seekers don't spend the time to research and analyze keywords and series language that should be included in the resume. They write their resumes from their memory of their job. And they don't actually do an analysis of the top skills from their current job to their target job. Matching transferable skills can be done with a set of keywords.

Announcement Analysis

Finding the top 6 to 10 keywords and phrases can take you 10 to 20 minutes. This is invaluable research and analysis for your federal resume. To find these all-important 6 keywords and skills, I copied and pasted the Duties, Qualifications, and KSAs into a Word file. Then I highlighted the words that seemed critical for the position. Then I made a list of these keywords and analyzed the list for the top 6 keywords and phrases.

Where to Look for Keywords

You can find keywords for your federal resume in the Duties; Qualifications; and Knowledge, Skills and Abilities sections of the announcement. The words in bold are keywords that will be important for your federal resume. The long list of keywords can be boiled down to about six to eight all-cap headings for your Outline Format federal resume.

DUTIES

You will coordinate and perform a wide variety of **administrative and management services** essential to the operations of the office and serve as an **advisor to management** on assigned administrative matters. In addition, you will conduct or participate in the **evaluation of administrative programs,** systems, and methods and identify ways to **improve the efficiency and effectiveness** of these services at the local level. You will also **represent the office** in meetings and **dealings with vendors** and organizations within and outside the agency that have primary responsibility for these services.

KNOWLEDGE, SKILLS AND ABILITIES:

- Skill in reviewing and evaluating administrative procedures to determine if the existing procedures are effective

- Ability to **plan, organize** and adjust fluctuation of assignments and **workload** to meet deadlines

- Knowledge of various techniques for **analyzing projects and programs**

Keywords from the Announcement

- Administrative and management services
- Advisor to management
- Evaluation of administrative programs
- Improve the efficiency and effectiveness
- Represent the office
- Dealings with vendors
- Plan, organize workload
- Analyze projects and programs

These could be the six major all-cap headlines for your Outline Format federal resume:

- Administration and Management
- Improving Efficiency and Effectiveness
- Identify Productivity Standards and Performance Measures
- Resource Utilization
- Analyze Projects and Recommend Solutions
- Advisor and Technical Assistant

Nine Announcements with 4 to 13 Keywords, Phrases, and Skills

When you are writing your federal resume, you will learn how to analyze a vacancy announcement to use the terminology from the announcement in your resume. These lists demonstrate that the keywords for certain jobs or occupational series can be developed from vacancy announcements, the agency mission statement, and the OPM's Qualification Standards. Every vacancy announcement can be analyzed for 4 to 13 keywords.

Here are some tips on how to find the keywords:

- Keywords are repeated many times in the vacancy announcement.
- Keywords are in the first one or two sentences in the Duties section.
- Keywords are proper names, nouns, or verbs.
- Keywords are not the old-style buzzwords, such as *plan, implement, manage, coordinate, review,* and *schedule.* They are more technical and specific to the job series.

In this section you'll find keyword lists for the following positions. We included the occupational series, grade ranges, and range of salaries for your interest. It's interesting that the keywords are technical no matter what the grade level, from GS-7 through GS-13.

- Supervisory Police Officer, GS-0083-11/11, $57,408–$74,628/year
- Management and Program Analyst, GS-0343-9/11, $51,630–$81,204/year
- Accountant, GS-0510-13/13, $89,033–$115,742/year
- Intelligence Specialist (Operations Support), IA-0132-03/03, $62,467–$115,742/year
- Criminal Investigator (Special Agent), GL-1811-07/09, $43,964–$74,891/year
- Park Ranger (Law Enforcement/Refuge), GL-0025-07, $38,790–$61,678/year
- Attorney-Advisor (Contract), GS-0905-13/13, $81,823–$106,369/year
- Supply Management Specialist, GS-2003-09/09, $47,448–$61,678/year
- Smuggling Interdiction and Trade Compliance Officer, GS-0401-07/11, $38,790–$74,628/year

Supervisory Police Officer, GS-0083-11/11

> Serves as Deputy Chief; **advises law enforcement personnel** on changes in policies, procedures, etc. **Establishes funding requirements** and **manages** the branch **operating budget.** **Adjusts personnel assignments** to meet deadlines; plans, **manages, and directs Depot police/security officers in** policies and procedures pertaining to **team operations.** Assures proper **cross-training** to assure a well-balanced and effective work force; performs police officer duties when needed to assist in police operations, including enforcement of federal laws. Assists in confinement of apprehended personnel; **supervises, plans, directs, and assigns staff assignments.** Provides **on-the-job training,** instructs personnel in specific tasks and job techniques, arranges for staff development to broaden personnel training, provides back-up skills by cross-training, and recommends formalized training. **Communicates performance plans** to personnel, evaluates performance, **counsels personnel, and recommends disciplinary actions.**

Keywords for Your Federal Resume

1. Law Enforcement Advisor
2. Establish funding requirements
3. Manage operating budget
4. Adjust personnel assignments
5. Manage and direct police/security officers in team operations
6. Cross-training, on-the-job training
7. Supervise, plan, and direct staff assignments
8. Communicate performance plans
9. Counsel personnel
10. Recommend disciplinary actions

Management and Program Analyst, GS-0343-9/11, Department of Homeland Security, Office of Intelligence & Analysis

> Major Duties:
>
> - Incumbent serves in a dual capacity as the **Program Analyst** and **Commercial Activity Officer.**
>
> - Incumbent performs functions directly related to **financial management, budget formulation and execution,** program review and analysis, organizational analysis, manpower utilization and control, internal controls, contract and procurement management.
>
> - Prepares **management studies** and reviews including a full range of data gathering and analysis related to **work processes** and information flow often requiring the adapting of existing **analytical tools** and methods to the unprecedented requirements of the review.
>
> - Provides **management advice** to supervisors and staff relative to operating plans and policies, reorganizations, budget, and other resources that have moderate financial and operational implications.
>
> - Performs full range of **financial and budget management** functions within the Business Office.

Keywords for Your Federal Resume

1. Program Analyst
2. Commercial Activity Officer
3. Financial management
4. Budget formulation and execution
5. Management studies
6. Work processes
7. Analytical tools
8. Management advice
9. Financial and budget management

Accountant, GS-0510-13/13

IRS Chief Financial Officer (CFO) Organization, Internal Revenue Service, U.S. Department of the Treasury, Washington, D.C., Metro Area

The incumbent will serve as a senior accountant in the CFO area responsible for establishing and applying **accounting theories, concepts, principles**, and standards to the financial activities of the IRS. The incumbent ensures that the Service's **financial systems, operations, and reports** meet the requirements of law and regulation.

Specialized experience involves work in which the applicant: Interprets, analyzes, and develops **accounting and financial management policies, standards, and procedures** that implement **broad accounting requirements** established by the Department, OMB, GAO, Treasury, and Congress. Examples of Specialized Experience include:

1. Preparing, **analyzing, interpreting**, and presenting **accounting data**;
2. Operating, maintaining, and modifying **internal control processes and systems**;
3. Using accounting information to recommend **solutions to management problems and structuring of organization programs**;
4. Managing, operating, and analyzing **cost accounting systems** in connection with manufacturing or other business activities

Keywords for Your Federal Resume

1. Accounting and financial management theories, concepts, principles, policies, standards, and procedures
2. Financial systems, operations, and reports
3. Broad accounting requirements
4. Financial analysis and evaluation
5. Internal control processes and systems
6. Financial and management structure, operations, and practices
7. Cost accounting systems

Intelligence Specialist (Operations Support), IA-0132-03/03

US Army Intelligence and Security Command, Mission Support Cmd/ACofS, G3, IOC/SIGINT Tech Dev Act, STDA Ops Branch, Fort Belvoir, VA.

Major Duties: You will be a **Signals Intelligence** (SIGINT) analyst and reporter performing classic cryptologic functions to include a wide variety of duties encompassing functional area of **information research, target development, and technical reporting**. Direct **collection, processing, and analytical efforts**.

SPECIALIZED EXPERIENCE: Specialized experience is identified as progressively responsible experience that includes **intelligence-related research, analysis, collections and/or operations**. This experience should have included **intelligence analysis and/or production, intelligence collection and/or operations, counterintelligence, or threat support** directly related to the position to be filled.

Keywords for Your Federal Resume

1. Signals Intelligence
2. Information research, target development, and technical reporting
3. Collection, processing, and analytical efforts
4. Intelligence-related research, analysis, production, collections and/or operations, counterintelligence, or threat support

Criminal Investigator (Special Agent), GL-1811-07/09

Department Of Homeland Security, United States Secret Service; site to be determined after selection is made.

Major Duties:

During the course of their careers, special agents carry out assignments in both of the following areas and may be assigned to multiple duty stations throughout the U.S. and abroad.

PROTECTION: Special Agents protect the United States President, Vice President, President-elect, Vice President-elect, their immediate families, former Presidents, their spouses and minor children until age 16, visiting foreign heads of states/governments, their accompanying spouses, major Presidential and Vice Presidential candidates, their spouses, and others designated by law.

INVESTIGATIONS: Special Agents **conduct criminal investigations** pertaining to the counterfeiting of United States and foreign government obligations and securities; fictitious and fraudulently negotiated government and commercial securities, identity theft, false identification, computer crimes, access device fraud, telecommunications fraud, telemarketing fraud, electronic funds transfer fraud, and fraud concerning federally insured financial institutions.

At least one year of specialized experience equivalent to the GL-7 level, which is in or directly related to **investigating complex criminal cases** (including but not limited to: felony crimes, narcotics, violent and serial crimes, child abuse, sexual exploitation, computer and technology-related crime, bias-related crimes, auto theft, consumer product tampering, organized crime, etc.) requiring the use of recognized investigative techniques, **interviews, interrogations, and/or surveillance**; **preparing investigative reports** and/or information to present to District or US Attorney's office; **leadership of a criminal investigative team** or component in which the principal duties consisted of **security investigation, intelligence gathering or criminal prosecution.**

Keywords for Your Federal Resume

1. Protection
2. Conduct criminal investigations
3. Investigate complex criminal cases
4. Conducting surveillance, interviews, or interrogations
5. Prepare investigative reports
6. Leadership of a criminal investigative team
7. Security investigation, intelligence gathering or criminal prosecution

Park Ranger (Law Enforcement/Refuge), GL-0025-07

Department Of The Interior, U.S. Fish and Wildlife Service, 1 vacancy—Gulf Shores, AL

Major Duties:

Apprehend, detain, arrest, and/or issue citations to violators of Federal, State, and local laws, rules and regulations

Detect and investigate criminal activity pertaining to Service lands and responsibilities, including arson, theft, breaking and entering, vandalism, air and water pollution, and destruction of property

Enforce laws and regulations concerning the possession, use, distribution, trafficking, cultivation, and manufacture of controlled substances on Fish and Wildlife Service lands

Prepare and submit requests for warrants for defendants who fail to appear in court

Participate in ground and air surveillance which may involve flying as a passenger in an aircraft to identify suspects and/or illegal activity

Enforce and investigate violations. Knowledge of Federal Refuge laws and regulations, state fish and wildlife laws on service lands, and Migratory Bird Treaty Act

Provide and/or obtain first aid or emergency medical assistance

Have one year of specialized experience, equivalent to the GS-5 grade level in the federal service. Examples of qualifying specialized experience include the following: park guide or tour leader; **law enforcement or investigative work;** archeological or historical preservation research work; **forestry and/or fire management work in a park, recreation, or conservation area;** management, assistant, or program specialized work involving the **development and implementation of policy related to protection, conservation, or management of park areas** or similar operations.

Keywords for Your Federal Resume

1. Apprehend, detain, arrest, and/or issue citations

2. Detect and investigate criminal activity

3. Enforce laws and regulations

4. Participate in ground and air surveillance

5. Enforce and investigate violations.

6. Knowledge of Federal Refuge laws and regulations, state fish and wildlife laws on service lands, and Migratory Bird Treaty Act

7. Law enforcement or investigative work

8. Forestry and/or fire management work in a park, recreation, or conservation area

9. Development and implementation of policy related to protection, conservation, or management of park areas

Attorney-Advisor (Contract), GS-0905-13/13

Department Of The Army, Army Installation Management Command, USAG, Staff Judge Advocate, Administrative/Civil Law Branch, Ft. Leonard Wood, Missouri 65473

About the Position: The Administrative Law Division provides advice/opinion relating to the organization, powers, functions, employment of the Army and the powers and authority of the commander, other managers/supervisors in relation to their official duties. In addition to performing duties in the specialized area of **contract and fiscal law**, all attorneys in the Administrative Law Division **conduct legal research,** provide advice, and **prepare legal opinions** on questions of law on the entire range of legal issues confronting a major Army and Joint Service Training Center. Advises/assists Civilian Personnel.

Major Duties:

In this position, you will serve as an advisor to the Commanding General, Installation Commander, and subordinate units. As a **legal advisor and consultant** for the Ft. Leonard Wood Commercial Activities (CA) Program, you will provide reviews of performance work statements, management studies, **contract administration** plans, quality assurance plans, award fee plans, source selection plans, solicitations, and other documents for legal adequacy, accuracy, and compliance. Participates as legal advisor during the source selection process and review of administrative appeals. Prepares legal memoranda for the Trial Attorney's Litigation File (TALF) for appeals before the Armed Services Board of Contract Appeals (ASBCA). Reviews proposed awards of all contracts and modifications of $100K or more. **Prepare legal opinions.**

Keywords for Your Federal Resume

1. Contract and fiscal law

2. Conduct legal research

3. Prepare legal opinions

4. Legal advisor and consultant

5. Contract administration

6. Review performance work statements

7. Prepare legal memoranda

8. Review proposed legal contracts

Supply Management Specialist, GS-2003-09/09

Us Army Installation Management Command, USAG Fort McCoy, Directorate Of Logistics, Supply & Services Division, Fort McCoy, WI

Major Duties:

Serve as the **Supply Management** Specialist in the Customer Service Branch of the Logistics Directorates Supply & Services Division. Responsible for managing transactions such as **requisitions**, issuing of warehouse stocks, **inventory** and **turn in of reparable/accountable supplies**. Researches and reconciles any required financial reports. Responsible for the day to day operations, troubleshooting connectivity issues, system errors and **loading ICP changes into the SARSS-1 (Standard Army Retail Supply System-1)**. Familiar with the **government catalog systems**, **establishes procedures and controls**, **utilizes automated databases**, and **performs quality control**. Coordinates supply requirements with National Inventory Control Points, headquarters and shipping depots. Coordinates, determines, and executes Government policies, Army regulations, and guidance regarding **accountable records**. Will utilize **Army regulations related to supply**. Performs causative research to **resolve critical inventory discrepancies**. **Ability to communicate orally and in writing.**

Keywords for Your Federal Resume

1. Supply management
2. Requisitions
3. Inventory
4. Turn in of reparable/accountable suppliers
5. Loading ICP changes into the SARSS-1 (Standard Army Retail Supply System-1)
6. Government catalog systems
7. Establishes procedures and controls
8. Utilizes automated databases
9. Performs quality control
10. Accountable records
11. Army regulations related to supply
12. Resolve critical inventory discrepancies
13. Ability to communicate orally and in writing

Smuggling Interdiction and Trade Compliance Officer, GS-0401-07/11

Department of Agriculture, Animal & Plant Health Inspection Service, Marketing & Regulatory Programs, Lincoln, NE; Omaha, NE; Des Moines, IA

Job Summary: The incumbent performs a variety of highly specialized duties involving the development, implementation, and maintenance of an active **Smuggling, Interdiction, and Trade Compliance (SITC) program**. Duties and functions performed by the SITC Officer play a vital role in **APHIS PPQ's (Plant Protection & Quarantine) mission** and program efforts to **safeguard US agriculture from plant and animal pests and diseases**, with responsibility to **identify and verify prohibited and/or non-compliant imported products** found at ports of entry and in commerce.

Major Duties: Incumbent is responsible for the operational planning, development, implementation, coordination, and evaluation of **operations designed to prevent the entry of prohibited agricultural products** and remove them from distribution. The incumbent **identifies pathways and methods for mitigating the dissemination of products** that carry these federally significant pests. **Conducts formal reviews** and **provides timely written recommendations** based on **systemic evaluation and monitoring of trade and agricultural smuggling activities**. **Develops** comprehensive **multifaceted strategies**, plans, and activities that would include interagency or work blitzes, market surveys, intensified inspections, devanning of cargo containers, and public outreach.

Keywords for Your Federal Resume

1. Smuggling, Interdiction, and Trade Compliance (SITC) program
2. APHIS PPQ's (Plant Protection & Quarantine) mission
3. Safeguard US agriculture from plant and animal pests and diseases
4. Identify and verify prohibited and/or non-compliant imported products
5. Operations designed to prevent the entry of prohibited agricultural products
6. Identifies pathways and methods for mitigating the dissemination of products
7. Conducts formal reviews
8. Writes reports and timely recommendations
9. Systemic evaluation and monitoring of trade and agricultural smuggling activities
10. Develops multi-faceted strategies.

Summary

Keywords are critical for fast-reading HR specialists. You will add your keywords to your resume when you are creating your outline, writing your accomplishments, and using language from the job announcement to improve the description of your duties. Using keywords shows that you are qualified for the job and that you took the time to analyze the target announcement.

Part 2

Plain Language and Value-Added Lessons

CHAPTER 7

Plain-Language Writing Lessons

How do you look on paper? How impressive is your resume? It's high time for civilians and current federal employees to learn to write about their career accomplishments in a concise, clear, and nonbureaucratic style. You must communicate your skills and accomplishments, and even brag a little. However, a three- to five-page resume does not afford space for every detail of your work. You must select the key experiences and write the resume in a new style, which I call *plain language.*

This chapter might be one of the most important in this book. By following the 10 resume-writing principles spelled out in this chapter, you will produce a well-written, easy-to-read, likable, impressive, factual, concise, and marketable resume. And a well-written resume will help you be selected for a promotion, increase your salary, and add to your retirement fund. All of your writing and editing effort will pay off!

Although this chapter is primarily about writing resumes, the tips apply equally well to other types of writing. These tips are useful for writing KSA accomplishments for your resume, essay narratives for your questionnaires, cover letters, your annual evaluation self-assessment, or even your Executive Core Qualifications for a Senior Executive Service application.

Most people don't give themselves enough credit in their resumes. Sometimes this is due to misplaced modesty. Sometimes it's because of the "I can't take full credit for that because we work as a team" attitude. More often, though, it's either a failure to recognize the significance of your performance or an inability to articulate your performance in a way that sounds meaningful.

Fortunately, writing a good resume can be manageable, simple, and even easy, if you follow a few guidelines. Although there's no substitute for experience, even a first-time resume writer can produce a perfectly fine resume. And the more you practice, the better you will become.

To write a good resume, you have to be able to do three things:

- Write well. Face it: You can't make a good resume out of poor sentences. You will learn how to write well by following the principles in this chapter. If you work at it, you can do it.

- Perceive your abilities and accomplishments clearly and objectively, neither diminished through false modesty nor exaggerated through undue pride.

- Assemble the well-written and accurate description of your qualifications into a compact, focused package.

Many people feel that their writing is not good. Even professional writers struggle with this feeling. And many people who need to put together a resume don't do much writing and have had little practice. At the same time, however, most people are good at telling a story to a friend—perhaps a funny thing that happened at the market, or an interesting program they saw on television. This ability is all you need to write a good resume. Your resume is really just a story about you.

You start with good content. If you are a poor worker and have accomplished little, your resume will not be impressive. But the fact that you are reading this book means that you are dedicated to improving your situation, and that's a sign of a good worker. If you have been reading and working with the chapters in Part 1 of this book, you have some good content by now. Now let's make it work for you.

I have identified 10 principles of good writing. They are neither hard nor complicated to learn and follow, and they work. Apply them yourself and see!

First Principle: Use Plain Words and Write About What You Really Do at Work

The purpose of a resume is to impress the reviewers with your qualifications for the job. But before you can impress them, they have to understand what you are writing. Overly embellished writing can be a turn-off or make you seem pompous. If writing is used incorrectly, you fail to seem impressive; you might even appear obtuse. Unspecific writing will not reach the essence of your duties, fails to explain the correlation between actions and results, and prevents the reader from understanding your job.

Here's an example of some generic writing that does not explain the "real job":

Halliburton (KBR) Operations (IRAQ)

Operations Specialist (01/06-present)

Ensure reports are completed in accordance with deadlines and undertake report editing where necessary. Ensure all security incidents are appropriately recorded and reported to project managers and relevant parties. Receive, analyze, disseminate, and submit to higher headquarters significant activity reports.

The real story is here:

Halliburton (KBR) Operations (IRAQ)

Operations Specialist (01/06-present)

FACILITY SUPPORT CUSTOMER SERVICES REPRESENTATIVE:

As one of 20 Operations Services Staff, I ensure a high quality of life and living services for contractors and federal civilians supporting the fighters in Iraq, Afghanistan, Kosovo, and other international sites. Receive requests for new services and solve problems for facilities maintenance requests. Provide accommodations for incoming staff. Oversee support for morale and health activities. I manage the status of more than 50 incoming project requests on a daily basis.

Tip: Here's a simple way to test whether your resume contains any overblown or nonspecific writing. Read it aloud to a friend. Can you keep a straight face? Or are you embarrassed? If you read it out loud to someone else, does he or she understand your job? Plain language is the single most important key to good resume writing. But if your resume does not pass the "straight face" test, how do you go about making it simple? You must look critically at *every single word* in your resume. Every word must pull its weight. You must mercilessly chop out every word that does not pack a punch. Use the fewest words possible to say the most.

Second Principle: Use Short Sentences

Long sentences are confusing and boring. They do not belong in your resume. Short sentences crackle with excitement! Abraham Lincoln once made the statement, "If you need me to give a long speech, I am ready now. If you want me to give a short speech, it will take me some time to prepare." No wonder the Gettysburg Address consists of just 10 short sentences. What is true of speeches is even more true of resumes. The last thing you need in your resume is a string of long sentences that take the reviewer a lot of time and effort to figure out.

Ideally, a sentence conveys only one clear thought. It flows logically from the preceding sentence and leads into the next sentence. There is no magically prescribed length for a good sentence. Good writing generally alternates between sentences of medium length and sentences that are much shorter. This creates variety and can set up a rhythm that keeps the reader's attention. See?

If your sentences have grown too long, you can break them into smaller sentences. Each small sentence can convey one piece of the full thought. Don't put a "laundry list" of ideas into one sentence. Here's an example:

Before:

> Provide logistics and information management support for designated programs/projects managed by the Advanced Undersea Systems Program Branch in order to identify specific requirements for money, manpower, material, facilities, and services for logistics and information management through one or more of the following phases of the program/project lifecycle: concept formulation, demonstration and validation, full-scale development, and production development.

After:

> As the Logistics Management Specialist in the Advanced Undersea Systems Program Logistics Branch, I directed logistics and information management support. Administered funding for manpower, materiel, facilities, and services. Managed full lifecycle projects from concept formulation, demonstration and validation, full-scale development, and production development.

Third Principle: Use "I" Intelligently

In the old days, there was no *I* in *resume*. The personal pronoun "I" was taboo. This was probably because it is easy to fall into the trap of starting every sentence with "I," which quickly becomes tedious and egocentric-sounding. The downside to avoiding "I" is that the sentences can end up as verbal contortionism. Today, the resume writer must strike a balance between these extremes.

We received a copy of an e-mail from a USMC civilian employee regarding the use of "I" in resumes for the U.S. Department of the Navy online application system (DONHR) system:

> *Human resources has passed the word that all resumes submitted through Resumix should be in first person (worded as if you are speaking). The person does affect the pulling of the resumes.*

Many reviewers still cringe at an "I" in a resume, but there is a growing trend toward including it. This is part of an overall shift away from a stilted resume and toward a resume that flows more naturally. The modern rule of thumb is to use "I" to personalize your resume, but not so often as to become obnoxious.

Electronic federal resumes have become bureaucratic, filled with acronyms and position description-like language, and mostly devoid of accomplishments. Federal HR specialists are trying to encourage writing that reflects what an employee really did in his or her job. What were the challenges? Who were the customers? What extra value did you bring to the job? This more personal style of writing can result in telling the "real story" about your job.

New Resume Use of "I Rules"

- *Don't* use "I" to start every sentence.
- *Don't* use "I" twice in the same sentence, or in two sentences in a row.
- *Do* use "I" when it makes your sentence flow smoothly.
- *Do* use "I" three to five times per page.
- *Do* use "I" with descriptions of accomplishments or "KSAs in the resume."
- *Do* use "I" in a compelling sentence emphasizing complexity, uniqueness, challenge, or outstanding service.
- *Do* use "I" in a summary of skills or competencies.
- *Do* use "I" in project descriptions where you are performing a particular role.
- *Do* use "I" in your Other Qualifications or Summary of Skills section. You can use "I" more frequently in a summary of your personal values, core competencies, and skills.

Here's an example in which it makes good sense to use "I" in a specific project description:

> My Division Director ordered an audit to be conducted within two business days. The task appeared nearly impossible. After getting input from other team members, I proposed a division of labor that made the challenge more manageable. We completed the audit a half-day ahead of schedule, and the Director awarded me a Certificate of Recognition for my contribution.

Notice that in this example, the last sentence does not say "I received a Certificate…." By saying "the Director awarded me," I avoided "I" and also made the sentence active rather than passive (see the Tenth Principle). This example also showcases a more personalized writing style.

Following are some other examples of the use of "I," which personalizes the example of success.

Project example:

> After extensive research I was able to convey to all personnel covering 7 different agencies the proper use/dispatch of government vehicles within Europe. Status of Forces Agreement (SOFA) stipulates if a European Country is not part of this agreement, government vehicles cannot be driven there without proper authorization.

Compelling example:

> As a Natural Resource Specialist, I complete difficult and innovative assignments, including unparalleled watershed analysis partnerships and a unique outreach partnership with Nestucca High School. Provide effective liaison to the public in wildlife and forest conservation issues. Fulfill a variety of roles centered on team leadership, fostering partnerships, providing expertise and advice on animal populations, performing wildlife surveys, and supervising summer crews for timber sale layout.

In the Summary or Profile or Other Qualifications sections:

> **PROFILE**
>
> Natural Resource Specialist with 24 years of extensive Bureau of Land Management ecosystem-based management experience. I am valued by managers for my expertise in completing innovative and challenging special projects. Possess strong skills in coordinating interagency partnerships and interdisciplinary team efforts. Specialize in public speaking, timber project layout leadership, wildlife surveys, habitat restoration, cooperative agreements, public outreach to school groups, and representing BLM goals to outside interest groups. My experience includes successful resolution of multiple-use conflicts involving wildlife, forest, and botanical resources. I have excellent communication, supervision, and negotiation skills.

First sentence in Work Experience after title:

> As a Wildlife Biologist, I practiced ecosystem-based management in a self-directed work team atmosphere. Wildlife Biologist on the Lower Deschutes eco-team assigned to evaluate and improve wildlife and fish habitat. The last four months of this employment period were spent detailed to the wildlife staff of the Lakeview District BLM, Klamath Falls Resource Area.

Fourth Principle: Use Powerful Words

If you use plain language in short sentences, how is your resume going to impress anyone? Through the use of powerful words! Powerful words convey strong and unambiguous meaning. You should use a thesaurus to find stronger substitutes for weak words in your resume. This is even more important in the age of the resume builder, where the character count may be strictly limited. But this won't take you all the way. To clear away the debris of weak words, you need to think about writing in a new way. For example, consider the following statement:

> Serve as point of contact for all matters pertaining to personnel.

Serve as is not impressive. It does not tell the reader anything. Chop it. *Point of contact* is good, but *chief liaison* is better. *Sole liaison* is better still (if true). *Pertaining to* adds nothing, so eliminate it. Just say, *all personnel matters.* Thus, the following statement is a good phrase:

> Sole liaison on all personnel matters.

Every single word in it contributes significantly to the idea. See how if you remove any word now, the sentence becomes weaker? That's how you know your sentence is truly strong.

Here are a few examples of powerful words that you might see frequently in federal vacancy announcements:

- Complex or highly complex
- Unique
- Energetic
- Creative

The following list is a compilation of more than 100 powerful words for resume writing based on more than 15 years of professional resume writing experience. There are undoubtedly many more. Keep this list near your computer or wherever you work on your resume as a handy reference. It will be a great tool when you are stuck for a word. The list is arranged into categories. Just by picking words for the various categories and modifying them as needed, you will be halfway to a quality resume already.

These words are nouns and verbs, quantifiers, interpersonal traits, abilities, core competencies, and industry jargon. These exceptional words will demonstrate your level of independence and impress the reader.

Creation

These verbs demonstrate initiative, resourcefulness, organizational skills, and creativity.

assemble	conceive	convene	create	design
forge	form	formulate	invent	implement
initiate	realize	spearhead	plan	

First or Only

The Navy Job Kit gives these instructions: "Use modifiers to define the frequency at which you perform tasks, i.e., occasionally, regularly, once or twice per year, monthly, weekly, daily. Use words that define the level and scope of your experience and skills." These quantifiers are important. If you do not tell readers you were the sole support for 15 professionals, how will they know it?

chief	first	foremost	greatest	most
leading	number-one	singular	one	only
prime	single	sole	unparalleled	top
unique	unrivaled			

Outcomes

To demonstrate that you can "get things done," use these words to demonstrate action and results.

communication	cooperation	cost-effective	efficiency	morale
outcomes	output	productivity		

Employment

These words demonstrate movement, action, and decision-making abilities.

deploy	employ	exercise	use	utilize

Leadership

Leaders are in demand—whether you are a manager, administrative staffer, or tradesperson. If you are a team leader, foreman, supervisor, or lead, define your leadership responsibilities.

(be) chief (of)

(be) in charge of

(be) responsible for

administer	control	direct	govern	head up
lead	manage	oversee	run	supervise

Primacy

How important are you to the project? Are you a subject-matter expert? If you are, say so.

advisor	coworker	key	major	expert
primary	principal	subject matter	source person	lead
sole source				

Persuasion

The ability to persuade is a significant trait for success. Persuasive skills and language can be used in describing teamwork.

coach	galvanize	inspire	lobby	rally
persuade	(re)invigorate	(re)vitalize	unify	unite

Success

The word "success" suggests results and positive thinking. The reader believes you are successful because you have written it in your resume.

accomplish	achieve	attain	master
score (a victory)	succeed	sustain	

Authorship

Writing is one of the principal skills needed in a civilian job. If you write and edit documents, include these skills.

author	create	draft	edit
generate	publish	write	

Newness

Are you part of a project that is being done for the first time? Tell readers or they won't know this is an innovative, state-of-the-art program designed to improve services and enhance the program.

creative	first-ever	first-of-its-kind	innovative	novel	state-of-the-art

Degree

Quantify your successes and results—with a percentage, if possible. Your resume will be more interesting, complete, and exciting.

100% (or other percentage that is impressive)

completely	considerably	effectively	fully
especially	extremely	outstanding	greatly
particularly	powerful	seasoned	highly
significantly	strongly	thoroughly	solidly

Quality

Qualify your work efforts. Was it excellent, outstanding, or high quality? Positive thinking and writing about outstanding achievements will sell the selecting official on your capabilities.

excellent	great	good	high quality	outstanding quality
special	superb			

Competencies

Writing about your knowledge, skills, and abilities in your resume requires that you state you are adept in concise, focused writing; expert in certain laws and regulations; capable in facilitating meetings; and skilled in network administration.

able	adept at	capable	competent	demonstrated
effective	expert	knowledgeable	proven	
skilled	tested	trained	versed in	

Words to Edit Out of Your Resume

Just as there are powerful words that serve you well in a resume, there are simple words and phrases to avoid. Here are a few before-and-after examples of the old writing style and the new, more succinct writing style.

Currently I am working as the Manager of Operations.
Manage operations.

I also have experience with planning meetings.
Plan and coordinate meetings.

I have worked for the Office of Training Programs.
Cooperate with Office of Training Programs.

I have helped set up office systems.
Organized new office systems.

Major duties include working with other staff.
Cooperated with staff.

I used a variety of equipment.
Equipment skills include….

Major duties were to write and edit.
Write and edit….

I provide….
Select a verb that will be more descriptive than "provide," such as design, research, coordinate, or facilitate.

Worked in the capacity of management analyst.
Management Analyst.

I was responsible for managing the daily operations.
Managed daily operations.

I also have experience in designing audit reports.
Design audit reports.

When needed, supervise team members.
Supervise team members on occasion.

As the department's user support….
User support for the department.

Worked with team members.
Member of a team.

Being the timekeeper for the office.
Timekeeper for the office.

Assume duties of the education specialist.
Education specialist planning programs and curriculum.

Also responsible for preparing payroll information.
Prepare payroll for 250 employees.

Helped with writing, editing.
Wrote, edited, planned, coordinated… any verb that describes the activity.

Tasks included compiling, organizing, and researching information.
Compile, organize, and research information.

Assisted with planning, researching, and designing.
Co-planned, researched, and designed….

As a member of a team, planned, researched, and designed.
Planned, researched, and designed as a member of the interagency team.

Responsible for all aspects of the critical reviews and narrative reports.
Wrote critical reviews and narrative reports.

I provide the leadership to maintain benchmarks to meet project deadlines.
Plan and lead team to maintain benchmarks to meet project deadlines.

Concurrently monitored project….
Managed details for the _____ project.

My other duties consist of customer services, research, and problem-solving.
Research and resolve problems for customers.

The information is gathered from….
Complied, organized, and managed information gathered from….

I have to do systems analysis and planning.
Manage systems analysis and planning for projects.

Assisted in all aspects of….
Involved in all aspects of….

Those are just some of the phrases to avoid; there are stronger ways to express yourself. The key is to review every single word and phrase in your resume. Then ask yourself two questions:

- If I cut it out, would the sentence be less meaningful?
- Is there any shorter or clearer way to say it?

If you can honestly answer no to both questions, leave it in. I look at it this way: You have to work hard; so should each word in your resume!

Fifth Principle: Beware of Acronyms

We know that federal employees depend on acronyms to communicate. And this is okay at work among your coworkers. But in a resume where you may be applying to another agency, your resume could be Greek to the new HR specialist. And, the electronic Resumix system at DOD might not recognize your acronyms as keywords. The Resumix keyword system does not include any of the unusual acronyms.

Solution: Describe your experience with both acronyms and descriptions to be safe. The Defense Finance & Accounting Service Human Resources Specialist gives this advice to employees to maximize success with the Resumix resume system:

> Please write a generic description of your proprietary systems, so that the automated system can search for your software and skill knowledge.

Here's an example. WAWF (Wide Area Work Flow) should be described this way in your resume:

> Train and provide technical assistance to customers in the use of Wide Area Work Flow (WAWF), Department of Defense Receipts & Acceptance system.

Sixth Principle: No Bureaucratese or Position Description (PD)–Style Writing

If you are writing a federal electronic resume based on your position description, beware of the temptation to write your resume the same way the HR specialist wrote the position description. You can write in a more clear and meaningful style without the bureaucratese or position description–style writing.

Bureaucratese is a style of language characterized by jargon and euphemisms that is used especially by bureaucrats. It is often confusing, cold, intimidating, and cloudy. All of us, but particularly those of us who work for the public, have a responsibility to handle language with care. We need to be accessible and clear. We need to avoid jargon and bureaucratese. Examples of jargon include the following:

- Overuse of the passive voice (see the tenth principle for more on this)
- Using federal and state program names without explaining what the programs are
- Using and misusing words such as *impact, interface, prioritize, modality,* and *ascertain*
- Using phony words and phrases such as *analyzation, conduit, augment,* and *determine the nature of*

Before: Bureaucratic writing style

> **Administrative Support Specialist:** Serves as deputy to the supervisor of the Administrative Personnel Processing Office (APPO), with responsibility for overseeing and assuring the quality and accuracy of a variety of support functions associated with the APPO of the Transatlantic Program Center (TAC). Manages assigned activities through a continuous review of operations support program accomplishments, against established objectives and goals. This process encompasses every aspect of personnel deployment to include temporary change of station (TCS) and temporary duty (TDY) requirements; pre-deployment package actions; travel itineraries; timekeeping; and final return to home station actions. Provides technical advice on operations support functions and quality assurance oversight to the supervisor. Plans, organizes, coordinates, and assists in the implementation of the mission requirements of the APPO. Manages, coordinates, and oversees the quality and accuracy for day-to-day support operations.

After: Active writing style that is more friendly and direct

> As the deputy to the supervisor of the Administrative Personnel Processing Office (APPO), I oversee efficient administrative and support operations for the Transatlantic Program Center (TAC). Coordinate deployment services for an average of 1,500 U.S. Army Corps of Engineers civilians deployed to Iraq and other reconstruction areas per year. As the lead of the Support Team, we ensure continuous review and update for the following deployment services: temporary change of station and temporary duty requirements. The team also manages customer services for pre-deployment package actions, travel itineraries, and final return to home station actions. I am the technical advisor to the supervisor on all mission requirements of the APPO.

Seventh Principle: Tell a Story or Describe a Project

The best resumes flow with well-written, interesting prose—almost like a story. Many federal employees are involved in major projects in their work. Their entire resumes can be composed of descriptions of projects.

What Is Your Top 10 List of Accomplishments?

The human resources specialists and supervisors enjoy a good story that demonstrates your accomplishment, outstanding service to the office or customer, and added value to the office. If you write 10 accomplishments and combine them into your resume, you will achieve a genuine personal statement of success, demonstrate your skill level, and keep the HR specialist spellbound.

Here are impressive stories:

Project: National Emergency Response Team (NERT):

Currently assigned to the NERT activated by the Director, FEMA; respond to incidents of national significance. I am a key participant in the design and implementation of IT and telecom solutions to meet the needs of emergency-management teams in response to critical events, including Hurricane Katrina. Prepared an Interagency Operations Plan that coordinated the joint operations of multiple federal and civil organizations including FEMA, the FBI, the U.S. Secret Service, the Port Authority NY/NJ, and the New York City Police.

Story: Irate Passenger at BWI

As a Lead Security Screener, I negotiated a solution with an unruly passenger recently at BWI airport. The passenger was highly irate because he could not take a special garden cutting tool to his mother for Mother's Day. When the screener originally presented the passenger with his options, he quickly escalated to the point where he was intimidating the female officer. I was presently on another lane and quickly went over to the location, where I immediately assumed control of the situation. Again in a calm, firm, clear, and precise manner, I explained all of the passenger's options. After the passenger took the information in, he yielded, decided to relinquish the item, and then apologized to the female TSO and to me for his actions.

Project: TSA Customer Service Survey

As the Lead Screener, I have created a TSA New Customer Service Survey and have trained more than 27 screeners in the survey administration. The survey information is managed in Excel and tracks problem data and monitors trends. **RESULTS:** These surveys have proven to be a valuable two-way tool to both gather data on the screening process and give the screening officers who have administered the survey valuable insight into passenger behavior.

Technology Out of This World

A potential customer approached me to design a new type of aerial imaging equipment. I explained that I was well qualified for this job, as I had designed a similar instrument, which was already in use. The customer asked to see the instrument. I explained, "I'd love to show it to you, but it's aboard MIR, the Russian Space Station." I got the account.

These stories show that you can work under pressure, can lead teams, can handle and negotiate problems, are resourceful, and can multitask very well. They also show you are a decision-maker and proven leader. Examples like these demonstrate that you can negotiate working partnerships with a plan of action. They also show you are highly technically skilled.

Eighth Principle: Be Consistent with Verb Tenses

The rule about tense in resumes is to use the present tense for all present responsibilities and skills and the past tense for all past responsibilities. Here are a few examples:

SENIOR COMPUTER TECHNICIAN (September 20XX to present)

- Senior Computer Technician serving a fast-paced metropolitan retail outlet for Best Buy, one of the nation's leading retailers and resellers of technology products and services. Lead for the Technical Service Group, a 7-person team providing warranty repair services for the broad range of computer and personal electronics products sold by the company. Repair desktop and laptop computer systems, including digital camera equipment, smartphones, printers, and other computer peripherals.

SENIOR COMPUTER TECHNICIAN (September 20XX to June 20XX)

- Systems administrator for a scientific workgroup computing environment. Planned and delivered customer support services to the organization. Installed, upgraded, delivered, and provided troubleshooting for hardware and software components. Performed file back-ups and restores, system and peripherals troubleshooting, and component repair.

- Provided a high level of customer service for a wide variety of computer and network problems. Monitored, analyzed, and resolved end-user issues and provided informal training and assistance.

- Researched and reported on new technologies, equipment, and software with application to the Naval Surface Warfare Center.

Ninth Principle: Avoid the Passive Voice and Words *Not* to Use in Your Resume

Human resources professionals write vacancy announcements in the passive voice. Many civilians became accustomed to writing their resumes in the passive voice. Now, however, you should avoid doing so. Use the active voice whenever possible. It's best if you can start your sentences with a verb or noun.

Terms to Eliminate from Your Resume

- Responsible for or Responsibilities include
- Duties include
- Additional duties include
- Tasks include
- Helped with, worked with, assisted with

Here is a typical example of passive voice followed by the more impressive version rewritten in active voice. The passive-voice example does not reflect that the employee really did anything. Someone else did the work, or the statement is simply a statement without action.

Before:

Lead Security Screener, TSA

Responsible for oversight of Security Screener operations to ensure performance of security screeners; provide security and protection of air travelers, airports, and aircraft. Tasked with oversight of passenger screening and baggage screening. Serve as primary interface between senior management and workforce and communicate operational and administrative information up and down chain of command. Other duties include obtaining and collating passenger flight data. Assisted with correcting the improper use or application of equipment, provided guidance to subordinates, and answered routine and non-routine questions. Additional duties include collecting performance metrics to process improvement areas.

After:

Lead Security Screener

Provided direct leadership to approximately 60 screeners per shift.

Operations Management: Optimized situational awareness, serving as primary interface between senior management and workforce; communicated operational and administrative information up and down chain of command. Obtained and collated passenger flight data and flight departure information, and interacted with checkpoint supervisors to ensure operational readiness. Recognized and recommended correction of improper use or application of equipment, provided guidance to subordinates, and answered routine and nonroutine questions. Managed and supported collection of performance metrics to process improvement areas and systemic or individual weaknesses, vulnerabilities, or inefficiencies in screening processes. Recognized customer service needs of traveling public and balanced them with safety and security. Moved screener forces to accommodate and balance wait times. Ensured accountability at all levels. Monitored individual performance and provided frequent communication to promote screener development.

Tenth Principle: Tell the Truth and Brag a Little

People are taught by their mothers and grandmothers to not brag about themselves. But in a federal job search, you have to be confident, proud, and able to talk about your best accomplishments.

In the same category, avoid superlatives as a general rule. Phrases such as *all, very, every, the greatest, the only,* and so forth raise a red flag. Use superlatives only for objectively quantifiable accomplishments or when reciting the opinion of a knowledgeable person. Example: "My supervisor has praised me as being the most efficient office manager he has ever known." Though subjective, the opinion of a supervisor is meaningful.

Summary

Because your resume reflects who you are, you should feel comfortable with it. Can you speak it out loud without embarrassment? If not, you could end up being embarrassed if the interviewer asks you about your accomplishments as recorded on the resume.

Resumes should be written in a way that allows you to read them aloud in a natural and comfortable fashion. What works for one person might not work for another. How would you speak about your experience to a friend? Look at the passive-voice examples in the Ninth Principle section. Do you see the difference in readability between the passive voice and the active voice?

The new writing style is more personal without being too casual, the flow of the prose tells a story, and the sentences are complete and written in active voice. These paragraphs are written as you would speak them.

CHAPTER 8

Researching the Agency's Core Competencies

Many federal agencies have developed a list of the top core competencies desired in employees. The agencies might integrate the competencies into their applications. The core competencies are used for recruiting the best candidates, for promoting employees to the next level, and as behavior-based interview questions (read more in Chapter 27). This chapter shows you how important core competencies are to your application for a federal job, in terms of your resume and the essays or examples that you will be asked to write to demonstrate your performance.

If you read the vacancy announcement, it gives you the technical "duties" of the job. It then lists the "specialized qualifications" desired for the job. Some vacancy announcements mention core competencies and others do not. This chapter includes the core competencies for five federal agencies, including Office of Personnel Management's Competencies for Supervisors for any agency.

In some agencies, the competencies seem like "value-added" skills to a technical set of skills. To stand out, it's great to include top competencies in your resume within various sections, such as Work Experience, Other Qualifications, or Summary.

What Are Your Core Competencies and How Can You Include Them in Your Resume?

As you read this chapter, underline the competencies that you consider to be yours as well. Because federal agencies are using the new behavior-based interview style, you should be prepared to write your best examples and practice speaking them for the interview.

 Note: Dr. Daniel Goleman wrote a great book that focuses on work-based competencies: *Working with Emotional Intelligence* (Bantam). He makes it clear that your core competencies are critical to the success of your job performance.

When including your core competencies in the text of your resume, you should blend them with language from your current and past position descriptions, the vacancy announcement's "duties" section, and your own statements of responsibility. Resume sections that can include core competencies are Work Experience descriptions, your Profile or Summary of Skills section, or a section near the end of the resume called Other Qualifications.

Using Core Competencies as Transferable Skills When Changing Careers

If you are changing careers, you will want to use this chapter to find your transferable skills, which can take you from one job series to another. Most jobs require skills in customer service, project management, teamwork, working under deadlines, and attention to detail. You can integrate these competencies to match your current skills to the skills that the new job requires.

Every agency has its own list of required competencies and its own interests. If you study the various core competency lists and agency descriptions, you will see that they require diverse values, soft skills, knowledge, and specialized skills for particular occupations. Some of the competencies are similar between agencies, such as customer service, flexibility, decision-making, problem-solving, teamwork, and resourcefulness.

 Note: The OPM's definition of core competencies is the following: "Observable, measurable pattern of skills, knowledge, abilities, behaviors, and other characteristics that an individual needs to perform work roles or occupational functions successfully." (U.S. Office of Personnel Management, Op. Cir., Glossary.)

Agency and Company Core Competencies

More and more agencies are developing their own sets of competencies. You can find a few of these lists by going to www.opm.gov and searching for "core competencies." You can also go to the sites for specific agencies and use their search engines to find "core competencies." Some agencies list them on their sites; others do not.

 Note: Chapter 22, "Senior Executive Service, Executive Core Qualifications," includes samples and descriptions of OPM's Executive Core Qualifications. These are the core competencies for executives in government.

In this section we provide example sets of core competencies for five federal agencies:

- **Supervisor Core Competencies—any agency:** Focuses on the important competencies for supervisors, team leads, and managers.
- **Veterans Administration:** The Department of Veterans Affairs developed one of the first sets of core competencies and still looks for these competencies in applications.
- **Department of the Interior, U.S. Forest Service:** Its core competencies have been widely used as KSAs and interview questions for years.
- **Central Intelligence Agency—Clandestine Agent:** These core competencies were found in a job announcement.
- **Defense Logistics Agency:** The DLA uses these core competencies for management promotions, evaluations, and interviews.

Core Competency Set 1: OPM's 10 Competencies Most Important for Supervisory Work

- **Accountability:** Holds self and others accountable for measurable high-quality, timely, and cost-effective results. Determines objectives, sets priorities, and delegates work. Accepts responsibility for mistakes. Complies with established control systems and rules.

- **Customer Service:** Anticipates and meets the needs of both internal and external customers. Delivers high-quality products and services; is committed to continuous improvement.

- **Decisiveness:** Makes well-informed, effective, and timely decisions, even when data are limited or solutions produce unpleasant consequences; perceives the impact and implications of decisions.

- **Flexibility:** Is open to change and new information; rapidly adapts to new information, changing conditions, or unexpected obstacles.

- **Integrity/Honesty:** Behaves in an honest, fair, and ethical manner. Shows consistency in words and actions. Models high standards of ethics.

- **Interpersonal Skills:** Treats others with courtesy, sensitivity, and respect. Considers and responds appropriately to the needs and feelings of different people in different situations.

- **Oral Communication:** Makes clear and convincing oral presentations. Listens effectively; clarifies information as needed.

- **Problem Solving:** Identifies and analyzes problems; weighs relevance and accuracy of information; generates and evaluates alternative solutions; makes recommendations.

- **Resilience:** Deals effectively with pressure; remains optimistic and persistent, even under adversity. Recovers quickly from setbacks.

- **Written Communication:** Writes in a clear, concise, organized, and convincing manner for the intended audience.

Technical Requirements

Many supervisory positions have specific subject-matter knowledge and skill requirements (in other words, technical requirements) candidates must meet. When the supervisory position has technical requirements, the employing agency must use an occupation-specific qualification standard. *The Supervisory Qualification Guide* is used in conjunction with the occupation-specific qualification standard.

Other Competencies Related to Leadership Positions

When filling supervisory positions, agencies may consider using additional competencies beyond the 10 recommended competencies in the preceding list. Agencies may choose from among any of the leadership competencies in the following list. Or, based on job analysis, agencies may develop their own competencies/Knowledge, Skills, Abilities (KSAs).

- **Conflict Management:** Encourages creative tension and differences of opinions. Anticipates and takes steps to prevent counterproductive confrontations. Manages and resolves conflicts and disagreements in a constructive manner.

- **Continual Learning:** Assesses and recognizes own strengths and weaknesses; pursues self-development.

- **Creativity and Innovation:** Develops new insights into situations; questions conventional approaches; encourages new ideas and innovations; designs and implements new or cutting-edge programs/processes.

- **Developing Others:** Develops the ability of others to perform and contribute to the organization by providing ongoing feedback and by providing opportunities to learn through formal and informal methods.

- **Entrepreneurship:** Positions the organization for future success by identifying new opportunities; builds the organization by developing or improving products or services. Takes calculated risks to accomplish organizational objectives.

- **External Awareness:** Understands and keeps up-to-date on local, national, and international policies and trends that affect the organization and shape stakeholders' views; is aware of the organization's impact on the external environment.

- **Financial Management:** Understands the organization's financial processes. Prepares, justifies, and administers the program budget. Oversees procurement and contracting to achieve desired results. Monitors expenditures and uses cost-benefit thinking to set priorities.

- **Human Capital Management:** Builds and manages workforce based on organizational goals, budget considerations, and staffing needs. Ensures that employees are appropriately recruited, selected, appraised, and rewarded; takes action to address performance problems. Manages a multisector workforce and a variety of work situations.

- **Influencing/Negotiating:** Persuades others; builds consensus through give and take; gains cooperation from others to obtain information and accomplish goals.

- **Leveraging Diversity:** Fosters an inclusive workplace where diversity and individual differences are valued and leveraged to achieve the vision and mission of the organization.

- **Partnering:** Develops networks and builds alliances; collaborates across boundaries to build strategic relationships and achieve common goals.

- **Political Savvy:** Identifies the internal and external politics that impact the work of the organization. Perceives organizational and political reality and acts accordingly.

- **Public Service Motivation:** Shows a commitment to serve the public. Ensures that actions meet public needs; aligns organizational objectives and practices with public interests.

- **Strategic Thinking:** Formulates objectives and priorities, and implements plans consistent with the long-term interest of the organization in a global environment. Capitalizes on opportunities and manages risks.

- **Teambuilding:** Inspires and fosters team commitment, spirit, pride, and trust. Facilitates cooperation and motivates team members to accomplish group goals.

- **Technical Credibility:** Understands and appropriately applies principles, procedures, requirements, regulations, and policies related to specialized expertise.

- **Technology Management:** Keeps up-to-date on technological developments. Makes effective use of technology to achieve results. Ensures access to and security of technology systems.

- **Vision:** Takes a long-term view and builds a shared vision with others; acts as a catalyst for organizational change. Influences others to translate vision into action.

Core Competency Set 2: Veterans Administration

If you are applying for jobs at the Veterans Administration or other federal agencies, you can include some of this language in your federal resume KSAs and prepare for your interviews based on these important core competencies.

- Interpersonal Effectiveness
- Customer Service
- Systems Thinking
- Flexibility/Adaptability
- Creative Thinking
- Organizational Stewardship
- Personal Mastery
- Technical Competency

Core Competency Set 3: Department of the Interior, National Park Service, Universal Competencies

These competencies are a combination of employee competencies/values and specific knowledge of the agency policies, legislation, and programs. You can read more about this agency at the National Park Service website: www.nps.gov/training/uc/home.htm.

- **Mission Comprehension:** This competency requires a thorough background and understanding of the 1916 NPS Organic Act and its many ramifications and the additional responsibilities that have been added to the NPS throughout its history; and a perspective of how the National Park System began as a part of the Conservation Movement that continues today.

- **Agency Orientation:** This competency requires a basic comprehension of the structure and organization of the NPS at the park, cluster, field area, and Washington Office levels; an understanding of the structure and organization of the Department of the Interior and its place in the federal government; and the development of an insight into an individual employee's role in the NPS in particular, and in the federal government in general.

- **Resource Stewardship:** This competency requires an overall understanding of the spectrum of resources protected by the NPS; the range of NPS responsibilities in managing these resources; the individual's role in resource stewardship; the planning process and its purpose in the NPS; and working with partners outside the agency to promote resource stewardship.

- **NPS Operations:** This competency encompasses a general comprehension of the basic operations of the NPS, especially at the park level; how these operations interact to fulfill the mission of the NPS; and why visitors come to parks and how the NPS "manages" them.

- **Fundamental Values:** This competency focuses on an employee's ability to exhibit certain attitudes and behaviors to accomplish an assigned job and to contribute to the overall health of the organization. These include leadership and teamwork behaviors; ethical behavior toward people and the organization; support of cultural diversity and fairness issues in the workplace; support of accessible parks and workplaces; an attitude toward safe behavior for one's self and for others; and mental and physical fitness.

- **Communications Skills:** This competency encompasses the ability to communicate effectively with the public and employees in writing and speech; to use interpersonal skills to be an effective employee; and to exhibit basic computer abilities.

- **Problem-Solving Skills:** This competency deals with the ability to analyze a problem, build consensus, make decisions, and practice innovation in various aspects of one's job.

- **Individual Development and Planning:** This competency considers an individual's being able to work with one's supervisor and agency to plan a course of action for one's performance, career, and ultimately, retirement.

Core Competency Set 4: Central Intelligence Agency

The CIA's top competencies are a combination of specialized, technical skills and soft skills, including spirit, self-starter, and courage. This is a great list of competencies.

Qualifications: Central Intelligence Agency's Clandestine Service Trainee Program is the gateway to a unique overseas experience. To qualify you must have first-rate qualifications: a bachelor's degree with an excellent academic record, strong interpersonal skills, the ability to write clearly and accurately, and a burning interest in international affairs. A graduate degree, foreign travel, foreign language proficiency, previous residency abroad, and military experience are pluses. **We are particularly interested in candidates with backgrounds in Central Eurasian, East Asian, and Middle Eastern languages**, and those with degrees and experience in international economics and international business as well as in the physical sciences. Entrance salaries range from $43,500 to $60,400, depending on credentials.

They also require the following core competencies:

For the extraordinary individual who wants more than just a job, we offer a unique career—a way of life that will challenge the deepest resources of your intelligence, self-reliance, and responsibility. It demands an adventurous spirit, a forceful personality, superior intellectual ability, toughness of mind, and a high degree of personal integrity, courage, and love of country. You will need to deal with fast-moving, ambiguous, and unstructured situations that will test your resourcefulness to the utmost. It takes special skills and professional discipline to produce results.

Core Competency Set 5: Defense Logistics Agency

These competencies are a combination of employee competencies/values and specific knowledge of the agency policies, legislation, and programs.

- Mission Comprehension
- Customer Services
- Professionalism
- Resource Stewardship
- Innovation and Initiative

- Leadership
- Teamwork
- Oral and Written Communications
- Strategic Focus
- Responsibility/Accountability

Sample Resume with Leadership, Customer Service, and Teamwork Core Competencies

This sample federal resume is for a civil engineer who achieves success with specialized knowledge in engineering, project management, and complex projects with important core competencies in leading teams, communicating, advocating for his projects, solving problems, and multitasking.

Target Job: Civil Engineer/Project Manager, GS-1101-12.
Resume Format: USAJOBS, Outline Format.
Core competencies are marked in bold.

Ronald F. Zimmerman

39982 Apache Trail

Beavercreek, OH 45410

(410) 998-2213 HOME

(410) 887-2539 WORK

Email: rfzimmerman@hotmail.com

PROFESSIONAL EXPERIENCE

Project Manager/Professional Engineer

Haliburton, Inc.	August 1988–February 2009
8239 Grand Lake Ave.	40+ hours/week
Dayton, OH 45440	Salary: $111K/year

SOLID **MULTI-TASKING** MANAGEMENT TALENT

While employed with the Haliburton Corporation, simultaneously and successfully fulfilled the duties and responsibilities of two crucial senior positions: that of Project Manager and Professional Engineer.

Project Management Professional (PMP)

ROUTINELY EXHIBITED **LEADERSHIP** AND MANAGEMENT ABILITY SKILLS. HANDPICKED as the project owner's primary Point of Contact (POC) on multiple projects. **Efficiently led interdisciplinary teams in** the successful execution of major construction; engineering; and Environment, Health & Safety (EHS) capital projects. Managed all planning, engineering design, construction, and permit considerations.

Managed multiple project teams; provided weekly status reports to stakeholders pertaining to each project's ongoing status comprising the monitoring of milestones, including cost, schedule, and compliance, along with design/construction specifications. **Consistently improved project performance results** with key metrics: on-time completion (schedule), completion within budget (cost), and product consistency/quality.

- Skilled in **problem-solving** and workflow management. Established a consistent project management process comprised of a standard schedule, budget, and other project documents pertaining to a $35M multi-facility site-remediation program, together with 15 different consultant/contractor teams. Resulted in 5% reduction in annual project management costs and a 15% improved on-time acheivement of key milestones.

INTERPRETED SCOPE OF WORK AND **PROVIDED RESPONSIVE CUSTOMER SERVICES** required for starting the project needs/scope development phase. As Lead Project/Program Manager of a business consolidation program, relied heavily upon that knowledge and experience for the renovations of 55 administration/manufacturing facilities.

- **Lead 20 consultant/contractor teams** in support of a strategic element of the $1.2B business acquisition. Achieved renovation program cost savings of over $75K of actual vs. planned.

SAVVY NEGOTIATOR possessing not only the unique ability to parlay with third parties, but with government agencies as well.

- Negotiated terms and conditions for a master contract with the goal of retaining more than 15 consultant/contractor teams to complete a major project.

- **Negotiated and resolved collaborative agreement** with engineering service firms to provide engineering and EHS assessment support for a $1.2B business acquisition/restructuring project.

OUTSTANDING VERBAL AND WRITTEN COMMUNICATOR

Improved skills far beyond technical expertise by preparing project plans, presenting business cases for funding approval, and managing consultant/contractor teams in deployment of company-wide strategic programs.

Summary

To stand out with your federal resume, including relevant core competencies that you have developed (and that the agency is seeking) will help you get referred and selected for an interview. If you can add some of the critical competencies for an agency into your resume, KSAs, or essays, you will be closer to being referred and selected for an interview. If you can write examples for the top competencies, you will be prepared for job interviews. Many agencies use their core competencies as a basis for interview questions. You will clearly be including specialized experience; to stand out, however, a few significant core competencies will help you to be more competitive.

Part 3

KSAs, Questionnaires, and Essays in the Resume and Cover Letters

CHAPTER 9

KSAs in the Application: Presenting Your Accomplishments

This chapter represents the biggest federal application change in this entire book! It started on May 11, 2010, when President Barack Obama issued a presidential memorandum ("Improving the Federal Recruitment and Hiring Process") that directed federal agencies to

> *eliminate any requirement that applicants respond to essay-style questions when submitting their initial application materials for any federal job.*

These essay-style questions—known as KSAs because they address job seekers' knowledge, skills, and abilities—have historically been a barrier for many federal job seekers. A job seeker might not have applied for a job that required KSAs as part of the application process because of the dread of writing the full-page narratives about job experiences.

What's confusing about this presidential memorandum to eliminate essays is that KSA terminology is still listed in vacancy announcements. So KSAs are not totally eliminated—your descriptions of your knowledge, skills, and abilities for the position are still an important part of your federal application.

There are several ways to cover the knowledge, skills, and abilities in your federal application. This chapter and the next two will give you insight into the importance and methods of describing your KSAs and specialized experience in a resume, a questionnaire, and a cover letter.

Understanding the Role of KSAs

KSA stands for knowledge, skills, and abilities, which the government (specifically the Office of Personnel Management) defines as follows:

- **Knowledge:** An organized body of information, usually of a factual or procedural nature, which, if applied, makes adequate performance on the job possible.
- **Skills:** The proficient manual, verbal, or mental manipulation of data, people, or things. These are observable, quantifiable, and measurable.
- **Abilities:** The power to perform an activity at the present time. Implied is a lack of discernible barriers, either physical or mental, to performing the activity.

The term *KSA* refers to these types of specified qualifications for a federal job, but it also has come to represent what applicants have to write in order to prove that they have those qualifications. In the past, KSAs took the form of long, one-page, 8,000-character narratives that described experiences that served as proof of an applicant's knowledge, skill, or ability in each required area of expertise. These narratives were then formally "rated and ranked" with a scoring system based on the complexity of the experience.

The difference that has come as a result of President Obama's federal hiring reform is the way KSAs are incorporated into federal applications. Most federal applications now are composed of two or three parts:

1. The federal resume with KSA Accomplishments within the resume.

2. A questionnaire with self-assessment questions and sometimes essay narratives as a part of the application process.

3. Additional requested documents.

KSAs now go into the resume in the form of accomplishment statements of up to 150 words, and the questionnaires are graded, serving a similar purpose to the old KSA narratives. You also might still see the request for short (4,000 characters) essay answers about KSAs as part of the question-naire (the focus of Chapter 10, "Questionnaires That Assess Your Knowledge, Skills, and Abilities"). The highest-scoring applicants from the questionnaires are placed on the "List of Certified Eligibles," and the resumes are forwarded to the hiring manager.

You can think of KSAs in the resume and questionnaire essays as a writing test. Your responses to the qualifications in the vacancy announcement and the items on the questionnaire will demon-strate whether you can analyze a question and answer it, understand the agency's mission, and write a narrative that relates your experience to the special needs of the position and organization. The reviewers are also looking to see whether you can follow directions closely and apply good computer and writing skills in developing a document that clearly articulates your job knowledge, skills, and abilities.

Ideally, the accomplishments you describe when addressing KSAs in the resume and the question-naire essay will be good examples that are also interesting to the reader. The hiring manager may have a stack of 30 to 150 qualified candidates to consider. Including memorable examples written in clear and easy-to-read text will go a long way toward getting your application into the list of Best Qualified candidates.

> **Note:** KSAs written in the first person ("I did this and that") are more compelling and real to the reader.

The KSA accomplishment stories that you write for your resume and questionnaire also become the foundation of your preparation for the interview (the focus of Chapter 27, "Preparing for a Structured, Behavior-Based Interview"). The section "Using the Three KSA Formats" later in this chapter shows how to present the same accomplishments in the different formats you will need throughout the federal hiring process.

Finding KSAs in Vacancy Announcements

The Qualifications and Evaluations section of the vacancy announcement describes the requirements for the position. In this section, you will see language such as knowledge, skills, abilities, competen-cies, essays, examples, narratives, questionnaires, supplemental statements, quality ranking factors, and specialized experience to describe the attributes you need to give examples of in your resume.

The HR specialists who post these announcements give you a lot of information about the position so that you can match your resume to those qualifications. Announcements typically contain an average of four to six KSAs or specialized experience elements, each of which could require you to provide an accomplishment to prove your expertise.

The following excerpts from vacancy announcements show sample instructions regarding how to include your knowledge, skills, and abilities in the resume and questionnaire. Note that the instructions on how to include KSAs in your resume or as separate narratives are not yet consistent. Some agencies are listing their KSAs in the announcement and are telling you to include them directly in the resume. Other agencies are not so clear about where to cover the KSAs. I recommend that you cover the KSAs in the resume no matter what the instructions are in the announcement.

Note the boldfaced text in the following vacancy announcement for a program analyst. It mentions that the questionnaire will cover KSAs, but it also explicitly asks for KSAs in the resume. (It also asks for the resume to be in Outline Format, which is covered in Chapter 3, "Work Experience and the Outline Format.") In particular, it asks applicants to address the knowledge listed in number 1 and the ability listed in number 2 in the KSAs listed in the "How You Will Be Evaluated" section.

This vacancy announcement also specifies a length for KSA examples—50 to 150 words—and asks for one example for each KSA in the announcement. These guidelines are good rules of thumb to follow if the announcement you are responding to doesn't offer instructions regarding length or number of examples. It's also important to include the result of your accomplishment. This amount of information may seem like a lot for a resume, but keep in mind that the average length of a federal resume is four to five pages.

GSA, Program Analyst, GS-0343-13

Instructions: These KSAs will be covered in the multiple-choice questionnaire. You should also cover these KSAs in your resume in the Outline Format. It will be critical that you give an example of your experience with travel management business practice and how you can communicate effectively. Give one example for each if you can, 50 to 150 words for each example.

HOW YOU WILL BE EVALUATED:

If you are found qualified for the position, your responses to the self-assessment vacancy questions will be used to assign a numerical score. If your responses to the vacancy questions are not supportable by your resume, then your score may be adjusted lower by the HR specialist. Veterans' Preference points will be added to a passing numerical score only if the appropriate documentation is submitted.

You will be evaluated on the vacancy-related questions that were designed to assess your overall possession of the following competencies/knowledge, skills, and abilities:

1. Knowledge of the commercial travel industry and travel management business practices.

2. Ability to communicate effectively orally and in writing.

3. Knowledge of management principles, methods, and techniques to implement and evaluate significant programs and activities.

4. Knowledge of qualitative and quantitative analytical techniques required to analyze the effectiveness and efficiency of assigned programs.

5. Knowledge of federal laws and regulations, executive orders, and agency directives and guidelines pertaining to designated program requirements and GSA compliance provisions.

The instructions in the following vacancy announcement for a paralegal also ask for the Outline Format for the resume. The instructions specifically tell you that the KSAs are covered in the questionnaire, but that you also should cover the specialized knowledge and KSAs in your resume. They are asking for examples of your KSAs as well within your resume.

U.S. Dept. of Justice, U.S. Attorney's Office, Paralegal Specialist, GS-0950-9

Instructions: You will complete an assessment questionnaire that will cover the KSAs, specialized experience, and competencies. You should cover these skills and competencies in your federal resume. The Outline Format can feature the important skills that will be of most interest to the HR specialist and hiring manager. Write examples of your experience in doing legal research, interpreting legal decisions, and examining legal documents. Add into your accomplishments that you have attention to detail, skill with technology (data management), responsiveness to customers, and the ability to write.

QUALIFICATIONS REQUIRED:

To be eligible at the GS-09 grade level, you must have at least one full year of specialized experience equivalent to the GS-07 grade level as defined below; or two full years of progressively higher level graduate education or master's degree in a related field (e.g., criminal justice, law) or an equivalent graduate degree such as an LL.B. or J.D.; or a combination of both specialized experience and education as explained below.

Specialized experience is defined as experience performing paralegal or legal work that demonstrates a basic knowledge of legal research and the ability to interpret legal decisions. Examples of specialized experience may include the following: examining and processing a variety of legal documents; conducting research, analysis, and evaluation of data in response to complex or sensitive requests; drafting briefs, pleadings, litigation recommendations, or other legal documents and correspondence; using a variety of electronic or manual filing systems to acquire and store information; finding documents and preparing recommendations; and searching and reviewing legal references, case files, and other sources for information and data required by attorneys or court personnel.

HOW YOU WILL BE EVALUATED:

Once the application process is complete, a review of resume and supporting documentation will be made and compared against your responses to the assessment questionnaire to determine whether you are qualified for this job. If, after your resume and or supporting documentation is reviewed, a determination is made that you have inflated your qualifications and or experience, you may lose consideration for this position. Please follow all instructions carefully. Errors or omissions may affect your eligibility.

Your qualifications will be evaluated on the following knowledge, skills, abilities and other characteristics:

- Attention to Detail
- Customer Service
- Oral Communication
- Self Management
- Technology Application
- Writing

The instructions in the following vacancy announcement for a program communication specialist clearly state that KSAs are covered in the questionnaire and should also be part of the resume. The instructions list specific skills applicants should describe in both the resume and the questionnaire.

Note that the basic qualifications for a GS-9 position list two areas of knowledge as qualifying specialized experience. These areas of knowledge should be incorporated into resume accomplishment statements as well. To find additional KSA information in this case, you would have to look at the questionnaire. Most vacancy announcements include a link to the questionnaire so that you can preview it.

HHS, Program Communication Specialist, GS-0301-9/12

Author's Instructions: The KSAs are covered in the questionnaire, and there will be a few essays to write. The essays/examples that you write should include examples of improving administrative procedures, screening and handling correspondence for the supervisor, drafting replies, and utilizing automation to manage correspondence. Also cover the KSAs in your resume!

QUALIFICATIONS REQUIRED:

Basic Qualifications

FOR GS-9:

You must have one (1) year of specialized experience that has equipped you with the particular knowledge, skills, and abilities to perform successfully the duties of the position, and that is typically in or related to the work of the position to be filled. To be creditable, specialized experience must have been equivalent to at least the GS-7 level in the federal government.

Qualifying specialized experiences are listed below:

- Knowledge of administrative principles, concepts and methodology and skill in carrying out basic assignments, operations, and procedures.
- Knowledge of technical methods to perform assignments such as carrying out limited projects that involve specialized techniques.

The following vacancy announcement for a work/life specialist clearly specifies what information applicants are expected to provide in their resumes. First, the instructions provide keywords for a resume in Outline Format. Second, the KSAs section lists the specific characteristics that applicants are evaluated on. Last, the preview of the questionnaire shows the KSAs in terms of the specific duties of the position. These questions clarify what details will be important to emphasize in KSA accomplishment statements on the resume. This announcement also provides a thorough explanation of how important it is that the information you provide about your accomplishments be accurate and consistent through all parts of your application.

Dept. of Air Force, Lajes Field Azores, AE, Work/Life Specialist, GS-0101-9

Instructions: The KSAs required for this position are clearly presented in the announcement. They will be covered in the questionnaire, but you should cover these in your resume. Your Outline Format could be: social services delivery, personal financial management advisory services, conducting interviews with clients, establishing working relationships with others, and communicating effectively.

HOW YOU WILL BE EVALUATED:

Your resume and responses to the self-assessment job questions are an integral part of the process for determining your basic and specialized qualifications for the position. Therefore, it is important to support your responses to the applicant assessment questions by providing examples of past and present experience when requested.

High self-assessment in the vacancy questions that is not supported by information in your resume, essay responses, and/or supporting documents may eliminate you from best-qualified status or result in a lowered score.

There are several parts of the application process that affect the overall evaluation of your application:

1. Your resume, which is part of your USAJOBS profile

2. Your responses to the core questions

3. Your responses to the self-assessment job-specific questions

4. Your supporting documents, if requested

Your latest resume will be used to determine qualifications as vacancies occur.

Once the application process is complete, a review of your application will be made to ensure you meet the job requirements. Your resume must reflect the experience identified on the questionnaire. The human resource specialist uses your responses to the occupational questionnaire, along with your resume and supporting documentation, to determine if you meet regulatory appointment authority and qualifications as listed in this vacancy announcement.

If, after your resume and/or supporting documentation is reviewed, a determination is made that you have inflated your qualifications and/or experience, your score may be adjusted to more accurately reflect your abilities. Please follow all instructions carefully. Errors or omissions may affect your rating.

KNOWLEDGE, SKILLS AND ABILITIES (KSAs): Your qualifications will be evaluated on the basis of your level of knowledge, skills, abilities, and/or competencies in the following areas:

1. Knowledge of social services delivery systems as well as concepts, principles, theories, and practices relating to one or more of the social or behavioral science fields.

2. Knowledge of personal financial management practices and techniques to provide clients with appropriate financial data and practical financial skills to enable them to make informed personal financial management decisions.

3. Skill in conducting interviews to establish the nature and extent of concerns/issues, provide assistance in developing goals and plans, and determine appropriate referral services/options.

4. Skill in establishing and maintaining effective working relationships using tact and diplomacy in interactions with individuals/families and with program representatives and officials.

5. Ability to communicate effectively both orally and in writing.

Work/Life Specialist

Preview Occupational Questionnaire

For each of the following tasks, choose the statement from the list below that best describes your experience and/or training. Darken the oval corresponding to that statement in Section 25 of the Occupational Questionnaire, OPM Form 1203-FX. Please select only one letter for each item.

A. I have not had education, training, or experience in performing this task.

B. I have had education or training in performing the task, but have not yet performed it on the job.

C. I have performed this task on the job. My work on this task was monitored closely by a supervisor or senior employee to ensure compliance with proper procedures.

D. I have performed this task as a regular part of a job. I have performed it independently and normally without review by a supervisor or senior employee.

E. I am considered an expert in performing this task. I have supervised performance of this task or am normally the person who is consulted by other workers to assist them in doing this task because of my expertise.

1. Interviews clients to make an independent evaluation of the situation, including the client's ability to deal with the problems, and assess appropriate options.

2. Plan, implement, and administer services and activities relating to military lifestyles (deployments, relocation, career planning/transition), individual and/or family development and relationships, and personal financial management.

3. Provide support services to individuals and/or families during deployments, mobilizations, local and national emergencies/disasters, and evacuations.

4. Gather data, compile statistics and subject matter resources, and prepare reports concerning community needs and development of new support services.

Using the Three KSA Formats

There are three basic ways to present your KSAs:

- Resume statements
- Questionnaire essays
- Interview bullet points

The following sections explain each of these formats in more detail. Whether you write KSAs in your resume or questionnaire essays, or tell a KSA story during your interview, you should provide specific examples of paid and nonpaid work experience, education, training, awards, and honors that support the skills required for the position.

KSAs in the Resume

KSAs take the form of accomplishment statements in resumes. Remember that you should have KSA accomplishments in your resume regardless of whether the announcement instructions specifically mention them. Also, you need to include the result of each accomplishment.

Using the Outline Format, type the keywords from the KSAs listed in the vacancy announcement in all uppercase letters in the resume. Then write at least one example from your Accomplishment Record that demonstrates you have the experience called for in the KSA. This short accomplishment example could include elements of the Context, Challenge, Actions, and Result (CCAR) formula that tells a complete story (the formula is explained later in this chapter). These accomplishments should be 50 to 150 words.

Accomplishment Records (ARs)

According to the Office of Personnel Management, the accomplishment record is a systematic procedure used to collect information about applicants' training, education, experience, and past achievements related to critical job competencies. The accomplishment record is based on the behavioral consistency principle that past behavior is the best predictor of future behavior. Applicants are typically asked to submit information on personal accomplishments to best illustrate their proficiency on critical job competencies (generally between four and eight). See http://apps.opm.gov/adt/Content.aspx?page=3-01&AspxAutoDetectCookieSupport=1&JScript=1 for more information on accomplishment records.

Keep in mind that the resume is an examination: You will be graded on what you have written. The reason for adding the accomplishment directly under the language of the KSA is so that the HR specialist can find the accomplishment easily in order to match it to the listed qualifications for the job. This can help you get referred to a hiring manager and even land an interview. If the HR specialist forwards your resume to a hiring manager, you want that manager to be impressed by your accomplishments that prove you have the knowledge, skills, and abilities to perform the job.

 Note: The sample resumes in this book all include accomplishments within the Outline Format. Some accomplishments are in the middle of the Work Experience section to support a specific skill. Other accomplishments are listed at the end of the resume, which are generalized accomplishments.

Questionnaires That Cover the KSAs

The newest component to the federal application, the questionnaire, is an examination: You will be graded on your answers. Some questions ask you to rate yourself on skills that are important to the position. If you rate yourself as being expert or almost expert, you will need to prove this in your resume. A few questionnaires will ask for essays, which are basically KSA narratives. But there are fewer and fewer of the essays within the questionnaires. The essays are not "rated and ranked" like the answers to the questions themselves. They are requested so that the HR specialist can determine whether you really are an expert in this area. You are proving your assessment rating with your example. (Chapter 10 has more information about questionnaires.)

A questionnaire essay is the same as a narrative KSA example of several paragraphs (4,000 characters). It includes the full details of an accomplishment story and both long and short sentences. It could include the full Context, Challenge, Actions, and Result (CCAR) formula that tells a complete story or an example that demonstrates competency in a certain area.

KSAs for Interview Preparation

If you are lucky enough to land an interview for a federal job, the hiring manager or panel will ask you 5 to 10 questions that relate to the KSAs and competencies listed for the position. The interview is an examination, and you will be evaluated on how well you address these questions.

The best way to demonstrate your expertise in an interview is by telling stories about what you have accomplished in similar work. To do this well, you need to practice your KSA accomplishment storytelling so that you will be memorable and compelling in your interview.

A good strategy to use is to make a bulleted list for each of your accomplishments from your resume so you can practice and memorize the story. Don't forget the suspense in telling the story or accomplishment, especially the challenge and the results. This list will become the basis of your practice and preparation for the interview. Chapter 27 has more information about preparing for the interview stage of the federal hiring process.

The Context, Challenge, Actions, Result (CCAR) Format

Remember that your resume, questionnaire essays, and interview answers have two goals. First, you want to present convincing evidence that your knowledge, skills, and abilities are a close match to those that the advertised position requires. Second, you want to tell an engaging story or relevant example that rings true to the reader and presents you as a person of depth and character. Therefore, your KSA should include the elements of a good story:

1. An appealing opening that makes some general statement about you, your experience, your opinions, or what you think is important about this KSA.

2. One good example could also be effective, if the example is excellent and demonstrates the KSA.

3. A closing that draws it all together.

OPM recommends that if you are writing a narrative KSA (used in questionnaire essays and, to a lesser extent, in resumes and interview answers), you should include the Context, the Challenge, your Actions, and the Result (CCAR) for each example that you cite:

- **Context:** What was the specific circumstance that led to the task or challenge you are going to describe? Where were you working? Had you just started the job, or had you been there for quite a while? Were you assigned the task, or did you show initiative by identifying a problem yourself that you felt needed resolution? What was the situation that made this issue critical to the organization?

- **Challenge:** What was the specific task you had to resolve? What obstacles did you have to overcome? What made completing this example a challenge—A short time frame? Gaining cooperation from others? First-time project? The challenge(s) of your project can earn more points because it shows why you were working on the project.

- **Actions:** What were the detailed steps that you took to resolve the challenge? These do not have to be earth-shaking. The fact that you met with your team or management, pulled together a plan, and then executed it is just fine. By providing details, you bring the situation to life and set yourself apart from the competition. The reader will know that you really were there and lived through this—that you are not just recounting a general circumstance that anyone might conjure up.

- **Result:** What happened? In some cases, you might be able to provide quantitative results (for example, your actions resulted in saving significant costs or time). In other cases, you might have received an award or at least a personal thank-you from your supervisor or another party. You might even be able to use an example in which the resolution was not ideal, but in which you made the best decision in a difficult scenario and at least mitigated the outcome.

 Note: You can use this same CCAR model for writing SES executive core qualifications (see Chapter 22, "Senior Executive Service, Executive Core Qualifications," for more on applying for SES positions).

Examples of KSAs in Each Format

This section is a collection of excerpts from federal applications that show how to demonstrate required knowledge, skills, and abilities on a resume, in the questionnaire essays, and during preparation for an interview.

Example: Social Worker

The vacancy announcement for this social worker position listed the following KSA in the Qualifications and Evaluations section:

KSA 1: Ability to evaluate a veteran's situation, abilities, and capabilities and arrive at a reasoned conclusion to include assessment of vulnerability and prioritization for emergency intervention.

Here's how the applicant addressed this KSA on her federal resume:

DIRECT SOCIAL SERVICES FOR THE HOMELESS from various socioeconomic cultural, ethnic, and educational backgrounds. Work under FEDERAL GRANT from McKinney Vento Homeless Education Assistance Act to serve more than 400 homeless families per year, totaling 2,800 homeless families within the San Antonio area. Approximately 15 percent of my clients are homeless veterans and their families.

INDEPENDENTLY ASSESS FAMILY NEEDS FOR EMERGENCY INTERVENTION by addressing their physical, mental, social, and educational situation. Identify family problems, strengths, weaknesses, coping skills, and types of assistance needed. Formulate and implement treatment plan. Provide counseling and crisis intervention.

- I assessed emergency needs for a homeless single father and his two children who were living in their car. First, I met with the father and evaluated the family's situation. I referred them to the transitional housing resources and to the San Antonio Housing Authority so that they could obtain more permanent housing. I contacted the school administrator and facilitated transportation with two different school districts in order to get the children back and forth to school.
- RESULT: The father and his children were able to obtain temporary housing and apply for more permanent housing. The children's education was not disrupted, and they were provided transportation to and from school.

The following excerpt from the questionnaire for this social worker position deals with this same ability.

For each of the following tasks, choose the statement from the list below that best describes your experience and/or training. Please select only one letter for each item.

A. I have not had education, training, or experience in performing this task.

B. I have had education or training in performing the task, but have not yet performed it.

C. I have performed this task on the job. My work on this task was monitored closely by a supervisor or senior employee to ensure compliance with proper procedures.

D. I have performed this task as a regular part of a job. I have performed it independently and normally without review by a supervisor or senior employee.

E. I am considered an expert in performing this task. I have supervised performance of this task or am normally the person who is consulted by other workers to assist them in doing this task because of my expertise.

If you selected D or E, please give example in 4,000 characters.

Social Worker, GS-12:

Ability to evaluate a veteran's situation, abilities, and capabilities and arrive at a reasoned conclusion to include an assessment of vulnerability and prioritization for emergency intervention.

The applicant answered E for this question, so she had to write a 4,000-character essay to give an example of this ability. Any announcement may require such narratives as part of a questionnaire or as separate statements. To prove that she had this ability, the applicant used the homeless veteran story from her resume, but included more detail:

In my work under the McKinney Vento Homeless Education Assistance Act, I have gained the ability to evaluate my clients' situations, abilities, and capabilities. I assess their vulnerability and prioritization for emergency intervention. About 15 percent of my clients are homeless veterans and their families.

One of my most challenging cases was that of a veteran and his family: a homeless single father and his two children. The father's work hours had been reduced, resulting in the loss of the family's apartment. They had been homeless for two days and were living in their vehicle. The father was distraught and became emotional after expressing his embarrassment about having to live in his car and not having a home for the children.

First, I met with the father and evaluated the family's situation. I prioritized its needs and developed a plan to help the father improve his family's situation. I contacted six emergency shelters and discovered one that had availability for males with children. After providing them with shelter, I referred the father to transitional housing resources and to the San Antonio Housing Authority so that the family could obtain more permanent housing.

I contacted the school administrator from the district where the children had attended school, and I ensured that they could continue to attend their previous school for the remainder of the school year. I facilitated transportation with two different school districts in order to get the children to and from school.

(continued)

(continued)

> As a result of my ability to evaluate and assess this family's needs in the emergency situation, this father and his children were able to obtain temporary housing and apply for more permanent housing. The children's education was not disrupted, and they were provided transportation to and from school.

After examining the vacancy announcement and questionnaire, this applicant came up with the following question that was likely to be asked during a structured interview:

> Can you tell me about a time when you evaluated a veteran's situation and provided emergency intervention? What did you recommend?

The applicant prepared the story about the homeless veteran and his two children to answer just such a question during the interview:

> Story Title: Veteran and His Children Living in Their Car
>
> Context: Current job as social worker
>
> Challenge: A homeless single father and his two children living in their vehicle
>
> Actions:
> - Evaluated my clients' situations, abilities, and capabilities
> - Assessed their vulnerability and prioritization for emergency intervention
> - Contacted six emergency shelters and discovered one that had availability for males with children
> - Referred them to transitional housing resources and to the San Antonio Housing Authority
> - Contacted the school administrator from the district where the children had attended school
>
> Result:
> - Family able to obtain temporary housing and apply for more permanent housing
> - The children's education was not disrupted, and they were provided transportation to and from school

Example: Federal Air Marshal

The following ability was listed in the Qualifications and Evaluations section of the vacancy announcement for a federal air marshal:

> Ability to communicate effectively in curriculum design to support changing missions.

The applicant described his experience as a senior instructor in the military to show this ability on his resume:

As USMC Senior Marine Instructor/Operations Chief, I directed a staff of 21 instructors and reported to the Commanding Officer and Curriculum Development Officer.

CURRICULUM DESIGN TO MEET CHANGING MISSIONS: I managed two training schools with military occupational specialties of the small arms technician and electro-optical ordnance repairer in Iraq. The department had failed an inspection. I analyzed the program, curriculum, course objectives, and timeline to train the specialty and designed a new course and program to meet mission objectives.

I restructured to a highly efficient and effective one-week program with 20 hours of classroom time and 20 hours of bench practice. I saved two weeks and produced trained specialty electronics technicians in one-third the time. More than 750 marines have completed the program with high performance reviews in the field. The commander has been briefed and has given wide approval for the more efficient training programs.

He expanded this description when he wrote a questionnaire essay about the same ability. Note the use of the CCAR format:

Introduction: Throughout my career, I have created and updated curriculum, assessed the need to change and streamline training, and implemented new training curricula on at least five occasions in the last 10 years.

Context: In my last position with USMC, as Senior Marine Instructor/Operations Chief, I directed a staff of 21 instructors and reported to the Commanding Officer, Executive Officer, Chief Instructor, and Curriculum Development Officer.

Challenge: My predecessor had been relieved of his duty for performance issues, the training schools were not meeting training objectives, and mission/theater needs in Iraq were growing. The department also had failed an inspection. I was tasked with restructuring the training schools, ensuring that students received the necessary information and the curriculum supported that objective.

Actions: The two schools I managed were the military occupational specialties of the small arms technician and electro-optical ordnance repairer. Although I was experienced in the former, I was not familiar with the latter. Given that, I needed to learn the subject matter quickly, analyze the relevant training, and recommend and implement reforms as needed. This process was a major change for the instructors who had been inadequately managed, so my communications with them and senior management were crucial.

One significant issue I uncovered was that the electro-optical ordnance class was overly long, taking three weeks to teach one week of material. This was a significant waste of instructor resources, as well as poor use of student time—the faster students were trained, the faster they could begin working in new jobs.

Result: The new curriculum was restructured to a highly efficient and effective one-week program with 20 hours of classroom time and 20 hours of bench practice. I saved two weeks and produced trained specialty electronics technicians in one-third the time. More than 750 marines have completed the program with high performance reviews in the field. The commander has been briefed and has given wide approval for the more efficient training programs.

The applicant prepared this same material for the interview as well:

Title of Story: Turnaround of Iraq Arms Training School Curriculum

Context: New position as Senior Marine Instructor/Operations Chief, Iraq, Small Arms and Electro-optical Ordnance Repairer

Challenges:

- Predecessor relieved of his duty for performance issues
- Growing mission/theater needs in Iraq
- Department inspection failure

Actions:

- Restructured the training schools
- Learned the subject matter quickly, analyzed the relevant training, and recommended and implemented reforms as needed
- Retrained the instructors
- Restructured three-week course into one week

Result:

- A highly efficient and effective one-week program for the new curriculum with 20 hours of classroom time and 20 hours of bench practice
- Produced trained specialty electronics technicians in one-third the time
- More than 750 marines who have completed the program received high performance reviews in the field

---

Example: Accountant

The following was listed in the Qualifications and Evaluations section of the vacancy announcement for a GS-9 accountant for the Defense Finance and Accounting Service (DFAS):

Apply financial management theories, concepts, principles, and methods to the financial management functions you have performed.

Here's how the applicant addressed this KSA on his resume:

FINANCIAL MANAGEMENT METHODS FOR SUSPENDED ACCOUNTING TRANSACTION ANALYSIS. Experience in financial management theories and methods to ensure efficient accounting and financial data resulted in efficient financial reports and advice to senior managers on suspended accounting transactions. Coordinated financial data, utilized financial tools, and interpreted financial reports to improve operation for DFAS customers.

I prepare a complex monthly management report for the Treasury Index 97 and 21 appropriations Suspense Account Report (SAR), which summarizes and captures pending clearing accounts of receipts, collections, remittance, and disbursements suspense accounts. I monitor, reconcile, prepare, report, and populate the numerical data into spreadsheets and ensure it is

---

> accurate and timely to cover the number, amount, and age of suspended accounting transactions for upper management. Once the data is compiled, I reconcile and balance the information on a collective spreadsheet that compares current month and prior month data. The data is applied to various financial reports and forwarded to headquarters for further comparison within a specific deadline.
>
> Results: My reports help to assess suspended accounting transactions and whether the organization is in compliance with various government accounting regulations.

The questionnaire for this position asked for a response to the following:

> In 500 words or less, provide specific examples that describe your level of experience in applying financial management theories, concepts, principles, and methods to the financial management functions you have performed.

The applicant responded as follows:

> During my 20-plus-year federal career as an Accountant, I have gained and utilized knowledge and skill in applying financial management theories, concepts, principles, and methods to a variety of financial management functions. I have held positions in accounting and payroll and have learned specialized job procedures, problem solving discipline, and proficiency in applying statistical theories, practical concepts, and policies for administrative program operations and business line objectives.
>
> In my present DFAS Accountant position, one of my critical tasks is to prepare a monthly management tool for the Treasury Index 97 and 21 appropriations Suspense Account Report (SAR), which summarizes and captures pending clearing accounts of receipts, collections, remittance, and disbursements suspense accounts. I monitor, reconcile, prepare, report, and populate the numerical data into spreadsheets and ensure it is accurate and timely to cover the number, amount, and age of suspense accounting transactions for upper management. Once the data is compiled, I reconcile and balance the information on a collective spreadsheet that compares current month and prior month data. The data is applied to various reports and forwarded to headquarters for further comparison.
>
> RESULT: My reports help to assess suspended accounting transactions and whether the organization is in compliance with various government accounting regulations.

After examining the vacancy announcement and questionnaire, this applicant came up with the following question that was likely to be asked during a structured interview:

> Can you give us an example of utilizing financial management theories to improve accounting operations?

The applicant organized his past work experience into bullet points in the CCAR format to prepare for such questions during a structured interview:

Context: Accountant with DFAS, skilled in using financial management theories and tools to generate important accounting reports and information for senior management

Challenge: Large volume of suspended accounting transactions impacts customer service

Actions:

- Utilize the monthly management tool for the Treasury Index 97 and 21 appropriations Suspense Account Report (SAR)
- Prepare a monthly management report
- Summarize and capture pending clearing accounts of receipts, collections, remittance, and disbursements suspense accounts
- Produce detailed spreadsheets
- Reconcile and balance the information on a collective spreadsheet that compares current month and prior month data
- Forward data to headquarters for further comparison

Result:

- Have discovered more than 500 suspended accounts
- Have delegated the resolution of more than 95 percent of the suspended accounts throughout the accounting team within 90 days

---

Writing Effective KSA Accomplishments in the Resume

KSA narratives require writing about an accomplishment that proves your ability to perform a certain task at a certain level. So you can simply manage a team or you can lead a culturally diverse team that was working under tight deadlines. It's all in the story.

This next example shows how the way you tell an accomplishment story can change its effectiveness. In the first federal resume, the KSA accomplishment of the pilot program is buried in the text. The basic facts are there, but they are not put into context. The revised resume draws attention to this applicant's impressive accomplishments by changing formatting and the order of information and adding detail.

Before:

05-2007 to present; 40 hours; Regional Vocational Rehabilitation Specialist, Department of Labor (DOL); 200 Granby St., Norfolk, VA, 23510; Phone: (757) 441-3071; Supervisor: Theresa Magyar—Please do not contact until employment offer is made; Salary: $71,102.00

REGIONAL PROGRAM MANAGER who governs all aspects of a vocational rehabilitation program sanctioned under U.S. Department of Labor merit system principles and guidelines; oversees rehabilitation efforts of 29 local and 13 regional contracted counselors in Virginia, Maryland, and Pennsylvania and directly supervises performance management. RESOURCEFUL: Identifies and uses contingency counselors for clients living outside assigned jurisdiction, but have compensatory records housed in appointed region.

RECRUITING AND CERTIFYING OFFICAL who manages all facets of the initial screening, recruiting, selecting, staffing, and training of candidates considered for certification as a DOL Vocational Rehabilitation Counselor. Have trained and certified 29 counselors in less than 60 days. Monitor and evaluate counselors' performance and extend certifications annually for 4 optional years. Renewals are based on the best qualified candidates, as the program is aimed at ensuring the highest-quality workforce and is a representative of the Department of Labor's Vocational Rehabilitation Program. Directly determine and augment staffing needs as appropriate, and adjust manpower demands as caseloads dictate.

SPEARHEADED THE EXECUTION OF THE PILOT INITIATIVE IMMEDIATE CONTACT PROGRAM (ICP), which targeted compensatory longshoremen out of work 8 weeks or less with imminent return-to-work dates. Rehabilitation specialist identified and contacted candidates, explained provisions, and assigned a counselor to assist in the reemployment transition, ensuring medical restrictions were honored and not impeded by employers. As a result of the pilot program, Norfolk, Virginia, captured 59 successful rehabilitations for the year (more than its quota), and the Norfolk Longshore Office received the U.S. Department of Labor's Secretary's Exceptional Achievement Award for 2010. The Baltimore Office also achieved its quota of 9 successes. The National Office praised my efforts in this program.

After:

05-2007 to present; 40 hours; Regional Vocational Rehabilitation Specialist, Department of Labor (DOL); 200 Granby St., Norfolk, VA, 23510; Phone: (757) 444-4444; Supervisor: Tom Smith; Salary: $71,102.00

AS PROGRAM MANAGER, SPEARHEADED THE EXECUTION OF THE PILOT INITIATIVE IMMEDIATE CONTACT PROGRAM (ICP), which targeted compensatory longshoremen out of work 8 weeks or less with imminent return-to-work dates. Baltimore achieved a record-setting 9 successes, meeting its targeted quota and ending a 10-year slump in achieving its goal.

Rehabilitation specialists identified and contacted candidates, explained provisions, and assigned a counselor to assist in the reemployment transition, ensuring medical restrictions were honored and not impeded by employers.

- RESULT: Pilot program yielded results far greater than expected—Norfolk, Virginia, captured 59 successful rehabilitations for the year, doubling the standards set by the National Office of 24.

- Received highest praise from the National Office for firm leadership and direction, coupled with steadfast and dedicated efforts to achieve this milestone. Efforts also contributed to Norfolk Longshore Office receiving the U.S. Department of Labor's highly coveted Secretary's Exceptional Achievement Award for 2010.

REGIONAL PROGRAM MANAGER. Direct all aspects of a Vocational Rehabilitation Program sanctioned under U.S. Department of Labor merit system principles and guidelines; oversee rehabilitation efforts of 29 local and 13 regional contracted counselors in Virginia, Maryland, and Pennsylvania and directly supervise performance management. RESOURCEFUL: Identify and use contingency counselors for clients living outside assigned jurisdiction, but have compensatory records housed in appointed region.

(continued)

(continued)

RECRUITING AND CERTIFYING OFFICIAL who manages all facets of the initial screening, recruiting, selecting, staffing, and training of candidates considered for certification as a DOL Vocational Rehabilitation Counselor.

- I have trained and certified 29 counselors in less than 60 days.

Monitor and evaluate counselors' performance and extend certifications annually for 4 optional years. Renewals are based on the *best* qualified candidates as the program is aimed at ensuring the highest-quality workforce is representative of the Department of Labor's Vocational Rehabilitation Program. I directly determine and augment staffing needs as appropriate and adjust manpower demands as caseloads dictate.

To see how KSA accomplishments work in a complete federal resume, look at the resume for TSA security inspector Paul Graham.

Target Position: TSA Supervisory Transportation Security Inspector (Aviation).
TSA security inspector seeking promotion.
Targeted, written, and designed by Julie Jasper with accomplishments by Roderick Jussim, Certified Federal Resume Writers.

PAUL GRAHAM
1234 Home St.
Fond du Lac, WI 53221
(444) 444-4444
email@email.net

HIGHEST FEDERAL GRADE: Lead Transportation Security Inspector-Aviation, SV-1801-I, Transportation Security Administration, Compliance Division, Department of Homeland Security.

OBJECTIVE: Supervisory Transportation Security Inspector (Aviation), SV-1801-J, Transportation Security Administration, Department of Homeland Security. Job Announcement Number: XXX-10-286352

PROFILE
Experienced TSA Lead Inspector with extensive knowledge of laws, policies, and regulations and ability to lead security programs to support specific and immediate security objectives as well as DHS's overall security mission. Advise leadership as a technical specialist using sound judgment and consistent decisiveness, based on research and experience, to promote operational enhancements and procedural efficiencies. Plan and set priorities of subordinates' work effort using team approach, maintaining accountability of actions. Excellent record of solving complex issues by fostering innovation and cooperation of team and coordinating actions with stakeholders. Communicate security procedures and requirements to team in easily understood terms. Maintain composure under difficult, pressure-filled circumstances. Outstanding role model displaying integrity, consistently volunteering for special projects, and completing projects under tight and restricted deadlines.

CLEARANCES
Secret Clearance

PROFESSIONAL EXPERIENCE
10/20XX–Present: Lead Transportation Security Inspector-Aviation, SV-1801-I, Transportation Security Administration, Compliance Division, Department of Homeland Security, Omaha, NE. $75,551.00/year; 40 hours/week; Supervisor: Larry Thompson, 444-666-1111. Permission to contact.

PRINCIPAL ADVISOR to leadership relative to the applicable security programs/TSA security directives and requirements. Assess impact of management decisions on daily operations. Report courses of action to management in a concise, professional, and unbiased manner. Conduct cost/benefit analysis to ensure appropriateness of recommendations.

Serve as ACTING ASSISTANT FEDERAL SECURITY DIRECTOR on multiple occasions when Assistant Federal Security Director is detailed to other locations. Managed seamless transition of duties for a 3-month period while Assistant Director was detailed to headquarters with no disruption in operations.

(continued)

(continued)

SOLVE COMPLEX SECURITY PROBLEMS: Apply experience and comprehensive technical knowledge and understanding of new technologies and methodologies. Evaluate mission-critical programs and operational requirements. Identify and evaluate underlying causes of issues; distinguish relevant from irrelevant information; weigh alternative solutions in advance of deadlines with limited guidance. Conduct RISK ANALYSIS and develop specific contingency plans to overcome risks.

- My ingenuity boosted gateway security and resolved a dispute with a carrier. The carrier was facing fines for gateway violations. I negotiated with the carrier and convinced it to commit to reasonable security improvements instead of paying fines.

- RESULT: No security violations from this carrier since implementing my solution.

LEADER/PROGRAM MANAGER for Ronald Reagan Washington National Airport (DCA) Access Security Program (DASSP) to support new designation of local airport as a Gateway Airport. My work put planes in the air.

- I encouraged local corporate flight departments and the local fixed-base operator to cooperate. I successfully managed the access security program, evaluated performance improvements, and ensured compliance with laws and regulations.

- RESULT: The airport achieved gateway approval in early June 20XX. Flights began shortly afterwards. I received a time-off award for superlative work.

LEAD TEAMS/SUPERVISE STAFF as Team Lead for Aviation Inspectors. Am role model and peer-to-peer coach. Consistently volunteer services, on short notice, to meet unexpected challenges and circumstances. CONFLICT MANAGEMENT: Engage team and subordinates in project planning and tasking; gain project buy-in through involvement. Ensure understanding of mission and objectives; troubleshoot problems to develop solutions.

- I maximize my team's performance and let individuals shine. When one individual was faltering, I mentored that individual, ensured tasks were equally distributed, and specifically deleted tasks to keep projects on schedule.

- RESULT: I have created an inclusive environment, motivated the staff, and improved overall performance. The staff has provided positive feedback about my inspections.

APPLY KNOWLEDGE OF LAWS/POLICIES/DIRECTIVES: Implement TSA's SOPs and Security Directives to conduct inspections. Adhere to directives/policies in making decisions; recognize implications of decisions relative to laws and regulations. Substantial knowledge of Title 49 Code of Federal Regulations, TSA National Investigation and Enforcement Manual Procedures, and TSI Handbook.

INDEPENDENTLY CONDUCT INSPECTION/COMPLIANCE ASSESSMENTS. Investigate security concerns; establish preventative methods/procedures. CONDUCT VULNERABILITY

ASSESSMENTS to test effectiveness of airports' current security systems and procedures. Support safe execution of large public events.

- Resolved a major significant golf bag problem that required hand carrying, due to late flight for a significant tournament deadline. Recognized for outstanding customer services by top golf pro in the country.
- During a championship tournament, which brought a large number of visitors and high-profile VIPs to the local county airport, I liaised with tournament planner concerning schedule in order to plan and alert screeners of heavy flight activities and equipment being carried on board.

Execute SPECIAL EMPHASIS INSPECTION (SEI) as directed by headquarters. Train screeners and personnel in new No Fly and Selectee lists, including knowledge of the laws and regulations, and training in communicating with potential No Fly passengers.

- Co-managed a tense situation with a No Fly passenger who was on the list in error. Was able to resolve the problem without the passenger missing the flight, but also ensuring a safe and secure flight.

PROVIDE TRAINING to new inspectors. Developed the Transportation Security Inspector on-the-job training program. CREATED REPORT WRITING CLASS and presented information to all local Supervisory Transportation Security Officers and Transportation Security Officers.

- Successfully completed development of training program within 1 month despite original timeline of 9 months so Assistant Federal Security Director could reveal the program at a statewide TSA Conference and later at the National Assistant Federal Security Director's Conference in 20XX.
- Training program was submitted to the Compliance Division and posted nationally on the TSA employee Web board.

2/19XX–10/20XX: Police Officer, Houston Police Department, Houston, TX. $48,800 per year; 40 hours per week; Supervisor: Sergeant Name: Hugh Rogers, 111-222-3333. Permission to contact.

ENFORCED LOCAL, STATE, AND FEDERAL LAWS. Conducted arrests and processed suspects who violated laws. PROVIDED DIRECTION/LEADERSHIP to district police officers as Acting Desk Sergeant. Supervised 39 of the district's sworn and civilian office personnel.

ADMINISTERED OPERATIONS: Ensured that personnel performed duties according to laws/regulations/SOPs. Accounted for currency taken in by all shifts; filed appropriate reports. MANAGED EVIDENCE INVENTORY, ensuring proper storage. Monitored booking procedures of all prisoners coming into the district for processing.

COMMUNICATED ORALLY, providing courtroom testimony in both criminal and civil court. TOOK DECISIVE ACTION to include making sound, though sometimes unpopular, decisions

(continued)

(continued)

in situations of greater than normal pressure, adverse circumstances, and heightened complexity. Based decisions on analysis of facts and data with minimal or no supervision.

- I stopped a suicide and saved a life when I took DECISIVE ACTION. I followed standard procedures but relied on experience and knowledge amid adverse circumstances and greater than normal pressure.
- RESULT: The subject was rescued without harm.

INVESTIGATED EMERGENCY AND NONEMERGENCY REQUESTS: Responded to calls including medical emergencies, suspicious activity, domestic disputes, homicide, personal assaults, property crimes, civil disturbances, and general assistance to community members. Examined crime scenes and investigated criminal activity; collected and controlled evidence; interviewed witnesses and determined relevant information.

DEVELOPED WRITTEN REPORTS of investigations, including criminal acts or local ordinance violations. Completed necessary forms, including, but not limited to, incident reports, accident reports, sobriety forms, field interview cards, custody forms, detention evaluations forms, domestic violence forms, prosecution report forms, internal memos, and mental health emergency detention forms. Wrote with clarity, ensuring accuracy of all information.

TRAINED AND MONITORED SUBORDINATES as Field Training Officer. Trained recruits in application of laws using real-life circumstances. Provided safety, location awareness, and report writing instruction. EVALUATED PERFORMANCE of officers' investigation progress and filed evaluation reports to document their progress.

COMPUTER PROFICIENCIES
Microsoft Office Suite, PARIS, ASAP database, Ishare

PUBLIC SPEAKING
Report Writing. Created and presented class instruction to 250 local Supervisory Transportation Security Officers and Transportation Security Officers, 20XX. Presentation was reviewed beforehand by North Central Region's legal counsel, who in return asked if it could use my material to present to airports in our region.

PUBLICATIONS
Aviation Security Inspector Procedures, 20XX.
On The Job Training Evaluation Checklist, 20XX. Document was prepared for TSI and, due to its valuable content, was subsequently provided to the Compliance Division and posted nationally on the TSA employee Web board.

HONORS AND RECOGNITIONS
Dependability/Reliability Award from DHS/TSA, 20XX.
Chief of Police Superior Achievement Award, 19XX: Awarded merit citation for calm and quick thinking in preventing a suicide attempt of a subject attempting to jump from a viaduct.

Certificate for Scholastic Achievement by MATC and PHI THETA KAPPA Honorary Society for maintaining an honors standing, 19XX.

SPECIALIZED TRAINING
Chemical-terrorism Vulnerability Information, 1-day course, DHS Office of Infrastructure Protection, 20XX
Introduction to the Incident Command System (ICS)-100, 1-day course, FEMA, 20XX
ICS-200 for Single Resources and Initial Action Incidents, 1-day course, FEMA, 20XX
ICS-300, 2-day course, Waukesha County Technical College, 20XX
Behavior Recognition Training, Transportation Security Administration, 20XX
Planning Considerations for Terrorism Response, 2-day course, St. Petersburg College, 20XX
Evaluating Truthfulness, The Ekman Group, 2-day course, 20XX
Introduction to Railroads Course, Transportation Technology Center, 20XX
Reid Technique of Interviewing and Interrogation, 2-day course, John Reid and Associates, 20XX

EDUCATION
Associate degree, Police Science, Minor: Psychology, Milwaukee Area Technical College (MATC), Milwaukee, WI, 19XX.
GPA: 3.818, Major GPA: 3.895, 66 total credits.
Honors Standing: Received Certificate for Scholastic Achievement by MATC and Phi Theta Kappa Honorary Society for maintaining an honors standing.

When you write your resume, give yourself credit for your successes, initiatives, and new ideas. Now is the time to tell the HR specialist and supervisors that you can perform the position and can prove it through your past performance. Be inspired to write the best accomplishments that you can in your resume. This can result in getting a Best Qualified rating and hopefully being interviewed for a new position.

Summary

Even with recent hiring reforms, you can't get away from KSAs on your federal application. Writing a resume, answering essay questions on the questionnaire, and preparing for the interview are all about highlighting accomplishments, explaining examples, and telling stories that prove you have the knowledge, skills, and abilities to do the job. Start with 5 or 10 accomplishments and determine the most interesting ones. Prepare these accomplishments for your resume, select the right skill level in the questionnaire, and get ready for the interview by practicing your KSA stories.

The next chapter reviews the questionnaires in more detail. The questions can be multiple choice or can result in an essay that describes an example to demonstrate your performance.

CHAPTER 10

Questionnaires That Assess Your Knowledge, Skills, and Abilities

This chapter focuses on the popular questionnaires that are a typical part of the federal application. More than 150 federal agencies are using the USAJOBS online federal resume plus questionnaire format (as well as providing supporting documents, such as transcripts and forms regarding veteran status) as their application style. This chapter explains the best way to answer the multiple-choice, check all that apply, yes/no, and essay questions that you might see on a questionnaire.

Understanding Questionnaires

The assessment questions on questionnaires are written by HR specialists and managers to enable them to find the best candidates for their position. The questionnaire serves as an examination to determine your level of knowledge, skills, abilities, and competencies for the job.

The questionnaire is a mandatory part of the federal application. Some people who apply to federal jobs lose consideration for a job because they do not complete one of the components of the application. If you are a serious candidate for a certain job, you must follow the directions, answer the questions, submit your essay answers, and send in your additional information. You will be found ineligible if you do not respond to the questionnaire.

The best way to complete your questionnaire is to copy and paste the entire questionnaire into a Word file. You can then check off your answers and write your essays ahead of time. Then you can go back online and answer the questions and copy and paste your essays fairly quickly.

 Note: Be sure to leave enough time before the application deadline to copy and paste the answers and information online. Some electronic submission systems take up to 24 hours to register your submission.

The questionnaire will ask you what your skill level is in various areas that are relevant to the position. If you choose an option that indicates a high level of skill, you may be asked for a short essay to demonstrate this level of experience.

 Note: Always look for the questionnaire before you apply for the position. (There is usually a link to it on the vacancy announcement.) Check the questions to make sure you can assess your skills high. If you cannot state that you are very well qualified with the questionnaire, then you may not qualify for the position.

HR specialists will grade you based on your self-assessment. The HR specialists will *not* grade your essays. The essays you write exist only to demonstrate and support the skill level you choose in the question.

The following two paragraphs are instructions written by an HR specialist about rating an applicant's qualifications. You can see that eligible applicants will receive a rating based on their responses.

 Note: This excerpt warns that HR specialists will review your resume against your questionnaire. If your resume does not reflect the skill level you chose on the questionnaire, the HR specialist can reduce your score. Make sure your resume matches your answers in the questionnaire by using the questions as a guideline to help you update your resume.

BASIS OF RATING

Applicants will be rated on the extent and quality of experience, education, and training relevant to the duties of the position. Eligible applicants will receive a numerical rating based on their responses to the application questions for this position submitted online. These responses must be substantiated by your online resume (passing scores range from 70 to 100 before the addition of Veterans' Preference points). Applicants who do not respond to the application questions may be rated ineligible.

WARNING! Your answers will be verified against information provided in your online resume. Be sure that your resume clearly supports your responses to all the questions by addressing experience and education relevant to this position. If you exaggerate or falsify your experience and/or education, you may be removed from employment consideration. You should make a fair and accurate assessment of your qualifications.

 Tip: To find out what your score is on your total application, you can send an e-mail to the human resources specialist and ask.

You can see two full samples of questionnaires in Chapter 12, "Understanding Vacancy Announcements."

Responding to Self-Assessment Questions

The following questionnaire styles are popular on federal applications. Get ready to check all that apply, select your skill level, and back it up with examples.

 Note: Although you should never exaggerate your qualifications, you should give yourself all the credit that you can when answering the questions. Be truthful with your self-assessment, but also be sure to consider carefully all of your skills and abilities. If you can do this job, think about your skills from all of your past history, not just your current position.

Multiple-Choice Questions

The following is an example of a standard self-assessment question. The best answer to this question is number 5.

Conducts on-site visits to assess the condition of institutions that have closed or that are in imminent danger of closing in order to take action to secure agency interests by seizing records, promissory notes, and other assets.

1. I have not had education, training, or experience in performing this task.
2. I have had education or training in performing this task, but have not yet performed it on the job.
3. I have performed this task on the job, with close supervision from supervisor or senior employee.
4. I have performed this task as a regular part of the job, independently and usually without review by supervisor or senior employee.
5. This task has been a central or major part of my work. I have performed it myself routinely, and I have trained others in performance of this task and/or others have consulted me as an expert for assistance in performing this task.

The following sections present examples of the variations of this type of question that you might see on a questionnaire.

General Self-Assessment Questions with Essays

Number 5 is the best answer in the following example.

Select the statement that best describes your level of experience applying analytical and evaluative methods and techniques to issues or studies concerning the management of space.

1. I have not had education, training, or experience administering, working with, or performing this task or function.
2. I have had education or training administering, working with, or performing this task or function, but have not yet used it on the job.
3. I have administered, worked with, or performed this task or function with close review and assistance from a supervisor, a senior employee, or a senior consultant.
4. I have administered, worked with, or performed this task or function as a regular part of a job and only in unique or unusual situations did I require assistance or review by a supervisor, senior employee, or senior consultant.
5. I have administered, worked with, or performed this task or function as a regular part of a job. I do not require assistance or review by a supervisor, senior employee, or senior consultant, even in unique or unusual situations.

Please describe your experience in space management to include space programming and your ability to efficiently move an organization from one location to another.

(Essay Question)

In 1,000 characters or less, please describe an analysis of a program that you have conducted, including the methodology and tools used to conduct the analysis, alternative courses of action, and the result of your analysis.

(Essay Question)

In 300 words or less, describe a situation where you had technical authority to authorize or disapprove funding requests, obligations, and expenditures of funds based on your interpretation of relevant law, regulation, or policy.

(Essay Question)

Select the response that best reflects your highest level of experience in processing administrative employment discrimination complaints in the federal sector with regard to disciplinary actions (counseling, reprimand, warning, suspension, demotion, leave restriction, removal).

1. I have not had the education, training, or experience in performing this task.

2. I have had specific training or education directly related to this task, although I have not performed this task on the job.

3. I have performed this task on the job with assistance from a team leader, supervisor, or other employee to ensure compliance with proper procedures.

4. I have performed this task on the job independently with approval of the final product by a team leader or a supervisor.

5. I have served as technical expert authority on this task, providing guidance or supervision to others because of my background.

If you selected choice 4 or 5, please provide a narrative supporting your answer to the above question, including information on the circumstances, the complexity of the work performed, the length of time, and the organization where the work was performed. Please limit response to 1/2 page (1,500 characters).

(Essay Question)

Specific Job Skill Questions

Read the provided answers for these questions carefully. The most complex answer is typically the best one to choose, if it fits your experience. In the following example, the best answer is number 6 because it includes the broadest range of experience.

Select the statement that best describes your highest level of experience in planning and implementing space renovations for and relocations of an entire organizational unit.

1. I have education, training, or experience in planning relocations and space renovations.

2. I have training or education in planning space renovations and relocations, but have not applied it on the job.

3. I have performed this task at an organization's headquarters level.

4. I have performed this task at an organization's field office.

5. I have performed this task among several field offices.

6. I have performed this task at both a field office and the headquarters level.

7. I have performed this task among several large organizational/departmental offices.

8. None of the above.

Tricky Questions

Answer number 4 is an acceptable response for the following example, but 5 is better. Numbers 3, 4, and 5 are very similar; you have to study the selections carefully.

Select the response that best describes your experience applying analytical and evaluative methods and techniques to assess program development or execution in order to improve organizational effectiveness and efficiency.

1. I have not had experience applying analytical and evaluative methods and techniques to assess program development or execution in order to improve organizational effectiveness and efficiency.

2. I have completed education or training in applying analytical and evaluative methods and techniques to assess program development or execution in order to improve organizational effectiveness and efficiency, but have not yet performed this task on the job.

3. I have applied analytical and evaluative methods and techniques to assess program development or execution in order to improve organizational effectiveness and efficiency under close supervision by a supervisor or senior employee.

4. I have applied analytical and evaluative methods and techniques to assess program development or execution in order to improve organizational effectiveness and efficiency as a regular part of a job, independently and usually without review by a supervisor or senior employee.

5. I have applied analytical and evaluative methods and techniques to assess program development or execution in order to improve organizational effectiveness and efficiency routinely as a major part of my work. I have supervised or trained others in performing this task and/or others have consulted me for expert assistance in performing this task.

"Check All That Apply" Questions

The best answer for this first sample question would be to check all of the options given.

Which of the following types of documents have you written?

Check all that apply:

- ❏ Correspondence
- ❏ Technical reports
- ❏ Regulatory/statutory material
- ❏ Policy or procedures
- ❏ Analyses of proposed policy, legislative, or management initiatives
- ❏ Memos
- ❏ Newsletters
- ❏ Training materials

Some "check all that apply" questions are not as straightforward. In the following two examples, you ideally would want to check all the options except the last one, "None of the above." Note that the last example asks for an essay to describe a specific example of when you accomplished the tasks listed in the questions.

Select the statements that describe your experience communicating project information to senior management officials.

Check all that apply:

1. I have met with policy officials on a continuing basis to discuss policy proposals.

2. I have met with policy officials to brief them on current project status.

3. I have briefed key leadership on costs, impact, feasibility, alternatives, issues and recommendations, and status of projects.

4. I have developed policies, regulations, procedures, or analyses for senior management.

5. I have presented policies, regulations, procedures, analyses, and recommendations to key leadership.

6. I have assisted in the preparation of policy recommendations, procedures, or analyses, providing data and background information to senior officials as requested.

7. I have developed comprehensive materials for reports, briefings, and meetings.

8. I have communicated program strategies, goals, objectives, and priorities to program personnel.

9. I have prepared briefing materials for use by or presentation to senior management officials.

10. I have contributed to Office of Management and Budget (OMB) 300 exhibits.

11. None of the above.

Please indicate which of the following describe your experience in providing support to the security adjudication process:

Check all that apply:

1. Initiated appropriate Bureau indices checks, arrest record checks, Central Intelligence Agency (CIA) information checks, ELSUR checks, and the like, in attempting to obtain pertinent identifying information relative to subject involved in each individual case.

2. Received and reviewed incoming material, such as applications, Changes in Marital Status forms, Personnel Status forms, and the like, for the purpose of discerning merit for granting, continuing, and/or revoking security clearance and access authorizations.

3. Assisted supervisor and/or coworkers with a segment of typical security clearance adjudications.

4. None of the above.

In the text box below, provide a brief summary of your experience providing support to the security adjudication process:

(Essay Question)

Yes/No Questions

"Yes" is the best answer in the following example:

> Do you have work experience that provided you with a comprehensive knowledge and application of legislation, regulations, policies, and procedures governing the Student Financial Assistance Title IV Family Federal Education Loan (FFEL) Program and the current policies and requirements relating to the administration of the Title IV FFEL program?
>
> Yes   No

Note that if you answer "Yes," you will be asked to write an essay about this experience.

 Tip: Make sure that your federal resume matches your questions and answers in the questionnaire. The HR specialist will review your resume against your questionnaire.

Answering Essay Questions

The writing style for essays can be any of the styles covered in Chapter 9: short accomplishment example and results statement, longer narrative CCAR format, or CCAR bulleted list. Be sure to follow the character- or word-limitation instructions carefully.

When writing your essays and giving examples, consider the duties, specialized experience, and other information listed in the vacancy announcement. If you can provide examples that are relevant to the target agency and position, the HR specialist will appreciate your skills even more. The following before and after examples for a private school headmaster seeking a GS-11 position as a course administrator for the FDIC show you how.

> The questionnaire for this position starts with the following statement:
>
>   1. I am qualified for the Course Administration Specialist CG-301-11 position because:
>
> Answer:
>
> Please provide a narrative supporting your answer to the above question, including information on the circumstances, the complexity of the work, the length of time, and the organization where the work was performed. Please limit your response to half a typewritten page (1,500 characters).

The headmaster's first attempt at answering this question was too short, only 619 characters (with spaces). It doesn't provide enough detail about the circumstances and complexity of his work to fully answer the question.

Before:

> Education: 3 postgraduate degrees for a total of 5 years of postgraduate education. One of those degrees is an education specialist degree that is considered a post-master's degree. I also have a MS degree in national security strategy and Master of Public Administration degree.
>
> Experience: I have a total of 15 years of experience working in education as follows: 3 years as an Executive Director at Notre Dame Academy in Lubbock, TX; 9 years as the Chief of Staff/ Business Manager at Hargrave Military Academy in Chatham, VA; and 3 years as an Instructor/ Division Chief at Marine Corps University in Quantico, VA.

The headmaster's second attempt provides a lot more relevant detail and comes in just under the 1,500-character limit.

After:

> **Experience: 12 years as a private school administrator and 3 years as an adult educator.**
>
> **Administrator:** As an **Executive Director** for the past **3 years** at Notre Dame Academy, a prestigious college preparatory Pre-K through 12 school, I have served as curriculum development specialist for the Academy. I planned the implementation of improved classroom technology into 20 classrooms to support course administration and student learning objectives.
>
> **The challenge of the technology and education implementation was budget management, classroom planning, teacher instruction, and curriculum changes for the technology-**oriented instruction.
>
> **I worked with a teacher committee to evaluate current curriculum and recommended the use of web-**based classroom lectures, student activities, and homework to integrate a more challenging curriculum for the students. Results: The 40 teachers were able to incorporate web-based lessons into at least one-third of their daily lessons with increased interest from both students and parents in new course administration and programs.
>
> **Adult Educator:** Taught mid-career, college-educated audiences for **3 years** as an **Instructor** at **Marine Corps University** (MCU), after completing an Instructional Management Course (5 weeks) to qualify. As an **MCU Department Chair**, drafted a curriculum for combat service support and taught most of the course.
>
> **Education**: **5 years combined postgraduate education:** Education Specialist, a post-master's degree in administration and supervision of instruction; Master of Public Administration; and Master of Science in National Security Strategy.

Note that Education information is included in this answer, even though the instructions did not ask for it. Specialized education can be mentioned within an essay to emphasize your major, curriculum, or degrees.

Here's another question on the questionnaire for the Course Administration Specialist position:

Select the type(s) of training programs that you have delivered:

- Classroom training
- Video training
- Paper-based training
- On-the-job training
- Automated or electronic job aids or manuals

Please provide a narrative supporting your answer to the above question, including information on the circumstances, the complexity of the work, and the length of time.

In this "before" example, the headmaster selected only three types of training programs: classroom, video, and paper-based. His examples for each include the basic information, but lack important detail.

Before:

Answer:

Classroom Training: I am a state-certified high school teacher with credentials that are current in Virginia and Texas. I taught U.S. Government for 2 years at Hargrave Military Academy in Chatham, VA, and Notre Dame Academy for 1 year. I was a classroom teacher for 3 years at Marine Corps University in Quantico, VA.

Video Training: I filmed military maneuvers and used film archives in class at Marine Corps University in Quantico, VA. Used video recordings as a high school tennis coach while at Hargrave Military Academy.

Paper-Based Training: Supported classroom learning with knowledge-based outlines, references outside of the classroom, and a detailed course syllabus.

In this "after" example, the headmaster thought more about his experience and was able to select all five types of training programs, enabling him to earn a higher grade on the questionnaire. His examples for each type include interesting, relevant details that show the HR specialist his range of skill.

After:

Answer:

Classroom Training: I have taught mid-career, college-educated adults for 3 years as an Instructor at Marine Corps University and U.S. Government to high school seniors for 3 years as a certified high school teacher with credentials that are current in VA and TX. To break up traditional lecture formats, I created in-class activities that included small group role-playing advocacy in point-counterpoint debates and Socratic teaching methods to stimulate class discussion. During my 9 years as an administrator at Hargrave Military Academy and 3 years at Notre Dame Academy, I ensured my teachers did not lecture for more than 15 minutes in 50-minute classes.

Video Training: Produced visual media to teach complex military maneuvers at Marine Corps University, filming and editing footage and integrating material from film archives. Videotaped high school player demonstrations as a High School Tennis Coach at Hargrave Military Academy for college coach reviews.

Paper-Based Training: Created self-paced texts of up to 25 pages for courses that were not taught in classrooms while assigned as an Instructor at Marine Corps University. The purpose of the self-paced texts was to convey basic knowledge to the students as a take-home exercise in order to save classroom lecture time.

On-the-Job Training: While serving in the Marine Corps, trained and certified basic-entry level skills for occupational specialties when formal school seats were cut. Performed supervisory role for student teaching certification while teaching at Hargrave Military School.

Job Aids: Drafted standing procedures for classroom management and protocol cards for crisis action in schools.

Summary

The questionnaire is an important part of the federal application. Your grade on the questionnaire determines whether you progress in the federal hiring process. A passing score ranges from 70 to 100.

Federal questionnaires are in a period of transition as agencies work to implement the latest hiring reform policies. Essays have become less important, serving as support to the answers given to the multiple-choice, check all that apply, or yes/no questions. Soon, the questionnaires won't include essays at all.

Yet even without essays, the questions that accompany federal applications can be challenging. You can never tell how many questions or what kinds of questions will be asked. It's important to review the "how to apply" instructions in the vacancy announcement when you are planning your time to apply for the position. You want to make sure you have enough time to thoughtfully answer all of the questions on the questionnaire.

CHAPTER 11

Cover Letters for Federal Jobs and Networking

As you learned in Chapter 9, "KSAs in the Application: Presenting Your Accomplishments," President Barack Obama issued a presidential memorandum in May 2010 (titled "Improving the Federal Recruitment and Hiring Process") that eliminated essay questions from the federal application process. That same memorandum directed federal agency heads to

allow individuals to apply for federal employment by submitting resumes and cover letters or completing simple, plain language applications, and assess applicants using valid, reliable tools.

This directive means that it's now possible to simply send a resume and cover letter to a federal hiring official and be considered for a federal job in certain circumstances. Those circumstances include

- Knowing the name and e-mail address for the hiring manager or other agency contact
- Qualifying for consideration under a special hiring authority by being, for example, a person with a disability, a veteran, a military spouse, or an undergraduate or graduate student
- Applying for a mission-critical job or another job that is in demand and is part of a government-wide or agency-specific direct-hire authority (many cybersecurity jobs are hired in this format)

The cover letter, which is the focus of this chapter, is important as way to address special hiring situations that might not be included as part of the resume. Even as part of a standard federal application, a cover letter provides another opportunity for you to highlight your skills and achievements, present some of your personality, address resume gaps, and prove why you are the best person for the job.

Federal Cover Letter Basics

A federal cover letter should be less than a page long and should be written in a formal, business style with no slang or contractions. It also should include the following items:

- **Your contact information:** List your name, address, phone numbers (home and cell, as appropriate), and e-mail address. This information goes at the beginning of the letter either in a standard return address format or in a format that matches your resume.
- **The date:** This fact follows your contact information at the beginning of the letter.

- **Hiring agency information:** After the date, include the name of the hiring department and agency and its address. Also include the name and title of the human resources recruiter (if you have this information in the vacancy announcement) or the contact to whom you are addressing the letter.

 Note: You should learn about the hiring agency before you apply for a position by, at the very least, reading its website. Then make sure you include some of what you learn in your cover letter. This kind of detail will show that you are truly enthusiastic about this job opportunity.

- **Job title, job announcement number, and/or vacancy identification number:** To make this information easy to find, you may want to list it before your greeting. Another option is to work it into your opening paragraph.

- **Your strongest qualifications:** Summarize how you match the qualifications listed in the job announcement. Emphasize any experience you have that connects you to the agency's mission and the requirements of the job.

- **An indication that your resume is enclosed:** Make sure the reader knows that you have provided additional information by mentioning your resume in the cover letter. Also mention any other supporting documents you may have enclosed, such as a DD214 (this is a Certificate of Release or Discharge from Active Duty that is required for any veteran-related special hiring authority). At the very least, include an enclosure line at the end of the document that lists the documents you have sent along with your cover letter.

- **Polite closing that indicates your interest in the job:** Emphasize the skills you are offering the agency and ask for the interview. End the letter with a professional closing, such as "Sincerely," and your name.

Cover Letters for USAJOBS and Other Online Application Systems

Although a cover letter is typically not required, some job applicants are choosing to add a cover letter to their federal job applications. You can upload a cover letter into USAJOBS or applicationmanager.gov. Figures 11.1 through 11.4 show samples of this type of cover letter.

Target Position: Social Worker

Melanie Santos

555 Park Boulevard, San Antonio, TX 78148 ◆ 210-555-5555 ◆ Melanies11@gmail.com

January 19, 20XX

Department of Veterans Affairs
Veterans Health Administration
Job Announcement Number: VA123456-789
Position: Social Worker, GS 0185-11

Dear Hiring Manager,

I am a dedicated and compassionate licensed social worker with an MSW and ten years of experience providing direct social services, conducting needs assessments, developing treatment plans, performing case management, and coordinating services and referrals. As a home care worker, I am well acquainted with the complex interplay of health and related psychosocial conditions.

Approximately fifteen percent of my current clients are homeless veterans and their families. I can offer your agency an in-depth knowledge of human development and human behavior and extensive knowledge of community resources. I work successfully with individuals from a wide range of socioeconomic, cultural, ethnic, educational, and other diversified backgrounds.

Thank you for your consideration in giving me the opportunity to expand the work I do to serve those who have served our country. My enclosed resume details my qualifications and accomplishments. I look forward to discussing with you in person how I can use these skills to improve services for Texas veterans.

Sincerely,

Melanie Santos

Enclosures: resume, references

Figure 11.1: This social worker uses a cover letter to emphasize her general expertise and specific knowledge of the people whom the hiring agency serves.

Target Position: Management and Program Analyst

MARY T. JONES
333 Third St.
Blacksburg, VA 22222
Home: 999-999-9999
Cell: 999-999-8888
Email: marytjones@yahoo.com

August 17, 20XX

Tony Agnello, Human Resources Specialist
Department of Agriculture
Office of Human Resources Management
546 Bay View Drive
Arlington, VA 20201

Re: Management and Program Analyst, GS-0343-13/14; Job Announcement Number DMY-10-0032-DE

Dear Mr. Agnello:

As my enclosed federal resume for the management and program analyst position shows, I am a human resources leader who offers more than 10 years of specialized experience analyzing processes and systems to address human capital planning and accountability and proven success in implementing effective changes.

I achieved these results by
- Developing, monitoring, and tracking the execution and reporting of information and performance data for human capital initiatives.
- Leading high-profile projects and human capital initiatives that increased the effectiveness and efficiency of HR operations and improved customer service.
- Representing my organization at high-level meetings with internal and external stakeholders to communicate program information, respond to questions, and champion new HR approaches.
- Serving as a Senior HR Manager for a program impacting 10,000 employees.
- Implementing HR policy and programs organization-wide and supervising staff.
- Researching and analyzing HR processes and systems and directing teams for a successful, large-scale Human Resources Information Systems (HRIS) integration to support future human capital planning.

The Department of Agriculture provides leadership both nationally and internationally in how to use food resources wisely. I look forward to discussing in an interview how I can help it use its own human resources wisely as well. Thank you for your time and consideration. I look forward to your response.

Sincerely,

Mary T. Jones

Enclosures: Federal resume

Figure 11.2: Using a substantial list of accomplishments and an assertive tone, this management analyst makes the case in her cover letter that she is worth interviewing.

Target Position: Management and Program Analyst

Sarah Smuckers
655 Rockabilly Way
Memphis, TN 38555
Home: 333-333-3333
Cell: 333-333-4444
Email: sarahsmuckers10@aol.com

November 2, 20XX

Veronica Smith
Internal Revenue Service
5333 Getwell Road
Stop 9417
Memphis, TN 38118

Dear Ms. Smith,

Enclosed is my application responding to **Job Announcement Number 08ME1-SBE0091-343-14-CH, Management and Program Analyst.** I have enclosed my federal resume, which highlights my professional accomplishments over the last decade.

I offer the Small Business/Self-Employed Business Unit of the IRS proven project management experience with an unusual combination of specialized, technical human resources leadership experience in the following areas:

- **Executive and Leadership Coaching and Development:** More than 11 years of experience in coaching and developing leaders and implementing training and formal programs as a human resources executive.
- **Human Resources Management:** Served as a Vice President of Human Resources and Organizational Development for three different organizations. Proven expertise in developing and managing human resources policies and procedures for dynamically changing organizations.
- **Strategic Hiring and Recruitment:** As VP, Human Resources, U.S. Food Service, designed and strategically recruited for a management development program that produced six top leaders for challenging markets.
- **Strategic Planning in Human Resources:** Focus on recruiting and retaining the best talent through all aspects of my human resources programs in order to meet the demand for creative, intuitive, and high-performing leaders.
- **Succession Planning:** Proven experience in devising, implementing, and leading succession plans for training, development, and refreshing the pipeline of management candidates and technical personnel.
- **Training and Management Development:** Experienced training director with vision and expertise in consulting with managers on required training, mission changes, and work demands.
- **Talent and Performance Management:** Designed and implemented performance-based leadership and employee programs for two major corporations.

I look forward to the opportunity to meet in person for an interview to discuss how my skills can help the IRS reach its goals. Thank you for your consideration of my application materials.

Sincerely,

Sarah Smuckers

Enclosure: Federal Resume

Figure 11.3: This executive uses bold text to make the job information easy to find and to highlight keywords from the job announcement to show that she has the expertise the IRS is looking for.

Target Position: Police Officer

Brandon Billings

304 Aalapapa Drive
Kailua, HI
(808) 222-2222
brandon.billings@gmail.com

May 10, 20XX

John Green, Human Resources Recruiter
Transportation Security Agency
7888 Leesburg Pike
Leesburg, VA, 20202

Dear Mr. Green:

Please find enclosed my federal resume for the position of Police Officer, GS-0083, Job Announcement Number 10101.

In particular, I believe the following experiences uniquely qualify me for this position:

- Working three years in visitor protection and law enforcement in the harbors and bays with the U.S. Coast Guard as a Boarding Team Member
- Training new hires in the handling of arms, ammunition, and pyrotechnic equipment as a Firearms Instructor
- Developing criminal investigative cases, including smuggling and illegal immigration cases
- Spending a year gaining specialized experience in law enforcement operation practices and techniques
- Honing the administrative skills that are necessary in law enforcement by completing training in Microsoft Office applications and sharpening my skill in writing reports

Thank you for your time and consideration. I look forward to discussing in an interview how I could be an asset to the TSA.

Sincerely,

Brandon Billings

Enclosures: Federal resume, DD-214

Figure 11.4: This applicant uses a cover letter to clearly connect his past work with the U.S. Coast Guard with the duties required of a police officer with the Transportation Security Agency.

Cold-Call Cover Letters

If you have the name of a hiring manager and would like to introduce your specialized experience and interest in his or her agency and office, you can send an e-mailed cover letter with a resume attached. You will also probably have to apply for positions through USAJOBS, but the direct cold-call e-mail message will just be another introduction.

Figure 11.5 shows an example of a veteran who qualifies for a 10-point preference contacting a hiring manger in the Department of Veterans Affairs. Because she can be hired through a special hiring authority and has a clear connection to the mission of this agency, she stands a good chance of getting some job leads (or possibly even an interview) in response to this cold-call cover letter.

Target Position: Administrative Officer

Sent: Friday May 20, 20XX
To: jjones11@va.gov
Subject: Opportunities for 30% Disabled Veteran: Administrative Officer, GS 9–11
Attached: marilynlogan_resume.docx, DD-214.pdf

Mr. John Jones, Acting Director
Veterans Benefits Administration, DVA
Atlanta, GA
Phone: (313) 999-9999

Dear Mr. Jones:

I read your comments in the *Atlanta Journal-Constitution* about the challenges of managing the veterans' benefits claims in the Atlanta center, and I want to help you meet these challenges. For the past five years, I have served as an Operations Manager for the National Guard. I know I could use this experience to contribute to the effectiveness of your claims office in an administrative or operations position.

My specific areas of expertise include the following:

- Leading evaluative studies to support changing National Guard requirements for readiness, materials, and administration
- Knowledge of and skill in analytical and evaluative methods to improve efficiency and effectiveness of the National Guard program operations
- Proven administrative officer capabilities, including generating reports, tracking information, and managing records
- Ability to communicate with senior officers, customers, and team members to achieve operations objectives
- Proficient computer skills, including data management, spreadsheet development, and report development

I have attached my resume to further detail my skills and experience. I would like the opportunity to speak with you in person about how my administrative, analytical, team leadership, and communications skills can be used at VBA to improve services and disability claims management and the administration to support these critical operations. I will contact you next week to confirm that you have received my application and to discuss how I might help the VBA in Atlanta fulfill its mission.

Thank you for your consideration.

Sincerely,

Marilyn Logan

MARILYN LOGAN
1111 Mystery Lane
Atlanta, GA 22222
E-mail: marilyn.logan@gmail.com

Figure 11.5: This e-mail message from an experienced administrative officer serves as a professional introduction to an agency that is likely to have many positions that match her experience.

Networking Cover Letters

Tell everyone you know that you are seeking a federal position and ask if they have any contacts or information about federal jobs, federal agencies, or special hiring programs. Follow up with any contacts you make by writing a cover letter and sending your federal resume. You may or may not get any results, but you are just telling everyone that this is your objective. It is surprising what people know. They could write back to you with hot tips on federal jobs.

Many job seekers have found that if you can get introduced to a hiring official, you can gain his or her interest in your background. Later on, if there is an actual vacancy announcement, your name could be remembered. If you come up on the List of Candidates, you might stand out because of your early networking and writing efforts.

Figure 11.6 is an example of a networking letter.

 Note: If you qualify for direct hire, Schedule A, or 10-point Veterans' Preference, you can get a job interview and get hired just based on a cover letter and resume—if the stars are lined up!

Target Position: HUD, other GS-7/9 positions

JOHN WHEELER
5212 Maple Drive
Waldorf, MD 20748
Mobile: (301) 333-3333
E-mail: jwheeler@aol.com

September, 21, 20XX

[Name of colleague, friend, or relative]

Dear [person's name]:

You may know that I have just relocated from Houston, Texas, to Washington, D.C. I am looking for a government or private-sector position in public housing. I would appreciate any leads or referrals to your friends, relatives, or colleagues who may work in government or the housing area.

My first preference would be to work for HUD. If you have any friends who work for HUD, I would like to know if they are hiring or planning expansion due to the housing problems here in the U.S. My public housing knowledge and experience, as well administrative and customer services skills, would be an asset to HUD in achieving its goal of improving housing for Americans.

For government positions, I am qualified for the following positions at the GS-7/9 grade level:

- Loan Specialist (Realty), GS-1165
- Housing Management Assistant or Housing Program Specialist, GS-1101
- Contract Specialist (my degree is complete), GS-1102

My areas of expertise include the following:

- **Public housing knowledge:** During my five years of experience in new home sales for public housing through the Accessory Dwelling Units (ADU) program, I have interpreted policies and procedures, interviewed buyers, and assisted with applications.
- **Administrative operations:** While working at District of Columbia Realty Taxpayer services, I improved administrative processing, resolved homeowner problems, and analyzed cases.
- **Customer communications:** In both positions I have held, I have been able to interpret complex policies in order to help customers understand public programs and policies, and rules and regulations. I also have excellent negotiating and problem-solving skills.

I appreciate any position or agency ideas that could be hiring in my field of work. I am currently working and would be available for an interview and to come to work within two weeks. If you want to talk, please call me at my cell (444) 444-4444 or write to me by e-mail at jwheeler@aol.com.

Thank you for your time and support for my new job search in the Washington, D.C. metro area.

Sincerely,

John Wheeler
Enclosure: Resume

Figure 11.6: A networking letter that lets friends and contacts know that the candidate is looking for a position and clarifies what he is interested in.

Special Hiring Authority Cover Letters

If you find an announcement that is a mission-critical hire, Schedule A (noncompetitive appointment for people with disabilities), or other special hiring authority for which you qualify, you can write your cover letter directly to a hiring manager for consideration. In this case, the cover letter serves as an introduction to an HR specialist, hiring manager, selective placement officer, or other individual who may be interested in your background. This hiring official may be interested in hiring through direct hire or other special hiring program and interview you about positions at his or her agency.

The cover letter should emphasize your specialized experience, interest in the agency, and your availability for an interview. In this situation, you also would attach your resume and your documents to prove that you are qualified for the hiring authority.

Figure 11.7 is a cover letter for a person who qualifies for Veterans' Preference hiring, and Figure 11.8 is an example of someone who can be hired under Schedule A.

Target Position: IT Specialist

AMOS N. FREDERICKS, JR.
1800 Friendship Road
Frederick, MD 20744
Home: 301-333-3333 • amosfredericks@hotmail.com

May 20, 20XX

CBP Indianapolis Hiring Center
6650 Telecom Drive
Suite 100
Indianapolis, IN 46278

Dear Human Resources Recruiter:

Enclosed is my application responding to Job Announcement Number IHC-287222-CDH-DE, Information Technology Specialist (Customer Support). In addition to my resume, I have enclosed my DD214 to demonstrate my qualification for a 10-point Veterans' Preference as a result of my service in the U.S. Air Force as an Electronics Technician during the Vietnam Era.

My specialized expertise in customer support includes five years of experience with the following duties:

- Diagnosing and resolving problems in response to customer-reported incidents
- Researching, evaluating, and providing feedback on problematic trends and patterns in customer support requirements
- Developing and maintaining problem tracking and resolution databases
- Installing, configuring, troubleshooting, and maintaining customer hardware and software
- Developing and managing customer service performance requirements
- Developing customer support policies, procedures, and standards
- Providing customer training and/or creating training programs
- Ensuring the rigorous application of information security/information assurance policies, principles, and practices in the delivery of customer support services
- Resolving technical and database problems

I am a proven team leader with a solid customer services ethic and strong problem-solving skills. I look forward to discussing how I can put these qualities to work for the Customs and Border Protection Agency.

Thank you for your consideration.

Sincerely,

Amos N. Fredericks, Jr.

Attachments: Federal resume, DD214

Figure 11.7: This Vietnam veteran uses this cover letter to emphasize his Veterans' Preference standing as well his technical support skills in response to a vacancy announcement posted on USAJOBS.

Target Position: Program Manager/Management Analyst

SAMUEL GERARD SIMPSON, BA, MBA, DC
10 HARBOR BREEZE LANE
BOSTON, MASSACHUSETTS 12345

Mr. Aaron Jones
Branch Chief, Special Emphasis Programs and Recruitment
Office of Human Resources
200 Constitution Avenue, NW
Washington, DC 20210

Dear Mr. Jones,

I am submitting my federal resume for consideration of positions within the Management and Administrative occupational family. Specifically, I am qualified for the following positions at the 11/12/13 grade level:
- Program Manager, GS-0301
- Management Analyst, GS-343

I offer the following assets:
- **Strong strategic and tactical thinking.** During my tenure with AT&T, I advanced from being a $6 million sales account manager to a $500 million Profit & Loss business manager in a fiercely competitive environment in a Fortune 500 corporation.
- **Outstanding written and oral communication skills.** While at AT&T, I regularly created and delivered presentations to audiences of 200+ business executives from the largest U.S. corporations. As a chiropractor, I delivered 200+ health-, wellness-, and safety-related talks in the western North Carolina area in the last 11 years.
- **Strong team leader and organization builder.** Serving as statewide chiropractic leader with roles in the North Carolina Chiropractic Association since 2002, I was elected to state district president (twice), was board treasurer, and currently am executive board secretary.
- **Results-driven leadership.** I opened a chiropractic clinic in 1998 that was profitable within 30 days and grew to $500K in five years and $1,000,000 in nine years. I managed staff ranging from 15 direct to 50 employees in a matrix management environment.

My relevant qualifications include

- Broad-based knowledge of business and organizational management, health care management, product/project management, marketing, business strategies, and sales.
- Outstanding administrative management skills, including budget management, human resources, contract management, procurement, inventory control, facility management, safety, and security.
- Adept at analyzing and applying laws, rules, and regulations.
- Well-developed quantitative and qualitative analytical problem-solving skills.
- Ability to multitask with changing marketplace demands, accommodating complex internal and external business drivers while adapting plans and priorities to successfully meet business needs.

I look forward to meeting you to discuss how my leadership and administrative management experience, technical ability, and exceptional collaboration and negotiation skills can support your organizational goals and objectives. Thank you for your time and consideration.

Sincerely,

Samuel G. Simpson

Enclosure: Federal resume, Schedule A certificate

Figure 11.8: This cover letter connects diverse career experiences for a chiropractor who wants to transition to being a federal management analyst and can be hired under the Schedule A special hiring authority.

Summary

Although cover letters have long been part of the corporate job search process, they are a relatively new part of the federal application. They provide a way to emphasize major accomplishments, explain career transitions, and address qualifications for hiring under special hiring authorities. Remember that the cover letter is a business letter, so you should follow a basic business letter format and keep your tone confident and professional. If you make the right connections and have the right qualifications, you might make it to the interview stage on the strength of your cover letter and resume alone!

Part 4

Navigating USAJOBS Announcements and Other Resume Builders

CHAPTER 12

Understanding Vacancy Announcements

$\mathbf{F}$ederal vacancy announcements are amazing! Yes, they are long, but they tell you all about the job, the agency, its mission, the office, the qualifications you need to have to get Best Qualified, and now even how they will grade your application.

Think of a vacancy announcement as a five- to eight-page federal job instructional guide. You will read it more carefully and with appreciation because if you follow the directions, you could get Best Qualified and maybe referred, interviewed, and hired! You have to read a manual to put together a bicycle, play a game, or even install an app on your iPhone. So, these vacancy announcements are simply the rules and procedures for applying for the position.

The key is to match your Outline Format federal resume to the vacancy announcement. Featuring the Duties keywords, Qualifications, Selective Placement Factors, Quality Ranking Factors, Knowledge, and Questionnaire Questions is critical. The Outline Format federal resume that is used throughout this book is successful. We use all-caps phrases on the resume to match the important qualifications that we find in the vacancy announcement.

Resume-Matching Example and Tips

Following is a federal resume abstract with all-caps keywords from the important qualifications sections of the announcement:

> CONTRACT MANAGEMENT: Administer realty contracts with a broad and diverse range of government agencies to perform contract management, close-outs, and terminations, including Social Security Administration, U.S Customs and Border Protection, Agricultural Marketing Services, Animal and Plant Health Inspection Service, Internal Revenue Service, Bureau of Indian Affairs, and Fish and Wildlife Service.
>
> CONTRACT ADMINISTRATION: Support 15 contracting officers, 30 project managers, and more than 300 projects. Manage paperwork, organize files, and provide general support while performing daily responsibilities. Knowledgeable of contractor and vendor performance parameters and the need for clear, concise, performance-based statements and measurements.
>
> - Created new procedures that reduced contract processing time and enabled the swift identification of key documents among thousands to be reviewed. Drafted checklists to aid in the review process.
>
> CONTRACT CLOSE-OUTS: Process 7 to 10 contract close-outs per month. Perform notification procedures to building service centers over the phone and in writing. Partner with contract officer. Correct documents as necessary. Create new agreements. Quality check documents to bill out correctly. Ensure that all paperwork, terms, steps, and procedures are complete so that contract is completed with absolute accuracy and integrity.
>
> - Slashed processing time of close-out procedures from months to hours. Suggested and helped implement personnel realignment so that key individuals now communicate critical steps, information, and updates. Devised inspection criteria to reduce processing time; errors are now spotted in minutes and missing information is easy to procure.

Following are important parts of the announcement to pay attention to when matching your resume:

- **Mission:** The Mission section is informative. It is very interesting and tells you about the agency, what services it provides Americans, and its purpose. You will have to decide whether you can get behind the mission of the position. For instance, if you want to work in a mission where the environment and lands are being protected (such as the Bureau of Land Management, Interior Department), you would not want to work for agencies that analyze numbers and collect taxes (such as the Treasury, Pension Benefit Guarantee Corporation). Carefully consider the mission before you apply to the position.

- **Duties:** The Duties of the position are a clear indication of what you will be doing for eight hours a day if you land this job. If you see certain words repeated many times, that will mean that you will be doing *a lot* of that duty in the position. If it says the word *accounting* or *purchase* five to eight times, that means you will be performing accounting or purchasing items a lot in that position. If you do not want a position crunching numbers and buying things for customers, do not apply to that position.

- **Qualifications and Specialized Experience:** The Qualifications and Specialized Experience is my favorite part of the announcement. If you read this carefully, it states that you must have one year of specialized experience equal to this position and have examples that demonstrate this. This is a very clear statement. If you do not have one year of specialized experience, do not apply. If you do have one year of specialized experience, feature this in your federal resume. If this experience is in your second-most-recent position, feature the earlier position and write the first position shorter.

- **Knowledge, Skills, and Abilities and Competencies:** The Knowledge, Skills, and Abilities and Competencies required are critical for the federal resume, and you should give examples that demonstrate these KSAs and competencies. The examples can be short (five lines long), but if you prove that you have this experience, you could get a better score on your application.

- **Occupational Questionnaire:** The Occupational Questionnaire will be multiple choice most of the time; you will have to select your skill level. Give yourself all the credit that you can on these questionnaires. The three announcements in this chapter range from 27 to 61 questions. The questionnaire is the closest thing to a valid, reliable assessment tool. It is important in getting Best Qualified with your score.

The rest of this chapter takes you through the steps of matching your resume to the vacancy announcement.

Step 1: Find Vacancy Announcements and the Occupational Questionnaire

You can find most federal vacancy announcements at the following websites. All jobs are posted on these websites, including jobs for the Army and Navy, which also have their own websites and job listings.

- **www.usajobs.gov:** The official Office of Personnel Management website
- **www.avuecentral.com:** Federal agency jobs website

In addition, you can find vacancy announcements through several other sources, which are detailed in the following sections.

Agency Websites

Most agencies list their jobs at their own websites, as well as at www.usajobs.gov. If you have targeted a specific agency, such as the Federal Bureau of Investigation, it would be much faster to search for jobs at www.fbijobs.gov than at the OPM's main site. Or if you wanted a job at the National Institutes of Health, you could go directly to www.hhs.gov.

Private-Industry Federal Job Sites

You can find federal jobs at privately owned and operated databases as well. These cost a few dollars for membership and access, but the databases are nicely managed, so you might be able to find specific jobs faster than on other websites. Here are a few examples of these types of sites:

- www.americajob.com
- www.fedjobs.com

Civilian Job Listings with Defense and Military Agencies

Looking for a job as a civilian on a military base? You don't have to join the military service to work as a civilian in a Department of Defense agency. You can look for job announcements at the following sites:

- **Navy/Marines:** https://chart.donhr.navy.mil/
- **Army:** www.cpol.army.mil
- **Department of Defense:** www.defenselink.mil/sites/c.html#CivilianJobOpportunities
- **Department of Homeland Security:** http://www.dhs.gov/xabout/careers/
- **National Guard and Reserve** (may require Dual Status of both being a civilian employee and joining the Guard or Reserves): www.usajobs.gov

 Note: When you go to the Navy Civilian website, you will see a message about its Security Certificate. It is safe to accept the certificate.

Your Network

Even if you apply for positions competitively on USAJOBS, you can still use your network to find out about positions that are coming up. And then your network can vouch for your qualifications for this position. Or you can send your federal resume and cover letter directly to a supervisor that you know as a basic introduction.

Do you know someone who works in government? What agency does this person work for? What is this person's job? Is this individual's agency growing or downsizing? Is it hiring? What kinds of people does the agency hire? How can you apply? Does the person you know have any clout with hiring managers? These are the questions you should ask your neighbor, golf partner, and fellow church-goer. This person's agency might be adding a new program and needing to hire more program managers, contract specialists, and computer specialists. This person might not know that you would like to work for the government and that you have expertise in a particular area. Network. Meet and talk with as many people as you can. You never know where you'll find a good lead.

Federal employees and others will tell you that your network is very important. Think long range. Listen for new programs and initiatives, especially those that will require specialized technical skills.

Reading, Listening to the News, and Keeping Your Eyes Open

Read federal newspapers, union newsletters, the federal page in your newspaper if it has one, the federal pages in the *Washington Post* (available online at www.washingtonpost.com), and *Government Executive Magazine* (also available online at www.govexec.com) to stay on top of what's going on in government.

 Tip: Save announcements that you apply to. You will need the announcement to prepare for an interview.

Step 2: Analyze the Vacancy Announcement and "How to Apply" Instructions

Read the highlighted sections to gain insight into each section of the announcement. Once you have found a job opportunity that interests you, save or print the vacancy announcement for thorough study. Don't be intimidated by the length and look of the announcement. We'll teach you how to discover the important information in the announcement and what the various sections mean. On USAJOBS announcements, scroll down to Print Preview. You can click on this, and the entire announcement can be printed and saved for future analysis and documentation.

 Tip: It's important to have a My USAJOBS account set up ahead of time so that you can follow the "APPLY NOW" instructions and complete the online questionnaire.

SSA Announcement: USAJOBS and Applicationmanager.gov

This vacancy announcement is typical now. It includes the important sections of the announcement: Mission, Duties, Specialized Experience, Benefits, and How to Apply. This application has two parts: the USAJOBS federal resume and the Occupational Questionnaire, which is multiple choice.

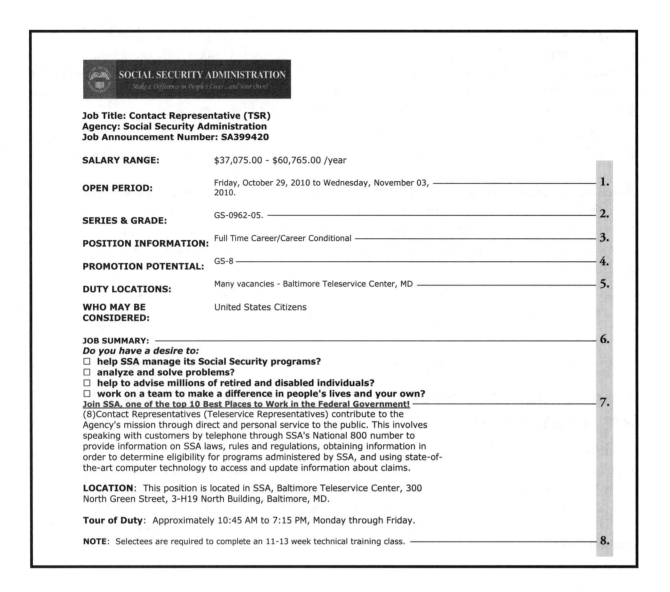

SOCIAL SECURITY ADMINISTRATION
Make a Difference in People's Lives...and Your Own!

Job Title: Contact Representative (TSR)
Agency: Social Security Administration
Job Announcement Number: SA399420

SALARY RANGE:	$37,075.00 - $60,765.00 /year
OPEN PERIOD:	Friday, October 29, 2010 to Wednesday, November 03, 2010. — 1.
SERIES & GRADE:	GS-0962-05. — 2.
POSITION INFORMATION:	Full Time Career/Career Conditional — 3.
PROMOTION POTENTIAL:	GS-8 — 4.
DUTY LOCATIONS:	Many vacancies - Baltimore Teleservice Center, MD — 5.
WHO MAY BE CONSIDERED:	United States Citizens

JOB SUMMARY: — 6.
Do you have a desire to:
☐ **help SSA manage its Social Security programs?**
☐ **analyze and solve problems?**
☐ **help to advise millions of retired and disabled individuals?**
☐ **work on a team to make a difference in people's lives and your own?**
<u>Join SSA, one of the top 10 Best Places to Work in the Federal Government!</u> — 7.
(8)Contact Representatives (Teleservice Representatives) contribute to the Agency's mission through direct and personal service to the public. This involves speaking with customers by telephone through SSA's National 800 number to provide information on SSA laws, rules and regulations, obtaining information in order to determine eligibility for programs administered by SSA, and using state-of-the-art computer technology to access and update information about claims.

LOCATION: This position is located in SSA, Baltimore Teleservice Center, 300 North Green Street, 3-H19 North Building, Baltimore, MD.

Tour of Duty: Approximately 10:45 AM to 7:15 PM, Monday through Friday.

NOTE: Selectees are required to complete an 11-13 week technical training class. — 8.

---

1. This announcement is open only three working days. SSA is hiring many people for this vacancy, so they have it open a short amount of time.

2. You can start only at a GS-5 for this position. The starting range is $37K to $44.2K at the GS-5. But there is promotion potential to a GS-8, which goes up to $60,765. Maybe you could negotiate your step within the grade. See OPM's Salary Table to understand the Steps and Grades.

3. This is a full-time position (not a temporary, or term position).

4. This position can grow to a GS-8 in four years.

5. Many vacancies—always a good sign!

6. Job Summary includes important tips/keywords for the resume and the interview if you are lucky enough to get referred and selected for the panel interview. Remember this short list!

7. SSA is one of the Top 10 Best Places to Work. You can see the entire list at www.ourpublicservice.org.

8. Formal training—great!

KEY REQUIREMENTS: ———————————————————————————— 9.
- U.S. Citizenship Required
- Registered for Selective Service. See Other Information tab
- Security and/or Background Investigation Required
- Selectees are required to serve a 1 year probationary period
- Selectees are required to complete a 11-13 week technical training class

Duties ———————————————————————————————— 10.
Many vacancies - Baltimore Teleservice Center, MD

<u>Teleservice Representatives</u> (TSR) <u>interview</u> <u>callers</u> to obtain information, to furnish information, and provide <u>guidance</u>, <u>resolve</u> <u>problems</u> with payments or eligibility status, <u>investigate</u> and <u>resolve</u> <u>situations</u> (i.e. nonpayment of benefits, premium reimbursements delays, cancellation of coverage) involving <u>Medicare Insurance issues</u> and <u>problems</u> with <u>disruption</u> of benefits as related to Medicare and other programs, and <u>redirect calls</u> to various social services, private, non-profit, and other government agencies.

Although this type of work is demanding, it is rewarding. The policy and provisions that govern SSA's programs are extensive, complex and subject to frequent changes in the law. The TSR is required to refer to numerous sources of Agency information, including <u>on-line technical manuals</u> and locally-prepared <u>guidelines</u>.

QUALIFICATIONS REQUIRED: ———————————————————— 11.

GS-05: Requires 1 year of specialized experience equivalent to the GS-4 level performing all or most of the following tasks: 1) <u>Applying laws</u>, rules or regulations and written guidelines; 2) <u>Communicating orally</u> in order to provide information, assistance, or instruction to members of the general public or their representatives; 3) <u>Performing administrative and clerical processes</u> using a computer to reconcile discrepancies, associate documents with related files/records, etc.; and 4) <u>Writing</u> routine correspondence in response to inquiries and draft a variety of other written products; **OR** a bachelors degree; **OR** 120 credits towards the completion of a bachelor's degree; **OR** a combination of college education beyond the first 60 credits/90 quarter hours and the specialized experience described above.

Substituting Education:

For more information on substituting education for experience, visit
http://www.opm.gov/qualifications/standards/group-stds/gs-cler.asp

SELECTIVE PLACEMENT FACTOR: ——————————————————— 12.

After meeting the qualifications requirements noted above, you will participate in a **panel interview to demonstrate your ability to serve the public**. To receive further consideration, you must demonstrate qualities such as <u>clarity of speech</u>, ability to <u>listen</u>, ability to establish <u>confidence</u> and put others at ease, and the

(continued)

9. Make sure you are aware of this info.

10. Duties: It is critical to match your resume to this section. Since the first sentence talks about INTERVIEWING CALLERS, this will be a skill to add into your resume. You will RESOLVE PROBLEMS and INVESTIGATE AND RESOLVE SITUATIONS for the callers.

11. You can be hired into this position only at a GS-5 level. This is the specialized experience that you must demonstrate in your resume to be Best Qualified: APPLY LAWS, COMMUNICATE ORALLY, PERFORM ADMINISTRATIVE, WRITE CORRESPONDENCE…or 120 credits toward a degree…or both (this is the BEST selection).

12. Selective Placement Factor is a "screen out." If you don't prove this in your resume, you won't get Best Qualified or even Minimally Qualified. Your voice has to be clear; you have to demonstrate that you can listen, establish confidence, calm people down, and be organized. This language should be added to your resume. You will also need to prove this in the panel interview.

(continued)

ability to <u>organize</u> and <u>express</u> <u>thoughts</u> clearly. If you do not pass the panel interview, you will not receive further consideration and will not receive further consideration and will not qualify for the job.

HOW YOU WILL BE EVALUATED: ———————————————— 13.

The evaluation you receive is based on your responses to the questionnaire. Your resume and supporting documentation will be compared to your responses to the occupational questionnaire, which is designed to capture the desired competencies for this position. These competencies include **oral and written communication**, **problem solving** and **planning**, **processing work** in a computer environment and organization. Please make sure you answer all questions and follow all instructions carefully. Errors or omissions may affect your evaluation. The questionnaire takes about 15 minutes to complete. To preview the questions, click the following link: <u>View Assessment Questions</u>

BENEFITS: ——————————————————————————— 14.

Social Security offers a comprehensive <u>benefits program</u> that you can customize for your individual medical and financial needs. In addition to traditional "dollars and cents" benefits, we offer a range of benefits to help you <u>balance life with Social Security to life outside of work</u>. Please visit our Careers site at <u>www.ssa.gov/careers</u> for additional information.

HOW TO APPLY: —————————————————————————— 15.
To apply for this position, you must provide a complete Application Package which includes:
1. Your Résumé ——————————————————————————— 16.
2. The Occupational Questionnaire ——————————————— 17.
3. Additional Required Documents (see Required Documents section below)

The complete Application Package must be submitted before midnight (EST) on Wednesday, November 03, 2010

———————————————————————————————— 18.
To begin the process, click the **Apply Online** button to create an account or log in to your existing USAJOBS account. Follow the prompts to complete the occupational questionnaire. Please ensure you click the (18)**Submit My Answers** button at the end of the process. —— 19.
To fax supporting documents you are unable to upload, complete the <u>United States Government Application Cover Page</u> using the following Vacancy ID: SA399420. Fax your documents to 1-**478-757-3144**. ————————————————————— 20.
Note: To check the status of your application or return to a previous or incomplete application, log into your USAJOBS account, select Application Status, and click on the more information link under the application status for this position. ——————— 21.

If you cannot apply online: ————————————————————— 22.

1. View and print the occupational questionnaire: <u>View Occupational Questionnaire</u>, —— 23.
and
2. Print the <u>1203FX Form C</u> to provide your response to the questionnaire and

---

13. The resume and your transcript will be compared to your responses in the Occupational Questionnaire. The answers need to match your resume. The competencies they will quiz you about will be written communication, problem solving and planning, and processing work in a computer environment. These should be keywords in your resume.

14. The benefits are fabulous, in addition to the traditional "dollars and cents" benefits.

15. This is a traditional application package: USAJOBS Resume, Occupational Questionnaire completed online, and then additional documents.

16. Your USAJOBS federal resume in the Outline Format with the keywords

from the announcement featured in ALL CAPS so that it is very easy to read. If you can add accomplishments or examples about how you solved problems for customers by phone, interviewed callers, referred to technical manuals, and updated files in a database, that could help you get Best Qualified.

17. Give yourself as much credit as you can when selecting the multiple-choice answers.

18. The Apply Online button is great. It would be best if you have your resume in USAJOBS already. And you can go back and edit and change some of the keywords in the Outline Format before you submit it for this position.

19. The Submit My Answers button is important. Look for it.

20. It's better if you can scan and upload your transcript and other documents into applicationmanager.gov, but you can fax them. Be sure to use the official US Government Fax Cover.

21. Check your status in both USAJOBS and Applicationmanager. Great information here (most of the time).

22. If you cannot apply online, just follow these directions.

23. You can view the questions here! Print them and review them before you submit your answers online. Give yourself all the credit that you can with the multiple-choice questions. Then be sure that the resume matches your selections, too.

3. Fax the completed 1203FX form and supporting documents to **1-478-757-3144**.

Due to our security procedures, our office will not accept any applications submitted via email or standard mail. The email address is listed only for inquiries about the position or the How to Apply process.

REQUIRED DOCUMENTS:

You must submit supporting documentation by the closing date of the vacancy announcement to claim certain types of preference or qualify on the basis of education.

VETERANS' PREFERENCE: If you are claiming veterans' preference under competitive procedures, submit a copy of your military discharge certificate (DD 214 member 4 copy), official statement of service from your command if you are currently on active duty, or other proof of eligibility. To be acceptable, the document must show Character of Service. If you are claiming 10-point veterans' preference, you must also submit an Application for 10-Point Veterans' Preference (SF 15) and the required documentation specified on the reverse of the SF 15. Preference will be granted based on the documents received. For more information visit http://www.opm.gov/veterans/html/vetguide.asp

PROOF OF EDUCATION: If you are qualifying on the basis of education or satisfying an educational requirement, submit a copy of your transcripts with the course title, number of credits, grade, and date of completion. To qualify, the degree must be from an accredited college or university recognized by the U.S. Department of Education. Education completed in a foreign institution must be certified as equivalent to coursework completed at a U.S. college or university. Certification of equivalency must be submitted at the time of application.

AGENCY CONTACT INFO: ─────────────────────────────────── **24.**

Christine D. Palmer
Phone: (215) 597-0587
Email:
CHRISTINE.PALMER@SSA.GOV

Agency Information:
SSA Philadelphia
Center for Human Resources -
7th floor
300 Spring Garden Street
Philadelphia, PA 19123   USA

WHAT TO EXPECT NEXT: ─────────────────────────────────── **25.**

Once you have successfully submitted your application materials, you can expect to receive the following email notifications concerning your application status: (1) Receipt of application; (2) Result of qualifications review; (3) Referred/Not Referred to the selecting official; and (4) Selected/Not Selected for the position.

24. Christine Palmer's phone and e-mail are right here. You could call or write to her if you had questions.

25. This information will be posted on your USAJOBS application-tracking page by Christine or someone in the human resources office in Philadelphia.

Following is the questionnaire for the Contact Representative. You will need to self-assess your skills (selecting A through E) for 42 questions. This is a typical questionnaire that is scored with automation and gives the HR specialist a valid, reliable assessment of your skill level for this position.

Occupational Questionnaire
Contact Representative (TSR)

Vacancy ID: SA399420   Announcement Number: SA399420   USAJOBS Control Number: 2081035

Occupational/Assessment Questions:

ABILITY TO COMMUNICATE ORALLY WITH INDIVIDUALS FROM VARIOUS SOCIO-ECONOMIC BACKGROUNDS AND INTELLECTUAL LEVELS IN ORDER TO EXPLAIN AND PROVIDE INFORMATION ON SOCIAL SECURITY ADMINISTRATION LAWS, RULES, REGULATIONS AND PROCEDURES AND TO OBTAIN INFORMATION FROM CLAIMANTS/THIRD PARTIES.

For each task in the following group, choose the statement from the list below that best describes your experience and/or training. Darken the oval corresponding to that statement in Section 25 of the Qualifications and Availability Form C. Please select only one letter for each item.

1. For questions 2 - 42 choose the ONE letter from the list below (A - E) that best describes your experience, education and/or training.

A- I have not had education, training or experience in performing this task.

B- I have had education or training in performing the task, but have not yet performed it on the job.

C- I have performed this task on the job. My work on this task was monitored closely by a supervisor or senior employee to ensure compliance with proper procedures.

D- I have performed this task as a regular part of a job. I have performed it independently and normally without review by a supervisor or senior employee.

2. E- I am considered an expert in performing this task. I have supervised performance of this task or am normally the person who is consulted by other workers to assist them in doing this task because of my expertise.

   2. Interview members of the general public to secure needed technical information and obtain and clarify relevant facts involving benefit problems related to welfare, unemployment, workers' compensation, disability, insurance claims, etc.

   3. Explain legal provisions, policies and regulations involving criteria for rights, benefits, or privileges in connection with a variety of programs (i.e., health care, insurance, pensions, taxation, naturalization, etc.) requiring assessing the individual's degree of understanding and adjusting the delivery of information accordingly.

   4. Respond to specific procedural and technical inquiries from the general public in person.

---

1. Be sure to give yourself all the credit that you can when selecting your skill level. Be sure to prove it in your resume as well.

2. Important: The item E. Be sure to review the three ways you can become an "E": Expert, supervised the test, or the person who is consulted by others. Any one of these three skill levels can earn you an "E."

5. Extract information from individuals who may be uncooperative, perturbed, bereaved, irate, etc. and analyze that information to determine an appropriate course of action.

6. Conduct personal or telephone interviews for the purpose of administering a benefit program such as: welfare, Aid to Families with Dependent Children, health or life insurance, retirement or pension plans, workman's compensation or unemployment insurance where you are dealing with the general public and are handling a large number of telephone calls or interviews a day.

7. Elicit information, using interviewing skills, with tact and diplomacy.

8. Explain (or elicit) sensitive or controversial information to (from) people of diverse backgrounds.

9. Explain complex technical procedures, regulations, laws or rules about retirement or health insurance program options such as benefits (disability, life, medical, homeowners), tax or legal issues, etc. by the spoken word, to members of the general public with antagonistic, hostile or opposing viewpoints.

10. Deal with customer's problems or complaints; or 4 or more college level courses dealing with human interaction or social issues such as: sociology, psychology, conflict resolution, counseling, mediation, etc.

3. – 11. Present information orally involving an academic or work related subject that has been evaluated for content, clarity, and accuracy (i.e., toastmasters, toastmistress, public speaking engagements, teaching/instructing, leading a group, etc.).

ABILITY TO INTERPRET AND APPLY LAWS, REGULATIONS, AND OPERATING PROCEDURES IN ORDER TO DETERMINE ELIGIBILITY FOR SOCIAL SECURITY ADMINISTRATION PROGRAM ENTITLEMENTS AND CONTINUING ELIGIBILITY AND TO PROVIDE INFORMATION TO CLAIMANTS AND TO MAKE APPROPRIATE REFERRALS.

12. Apply and interpret laws, regulations, rules, and written guidelines to make a determination about an individual's eligibility for a program, benefit, or entitlement such as: welfare, Aid to Families with Dependent Children, workers' compensation, unemployment insurance, or private health, life or pension/retirement programs.

13. Determine the eligibility or ineligibility to receive Supplemental Social Insurance benefits.

14. Research, interpret, and apply rules and/or regulations in order to obtain/provide information for a variety of individuals (i.e., social services representative, loan or credit advisor, tax, consultant, insurance representative, real estate agent, etc.).

15. Apply and interpret procedures or policies such as private insurance policies (i.e., automobile, fire, theft, etc.); or two or more college courses in business law, accounting principles, or business math, etc.

16. Consult a large and diverse body of laws, rules. regulations, instructions, etc., to determine the appropriate guideline(s) to apply to resolve a case or situation in question, (i.e., social insurance examiner/specialist, social insurance service representative, tax specialist, insurance claims adjudicator, unemployment representative, etc.).

(continued)

3. This is a KSA, really, but you don't have to write a long narrative.

(continued)

17. Identify Medicaid, Medicare or private medical insurance program needs of individuals.

18. Interpret and provide full explanations of Federal and/or state laws and regulations covering benefits, obligations or entitlements for a program such as: welfare, Aid to Families with Dependent Children, workers' compensation, unemployment insurance, or private health, life or pension/retirement programs.

19. Explain legal provisions, regulations and information to the general public, and provide assistance to the public on rights, benefits, privileges or obligations under a body of law.

20. Apply written instructions and procedures consisting of multiple steps such as assisting others to complete credit, loan, employment or claims applications.

4. – ABILITY TO PROCESS WORK IN A COMPUTER ENVIRONMENT IN ORDER TO MEET CUSTOMER NEEDS.

21. Use computers to retrieve information involving welfare, unemployment, workers' compensation, disability or insurance claims.

22. Provide immediate assistance to customers, by analyzing and answering customer questions and performing follow-up action to maintain customer accounts based on information accessed from a computer terminal utilizing complex databases with multiple subsystems.

23. Use complex database equipment that has access to other databases (i.e., one company database searching another company database - Internal Revenue Service searching Department of Motor Vehicle or various nationwide law enforcement office databases) in order to answer customer questions and perform follow-up action on customer/client accounts.

24. Operate a personal computer to complete or input information into a computer while dealing with clients/customers in person or by telephone.

25. Provide complex technical assistance involving benefits, tax or legal issues, insurance (disability, life, medical, homeowners, etc.) based on information retrieved or accessed from a computerized database system.

26. Use basic word processing software packages such as Word, Word Perfect, etc.) on a daily basis in order to prepare written documents.

27. Process or analyze data using computer systems or applications.

28. Operate a personal computer or computer terminal, or use a computer or word processor.

29. Operate a personal computer to create, edit, print, retrieve, and manipulate files.

ABILITY TO USE REASONING TO ANALYZE ISSUES IN ORDER TO MAKE DECISIONS AND RESOLVE PROBLEMS.

30. Research issues and makes decisions within the parameters of clearly established rules, regulations, or precedents.

31. Review documents, records, data or other materials identifying missing information or problems, determine and initiate appropriate corrective actions.

4. These questions support this knowledge, skill, and ability.

32. Listen to information provided by individuals and identify the nature and purpose of an inquiry by extracting relevant facts necessary to independently solve their problems.

33. Develop facts necessary to solve problems through probing and questioning an individual.

34. Research, gather and evaluate customer/client information and use appropriate guidelines and procedures to resolve complex problems concerning benefits, entitlements, related to insurance (medical, life, disability, homeowners, automobile) tax or legal issues.

35. Research, interpret, and apply complex laws, rules, regulations, and written guidelines in order to evaluate and approve applications, claims, or requests (i.e., determining eligibility requirements from information such as birth certificates, selective service records, financial records, academic transcripts, etc.).

ABILITY TO ORGANIZE, PRIORITIZE AND PROCESS A LARGE VOLUME OF WORK WITHIN ESTABLISHED DEADLINES.

36. Rearrange priorities for my own work to ensure deadlines are met.

37. Work successfully in positions that often had tight deadlines or high volume production.

38. Deal calmly and effectively with high stress situations (i.e., tight deadlines, hostile individuals, emergency situation or dangerous situations).

39. Manage and organize a large volume of claims related work (i.e., processing of public or private claims).

40. Experience in positions involving constantly changing priorities and timeframes.

41. Manage and organize a large volume of complex technical/administrative work such as work in accounting, payroll, financial, personnel and legal fields.

42. Frequently make adjustments in procedures due to changing laws, regulations, and/or written guidelines.

Census Announcement: Professional Position, GS 7/9, Target 12 with USAJOBS Federal Resume, Questionnaire, and Essays

This CBP announcement is open two weeks to hire a few accountants at either the GS-7 or GS-9 level. You can get promoted to a GS-12 in this position. The KSAs are covered in the questionnaire and must be written as narratives. There is a positive education requirement for this position.

Bureau Of The Census

Job Title: Accountant, GS-510-7/9; CENSUS-D-DP
Department: Department Of Commerce
Agency: Bureau of the Census
Sub Agency: 63 Bureau of the Census
Job Announcement Number: FIN-2011-0004

SALARY RANGE:	$42,209.00 - $67,114.00 /year
OPEN PERIOD:	Saturday, October 30, 2010 to Monday, November 15, 2010
SERIES & GRADE:	GS-0510-07/09
POSITION INFORMATION:	Competitive Service: Career or Career-Conditional Full-Time
PROMOTION POTENTIAL:	12
DUTY LOCATIONS:	few vacancies - Washington DC Metro Area (Suitland, Maryland)
WHO MAY BE CONSIDERED:	All qualified U.S. citizens. Department of Commerce employees eligible for the Career Transition Assistance Program (CTAP). Applicants eligible for the Interagency Career Transition Assistance Program (ICTAP).

1. — (SERIES & GRADE)
2. — (PROMOTION POTENTIAL)
3. — (DUTY LOCATIONS)

JOB SUMMARY:

This vacancy is for a FEW Accountant positions in the Assistant Division Chief for Financial Management and Reporting, Finance Division, located at the U.S. Census Bureau Headquarters in Suitland, Maryland.

Promotion Potential: GS-12
Relocation expenses may or may not be paid. ————— *4.*
This is a bargaining unit position.

This position may be filled through means other than the competitive process.

Come join the Census Team, where everyone counts. The Census Bureau ————— *5.*
produces quality data that help Americans better understand our
country - its population, resources, economy, society and culture. We
offer competitive salaries, flexible hours and work arrangements,
developmental opportunities, recognition for a job well done, a
variety of benefits and health insurance plans, and a host of other
employment incentives. If working in an environment that values your
individuality and diversity and allows you to innovate, engage in

1. You can start in this position at either the GS-7 or GS-9 level.
2. You can get promoted to a GS-12 in this position.
3. Many vacancies—good news!
4. If you are a good candidate, you can negotiate the relocation, depending on your background, qualifications, and resume.
5. Memorize this for the interview and add some of these keywords to your resume.

problem solving, and achieve your professional goals appeals to you, then the Census Bureau is the place for you. Come join the Census Team and be responsible for contributing to the fabric of our nation - where everyone counts.

KEY REQUIREMENTS:

- You must be a U.S. citizen.
- You must apply on-line through USAJOBS. Please see How to Apply section.
- If your resume is incomplete, you may not be considered for this vacancy.
- Employment subject to completion of satisfactory investigation/clearance.
- Requested supplemental documents must be faxed to USAJOBS and received
- by the closing date. This requirement applies to ALL applicants.

Duties

6. **Additional Duty Location Info:**

few vacancies - Washington DC Metro Area (Suitland, Maryland) The incumbent of this position provides **professional accounting services** in the Assistant Division Chief for Financial Management and Reporting. Duties typically performed include the following: **analyzing and reconciling a variety of accounts and transactions**; **formulating** a variety of routine **financial reports** and implementing **fiscal year-end closing** procedures for specific funds; developing procedures to be used in the **design or modification of automated accounting systems**; **providing** advice to management of organizations serviced; assisting management in **applying financial data** and **recommending alternatives** to **resolve difficult problems**; adjusting **differences** between the general ledger and subsidiary accounts; and **analyzing financial and statistical data** from domestic and/or foreign business firms.

Qualifications and Evaluations

QUALIFICATIONS REQUIRED: ————————————————— **7.**

MINIMUM QUALIFICATION REQUIREMENTS: You must have the education and experience listed below.

Basic Entry Requirements:

A. Degree: accounting; **or** a degree in a related field such as business administration, finance, or public administration that included or was supplemented by 24 semester hours in accounting. The 24 hours may include up to 6 hours of credit in business law. (The term "accounting" means "accounting and/or auditing" in this standard. Similarly, "accountant" should be interpreted, generally,

(continued)

6. The keywords are in this section. Add them to your resume in the Outline Format.

7. You MUST have these qualifications to apply for this position.

(continued)

as "accountant and/or auditor.")

OR

B. Combination of education and experience - at least 4 years of experience in accounting, or an equivalent combination of accounting experience, college-level education, and training that provided professional accounting knowledge. The applicant's background must also include one of the following:

Twenty-four semester hours in accounting or auditing courses of appropriate type and quality. This can include up to 6 hours of business law; A certificate as Certified Public Accountant or a Certified Internal Auditor, obtained through written examination; or Completion of the requirements for a degree that included substantial course work in accounting or auditing, e.g., 15 semester hours, but that does not fully satisfy the 24-semester-hour requirement of paragraph A, provided that (a) the applicant has successfully worked at the full-performance level in accounting, auditing, or a related field, e.g., valuation engineering or financial institution examining; (b) a panel of at least two higher level professional accountants or auditors has determined that the applicant has demonstrated a good knowledge of accounting and of related and underlying fields that equals in breadth, depth, currency, and level of advancement that which is normally associated with successful completion of the 4-year course of study described in paragraph A; and (c) except for literal nonconformance to the requirement of 24 semester hours in accounting, the applicant's education, training, and experience fully meet the specified requirements.

In addition to the basic requirements:

FOR GS:07:

Experience:
You must have one year of specialized experience as an Accountant at the GS-05 level in the Federal service or one year of equivalent professional work experience examining accounting documents for the proper accounting classification and authorization. You entered and processed data into various accounts and the general ledger, performed reconciliations and analyzed a variety of accounts. You recognized and adjusted differences between the general ledger and subsidiary accounts, reviewed financial data for completeness and prepared monthly trial balances and financial reports. You were under the direct and continuing supervision of a higher-level employee who provided specific directions that covered all aspects of

the assignment. Your work was closely reviewed while in progress and when completed for accuracy and compliance with instructions.

OR

Education: One full year of graduate education or superior academic achievement (GPA of 2.95 or higher. You must submit a copy of your college transcripts. See the Required Documentation section for more information.

FOR GS-09:

Experience:
You have at least one year of specialized experience as an Accountant at the GS-07 level in the Federal service or one year of equivalent professional work experience that required a knowledge of accounting concepts and principles to perform a variety of technical accounting assignments. You examined accounting documents for the proper accounting classification and authorization. You entered and processed data into various accounts and the general ledger, performed reconciliations and analyzed a variety of accounts. You recognized and adjusted differences between the general ledger and subsidiary accounts, reviewed financial data for completeness and prepared monthly trial balances and financial reports. Your work was assigned by the supervisor or a higher level accountant who gave instructions and explanations with each assignment and provided guidance on work in progress. You independently carried out recurring work assignments. Completed work was reviewed for accuracy, adequacy, and compliance with instructions and procedures.

OR

Education: Master's or equivalent graduate degree or 2 full years of progressively higher-level graduate education leading to such a degree that provided you with the knowledge, skills, and abilities to perform the work of an accountant.

Applicants must meet all qualification requirements by the closing date of this announcement.

Qualification requirements in the vacancy announcements are based on the U.S. Office of Personnel Management Qualification (OPM) Standards Handbook, which contains federal qualification standards. This handbook is available on OPM's website at: http://www.opm.gov/qualifications.

(continued)

(continued)

One year probationary period is required.

HOW YOU WILL BE EVALUATED:

The Human Resource Division's review of applications is a three-step process.

1. All candidates are evaluated to determine if they meet the basic eligibility requirements (i.e., are a U.S. citizen, meet the "who may apply" description).

2. If you meet the basic eligibility requirements, your RESUME and TRANSCRIPTS, if applicable, are reviewed to determine if your experience and/or education meet the qualification requirements described in this announcement. If so, you are considered basically qualified for the position.

8.—3. Once you are determined basically qualified, the next step is a review of your answers to the experience, awards, education, and training and self-development questions. The answers to these questions determine which candidates are best qualified for the position and will be referred to the selecting official for consideration. The best-qualified candidates will then be identified, or ranked, for referral to the selecting official.

Your application will be evaluated based on your ability to demonstrate the following knowledge, skills, and ——————————————— **9.**
abilities/competencies (KSAs):

1. Knowledge and understanding of a variety of financial transactions in order to modify and correct information in the accounting systems.

2. Ability to set priorities, identify and recognize issues, problems, and/or opportunities to determine whether action is needed.

3. Knowledge of Federal accounting regulations, procedures and policies to interpret, analyze and carry out assignments.

4. Ability to interpret financial data and determine the appropriate course of action to ensure compliance with regulatory guidance.

10.—You do not need to respond separately to each KSA above. Your answers to the on-line experience questions will serve as responses to the KSAs.

---

8. After HR reviews for basic eligibility, it reviews the questionnaire answers to determine whether you are Best Qualified. Then you will be ranked and maybe referred to a selecting official.

9. KSAs for the job. These can go in the resume, but they will be covered in the questionnaire and you will write 4,000-character essays (see the questionnaire here in this chapter).

10. This statement says that you do not need to respond separately, but the questionnaire asks for 4,000-character essays.

11. — NOTE: If you are found to have rated yourself higher in the self-assessment than is supported by the information in your on-line resume, essay responses, and/or supporting documentation, your score may be lowered to reflect your documented experience.
To preview questions please <u>click here</u>. ——————————————————————**12.**

HOW TO APPLY:

Applications and supplemental documents MUST be received by 11:59 PM (EST) of the closing date.

Application under this announcement requires the applicant to complete and submit a specially designed USAJOBS application. The submission of anything other than the USAJOBS application will result in your application not being considered under this announcement. If, however, you do not have Internet access, please contact the human resources specialist listed on the announcement in order to receive information on alternative methods for applying to this vacancy.

If you do not create a resume in USAJOBS, or if the resume is incomplete, then your application will not be considered under this announcement.

13. — For experience questions that require a narrative response, please give a complete and detailed answer. Do not enter "Refer to Resume" or copy and paste your resume to explain your answer.

14. — Applicants who do not provide a complete and detailed answer to the questions requiring narrative responses will not receive credit for the question.

15. — You may be directed to provide specific documentation to verify information about your civil service status, your education, your CTAP/ICTAP eligibility, your veteran's preference and/or other information.

Individuals who have special priority selection rights under the Agency Career Transition Applications will not be accepted after the closing date. There is no grace period.

REQUIRED DOCUMENTS:
You may provide supplemental documents at any time during the open period of a vacancy announcement. Please follow the instructions provided in the Documents section of the application process for uploading electronic documents and/or for faxing documents.

Veteran Information:
For information on Veterans' Preference please review the Vet Guide at
http://www.opm.gov/employ/veterans/html/vetsinfo.asp.

(continued)

11. Your resume has to match the answers in the questionnaire.
12. If you click on that link, you can view the questions before you actually apply for the position.
13. The essay narratives in the questionnaire are best written with examples from your work history or college courses/projects and papers.
14. The essays in the questionnaire are mandatory.
15. Get your documents ready ahead of time! They are critical.

(continued)

To receive **5-point veteran's preference**, you must submit a copy of your DD-214 (stating Disposition of Discharge or Character of Service) by the closing date of this vacancy announcement.

To receive **10-point veteran's preference** for a service-connected disability you must submit an SF-15, "Application for 10-Point Veteran Preference" (revised December 2004 or later), documentary proof from the appropriate branch of the Armed Forces or the Department of Veterans Affairs, and a copy of your DD-214 (stating Disposition of Discharge or Character of Service) by the closing date of this vacancy announcement.

Applicants on **active duty** claiming either 5-point or 10-point preference must show on their application that they have met the requirements for preference and submit appropriate proof and documentation at time of appointment.

If selected for this vacancy, you will be required to complete a Declaration for Federal Employment (OF-306) to determine your suitability for federal employment and to authorize a background investigation. You will be required to sign and certify the accuracy of all the information in your application. If you make a false statement in any part of your application, you may not be hired; or you may be fired after you begin work; or you may be fined or jailed.

ARE YOU USING YOUR EDUCATION TO QUALIFY? You MUST provide transcripts or other documentation to support your educational claims. Unless otherwise stated: (1) unofficial transcripts are acceptable, or (2) you may submit a list with all of your courses, grades, semester, year, and credit for the course. All materials must be submitted by the closing date of the announcement.

AGENCY CONTACT INFO:

Delegated Examining Unit
Phone: 301-763-3705
Fax: 000-000-0000
Email: deborah.l.proctor@census.gov

Agency Information:
63 Bureau of the Census
4600 Silver Hill Road
Room 2K038
Washington, DC 20233
Fax: 000-000-0000

16.— WHAT TO EXPECT NEXT:
Applicants will receive notice that their application has been received. Applicants can check the status of their application by accessing the USAJOBS, Applicant Site at http://usajobs.opm.gov and clicking "My USAJOBS". You will need to login and then click on "Track your online job application."

16. You can check the status of your application.

This is the Bureau of the Census questionnaire. You will need to self-assess your skills for this position.

Vacancy Questions Preview

Department of Commerce

Grade: 07

1. In addition to meeting the basic entry requirements, do you have one year of specialized experience equivalent to at least GS-5, or one year of related graduate level education, superior academic achievement, or a combination of both experience and education? (See the "Qualifications" section of the announcement for the definition of specialized experience).

    1. Yes

    2. No

Grade: 09

1. In addition to meeting the basic entry requirements, do you have one year of specialized experience equivalent to at least GS-7, or two years of progressively higher level graduate education leading to a master's degree or master's or equivalent graduate degree or a combination of education and experience? (See the "Qualifications" section of the announcement for the definition of specialized experience).

    1. Yes

    2. No

Grade: All Grades

You MUST have a complete resume entered into USAJOBs in order to be considered for this position.

You must respond to all essay questions. If you do not have experience in the subject, please indicate "N/A" in the block provided. "See my resume" is not an acceptable answer, nor is copying information directly from your resume.

I certify that I have read the "Who May Be Considered" AND the "Job Summary" sections of this vacancy announcement and I understand that if I am a previous or current Federal competitive employee (includes most Census employees) looking for a transfer, promotion, reassignment, or reinstatement, this vacancy may not afford me the best advantage. I understand my option to consult with the HR office listed on the vacancy if I have any questions.

* 1. Have you completed at least 24 semester hours in accounting courses? (may include up to 6 credits in Business Law)

    1. Yes

    2. No

(continued)

(continued)

* 2. Do you have experience interpreting legislative policies and procedures to ensure compliance with accounting requirements?

    1. Yes

    2. No

* 3. Please provide examples and describe your experience supporting your response to the previous question.
Maximum length of 4000 characters.

* 4. Which of the following software applications do you frequently use in your work?

    1. Microsoft Word

    2. Lotus 1-2-3

    3. WordPerfect

    4. Microsoft Excel

    5. Microsoft Access

    6. Microsoft PowerPoint

    7. Adobe Photoshop

    8. Quark Express

    9. Freehand Illustrated

    10. Dreamweaver

    11. Microsoft FrontPage

    12. Macromedia Flash

    13. None of the above

* 5. Describe your experience collaborating and/or coordinating with external organizations in order to accomplish organizational goals.

    1. As the head of an organizational unit, I have coordinated or collaborated with organization heads outside my agency or company regarding policy issues in order to accomplish organizational goals.

    2. I have been given authority to represent my organizational unit to representatives from outside my agency or company regarding policy issues in order to accomplish organizational goals.

    3. I regularly coordinate or collaborate with business interests outside my agency or company regarding common issues.

    4. I have little experience collaborating or coordinating with interests outside my agency or company.

    5. None of the above

* 6. Do you have experience devising ways to improve work unit performance?

    1. Yes

    2. No

* 7. Do you have experience applying independent judgment during times when specific and detailed instructions were not provided?

    1. Yes

    2. No

* 8. Please provide examples and describe your experience supporting your response to the previous question.
Maximum length of 4000 characters.

* 9. Do you have experience conducting research to verify or resolve inconsistencies in vendor and customer information?

    1. Yes

    2. No

* 10. Please provide examples and describe your experience supporting your response to the previous question.
Maximum length of 4000 characters.

* 11. I have experience researching, analyzing, reconciling and preparing financial accounting data for external financial reporting purposes.

    1. True

    2. False

* 12. Please provide examples and describe your experience supporting your response to the previous question.
Maximum length of 4000 characters.

* 13. Do you have experience identifying and resolving database performance problems in an Oracle environment?

    1. Yes

    2. No

* 14. Please provide examples and describe your experience supporting your response to the previous question.
Maximum length of 4000 characters.

SBA Announcement: USAJOBS and Applicationmanager.gov Occupational Questionnaire with 67 Questions That Support the Knowledge, Skills, and Abilities

This SBA announcement is open 12 days. You can apply to both GS-12 and GS-13 levels. This IT announcement requires that both technical skills and competencies be covered in the federal resume.

U.S. Small Business Administration

Job Title: Information Technology Specialist, GS-2210-12/13
Agency: Small Business Administration
Job Announcement Number: 10D-339-DB

SALARY RANGE:	$73,848.00 - $114,158.00 /year	**1.**
OPEN PERIOD:	Thursday, October 28, 2010 to Wednesday, November 10, 2010	
SERIES & GRADE:	GS-2210-12/13	**2.**
POSITION INFORMATION:	Full Time Career/Career Conditional	
PROMOTION POTENTIAL:	13	**3.**
DUTY LOCATIONS:	1 vacancy - Denver, CO	
WHO MAY BE CONSIDERED:	US Citizens and Status Candidates	**4.**

JOB SUMMARY:

5. Become a part of an Agency that touches the lives of every American! We are the U.S. Small Business Administration (SBA) and for over 50 years, we have successfully served the Nation's small business owners. Consider a career with SBA to help manage the credit and contracts for America's small business during this new era of economic responsibility. We recognize that small business is critical to our economic recovery and strength, to building America's future, and to helping the United States compete in today's global marketplace. We represent a highly skilled and motivated workforce and welcome those interested in furthering our mission.

6. This position is located at the Small Business Administration, Office of the Chief Financial Officer, Office of Financial Systems, Denver Branch, which is located in Denver, CO. This position is ideal for a new to experienced, mid-career professional seeking enhanced professional development, a teamwork environment and recognition for excellent performance. The SBA offers generous federal government health benefits, flexible work schedules and leave, and promotes work-life balance. This position is in the Office of Financial Systems.

KEY REQUIREMENTS:
- You must successfully complete a background investigation and credit check.
- You must be a U.S. Citizen to apply for this position.

7. **Duties.**

1 vacancy - Denver, CO

As an information Technology Specialist you will serve as an <u>expert on automated data processing systems</u> operated and/or developed and maintained by the OFS in support of the <u>Agency's Financial Management and Procurement</u> activities. Specifically, you wil<u>l install, maintain, patch and manage all OCFO Denver servers</u>, including <u>Windows servers</u> for Cold Fusion, Sybase, File Servers, Oracle, and other servers as necessary in support of all OCFO functions, including <u>loan accounting, procurement, and administrative accounting</u>; Install, maintain, patch, configure and manage all aspects of the OCFO SAN

---

1. You can start your position and negotiate the salary anywhere in this range based on your experience/resume.

2. You can apply for both GS-12 and GS-13.

3. If you want to get promoted to a GS-14, you will have to look for a new position.

4. Open to current federal employees, veterans, other Status Candidates, and all U.S. citizens.

5. This is critical information for the interview. Memorize this and expect an interview question about the mission.

If you have background with small businesses, be sure to use the term "small business."

6. If you have a background in financial systems, this could help you get Best Qualified because you have specialized experience in financial systems.

7. The keywords that you should be sure to include in your federal resume in the Outline Format are underlined. You should add project examples that could feature your experience in automated data-processing systems, especially for financial and procurement activities.

environment, including <u>storage arrays, drive cages, fiber switches, and other ancillary hardware and</u> software; Serve as <u>OCFO lead on disaster recovery efforts</u>, including documentation and testing; Support agency <u>data communications network</u>, including <u>switches</u>, <u>transceivers</u> and other hardware as necessary; <u>Provide end user support</u> in all aspects of desktop management; and provide <u>help desk support</u> for a wide variety of issues, including <u>financial and procurement operations.</u>

QUALIFICATIONS REQUIRED:

8. For all positions individuals must have IT-related experience demonstrating each of the four competencies listed below. The employing agency is responsible for identifying the specific level of proficiency required for each competency at each grade level based on the requirements of the position being filled.

1. **Attention to Detail** - Is thorough when performing work and conscientious about attending to detail.
2. **Customer Service** - Works with clients and customers (that is, any individuals who use or receive the services or products that your work unit produces, including the general public, individuals who work in the agency, other agencies, or organizations outside the Government) to assess their needs, provide information or assistance, resolve their problems, or satisfy their expectations; knows about available products and services; is committed to providing quality products and services.
3. **Oral Communication** - Expresses information (for example, ideas or facts) to individuals or groups effectively, taking into account the audience and nature of the information (for example, technical, sensitive, controversial); makes clear and convincing oral presentations; listens to others, attends to nonverbal cues, and responds appropriately.
4. **Problem Solving** - Identifies problems; determines accuracy and relevance of information; uses sound judgment to generate and evaluate alternatives, and to make recommendations.

AND

9. **GS-12:** One year specialized experience equivalent to the GS-11 grade level in the federal service performing duties such as <u>server management, SAN management, end-user support, vulnerability</u> <u>mitigation, data communications and disaster recovery.</u>

GS-13: One year specialized experience equivalent to the GS-12 grade level in the Federal service performing duties in server management, implementing back up strategies for multiple servers, SAN management, end-user support, <u>vulnerability mitigation, data communications, disaster recovery and</u> <u>addressing software and hardware issues.</u>

Education may not be substituted for experience for this position.

HOW YOU WILL BE EVALUATED:

We will review your résumé and/or transcripts(s) to ensure you meet the basic qualification requirements. Applicants meeting basic qualification requirements will further be evaluated on the information provided in the *Supplemental Questionnaire.*

10. To preview this questionnaire, click on the following link <u>View Assessment Questions</u>. You will receive a numeric rating based on your responses to the questionnaire. The score is a measure of the degree to which your background matches the knowledge, skills and abilities required of this position.

(continued)

8. In addition to the technical IT skills that are described in the Duties section, make sure these competencies are reflected in your accomplishments/ projects or duties statements. All of these are important to help you get Best Qualified…in addition to your technical skills in automated data processing in finance and procurement.

9. If you are applying for both grades, cover both sets of specialized experience. Be sure to feature the position in your federal resume that best demonstrates this one year of specialized experience.

10. Preview the questionnaire, print it, and be sure to give yourself all the credit that you can with the questionnaire answers. Then be sure to match your resume to your answers. The HR specialist will review the resume against this questionnaire.

(continued)

If, after reviewing your resume and or supporting documentation, a determination is made that you have inflated your qualifications and or experience your score can and will be adjusted to more accurately reflect your abilities.

11. RELOCATION EXPENSES WILL NOT BE PAID.

HOW TO APPLY:

12. To apply for this position, you must provide a complete Application Package which includes:
1. Your Résumé (your resume must contain the basic information outlined in the Optional Application for Federal Employment OF-612: http://www.opm.gov/forms/pdf_fill/of612.pdf).

13.
2. A complete Occupational Questionnaire
3. Additional Required Documents (see Required Documents section below)
The complete Application Package must be submitted by 11:59 PM (EST) on Wednesday, November 10, 2010.
To begin the process, click the **Apply Online** button to create an account or log in to your existing USAJOBS account. Follow the prompts to complete the occupational questionnaire. Please ensure you click the **Submit My Answers** button at the end of the process.

14.

15. **AGENCY CONTACT INFO:**

Dianna L. Burrell
Phone: (303)844-7791
Email: DENVERHR-DB@SBA.GOV

Agency Information:
Small Business Administration Denver
Office of Human Capital Management
721 19th Street Room 392
Denver, CO 80202
ANNOUCEMENT #_____

WHAT TO EXPECT NEXT:

16. Once the online questionnaire is received, you will receive an acknowledgement email that your submission was successful. After a review of your complete application is made you will be notified of your rating and or referral to the hiring official. If further evaluation or interviews are required you will be contacted. We expect to make a job offer within 40 days of the closing date of this announcement. You will be notified through Application Manager of the outcome.

11. Maybe you can negotiate the cost of relocation when you discuss the step within the grade that you are offered.

12. This is the traditional way most of the USAJOBS vacancy announcements will be posted: USAJOBS federal resume, occupational questionnaire, uploading documents, and submitting by 11:59 p.m. ET.

13. We don't recommend using the OF-612. If you do fill out the OF-612, maybe you can upload it into USAJOBS. But the USAJOBS resume builder will be easier to use.

14. Some people are missing the Submit My Answers button. So look for it and submit when you are finished.

15. If you have questions, you can call Dianna Burrell or write to her at this e-mail address. SBA Human Capital Management is very customer service oriented.

16. This is a new section created by the Federal Hiring Reform (Executive Order by President Obama, May 11, 2010) to be more informative about your federal application and also to make a job offer within 40 days of the closing date. I hope this can really happen. Be sure to check your applicationmanager.com tracking page to find out the step-by-step results of your application. This is exciting!

This is the questionnaire for the preceding announcement. You will need to self-assess your skill areas for the SBA position.

67 Multiple-Choice Occupational / Assessment Questions: Information Technology Specialist, GS-2210-12/13

Vacancy ID: AP400391
Announcement Number: 10D-339-DB
USAJOBS Control Number: 2077286

Occupational/Assessment Questions:

1. Select the one statement below that best describes your experience to meet the basic requirements for this position at the GS-12 level.

   A. I have at least one year of specialized experience equivalent to the GS-11 grade level in the federal service in server management, SAN management, end user-support, vulnerability mitigation, data communications, and disaster recovery.

   B. I do not have the specialized experience listed above.

2. Select the one statement below that best describes your experience to meet the basic requirements for this position at the GS-13 level.

   A. I have at least one year of specialized experience equivalent to the GS-12 grade level in the federal service in server management, implementation of back up strategies for multiple servers, SAN management, end user-support, vulnerability mitigation, data communications, disaster recovery and addressing hardware and software issues.

   B. I do not have the specialized experience listed above.

From the following items, choose the ONE statement from the list below that best describes your experience and/or training. Please select only one letter for each item.

   A. I have not had education, training or experience in performing this task.

   B. I have education or training in this task, but have not performed it on the job.

   C. I have performed this task on the job. My work on this task was monitored closely by a supervisor or senior employee.

   D. I have performed this task as a regular part of a job. I have performed it independently and normally without review by a supervisor or senior employee.

   E. I am considered an expert in performing this task. I have trained others and/or supervised this task or am normally the person consulted by others to assist them in doing this task.

3. Identify hardware and software performance gaps.

4. Recommend hardware and O/S configurations to meet performance and uptime requirements.

5. Design hardware and software solutions to meet business needs.

6. Integrate data communications into design configurations.

7. Install, rack, and cable servers in a rack dense environment.

8. Perform windows server 2003, 2008 and other O/S installations.

9. Perform O/S hardening and security configuration.

(continued)

(continued)

10. Create domain users

11. Create local users

12. Assign rights to groups and users

13. Implement O/S baseline configuration.

14. Perform installation and configuration of Cold Fusion.

15. Perform installation and configuration of Relational Databases

16. Implement NIC teaming

17. Configure DRAC cards for remote power/control.

18. Review security, application, and other relevant logs

19. Troubleshoot production issues

20. Coordinate automated reboots among various servers

21. Patch Servers

22. Develop programs using appropriate technologies to automate server management.

Skill in the design, implementation and support of a SAN environment

23. Perform requirements gathering and space usage analysis relating to SAN design.

24. Design SAN solutions appropriate for Database, Application server, and File and Print servers.

25. Configure Flare OS

26. Rack, cable, and connect SAN

27. Configure and Cable SAN hardware for maximum redundancy

28. Initialize SAN

29. Create disk pools

30. Manage disk pools

31. Assign disk pools to servers

32. Implement SAN specific DR techniques

33. Hot swap SAN hard drives

34. Hot swap SAN hardware (not hard drives)

35. Monitor SAN health

36. Patch SAN OS

Skill in design, implementation and management of disaster recovery (DR)

37. Develop and document DR plans relating to Cold Fusion

38. Develop and document DR plans relating to a relational databases

39. Test DR plans

40. Coordinate DR testing

41. Document result of DR test

42. Recommend corrective actions and improvements to DR strategy

Ability to mitigate a wide range of enterprise vulnerabilities

43. Interpret vulnerability scans and determine mitigation strategy

44. Mitigate POAM vulnerabilities

45. Mitigate foundstone or similar scanning tools vulnerabilities

46. Mitigate server vulnerabilities

47. Mitigate workstation vulnerabilities

48. Mitigate printer/print server vulnerabilities

49. Mitigate Network attached copier vulnerabilities

50. Mitigate switch vulnerabilities

Ability to provide end-user support to over 50 end users

51. Provide help desk support

52. Manage desktops from a centralized location

53. Develop scripts and programs to automate workstation management

54. Install software

55. Configure software

56. Remove software

57. Troubleshoot Windows XP problems

58. Troubleshoot Microsoft office problems

59. Troubleshoot application connectivity problems

60. Troubleshoot browser problems

Ability to communicate in writing

61. Create network diagrams using Visio

62. Write system documentation

63. Write Memorandums of Understanding (MOU) relating to data transfer

64. Write Interconnection Security Agreements (ISA) relating to data transfer

65. Lead requirements gathering sessions and translate into functional and technical requirements.

66. Write standard operating procedures, white papers, and technical documents.

67. Respond to internal and external information requests, auditor requests, etc.

Summary

Federal vacancy announcements are fairly long, but if you take your time and analyze critical sections, you can find the information you need to write the best possible federal resume for the position. The human resources specialists write detailed announcements to help you understand the job. You can use this information to your benefit. You can easily analyze the three announcements in this chapter by just carefully reviewing each duty, qualification, KSA, and question contained in the announcement. Take your time, focus, update your resume with keywords and skills, and you will stand a chance of being Best Qualified for your target position.

CHAPTER 13

USAJOBS and Other Federal Resume Builders

The first 12 chapters of this book were focused on writing great content in your federal resume. Now it's time to structure that great content into the resume builder for your agency.

This chapter is dedicated to giving you an overview of the resume builders you will find during your federal job search and application process. The good news is that once you have one good federal resume, you can use that resume for all of the resume builders—with some editing to fit the maximum character count of the builder headings/fields.

 Tip: Once you have your Outline Format federal resume written in your favorite software, you are ready to copy and paste it into any resume builder (with some editing and character counting).

The resume builder headings will help you analyze your resume sections and fit your content into the builders. You can count your characters using Microsoft Word. Highlight the content that you would like counted. Select Tools, Word Count from the menu. (In Word 2007, go to the Review tab and click the Word Count button.) You can count your characters with and without spaces.

These builder lists were designed to inform you that there is more than one resume builder and online application system. You will see that the federal agencies are using a variety of "how to apply" instructions, resume builder formats, character lengths, page lengths, and resume fields. You will be mixing and matching your resume sections into the resume builders. The important thing is to read the directions. The total application process beyond the resume builder might involve a resume, questionnaire, and faxing information to the HR office.

 Tip: Read the directions for the Profile, Resume Builder, Questions, Supplemental Data Sheet, Fax Information, and Submit sections. Make sure you hit APPLY or SUBMIT after you submit your resume and answer the questions.

Maximize Your Use of the Resume Builders

Even though the resume builders are inflexible in terms of organization of resume information (the old paper federal resumes were much more flexible), they are the door to the supervisor, and you should take time and effort to make your online resume look good. The samples in this book will show you techniques for improving content and readability of the words in your resume—even if the application is just a small field on a Web page.

Once you have your federal resume written, formatted like the samples in the book, and focused toward one or two occupational series, you are about 80 percent ready to apply for any job. The resume builder lists at the end of the chapter give an overview of the builders agencies are using today. This chart will be changing frequently, so don't be surprised if an agency has different instructions than published in this book.

If you count the characters of your Work Experience, Training, Awards, Additional Information, and other sections, you will be ready to edit slightly and copy and paste your content into the builders.

The USAJOBS Work Experience field is 3,000 characters. If your work experience description is 5,500 characters, and you can't bear to delete anything, you have two options: You can use two job blocks for Job 1 in USAJOBS or continue the information in Additional Information at the end of the USAJOBS resume builder. Either way, you should write at the end of the Duties section, "Continued in Additional Information" or "continued in Job Block 2." This way the human resources specialist and supervisor will know that there is a continuation of this Work Experience description.

 Tip: If you have more than 3,000 characters for your USAJOBS Work Experience section, you can continue in another job block or in the Additional Information section. Your most important work experience duties and KSA accomplishments should be written in the first 3,000 characters if possible.

The Most Popular Federal Resume Builders and Their Resume Headings

The most popular federal resume builders are listed in the following sections. We have collected the names of each of their resume sections and the number of characters that you can insert into each field. This is a handy guide for copying and pasting into many builders.

 Note: The Work Experience section is the most important section of your federal resume.

USAJOBS Resume Builder

USAJOBS is managed by Monster.com and is getting better all the time. The USAJOBS resume builder is almost mandatory for any federal job seeker. It's good to set up a My USAJOBS profile and submit a starter resume into the system. This way you can access questionnaires and further information easily.

The sections of the USAJOBS resume builder are the following:

1. Candidate Information.
2. Recent and Relevant Work Experience: You are allowed 3,000 characters per job block and can list an unlimited number of jobs. The optimum number of job listings is five to eight. The most important positions are within the last 10 years.
3. Education.
4. Relevant Coursework, Licensures, and Certifications: 2,000 characters.
5. Job Related Training: 2,000 characters.
6. References.
7. Additional Language Skills.
8. Affiliations.
9. Professional Publications: 2,000 characters.
10. Additional Information: Job-related honors, awards, leadership activities, skills (such as computer software proficiency or typing speed), or any other information requested by a specific job announcement, and work experience continuations. You are allowed 22,000 characters.
11. Availability: Be sure to check off all of your preferences.
12. Desired Locations.

 Tip: Remember that when you update your current resume in any of the Resumix builders, it will overlay the old resume on file. The only builder that allows more than one resume version is USAJOBS.

Avue Central

Avue Central (www.avuecentral.com) is owned and operated by Avue Digital Services. More than 25 federal agencies use the Avue system to collect resumes, assess candidates, and manage recruitment. If you set up an account and submit your resume into Avue Central's resume builder, you can apply for jobs with any of its customer agencies. Some of the agencies that use the Avue Digital Services include Peace Corps, USAID, U.S. Marshals Service, Millennium Challenge Corporation, U.S. Forest Service, Department of Justice, and Office of Justice Management. For these agencies you will actually submit your resume and apply for positions at this website. You can still find announcements for these jobs at USAJOBS, but then USAJOBS will take you to www.avuecentral.com

to submit your resume and documents, apply for the position, and complete the questionnaire. One of the best features of Avue Central's announcements is the position description that is also developed for the job.

Following are the headings for the Avue Central resume builder:

1. Personal Information.
2. Applicant Information.
3. Work History: 4,000 characters.
4. Eligibilities.
5. References.
6. Educational Background.
7. Relevant Information.
8. Awards, Community Service, Training, Certifications, Collateral Duties, Significant Details.
9. Other Considerations: Military details.
10. Additional Information: No maximum character space is indicated.
11. Supporting Documentation: You can add files by browsing and uploading.
12. "Prepare a hard copy of my resume:" This resume format is great!

Resumix

Resumix™ is owned by Monster.com and is the only system where the HR specialist and supervisor search for the Best Qualified candidates with a set of keywords and skills for the position. This system is a keyword system, and you should carefully study the language in your resume to make sure you have included the correct keywords (see Chapter 6 for more on keywords).

We describe the headings and characters for three Resumix builders in the following sections. These are the three largest DOD hiring agencies.

CPOL Resume Builder Headings

You can access the CPOL builder at www.cpol.army.mil. Headings for the builder are the following:

1. Contact Information.
2. Work Experience: 12,000 characters for all jobs.
3. Education: 2,000 characters for all education entries.
4. Additional Information (training, licenses, certifications, performance appraisals/ratings, awards, and so on): 6,000 characters for all information.
5. "Click here for worksheets:" You can click for worksheets, or simply copy and paste your content into the three fields above (which is much easier). If you do not use the worksheets, be sure that you include the right information for each position.

CHART Resume Builder Headings

You can access the CHART builder at https://chart.donhr.navy.mil/. (You will see a warning and will have to accept the Security Certificate.) Headings for this builder are the following:

1. Contact Information
2. Eligibility
3. Education
4. Work History: 7,500 characters
5. Other Work-Related History: Training, Licenses, and Certificates
6. Performance Ratings, Awards, Honors, and Recognitions: 1,500 characters
7. Other Information: 7,000 characters
8. U.S. Military Service
9. Additional Data Sheet

Summary of Resume Builder Headings

As you can see from the preceding heading listings, the builders are similar but not the same. We have reviewed four resume builders, but there are many more. When applying for jobs on USAJOBS, you will simply go to the Apply Now button and follow the directions.

Table 12.1 shows the various resume builders.

Table 12.1: Federal Resume Builder Chart

Name of Agency Builder	Agency Jobs Website	Recruitment Name	Job-Specific Assessment Questions?	Essays?
Agriculture	www.usda.gov/da/employ/director.htm	USAJOBS/Application Manager	Yes	Yes
Air Force	www.usajobs.gov	USAJOBS/Application Manager	No	KSAs in the res.
Army Civilian Personnel	www.cpol.army.mil	CPOL/Resumix	No	No
Avue Central	www.avuecentral.com	Avue	Yes	Yes
Bureau of Land Management	www.blm.gov/jobs/	USAJOBS	Yes	Yes
Central Intelligence Agency	www.cia.gov https://www.cia.gov/careers/index.html	CIA Builder	No	No
Citizenship	www.uscis.gov/	USAJOBS	Yes	Yes
Commerce	www.usajobs.gov	USAJOBS/Monster	Yes	Yes
Customs & Border Protection	http://www.cbp.gov/xp/cgov/careers/	USAJOBS/Application Manager	Yes	Yes
Defense Contract Management Agency	www.dcma.mil	Army Resumix	No	No
Defense Finance & Accounting Office	www.dod.mil/dfas/careers.html	USAJOBS/Application Manager	No	No
Defense Logistics Agency	www.dla.mil	USAJOBS/Application Manager	No	No
Environmental Protection Agency	www.epa.gov/ezhire/	USAJOBS/Monster	Yes	Yes

Name of Agency Builder	Agency Jobs Website	Recruitment Name	Job-Specific Assessment Questions?	Essays?
FAA	http://www.faa.gov/jobs/	ASAP	Yes	Yes
FBI	www.fbijobs.gov	FBIJOBS, QuickHire	Yes	Yes
FEMA	www.fema.gov/career	USAJOBS/Application Manager	No	Yes
Forest Service	http://www.fs.fed.us/fsjobs/	USAJOBS/Application Manager	Yes	
General Accountability Office	http://www.gao.gov/careers/index.html	GAO Careers/QuickHire	Yes	Yes
General Services Administration	www.gsa.gov (GSA Jobs link on right)	GSA Jobs/QuickHire	Yes	Yes
HHS Careers at Rockville	https://jobs.quickhire.com/scripts/hhs-rhrc.exe	USAJOBS/Application Manager	Yes	Yes
Homeland Security	www.dhs.gov/xabout/careers/	USAJOBS/Application Manager	Yes	Yes
Housing and Urban Development	www.hud.gov/jobs/index.cfm	USAJOBS/Application Manager	No	Yes
Interior	http://www.doi.gov/employees/index.cfm	USAJOBS/Application Manager	Yes	Yes
Justice	www.doj.gov	Avue Central	Yes	Yes

(continued)

(continued)

Name of Agency Builder	Agency Jobs Website	Recruitment Name	Job-Specific Assessment Questions?	Essays?
National Aeronautics and Space Administration	www.nasajobs.nasa.gov/	USAJOBS/Application Manager	Yes	Yes
Navy CHART	https://www.donhr.navy.mil/	Navy CHART/Resumix	No	No
Office of Secretary of Defense	http://www.defense.gov/osd/	USAJOBS/Application Manager	No	No
Peace Corps	www.avuecentral.com	Avue Central	Yes	Yes
Small Business Administration	www.sba.gov	USAJOBS/Application Manager	No	No
State Department	http://careers.state.gov/	USAJOBS/Gateway to State	Yes	Yes
Transportation	http://careers.dot.gov/	USAJOBS/Monster	Yes	Yes
Transportation Security Agency	http://www.tsa.gov/join/careers/careers_security_jobs.shtm	USAJOBS/Monster	No	Yes
U.S. Marshals Service	www.avuecentral.com	Avue Central	Yes	Yes
Veterans Administration	www.va.gov	USAJOBS/Application Manager	KSAs	Yes

Disclaimer: Research for this spreadsheet was completed on December 2, 2010. Please know that resume builders, website addresses, methods of collecting resumes, and other information may change from week to week.

Summary

If you write your resume in Word, save it, date it, and count the characters, you will be ready to copy and paste it into federal resume builders and apply for federal jobs. Remember that there usually are two, three, or four steps to actually applying for the job: creating your profile, submitting your resume, answering questions, and faxing other information. Be sure to follow the directions. After the resume is in the resume builder, you can keep reading and find the Occupational Questions or other instructions. And at the end, don't forget to actually click the button to apply, submit, or self-nominate for your job!

Part 5

Special Insight for Targeting Occupational Series

Science, Medicine, and Health Policy: Converting a Curriculum Vitae to a Federal Resume

By David Raikow, Ph.D.

This chapter compares the Curriculum Vitae (CV) and the federal resume. Then it gives step-by-step instructions for converting your CV to a CV/federal resume hybrid. Then it gives other hints for crafting your new resume and shows an example.

CVs Are Different

Scientists and graduate students are very familiar with the curriculum vitae (CV), the standard resume type for academic job applications. CVs are meant to catalog the sum total of your experience, and so differ substantially from business resumes. Whereas business resumes are usually limited to two pages and are highly focused or tailored to a job ad, CVs have no length limit and are generic. Business resumes are meant to be quickly scanned, whereas CVs are meant to be studied. Both the format and actual information presented in a business resume vary widely. CVs in general have standard sections, some of which are discipline-specific.

As a scientist or graduate student, you should already have a CV. Indeed, it's a good idea to update your CV every time you do something new such as publish, get a grant, or present a paper at a meeting. Some things like your publications never leave your CV. As you advance professionally, other things like the committees you served on as a graduate student are too old or no longer relevant to include on your CV. Even then, it's a good idea to save those deleted items in a separate file because you never know when you'll need to remind yourself of what you have done in the past. Building a CV is a continual process and should be taken seriously; that's why spending a few minutes to update it whenever necessary is important.

But in a difficult job market, savvy scientists and graduate students include all job market sectors in their searches. This means looking beyond the comfort zone of academia, be it "research-one" universities, community or small colleges, the private sector, nongovernment organizations, state and municipal governments, and crucially, the federal government. There are simply too many federal opportunities to ignore this sector. Yet there are major differences in the job application process between academia and the federal government that affect resumes even before you start to write.

Academia still uses standalone documents, such as actual Word or PDFs files that are typically e-mailed or uploaded. The federal job application process, in contrast, is now almost entirely online. Use by federal agencies of online application systems, chiefly USAJOBS, means that the most common federal resume you will use consists of information entered into web-form boxes. You still need a standalone document, however, because some federal postdoctoral programs call for CVs by name to be e-mailed. Agencies can do this by putting postdoctoral fellows in the Excepted Service, which allows nonstandard selection procedures. The Excepted Service is different from the Competitive Service. Excepted Service positions are not always posted on USAJOBS and individuals can be hired in a streamlined hiring process. Usually Excepted Service individuals have highly specialized skills and education for unique government missions.

Scientific federal resumes are different still from other federal resumes because common practices in science are not present in other careers. All federal scientists started in academia in order to obtain advanced degrees. As such, all federal scientists are familiar with CVs, just like you. In fact, some permanent scientific jobs, term positions, and postdocs in the federal government are evaluated as academic jobs are, complete with giving a seminar, meeting the primary investigators of a lab, interviews, and comments concerning applicants solicited from the scientific staff. Such a gauntlet usually follows evaluation and ranking by HR personnel, of course.

Such rigorous interviews are allowable because many of these jobs are in the Excepted Service. Jobs like postdocs in the Excepted Service have simple procedures, such as submitting a CV and cover letter. Selecting officials are usually the scientists you will be working with, and hence are not expecting you to limit your resume to five pages or so. Indeed, for those with more experience, limiting your resume to five pages will be detrimental to your application. But don't feel overwhelmed by the need to have a standalone CV, a standalone federal resume, and a USAJOBS federal resume, because scientists can bend the rules.

Hybrid CV/Federal Resumes

The solution is to start with the CV you have, create a standalone hybrid CV/federal resume, and use that to populate web-form boxes on USAJOBS. A hybrid document allows you more freedom than a generic federal resume, and can be used for federal job applications. With some simple edits, it can also be used for academic job applications. Hybrids look like federal resumes in that they have a summarizing first page (see Chapter 5, "Education, Job Related Training, and Additional Information").

Hybrids also have detailed descriptions of job duties and roles, and contain all the sections a generic federal resume would. But hybrids also contain any nonrepetitive section you would normally include in a CV, and can be as long as you like. It is still vital, however, that you include all required compliance information and make other information easy to glean.

Creating the CV/Federal Resume Hybrid

CVs have standard sections, including contact information and affiliation, education, professional experience, publications, and so on. Some of these sections can go by different names. Whether you use a section labeled Professional Activities or Academic Service; Teaching Experience or Courses Taught; Grants, Grants and Funding, Selected Grants, or Competitive Grants is not important here. You might even have sections that are not discussed here or sections that are particular to your field of study. Just match the sections discussed here with your own and follow the examples for sections with similar kinds of information in lieu of an exact match.

Table 14.1 is a quick comparison among traditional CVs, a standalone CV/federal resume hybrid, and edits to the hybrid for academic applications.

Table 14.1: Traditional CV Compared to Federal Resume Hybrid

Traditional CV	CV/Federal Resume Hybrid	Edits to Hybrid for Academia
No length limit	✓	
Contact information and affiliation	✓ + compliance information	Delete compliance information
No	Objective	Delete
No	Detailed Profile statement	Research Interest Summary
Education	✓ + high school	Delete high school, add advisor and thesis
Certifications	✓	
Honors	✓	
Grants	✓	
Employment summary	No	Employment summary
No	Detailed duties & responsibilities	Move section to later pages
Research Experience	Incorporated into detailed duties	
Teaching Experience	✓	
Professional Activities/ Academic Service	✓	
Continuing Education	✓	
Extension and Outreach/ Community Service	✓	
Current/Professional Memberships	✓	

(continued)

(continued)

Traditional CV	CV/Federal Resume Hybrid	Edits to Hybrid for Academia
Contributed Papers/ Presentations at Meetings	✓	
Collaborators	✓	
Students advised	✓	
References	✓	
Scientific Publications	✓	
Book reviews/other publications	✓	
Skill lists by class	No	

The First Page

The first page of this resume introduces the important credentials of the candidate, including education, certification, and a profile of expertise that relates to the position.

Contact Information and Affiliation

Use your name, affiliation, and contact information as you would on a CV, but add "compliance" information: citizenship, Social Security number, Veterans' Preference, and federal civilian status.

Objective

State the position for which you are applying, including title and job application reference number, just below your contact information. This is not a statement of goals, as you might include in a business resume.

Profile Statement

Include a Profile statement just below your objective. Define yourself based on the professional roles you've played. (See Chapter 3, "Work Experience and the Outline Format: How to Stand Out and Get Referred.") State what kind of scientist you are; in other words, your fields of expertise and the kind of experience you have. This is your first opportunity to include keywords from the announcement (see Chapter 6, "Keywords for Federal Jobs").

Here are two examples of a profile statement. In Figure 14.1, a recent graduate seeking a GS-11 position features specialized expertise: Environmental Scientist, Reviewer, Public Speaker, and Computer Skills. The second example, Figure 14.2, is a summary of a GS-11 seeking a GS-12 position featuring more technical scientific titles. You can see further progression, GS-12 seeking GS-13, in the sample resume.

SUMMARY OF QUALIFICATIONS

- **Environmental scientist:** Experience in a variety of ecosystems conducting and evaluating scientific studies in ecology and environmental science; experimental design, field sampling, laboratory analysis, and data exploration using advanced statistics including multivariate analyses; writing grant proposals, protocols, and status reports; and publishing results in scientific journals.

- **Reviewer:** Experience in evaluating the application of scientific principles, editing, critiquing, and recommending rejection, revision, or publication of manuscripts submitted to scientific journals; writing book reviews.

- **Public speaker:** Experience in presenting complex scientific concepts to scientists, students, laypeople, congressional delegates, and the media.

- **Expert:** Full suite of computer word processing, data management, chart/graph/image manipulation, and presentation creation skills.

Figure 14.1: Profile statement for recent graduate seeking a GS-11 position.

PROFILE

Federal Research Aquatic Biologist: Systems-thinking ESA Certified Ecologist; stream ecology, limnology, aquatic ecology landscape ecology, ecosystem ecology, community ecology, invasion biology, food webs, biogeochemistry, ecotoxicology.

Scientific Primary Investigator (PI): Develop, initiate, and lead biological research programs; write grant proposals to support research programs; create new methodologies; adapt existing methodologies to test new hypotheses; hire and supervise support staff, implement QA/QC measures; manage and explore data using spreadsheets, databases; statistically analyze data using standard, multivariate, and geospatial statistics; publish results in peer-reviewed primary scientific journals; present results at conferences.

Agency Representative: Represent NOAA, GLERL, and the NOAA National Center for Research on Aquatic Invasive Species at scientific and regulatory workshops, meetings, and conferences; confer and build new relationships with other agencies and organizations; critique scientific merit of proposed federal regulations.

Writer and Speaker: Write budgets, protocols, status reports, book reviews, book proposals, book chapters, and books; critique scientific manuscripts; critique grant proposals; present complex scientific concepts to scientists, students, untrained audiences, congressional delegates, and the media; teach students; create and present seminars and workshops for laypeople.

Figure 14.2: Summary for a GS-11 candidate seeking a GS-12 position.

Education

List your degrees, majors, and school name as you would on a CV, but add your high school, cities, states, and ZIP codes.

Certifications

List your certifications as you would on a CV.

Later Sections That Should Be Just Like a CV

These sections are the same as a regular CV: Honors, Grants, Current Memberships in Societies or Professional Organizations, List of Selected Collaborators, Students Advised or Mentored, Scientific or Peer-Reviewed Publications, Book Reviews/Non-Scientific/Non-Peer-Reviewed Publications, Conference Presentations, Other Presentations.

Modified Sections

Since the scientist holds several types of professional positions, including employment, teaching, and research, it's helpful to the human resources specialist and the supervisor to separate the types of positions into categories.

Employment

A traditional CV will have simple reverse-chronological listings of your positions, and academicians expect to see this on the first page. But in a federal resume or hybrid, the first page does not have this list. Instead, your positions with details of your duties should be large sections in themselves— for example, one entire page for a single professional position starting on page two. This is where you must add keywords or phrases from the job announcement.

You shouldn't need to embellish here; after all, you should be applying for jobs for which you have relevant experience. You will, however, need to phrase your descriptions so that the human resources personnel who are grading your application can see that you are indeed qualified. (See Chapter 3 for more on writing work experience descriptions.) Working on expanding job duties can also help to identify roles you've played during your career that can be summarized in the Profile section. You should include phrases like "write and obtain grants," even though the actual grants are listed in their own section.

If you're a graduate student or a recent graduate, delete the Employment section and highlight your experience under the Project Descriptions section. When editing your hybrid for academia, restore the position list on the first page, and then move down the detailed duties and responsibilities section to somewhere else in the document. Often page two of a traditional CV starts with your publications.

Research Experience

It can be useful to organize your scientific or technical experience in terms of the major projects you have undertaken. Many scientists early in their careers do this in their CVs. In federal resumes, project experience descriptions can substitute for a series of specific jobs or job titles that you don't have. The concept is the same as describing previous jobs. You need to name the project, state where you conducted it, state when you conducted it, state the number of hours a week you spent on it, and describe what you did. (See Chapter 3, "Work Experience and the Outline Format.") You might also have other relevant experience, such as a college internship, which could have its own separate section and short description.

Teaching Experience

Teaching experience can be its own section, but you can incorporate teaching experience into your skill lists or duties and responsibilities if your experience is not extensive (see "Skill Lists"). Just be careful not to bury it if it is specifically listed in the vacancy announcement.

Professional Activities or Service

Professional activities can be incorporated into skill lists or job descriptions. However, if you have a lot of experience here, you can use a section much like a CV. If the advertised position is administrative, you can include a specific Administrative Skill List (see "Skill Lists").

Continuing Education

Continuing education classes or training should be its own section to highlight your continuing commitment to professional growth and staying on top of new developments.

Extension and Outreach

If you have a lot of experience in this area, create a separate section.

References

Some people include a list of references in their CVs. Employers usually ask for lists of references separate from the resume. This is often the case for government positions, but you can include a list of professional references.

Other Hints for Crafting Your Federal Resume

There are a few other considerations to keep in mind as you convert your CV into a federal resume. These include tailoring the writing to your audience and compensating for a lack of formal experience outside of college.

Skill Lists

As a scientist, you have amassed many skills. Chances are, though, you've never had to actually think about it and list them all. Listing your skills can take some time, but it is extremely important in the federal resume. These skill lists can be presented in the federal resume as either individual top-level sections or subsections within a section labeled "Skills." Skill lists are very useful for graduate students and those who are at an early stage in their career.

I recommend grouping your skills into classes that are relevant to your field of study and the job announcement. For example, you might have laboratory skills, field-data-collection skills, and computer skills. You might want to group together specific types of computer skills. It's up to you. The different skill sets you organize give you a chance to creatively customize your federal resume to yourself and the job announcement.

To figure out exactly what skills you have, I recommend walking through the steps of the various projects that you have done and cataloging the skills necessary to do each step. For example, an ecologist might have studied the ecosystem of a stream. In order to do this, she took water samples, measured temperature and other parameters, collected organisms, and brought them back to the lab for analysis. Later she compiled her data and analyzed it. What specific skills were necessary to do all this? She may have had to design the study and choose field sites. She had to collect water samples without contaminating them. She had to run specific chemical tests in the lab. She had to know how to collect specific organisms, handle them, identify them, and preserve them. She had to manage her data in spreadsheets or databases and then analyze them statistically. The skill set derived from this project and listed on the federal resume will be specific and lengthy, and perhaps will contain discipline-specific terminology (more on jargon in the next section).

Be careful not to lump different skills under general titles. For example, "microscopy" is too vague. Instead, do you know how to prepare samples for microscopy, operate specific types of microscopes, identify microscopic organisms or tissues, or all of these things? If so, create a clear, technical list of those skills as in Figure 14.3.

Selected Field and Laboratory Skills
- Measure physical ecosystem parameters of streams, lakes, and wetlands.
- Sample water, organic matter, suspended sediment, sediment cores, sediment traps.
- Conduct in-situ tracer additions in aquatic ecosystems.
- Collect and analyze stable isotopes.
- Collect fish, benthic macroinvertebrates, mussels, zooplankton, periphyton, and phytoplankton.
- Identify benthic macroinvertebrates, mussels, zooplankton, and phytoplankton.
- Analyze chlorophyll, dissolved and particulate carbon, nitrogen, and phosphorus nutrient species.
- Use HPLC, GC, IC, CHN Analyzer, Spectrophotometer, and Mass Spectrometer.
- Prepare samples for microscopy and use compound, dissecting, and inverted microscopes.

Figure 14.3: List of skills.

Remember, skill lists could be separate sections for a grad, incorporated into a job description for an early career scientist, or removed from the document of a more advanced scientist and reserved for KSAs if relevant.

Balancing Jargon and Clarity

Scientists are used to speaking in their own technical language. The problem is that the people who evaluate applications are not scientists. Indeed, your application will be evaluated by human resources personnel who may not have technical training in your discipline. If the HR personnel cannot understand the language you use, you might not be rated as highly as you could be. So, make it easy for them to understand your qualifications.

At the same time, it is probably impossible to adequately describe your experience without some degree of technical specificity. Also, once you get past the first cut, your federal resume will be evaluated by someone with scientific or technical training. Additionally, resumes might be scanned for technical keywords. Thus, it is important to balance technical language or jargon with clarity for nonscientists.

You can achieve balance between jargon and clarity in several ways:

1. Scan the job announcement for keywords and phrases, and use them to describe your experience. Again, you don't need to embellish if you are applying for a job for which you have relevant experience and which is at the appropriate GS level. You're simply choosing to phrase your experience so that the HR personnel can recognize it.

2. Simplify the titles of projects if they are very technical. If you are using project descriptions, title the projects descriptively, but more simply than publication titles. For example, a project titled "Cellular mechanisms of protein transport" can be better than "Binding homologue identification using affinity purification in lymphocytes." You can then be more detailed and technical in the description as well as in your KSAs. The exception would be if technical keywords are present in the announcement.

3. If the job announcement calls for knowledge of something specific, such as statistics, do not simply list the statistical tests with which you have experience. Instead, say "statistical analysis" in a skill list, and then briefly list the tests you have performed, grouped and identified by type.

4. Be sure to expand all acronyms at their first use. Each discipline, region, department, and lab has its own "alphabet soup," so don't assume others will understand it.

Graduate Students and Recent Grads Versus Established Scientists

Graduate students or recent graduates face some issues that established scientists do not. Foremost is the fact that you have spent all your time in graduate school and not in different jobs with separate titles. To deal with this, list your experience as specific projects you've undertaken. If you don't have many grants, you can delete the Grants section and incorporate the grants you have into project descriptions to deemphasize having few grants.

Another issue is how to quantify your hands-on experience. The human resources personnel who will evaluate your application have strict guidelines concerning the calculation of time spent on the job. If you've just graduated, how do you quantify your experience in terms of hours spent per week? The solution is to count the semesters that you have been earning graduate-level credits for research and total them into years. You can count this as full-time work experience (40 hours per week), and your statements are supported by your transcripts.

All federal resumes should include narrative descriptions of past jobs or projects. But as scientists advance and gain experience, their skill sets increase, and established scientists might find that listing all their skills is redundant with detailed job or project descriptions. Because you should avoid redundancy in your federal resume, I recommend that you reach a balance between skill lists and narrative descriptions. Scientists early in their careers should certainly have narrative descriptions, but they should stress skill lists.

As you advance, the number and size of narrative descriptions should increase while skill lists become smaller and more general. Established scientists should have a minimum of skill lists, if any. Skill lists, having been removed from your resume, can be an efficient way of answering some KSAs. In addition, a Major Accomplishments section is best used by more senior-level scientists. If you include a Major Accomplishments section early in your career, it might backfire by implying that, for example, all you've done is get your degree.

Populate Your USAJOBS Resume-Building Form

Previous chapters discussed the USAJOBS resume-building form. Many of your CV/federal resume hybrid sections are represented in the web form, including Work Experience, Education, Job Related Training (continuing education), References, Professional Affiliations, and Publications. Use the Additional Information field for everything else, starting with your Profile statement. If you have enough room, you can sneak a cover letter in there as well.

Some agency job application systems, however, cannot accept the maximum number of characters generated by very large resumes pushed from USAJOBS to the agency system. If that happens, you will have to trim the Additional Information field in USAJOBS and resubmit your resume.

Edit Your Hybrid for Academic Applications

Some academicians may find the federal resume to be an odd format. So if you plan to apply for academic positions, these simple edits to your hybrid can make it more palatable to academia:

- Remove compliance information from your contact information and job descriptions (for example, your salary).
- Remove the objective.
- Delete the detailed profile statement and replace it with a research interest summary. The information from the profile statement can be addressed to a limited degree in your cover letter. Replace the detailed profile statement with two or three lines summarizing your field of expertise and experience. This will establish upfront what type of scientist you are.
- Delete high school from your education and add the name of your advisor and the title of your thesis.
- Add a summary of your employment to the first page.
- Move the detailed duties and responsibilities descriptions for each job from the second page to later pages.
- Move your publications and presentations up so they start on page two.

Sample Federal Resume/Curriculum Vitae

Here is real example of a hybrid CV/federal resume.

This hybrid contains more work experience than a traditional CV. Shortening it into a generic federal resume would reduce your chances of landing a job. The Profile section illustrates professional advancement compared to the previous examples. The Professional Experience sections are organized by role, project, and accomplishments. Note the use of sentence fragments in active voice. The length, at 10 pages, makes it more like a CV.

Target Job: Ecologist, GS-0408-13 from current position as Ecologist, GS-0408-12.
Resume Format: Federal paper resume/CV hybrid.
Federal to federal career promotion.

David F. Raikow, Ph.D.
1234 Anystreet, Cincinnati, OH 12345
(123) 456-7890 (Cell, U.S. Eastern Time Zone)
www.davidraikow.com, david@email.com
Vacancy: Ecologist, GS-0408-13; SSN: 000-00-0000; Citizenship: USA; Veterans' Pref: No.

Science Coordinator and Advisor: Create, plan, and administer original multidisciplinary and interagency research programs. Initiate and lead new research thrusts, oversee scientific contracts. Create interagency research teams. Create and manage budgets. Hire and supervise interns. Write interagency agreements, Quality Assurance Project Plans, project management plans, and work breakdown structures.

Ecologist: Federal Principal Investigator; stream ecology, lake ecology, community, ecosystem, and landscape ecology, food webs, biological invasion, ecotoxicology; benthic macroinvertebrates, phytoplankton, zooplankton, terrestrial insects, spiders, fish.

Agency Representative: Represent the National Oceanic and Atmospheric Administration (NOAA), the Great Lakes Environmental Research Laboratory (GLERL), and the NOAA National Center for Research on Aquatic Invasive Species (NCRAIS) at workshops, meetings, and conferences. Build new relationships with state and federal agencies, universities, and non-government organizations. Critique scientific merit of proposed federal regulations.

Writer and Speaker: Write grant proposals, protocols, status reports, technical memos, scientific papers, presentations, book reviews, book proposals, book chapters, and books. Critique scientific manuscripts and grant proposals. Present complex scientific concepts to scientists, untrained audiences, congressional delegates, and the media. Create workshops for, and present seminars to, undergraduates and the public.

EDUCATION

Ph.D.	2002	Ecology, Evolutionary Biology and Behavior (EEBB) and Zoology (dual degree), Department of Zoology and W.K. Kellogg Biological Station, Michigan State University, East Lansing, MI 48824.
M.S.	1996	Biological Sciences, Ecology and Evolution Program, Department of Biological Sciences, University of Pittsburgh, Pittsburgh, PA 15260
B.S.	1993	Biological Sciences, University of Pittsburgh
B.A.	1993	History and Philosophy of Science, University of Pittsburgh
Graduate	1988	Peabody High School, 515 Highland Ave., Pittsburgh, PA 15206

CERTIFICATIONS

"Ecologist," Ecological Society of America	2003
"Teaching College Science and Mathematics," Michigan State University	2002

(continued)

Figure 14.4: A traditional CV.

(continued)

PROFESSIONAL EXPERIENCE

RESEARCH ECOLOGIST GS-0408-12   Sept. 2006 to Present
U.S. Environmental Protection Agency (EPA)   40 hrs., $XX,XXX
National Exposure Research Laboratory (NERL)   Contact Supervisor: Yes
Ecological Exposure Research Division (EERD)   Brent Johnson
26 W. Martin Luther King Dr., Cincinnati, OH 45268   (123) 456-7890

SCIENCE COORDINATOR: Coordinate and lead interdisciplinary (e.g. ecology-hydrology, ecology-toxicology, aquatic-terrestrial), and interagency (e.g. EPA-NOAA-university) research projects and multi-project research programs. Manage scientific projects run by others under contract. Create scopes of work for scientific contract solicitations. Create formal Quality Assurance Project Plans, project work plans, work breakdown structures, timelines, and budgets. Regularly review quality of scientific results produced under contract in meetings with multiple internal and external contractors.

SCIENCE ADVISOR: Review scientific methodology proposed by colleagues and approve methodology proposed by contractors. Critically review and edit science reports, unsolicited manuscripts submitted to peer-reviewed primary scientific literature.

WRITER: Write peer-reviewed scientific publications and letters, technical reports, and internal research proposals. Create scientific posters and present results at national and international conferences. Maintain a blog and write scientific blog posts distributed by www.researchblogging.org.

SPEAKER: Create multimedia PowerPoint presentations (e.g. including original animations, original Google Map Pro movies). Present results orally at national and international conferences. Represent agency and give scientific presentations to federal and state agencies, non-government organizations, universities, and the public. Adjust complexity level of presentations to accommodate expertise level of audience.

ECOLOGIST: Apply knowledge of biology, ecology, hydrology, pollution, biogeochemistry, multiple ecosystems, and organisms. Design and conduct quantitative ecological research, including field studies, experiments, geospatial modeling, and database mining. Collect, manage, explore, and statistically analyze scientific and environmental data. Create databases. Manage geospatial data and create maps in geographic information systems (e.g. ArcMap/ArcINFO).

PROJECTS:
- Riparian zone contamination by aquatic subsidies (Landscape Scale).
- Methylmercury bioaccumulation across a productivity gradient (Ecosystem Scale).
- Spatial identification of material source-areas in watersheds (Landscape Scale).

ACCOMPLISHMENTS:
- $150,000 external grant obtained, $85,000 in internal research funds obtained.
- 2 peer-reviewed papers and 1 letter published, 1 paper in revision, 2 manuscripts in preparation.
- 4 invited seminars presented at federal agencies, universities, and non-gov. organizations.

RESEARCH AQUATIC BIOLOGIST GS-0401-11　　　　Nov. 2003 to Sept. 2006
National Oceanic and Atmospheric Administration (NOAA)　　　　$XX,XXX
Great Lakes Environmental Research Laboratory (GLERL)　　　　40 hrs.
2205 Commonwealth Blvd.　　　　Contact Supervisor: Yes
Ann Arbor, MI 48105-2945　　　　David Reid, (124) 456-7890

SCIENCE COORDINATOR: Coordinate and lead interdisciplinary (e.g. ecology-biological invasion), and interagency (e.g. NOAA-USGS) research projects. Recruit interagency, non-government, and international principal investigator collaborators for scientific proposals. Write memoranda of understanding and interagency agreements to govern projects. Create and manage budgets with spending authority and purchase card. Hire and supervise subordinate staff.

AGENCY REPRESENTATIVE: (50% time) Represent and support the National Oceanic and Atmospheric Administration (NOAA), the Great Lakes Environmental Research Laboratory (GLERL), and the NOAA National Center for Research on Aquatic Invasive Species (NCRAIS) at scientific and regulatory meetings, workshops, conferences. Alternate NOAA representative to the Great Lakes Aquatic Nuisance Species Panel. Forge and maintain new relationships between NOAA and scientific and regulatory federal agencies, state agencies, universities, and non-government organizations.

SCIENCE ADVISOR: Identify, prioritize, and recommend biological invasion research needs to agency. Provide advice on technical scientific approaches to peers. Analyze and critique scientific merit of proposed federal regulations. Review and comment on biological publications, studies, programs, proposals, and emergency response plans. Critique unsolicited scientific manuscripts and grant proposals.

BIOLOGIST: Apply knowledge of biology, ecology, hydrology, biological invasion, pollution, landscapes, ecosystems, and biogeochemistry in order to design and conduct quantitative ecological studies into biological, chemical, and physical ecological issues. Collect and statistically analyze data (standard, multivariate, Systat, SAS, SPSS). Develop new scientific methods. Collect, manage, explore, and analyze scientific and environmental data. Create and mine databases. Manage geospatial data; create maps in geographic information systems (ArcMap/ArcINFO).

SELECTED PROJECTS:
- Unaddressed Secondary Biological Invasion Vectors.
- Identifying, Verifying, and Establishing Options for Best Management Practices.
- Great Lakes Aquatic Nonindigenous Species Information System (GLANSIS database).
- The History of Species Invasion and Scientific Responses in the Great Lakes.

ACCOMPLISHMENTS:
- $35,000 external grant obtained.
- $38,000 in internal research funds obtained.
- Assembled 10-member federal, academic, private, and international research team for a $2.5M proposal.

(continued)

(continued)

TEACHING EXPERIENCE

Certification in Teaching College Science and Mathematics:
- Program of Michigan State University, College of Natural Science.
- Mentored Teaching Project: "Improving links between the elements of a field ecology course," 2002.
- 10 Workshops: Planning a course, Pedagogical changes, The systematic introduction of ethics, Designing group experiences, Academic myths we live by, Finding a job, Grading papers, Choosing tools, Online cheating, and Website building for classes.
- Class: Teaching College Science, NSC 870.

Great Lakes Summer Student Fellowship Program:
- Mentor undergraduate interns conducting research at GLERL, 2004, 2005.

Classes taught and assisted:
- Guest Lecture: "Biological Invasions," Community and Ecosystem Ecology (Graduate); Michigan State University, 2000–2004.
- Instructor: Genetics Recitation; Michigan State University, lead discussion, write quizzes, and grade tests, 2002.
- Instructor: Ecology Lab; Michigan State University and University of Pittsburgh; Run campus-based labs and assist in field-based courses, 1995, 2001.

OTHER EXPERIENCE

GRADUATE STUDENT, 1996–2002, Michigan State University, Kellogg Biological Station.
"How the feeding ecology of native and exotic mussels affects freshwater ecosystems"
- Discovered phytoplankton community dominance of toxic *Microcystis aeruginosa* in lakes invaded by zebra mussels. Identified competitive food-web interactions between zebra mussels and larval fish. Obtained $21,650 grant.

"The Lotic Intersite Nitrogen eXperiment (LINX)"
- Created three new experiments. Supported primary-stream food web and nutrient cycling experiments. Identified organic matter subsidy to stream mussels from upstream wetlands in a complex watershed.

"Long-Term Ecological Research (LTER)"
- Collected samples and measured parameters for long-term aquatic ecosystem monitoring.

GRADUATE STUDENT, 1994–1996, Dept. of Biological Sciences, University of Pittsburgh.

WRITER, 2002–2004, The Resume Place, 89 Mellor Ave., Baltimore, MD 21228.

PUBLICATIONS

Raikow, D. F., In Prep, Geospatial delineation of resource sheds driving nutrient and pesticide loading to rivers.
Raikow, D. F., J. T. Oris, C. Hammerschmidt, M. G. Mehling, A. K. Gevertz, D. M. Walters, In Prep, Mercury bioaccumulation across a stream productivity gradient.

Nietch, C. T., E. Quinlan, D. F. **Raikow,** others, In Prep, Antimicrobial exposure in a flow-through artificial stream ecosystem.

Raikow, D. F., and E. D'Amico, In Review, Temporal variation in spatial sources of mercury loading to rivers, *Environmental Science and Technology.*

Atkinson, J. F., D. F. **Raikow,** In Review, Delineation of resource sheds in large lakes, *Limnology and Oceanography: Fluids and Environments.*

Raikow, D. F., D. M. Walters, K. M. Fritz, M. A. Mills, 2010b, The distance that contaminated aquatic subsidies extend into lake riparian zones. *Ecological Applications.* DOI: 10/1890/09–1504.1.

Raikow, D. F., J. F. Atkinson, and T. E. Croley, 2010, Development of resource shed delineation in aquatic ecosystems. *Environmental Science and Technology, 44,* 329–334, DOI: 10.1021/es900562t.

Walters, D. M., K. M. Fritz, M. A. Mills, D. F. **Raikow,** 2010a, Spider-mediated flux of PCBs from contaminated sediments to terrestrial ecosystems and potential risks to arachnivorous birds. *Environmental Science and Technology, 44,* 284–2856, DOI: 10.1021/es9023139.

Croley, T. E., D. F **Raikow,** J. F. Atkinson, and C. He, 2008, Hydrological resource sheds. *Journal of Hydrologic Engineering, 13,* 873–885.

Raikow, D. F., D. F. Reid, and P. F. Landrum, 2007b, Aquatic invertebrate resting egg sensitivity to glutaraldehyde and sodium hypochlorite. *Environmental Toxicology and Chemistry, 26,* 1770–1773.

Raikow, D. F., D. F. Reid, E. R. Blatchley III, G. Jacobs, and P. F. Landrum, 2007a, Effects of proposed physical ballast tank treatments on aquatic invertebrate resting eggs. *Environmental Toxicology and Chemistry, 26,* 717–725.

Raikow, D. F., D. F. Reid, E. E. Maynard, and P. F. Landrum, 2006, Sensitivity of aquatic invertebrate resting eggs to SeaKleen® (Menadione): A test of potential ballast tank treatment options. *Environmental Toxicology and Chemistry, 25,* 552–559.

Sarnelle, O., A.E. Wilson, S. K. Hamilton, L. B. Knoll, D. F. **Raikow,** 2005, Complex interactions between the zebra mussel, *Dreissena polymorpha,* and the noxious phytoplankter, *Microcystis aeruginosa. Limnology and Oceanography, 50,* 896–904.

Raikow, D. F., 2004. Food web interactions between larval bluegill sunfish (*Lepomis macrochirus*) and exotic zebra mussels (*Dreissena polymorpha*). *Canadian Journal of Fisheries and Aquatic Sciences, 61,* 497–504.

Raikow, D. F., O. Sarnelle, A. E. Wilson, and S. K. Hamilton, 2004, Dominance of the noxious cyanobacterium *Microcystis aeruginosa* in low-nutrient lakes is associated with exotic zebra mussels. *Limnology and Oceanography, 49,* 482–487.

Technical Memos, Proceedings, Letters, Reviews

Raikow, D.F., 2010, Dose-response versus ANOVA, *Frontiers in Ecology and the Environment, 8,* 121–122.

Croley, T. E., C. He, J. F. Atkinson, and D. F **Raikow,** 2007, Resource shed definitions and computations, NOAA Technical Memorandum GLERL-141, Ann Arbor, Michigan.

(continued)

(continued)

Croley, T. E., J. F. Atkinson, and D. F **Raikow,** 2007, Hydrologic-hydraulic-ecologic resource sheds, The 18th International Association of Science and Technology for Development Conference on Water Resources Planning, May 30–June 1, 2007, Montreal, Canada.

Raikow, D.F., 2006, Unnatural Selection, *Wired Magazine, 14(4),* April.

Stevens, M. H. H., D. F. **Raikow,** M. R Servedio, R. J. Collins, T. L. Schumann, A. N. Tipper, and W. P. Carson, 1996, Hutchinson's chariot: A review of Species Diversity in Space and Time, by M. L. Rosenzweig. *Plant Science Bulletin, 42,* 48–49.

As Contributing Author

Troutman, K., 2007, *Federal Resume Guidebook*, 4th ed., JIST Publishing, Indianapolis, IN, ISBN: 978-1593574260.

Troutman, K., and E. Troutman, 2004, *The Student's Federal Career Guide: 10 Steps to Find and Win Top Government Jobs and Internships*, The Resume Place, Baltimore, MD, ISBN: 978-0964702561.

Troutman, K., 2004, *The Federal Resume Guidebook*, 3rd ed., JIST Publishing, Indianapolis, IN, ISBN: 978-1563709258.

USGS Nonindigenous Aquatic Species (NAS) database factsheets: *Dreissena polymorpha, Corbicula fluminea, Cercopagis pengoi, Daphnia lumholtzi, Alosa psuedoharengus, Morone America, Cordylophora caspia.*

GRANTS

$15K 2009 Additional support for effect of eutrophication on mercury biomagnification in stream food webs, EPA Research Award.

$70K 2008 Effect of eutrophication on mercury biomagnification in stream food webs, EPA Research Award.

$150K 2006 Resource shed delineation in Lake Erie, NOAA New York Sea Grant.

$19K 2006 Resting eggs, Great Lakes Aquatic Nonindigenous Species Information System, International Field Years on Lake Erie. NOAA Research Award.

$35K 2005 Great Lakes Aquatic Nonindigenous Species Information System. Great Lakes Fisheries Trust.

SELECTED COLLABORATORS

Atkinson, Joseph	Great Lakes Program, University at Buffalo
Croley, Tom	NOAA Great Lakes Environmental Research Laboratory
Fritz, Ken	EPA, National Exposure Research Laboratory
Fuller, Pam	USGS, Center for Aquatic Resources Studies
Hamilton, Stephen	Dept. of Zoology, Michigan State University
Landrum, Peter	NOAA Great Lakes Environmental Research Laboratory
Mills, Marc	EPA, National Risk Management Research Laboratory
Oris, Jim	Dept. of Zoology, Miami University

HONORS and AWARDS

Term Position Extension, EPA	2009
Superior Accomplishment Recognition Award, EPA	2007–2009

Service Recognition, GLERL, for "The Environmental Science Careers Seminar Series"   2006
Term Position Extension, NOAA   2005
Fellowship, Graduate Research Training Group (RTG), Michigan State University   1997–1999
Graduation Cum Laude, University of Pittsburgh   1993
Departmental Honors, Biological Sciences, University of Pittsburgh   1993
Departmental Honors, History and Philosophy of Science, University of Pittsburgh   1993

SOCIETY MEMBERSHIPS

American Society of Limnology and Oceanography   2000–present
Ecological Society of America   1997–present
North American Benthological Society   1993–present

CONTINUING EDUCATION

Groundwater Pollution and Hydrology	38 hrs.	Princeton Groundwater, Inc.	2010
Project Management	16 hrs.	Trainer Michael Greer	2006
Advanced Conservation GIS and Remote Sensing	32 hrs.	Smithsonian's National Zoological Park Conservation and Research Center	2006
Introduction to ArcGIS II	24 hrs.	ESRI	2005
Introduction to ArcGIS I	16 hrs.	ESRI	2005
Microsoft Access II	8 hrs.	Washtenaw Community College	2004
Microsoft Access I	8 hrs.	Washtenaw Community College	2004
Confined Space Entry	4 hrs.	Hazmat School	2004

PRESENTATIONS

Conference contributions:

Raikow, D. F., and E. D'Amico, 2010, Temporal variation in spatial sources of mercury loading to rivers, Third International Symposium on Ecology and Biodiversity in Large Rivers of Northeast Asia and North America, Memphis, TN.

Raikow, D. F., D. M. Walters, C. Hammerschmidt, M. Mehling, A. Gevertz, J. Oris, 2010, Methylmercury bioaccumulation across a productivity gradient in streams, North American Benthological Society, Santa Fe, NM.

Walters, D.M., M. A. Mills, K. M. Fritz, D. F. **Raikow,** 2010, Spider-mediated flux of PCBs from contaminated sediments to terrestrial ecosystems, North American Benthological Society, Santa Fe, NM.

Raikow, D. F., D. M. Walters, K. M. Fritz, M. Mills, 2009. Not without cost: ecological subsidy and the lateral extent of polychlorinated biphenyl (PCB) export from aquatic to riparian food webs. American Society of Limnology and Oceanography, Nice, France.

Walters, D. M., M. A. Mills, K. M. Fritz, D. F. **Raikow,** 2009, Using riparian spiders as sentinels of PCB export and risk at contaminated sediment sites, Society of Environmental Toxicology and Chemistry, New Orleans, LA.

Mehling, M., A. Gevertz, C. Hammerschmidt, D. F. **Raikow,** D.M. Walters, J. Oris, 2009, Effect of Eutrophication on Mercury Accumulation and Distribution in Stream

(continued)

(continued)

Ecosystems, Society of Environmental Toxicology and Chemistry, New Orleans, LA.

Raikow, D. F., J. F. Atkinson, and T. E. Croley, 2008. Delineating resource sheds in aquatic ecosystems. North American Benthological Society, Salt Lake City, UT.

Walters, D. M, K. M. Fritz, D. F. **Raikow,** M. Mills, R. R. Otter, 2008. δ13C and δ15N track contaminant flux from aquatic to terrestrial food webs. The 6th International Conference on Applications of Stable Isotope Techniques to Ecological Studies, Honolulu, HI.

Croley, T. E., C. He, C. DeMarchi, and D. F. **Raikow,** 2008. Managing Saginaw Bay nutrient loading by surrounding watersheds through near real time hydrologic resource sheds. International Hydrological Programme: The Role of Hydrology in Water Resources Management, Capri, Italy.

Raikow, D. F., J. F. Atkinson, and T. E. Croley, 2007. Applying resource sheds to coasts and lakes. American Society of Limnology and Oceanography, Santa Fe, NM.

Atkinson, J. F., D. F. **Raikow,** and T. E. Croley, 2007. Hydrodynamic Modeling for Resource Shed Delineation in the Great Lakes. American Society of Limnology and Oceanography, Santa Fe, NM.

Croley, T. E., J. F. Atkinson, and D. F. **Raikow,** 2007. Hydrologic-hydraulic-ecologic resource sheds. The Second IASTED International Conference on Water Resources Management, Honolulu, HI.

Raikow, D. F., J. F. Atkinson, and T. E. Croley, 2006. Resource shed delineation in Lake Erie. International Association of Great Lakes Research, Windsor, ON, Canada.

Raikow, D. F., D. F. Reid, and P. Landrum, 2006. Sensitivity of aquatic invertebrate resting eggs to proposed ballast tank treatment methods. International Conference on Aquatic Invasive Species, Miami, FL.

Seminars

Invited Seminar: "Aquatic insects transfer PCBs to riparian food webs creating exposure risk in birds," Environmental Protection Agency, Cincinnati, OH, 2010.

Invited Seminar: "Quantifying ecosystem connectivity," Biology and Geography Departments, University of Cincinnati, Cincinnati, OH, 2010.

Invited Seminar: "Ecological, hydrological, & chemical flows across the landscape," USGS North Appalachian Research Laboratory, Wellsboro, PA, 2010.

Management Briefing (Division): "Surface water source area delineation using resource shed analysis," Cincinnati, OH, 2009.

Public Seminar: "Legacy contamination of streams: forgotten but not gone," Powdermill Nature Reserve, Rector, PA, 2009

Invited Seminar: "Ecological subsidy and resource sheds: underused concepts in conservation." Great Lakes Office of The Nature Conservancy, Chicago, IL, 2008.

Workshop Presentation: "Commercial online professional networks," EPA Postdoc face-to-face meeting, Washington, DC, 2008.

Management Briefing (Laboratory): "Linking watersheds and coasts by delineating resource sheds," Environmental Protection Agency, Research Triangle Park, NC, 2007.

Invited Presentation: "Applying the dose-response model to ecological questions," Laboratory of Dr. Emma Rosi-Marshall, Loyola University, Chicago, IL, 2007.

Invited Presentation: "Linking watersheds and coasts by delineating resource sheds," Network of Cincinnati EPA Trainees (NCET), Cincinnati, OH, 2007.

NY Sea Grant Advisory Team Briefing: "Resource shed delineation and application," University at Buffalo, Buffalo, NY, 2007.

Management Briefing (Branch): "Resource shed delineation in Lake Erie," Ecosystem Research Branch, EPA-NERL, Cincinnati, OH, 2006.

Invited Seminar: "Aquatic invasive species: trends and challenges," Shared Waters: A Symposium on the Great Lakes, Western Michigan University, 2006.

Presentation: "Resource shed delineation in the Great Lakes," Michigan Department of Natural Resources, Traverse City, MI, 2006.

Presentation: "Resource shed delineation in the Great Lakes," Michigan Department of Natural Resources, Detroit, MI, 2006.

Funding Agency Briefing: "Resource shed delineation in the Great Lakes," NY Sea Grant, University at Buffalo, Buffalo, NY, 2006.

OUTREACH and COMMUNITY SERVICE

National Ocean Science Bowl, Moderator, Science Judge	2004–2006
Interviewee for newspapers, television, and radio concerning biological invasion	2000–2005
Invited Speaker, Lego Robotics Teams, Women in Science (University of Michigan)	2005
Volunteer at the NOAA Booth in the Detroit International Boat Show	2004
International Science and Engineering Fair, Grand Awards Judge	2000, 2004
Mentor local 7th-grade science project: "Will turtles eat zebra mussels?"	1998
Emergency Medical Technician, Medical Supply Officer, Secretary: Foxwall EMS	1989–1992

PROFESSIONAL SERVICE

Panels and Symposia:
- Member: Scientific productivity metrics committee, EERD reorganization, 2010.
- Attendee: EPA Integrated Modeling for Integrated Assessment Workshop, 2008, 2007.
- Invited Participant: "EPA Future Midwestern Landscapes Study Design Meeting," 2007.
- Alternate NOAA Representative to the Great Lakes Aquatic Nuisance Species Panel, 2005.
- Invited Panelist and Speaker on Invasive Species Research Priorities: IAGLR conference forum "Great Lakes Research Needs," MI Dept. of Environ. Quality (sponsor), 2005.
- Invited Participant: "Aquatic Nuisance Species and the Disruption of the Great Lakes Food Web Symposium," National Wildlife Federation (sponsor), 2005.

Written Contributions:
- Internal review: Evaluation of non-target effects associated with transgenic crops," EPA NRML report, 2008.
- Review of "An Analysis of the Effectiveness of Ballast Water Exchange in Controlling Aquatic Nonindigenous Species Introductions to the Great Lakes Basin and Chesapeake Bay," Report to Congress, 2006.
- NOAA Aquatic Invasive Species Program Five-Year Strategic Plan, 2006.

Symposium and Workshop Organization:

(continued)

(continued)

- "Quantifying Ecological Subsidy and Resource Sheds"; Propose and run a special session at the ASLO Conference, 2007.
- "Environmental Science Careers Seminar Series"; Create and present a four-part seminar series for undergraduate and graduate students, GLERL, 2005.
- "NOAA Aquatic Invasive Species Research Strategy Workshop"; Lead the Control and Management breakout workgroup, 2004.

Proposal Review:
- Cooperative Institute for Coastal and Estuarine Environmental Technology
- NOAA GLERL International Field Years on Lake Erie
- NOAA Great Lakes Ecosystem Research Program
- U.S. National Science Foundation
- NOAA Sea Grant

Manuscript Review:
- *Journal of the North American Benthological Society*
- *Canadian Journal of Fisheries and Aquatic Sciences*
- *Journal of Great Lakes Research*
- *Marine Environmental Research*
- *Marine Ecology Progress Series*
- *Limnology and Oceanography*
- *Marine Biology*
- *Hydrobiologia*
- *Wetlands*

REFERENCES

Stephen K. Hamilton, Ph.D., *Ph.D. major advisor,* Professor, W. K. Kellogg Biological Station, Michigan State University, 3700 East Gull Lake Dr., Hickory Corners, MI 49060, 123-456-7890, shamilton@email.edu

David M. Walters, Ph.D., *EPA mentor now at USGS,* Ecologist, U.S. Geological Survey, Fort Collins Science Center, 2150 Centre Ave., Building C, Fort Collins, CO 80526-8118, 123-456-7890, waltersd@email.gov.

Greg Toth, Ph.D., *Former Branch Chief,* Ecological Exposure Research Division, EPA National Exposure Research Laboratory, 26 West Martin Luther King Jr. Blvd., Cincinnati, OH 45268, 123-456-7890, toth.greg@email.gov.

David F. Reid, Ph.D., *NOAA supervisor,* Senior Research Physical Scientist, and Director, NOAA National Center for Research on Aquatic Invasive Species, NOAA Great Lakes Environmental Research Laboratory, 4840 S. State Rd., Ann Arbor MI 48108, 123-456-7890, david.reid@email.gov.

Editing for Academia

This is the first page of a hybrid document that has been edited for academia. Compliance information has been removed from the contact information. A brief summary has been substituted for the Profile section of the federal resume. The Education section has been expanded. A list of professional positions has been added.

David F. Raikow, Ph.D.
1234 Anystreet, Cincinnati, OH, 45243
123-456-7890 (Cell; U.S. Eastern Time Zone)
www.davidraikow.com
david@mail.com

ECOLOGIST

Applied and basic community and ecosystem ecology, ecosystem connectivity, source area delineation, land use and material loading to aquatic ecosystems, ecotoxicology, and contaminant cycling in streams, inland lakes, watersheds, and coasts.

EDUCATION

Ph.D. 2002 Ecology, Evolutionary Biology and Behavior (EEBB) and Zoology (dual degree), Department of Zoology and W. K. Kellogg Biological Station, Michigan State University, East Lansing, MI 48824. *Stephen K. Hamilton, Advisor. "How the Feeding Ecology of Native and Exotic Mussels Affects Freshwater Ecosystems."*

M.S. 1996 Biological Sciences, Ecology and Evolution Program, Department of Biological Sciences, University of Pittsburgh, Pittsburgh, PA 15260. *William P. Coffman, Advisor. "Substrate Heterogeneity and Macroinvertebrate Diversity in Linesville Creek, PA."*

B.S. 1993 Biological Sciences, University of Pittsburgh. *Kenneth W. Cummins, Honors Advisor, "Factors That Affect Coarse Particulate Organic Matter Retention in an Appalachian Mountain Stream."*

B.A. 1993 History and Philosophy of Science, University of Pittsburgh.

CERTIFICATIONS

Ecologist, Ecological Society of America   2003
Teaching College Science and Mathematics, Michigan State University   2002

PROFESSIONAL EXPERIENCE

Research Ecologist, GS-0408-12   9/2006–Present

U.S. Environmental Protection Agency (EPA), Cincinnati, OH.
National Exposure Research Laboratory (NERL), Ecological Exposure Research Division, Ecosystems Research Branch. Brent Johnson, Acting Branch Chief: 123-456-7890.

Research Aquatic Biologist, GS-0401-11   11/2003–9/2006

National Oceanic and Atmospheric Administration (NOAA), Ann Arbor, MI.
Great Lakes Environmental Research Laboratory. David Reid, Supervisor (retired).

Figure 14.5: First page of a hybrid document.

Summary

The hybrid federal resume/CV focuses on education, experience, and specialized qualifications. Your hybrid is an important document to demonstrate that you are a subject-matter expert. Your federal resume is your application and examination. If your resume is not detailed enough, the interview might not occur.

CHAPTER 15

Information Technology Resumes

Writing a resume for the IT world has some interesting challenges, whether the resume targets a job in private industry or the federal government. On one hand, you want to impress the reader with your technical expertise, and what better way to do that than to use lots of technical jargon (appropriately, of course)? On the other hand, your resume will likely also be read by a variety of nontechnical personnel, from the junior human resources specialist logging in the resume or performing an initial screening, all the way to the hiring manager, who may or may not have a technical background. How can you satisfy both of these audiences, plus position yourself as the "Best Qualified" for the position you want?

That's the purpose of this chapter: to help you first of all to understand the types of IT jobs available in the federal world so that you can do a good job of the most important step—selecting those positions that are the best matches for your career aspirations and experience—and then knowing how to present your IT education, training, and job experience in an effective marketing format that produces results.

Government IT Jobs in the 21st Century

The most interesting trend in federal IT jobs is that more and more, the government is taking its lead from industry. In all areas, government managers are challenged to think like entrepreneurs, to focus on the bottom line, and to build standard, repeatable business processes based in industry-wide best practices. Always remember in developing your federal resume, KSA accomplishments in your resume, your essays, your cover letter, and any other component of your application package that IT systems and software are *never* the end goal; they are merely the tools to build successful, mission-driven business systems. Every job duty and accomplishment you describe should maintain that focus.

What does this mean in the IT arena? First of all, look to the key business drivers in the IT industry and you will find the federal government in lockstep.

Industry Certifications

IT positions in both the government and industry increasingly require industry certifications. Those most in demand include the following:

- **Microsoft:** Microsoft Certified Systems Engineer (MCSE) is probably the most in demand, but Microsoft certifications of any type (and there are many) are highly valued. Search for "certifications" at www.microsoft.com for descriptions of the current Microsoft certifications (www.microsoft.com/learning/mcp/certifications.asp when this book went to press).

- **Cisco:** Like Microsoft, Cisco has a wide range of certifications, from Cisco Certified Network Associate (CCNA) and Cisco Certified Network Professional (CCNP) to Cisco Certified

Network Design Associate (CCDA) and Cisco Certified Network Design Professional (CCDP). Search for "certifications" at www.cisco.com for a description of the current Cisco certifications (www.cisco.com/web/learning/le3/learning_career_certifications_and_learning_ paths_home.html when this book went to press).

- **PMI:** The Project Management Institute (PMI) has become the standard for project management best practices for the federal government as well as for private industry. Increasingly, government contracts are requiring that the Project Manager be either PMI certified as a Project Management Professional (PMP) or have a Defense Acquisition Workforce Improvement Act (DAWIA) certification (available only as a government employee), particularly for any IT position that includes IT acquisitions. With the government under continued pressure to outsource all work not "inherently governmental," many government IT positions have core responsibilities centered on managing outsourced work products. Related disciplines that you should stress in your resume and KSAs include Risk Management, Configuration Management, Earned Value Management, Quality Assurance, and Communications Management.

- **ITIL:** Information Technology Infrastructure Library. This is actually an IT service delivery standard derived from the British government. As PMI focuses generically on project management issues across any industry, this is increasingly becoming PMI's IT companion. ITIL brings together many of the disciplines you have come to know in the IT world: Problem Management, Configuration Management, Release Management, and so forth. Check out www.itil-officialsite.com/home/home.asp for further details on this IT service management approach and its associated certifications. You should reference any and all of these disciplines and terms in your resume materials if you have this type of experience.

- **IT Security Certifications:** CISSP (Certified Information Systems Security Professional) is probably the most in-demand ("gold standard") certification in the market. Given the ever-present security threat to enterprise systems and data assets, if you have this or other IT security credentials, you probably will have a job!

- **IT Planning Certifications:** There are many opportunities as well for Enterprise Architecture (EA) and even Chief Information Officer (CIO) certifications. Take a look at the GSA CIO University for one example of a CIO certification widely respected in the federal government (www.cio.gov/index.cfm?function=cio_university) and at the EA certification provided by the Institute for Enterprise Architecture Developments (www.enterprise-architecture.info/ EA_Certification.htm).

- **CMM/CMMI:** Capability Maturity Model and Capability Maturity Model Integration (CMMI) are process-improvement standards developed and fostered by the Carnegie Mellon Software Engineering Institute (SEI). The federal government is increasingly pushing for both its own organizations and contractors to implement best practices for process management that are validated in a CMM or CMMI rating. Although this is really an organizational certification, any training or experience you have in assisting your firm or client to gain a CMM/CMMI rating should be highlighted. Read more at www.sei.cmu.edu/cmmi/.

If you have one of these or other certifications, you definitely will want to highlight this in the first half of the first page of your federal resume. If you do not have any certifications, there is no time like the present to get started. Although formal training is important, you can get started on many of these certifications through self-study, and the time and cost invested will be well paid back.

Enterprise Architectures

Both industry and government have realized that reinventing the wheel again and again is neither fiscally nor mission responsible. Many job positions posted by the federal government are derived from federal-wide initiatives to design "reusable," "interoperable," "accessible," "scaleable," "enterprise" systems and solutions. Start by taking a look at the President's Management Agenda (E-Government & Information Technology), which underscores the wider **E-Gov** initiative to improve services to citizens through the use of technology and includes such initiatives as IT Investment Management, Cybersecurity, Open Government, and Federal Enterprise Architecture.

Systems Development Life Cycle (SDLC)

The government has learned the lesson that the real cost for a system is the total life-cycle cost—from product or system inception through development, testing, acceptance, implementation, and then life-cycle support and even decommissioning. If you are a software developer or even plan, acquire, and then implement new systems, you have had to consider all of these life-cycle aspects. Again, incorporating the appropriate and accepted term for this experience into your resume demonstrates your expertise and awareness of the imperatives on the IT industry and federal IT initiatives.

Continuity of Operations (COOP)

Continuity of Operations (COOP) and Disaster Recovery Planning have been high on the federal government's to-do list since 9/11. One place to start is by consulting FEMA's Federal Preparedness Circular (FPC) 65 (www.fas.org/irp/offdocs/pdd/fpc-65.htm). It is very likely that you will have played some role in disaster preparedness in any IT position in which you have served. Highlighting this experience and relating it to the term "COOP" will ring true to the hiring manager for almost all positions.

Business Process Reengineering (BPR)

Remember the focus on documented, repeatable business processes? The buzzword in the business world for developing these is Business Process Reengineering (BPR). If you have been around awhile in the IT world, you have at some point had to think about how you currently manage a process (the "as-is" scenario) and how you could improve it in the future (the "to-be" process). If you have led or participated on projects to map processes like this, you have essentially been involved in BPR (and should take credit for it and use the correct term).

IT Planning

Whether you have formally served as a Contracting Officer's Technical Representative (COTR) in the federal government or at a minimum researched, recommended, and documented requirements for IT items or services to be procured, this is one area that you should definitely highlight. Become familiar with terms such as Statement of Work (SOW), Statement of Objectives (SOO), and Request for Proposals (RFP). Even for private-industry experience, try to cast your expertise in these terms. You should be aware of a number of initiatives, standards, and regulations related to IT Strategic Planning, Capital Planning, and Portfolio/Project Management (PPM), including the following:

- **IT Capital Planning and Investment Control (CPIC), OMB Exhibit 300s,** and **OMB Circular A-11,** which provides guidance on preparing the federal budget (www.whitehouse.gov/omb/circulars/a11/03toc.html). A few other interesting links include www.osec.doc.gov/cio/oipr/Ex300_instructions.htm and www.ocio.usda.gov/cpic/index.html.

- **OMB Circular A-130,** which establishes policies for the management of federal information resources (www.whitehouse.gov/omb/circulars/a130/a130trans4.pdf).

- **Federal Information Security Management Act of 2002 (FISMA),** which was designed to enhance computer and network security within the federal government by implementing regular security audits (www.dhs.gov/files/programs/gc_1281971047761.shtm).

- **Clinger-Cohen Act of 1996** or the Information Technology Management Reform Act, which requires the federal government to use performance-based management principles for acquiring information technology (http://govinfo.library.unt.edu/npr/library/misc/itref.html).

Data Management

Another key area for industry and government is managing critical "data assets." It is no exaggeration that after its personnel, the second most critical asset for any organization is its data. The imperative in industry and government is to define and implement systems and processes that ensure that the right data items are identified, managed, and made accessible to business processes. Think about any initiative in which you assisted your organization or client to identify key data items to be collected, stored, and published, and correctly identify this as Data Management. A close discipline to this is **Records Management**—managing as Controlled Items (CIs) the key personnel and business records and documents for the organization. Include references to any records-management systems you have used in your current or recent positions.

IT Job Series: How the Federal Government Has Organized IT Positions

The first step in conducting an effective job search for IT positions in the federal government is to understand the various job series that apply to IT-related positions (see www.opm.gov/fedclass and select Position Classification Standards under White Collar Positions; see www.opm.gov/fedclass/html/gsseries.asp to find detailed descriptions for each job series). Note that on USAJOBS (www.usajobs.gov) you can search for IT jobs first of all on the Basic Search tab by selecting Information Technology under the Job Category Search field. There is also a Series Search tab that allows you to select job announcements based on the target job series.

Jobs in Series GS-2210 and Beyond

The primary job series for most IT professionals is GS-2210, Information Technology Management. Although most IT-related positions are classified under this category, there are a few others of interest if you have very specific skills. The distinctions between these categories are as follows:[1]

- **GS-2210, Information Technology Management:** These jobs are characterized as "administrative IT technology work" and are positions that "manage, supervise, lead, administer, develop, deliver, and support information technology (IT) systems and services. Whereas many positions may require the skilled use of Automated Information Systems (AIS), the distinction is that these positions have Information Technology as their primary focus. *(See below for more details.)*

---

[1] *Definitions adapted from position descriptions found on www.opm.gov/fedclass/html/gsseries.asp.*

- **GS-2299, Information Technology Student Trainee:** These positions do not refer to the temporary, summer job types of employment, but for "student trainee positions made under career-conditional or career appointments in the competitive service. A student may be appointed to any position that leads to qualification in a two-grade interval professional, administrative, or technical occupational series and that provides an opportunity for the student's growth and development toward the target position."

- **GS-0332, Computer Operations Series:** This series covers positions where the primary duties involve "operating or supervising the operations of the controls of the digital computer system." If you have experience as a Computer Operator, you might want to check positions in this category as well as in GS-2210.

- **GS-0335, Computer Clerk and Assistant Series:** This series is closely aligned with GS-0335 in that it focuses on providing a clerical level of data-processing support. Sample duties as a Computer Assistant might be installing new desktop systems, issuing data media, maintaining system documentation, and receiving and resolving routine user trouble calls.

- **GS-0854, Computer Engineering Series:** These Computer Engineering positions are characterized as "professional" positions requiring extensive academic qualifications in computer hardware, software, and system architectures. The work revolves around the "research, design, development, testing, evaluation, and maintenance of computer hardware and systems software in an integrated manner." Sample positions might involve developing computer simulations or leading the design and integration of complex IT systems.

- **GS-1550, Computer Science Series:** This is the most scientifically oriented type of IT work and would typically require advanced degrees and skills in computer science, engineering, statistics, and mathematics, and involve "research into computer science methods and techniques."

More Details on the 2210 Series

The Office of Personnel Management (OPM) *Job Family Classification Standard for Administrative Work in the Information Technology Group, GS-2200* (www.opm.gov/fedclass/gs2200a.pdf), notes that the GS-2210 series covers the following:

> Two grade-interval administrative positions that manage, supervise, lead, administer, develop, deliver, and support information technology (IT) systems and services. This series covers only those positions for which the paramount requirement is knowledge of IT principles, concepts, and methods; for example, data storage, software applications, and networking.
>
> Information technology refers to systems and services used in the automated acquisition, storage, manipulation, management, movement, control, display, switching, interchange, transmission, assurance, or reception of information. Information technology equipment includes computers, network components, peripheral equipment, software, firmware, services, and related resources.

The GS-2210 series is considered an administrative position as opposed to a "clerical or professional" position. Usually a professional series requires education. For example, GS-1550 (Computer

Science) and GS-0854 (Computer Engineer) are considered professional series because they require a body of knowledge related to math and science (essentially a college degree with courses taken in math, engineering, statistics, or computer science). Because the 2210 is an administrative series, people who come in as a GS-2210-5 and have position potential to GS-2210-11 have the possibility of being promoted to GS-7/9/11 (two grades at a time). After you reach GS-11, you can be promoted only one grade at a time (to GS-12/13/14/15).

The GS-2210 series includes, but is not limited to, the specialties included in Table 15.1. Note the specialty abbreviation that is often included in the job title in the position description.

Table 15.1: Descriptions for the GS-2200 Occupational Series[2]

GS-2200 Specialty	Description
Policy and Planning (PLCYPLN)	Work that involves a wide range of IT management activities that typically extend and apply to an entire organization or major components of an organization. This includes strategic planning, capital planning and investment control, workforce planning, policy and standards development, resource management, knowledge management, architecture and infrastructure planning and management, auditing, and information security management.
Security (INFOSEC)	Work that involves ensuring the confidentiality, integrity, and availability of systems, networks, and data through the planning, analysis, development, implementation, maintenance, and enhancement of information systems security programs, policies, procedures, and tools.
Systems Analysis (SYSANALYSIS)	Work that involves applying analytical processes to the planning, design, and implementation of new and improved information systems to meet the business requirements of customer organizations.

[2]*Descriptions taken from Descriptions for the GS-2200 Occupational Series, www.opm.gov/fedclass/gs2200a.pdf.*

GS-2200 Specialty	Description
Applications Software (APPSW)	Work that involves the design, documentation, development, modification, testing, installation, implementation, and support of new or existing applications software.
Operating Systems (OS)	Work that involves the planning, installation, configuration, testing, implementation, and management of the systems environment in support of the organization's IT architecture and business needs.
Network Services (NETWORK)	Work that involves the planning, analysis, design, development, testing, quality assurance, configuration, installation, implementation, integration, maintenance, and/or management of networked systems used for the transmission of information in voice, data, and/or video formats.
Data Management (DATAMGT)	Work that involves the planning, development, implementation, and administration of systems for the acquisition, storage, and retrieval of data.
Internet (INET)	Work that involves the technical planning, design, development, testing, implementation, and management of Internet, intranet, and extranet activities, including systems/applications development and technical management of websites. This specialty includes only positions that require the application of technical knowledge of Internet systems, services, and technologies.
Systems Administration (SYSADMIN)	Work that involves planning and coordinating the installation, testing, operation, troubleshooting, and maintenance of hardware and software systems.
Customer Support (CUSTSPT)	Work that involves the planning and delivery of customer support services, including installation, configuration, troubleshooting, customer assistance, and/or training, in response to customer requirements.

Competency Model for Cybersecurity: Cybersecurity Competencies by Grade Level

The government is hiring "Critical Mission Skills" cybersecurity specialists, and it is considering professionals from the fields of IT, Electronics Engineering, Computer Engineering, and Telecommunications. The government will train you if you have the right set of competencies in your background and in your federal resume. Review the list of competencies the government is seeking and build project details and descriptions to support the competencies.

The following tables present the competencies that have been confirmed as appropriate for selection on a government-wide basis for cybersecurity work in the four series listed below and at the grades indicated. Agencies are responsible for conducting job analyses for work responsibilities outside the cybersecurity function. Similarly, agencies must determine the applicability of these competencies to positions that do not perform the full range of cybersecurity work. See a full list of General and Technical Competencies here:

www.chcoc.gov/transmittals/TransmittalDetails.aspx?TransmittalID=3436

Table 15.2: Occupations and Grades with Confirmed Competencies

Occupations	Grades
2210 Information Technology Management Series	9, 11, 12, 13, 14, 15
0855 Electronics Engineering Series	12, 13, 14, 15
0854 Computer Engineering Series	12, 13, 14, 15
0391 Telecommunications Series	9, 11, 12, 13

Cybersecurity Competencies by Occupation, 2210 Information Technology Management Series

General Competencies for a GS-12:

- Accountability
- Attention to detail
- Computer skills
- Customer service
- Decision making
- Flexibility
- Integrity/honesty
- Interpersonal skills
- Learning
- Memory
- Oral communication
- Problem solving
- Reading
- Reasoning
- Resilience
- Self-management
- Stress tolerance
- Teamwork
- Technical competence
- Writing

Technical Competencies for a GS-12:

- Communications security management
- Compliance
- Computer network defense
- Configuration management
- Information assurance

- Information systems/network security
- Information systems security certification
- Operating systems
- Security

Selecting the Right Job Announcement for You

Selecting the right job announcement in the first place is just as critical for IT positions as for any other job search. No matter how good your resume and KSA materials are, if you truly do not have the credentials required by the hiring manager, it is close to certain that you will not be in the Best Qualified range. So how can you tell from reading an IT job announcement whether you might be minimally qualified or seriously at the top of the pack?

Analyzing a Sample Announcement

Let's take a sample IT job announcement and really look at it. Here is an actual job announcement for an Information Security Specialist at the GS-11/12 level. Table 15.3 presents each sentence from the vacancy announcement and the skills required for the job, and an interpretation of the requirement for this skill.

MAJOR DUTIES:
IT Specialist (INFOSEC), GS-2210-11/12

The incumbent acts as the subject matter expert for the Information Assurance Group within the Network Security (NETSEC) Division and is responsible for ensuring that the DoD, OIG automated information systems (AIS) and networks are in compliance with the DoD Information Assurance (IA) policies, guidance, and standards. The incumbent is responsible for developing, implementing, maintaining and reviewing an information security program to assure compliance for all centrally maintained AIS and networks at all levels.

Ensures the integrity, availability, confidentiality, non-repudiation and authentication of DoD, OIG AIS's and networks via reviews and the use of auditing and security policy enforcement tools. Interprets current Department and Federal AIS Security laws, regulations, policies, standards and guidelines. Coordinates with the Office of Security in the certification and accreditations of centrally managed AIS's and networks; communicates security-related IA issues or items of interest affecting the DoD, OIG; and tests, verifies and assures adequate security controls exist with the AIS's and networks.

The first thing you should do is reduce the job announcement to bullets and highlight the key requirement expressed in each bullet. Then, for each bullet, you need to make a judgment call on whether the requirement is a clear, hard requirement (you must have experience in this very explicit application or system in order to qualify) or a more generalized skill that could be satisfied from a fairly different context.

Looking at the IT Specialist (INFOSEC) position, let's categorize the bullets (see Table 15.3).

Table 15.3: Analyzing Required Skills for an IT Specialist Position

Job Requirement	Skills and/or Experience You Must Have	Interpretation
The incumbent acts as the subject matter expert for the Information Assurance Group within the Network Security (NETSEC) Division and is responsible for ensuring that the DoD, OIG automated information systems (AIS), and networks are in compliance with the DoD Information Assurance (IA) policies, guidance, and standards.	• Have fairly senior technical knowledge of Information Security practices and principles. • Ensure that IT systems comply with DoD Information Assurance policies.	This is a fairly general statement. Good, solid experience in any technical IT security specialist role would probably meet this qualification. (But note below that you must have specific knowledge of federal security laws!)
The incumbent is responsible for developing, implementing, maintaining, and reviewing an information security program to ensure compliance for all centrally maintained AIS and networks at all levels.	• Actual experience developing an IT security program and plan.	Again, if you have experience, even in private industry, with evaluating IT security risks and vulnerabilities and designing and implementing a formal security plan, you would probably qualify here. Just implementing standard security measures on systems would likely not be sufficient.
Ensures the integrity, availability, confidentiality, non-repudiation, and authentication of DoD, OIG AISs, and networks via reviews and the use of auditing and security policy enforcement tools.	• Technical skills with IT security policy applications and tools. • Experience actually defining and implementing security audits.	Although hiring authorities are not requiring experience with a specific set of security tools, you should have real experience with at least one tools suite. Just reading about them is not enough.

Job Requirement	Skills and/or Experience You Must Have	Interpretation
Interprets current department and federal AIS security laws, regulations, policies, standards, and guidelines.	• Specific knowledge of federal security laws, policies, and actual experience interpreting them.	You would need actual demonstrated evidence that you have applied a knowledge of federal security laws, regulations, policies, and so on.
Coordinates with the Office of Security in the certification and accreditations of centrally managed AISs and networks; communicates security-related IA issues or items of interest affecting the DoD, OIG; and tests, verifies, and ensures that adequate security controls exist with the AISs and networks.	• Experience guiding an organization through the C&A of a government computer system or network. • Identifying and mitigating IT security vulnerabilities. • You should at a minimum have actual experience participating in or leading a C&A process for a system or network.	This second bullet could probably be satisfied with either hands-on technical experience or more IT security management experience.

Summarizing Table 15.3, if you were applying for this position, you would want to ensure that you have clear bullets and accomplishments highlighting your experience in the following areas:

1. Leading formal C&A efforts to certify new computer systems or networks.
2. Developing and implementing formal System Security Plans (SSPs) and other formal IT security plans.
3. Using security application suites, auditing tools, and so on.
4. Interpreting and applying federal security laws, policies, and so on.

If you also included a general discussion of your IT security roles, responsibilities, and accomplishments in current and past positions, you would have a very competitive resume. You can see how critical this process is in selecting a position that is genuinely a good match for your skills and experience. If after this type of analysis, you find that you really do not have one of the key required skills, it is highly unlikely that you would ultimately be selected for the position.

When You Don't Match the Requirements Exactly

The toughest call is when the announcement mentions a specific government application or system that you could have used only if you were already in that job or agency. In this case, consider several factors, including the exact language used (is this *required,* or *desirable?*) as well as the overall announcement itself. If there is one position and the posting time is short, the requirement is probably very firm. If there are multiple positions available, you might have a better chance of gaining an interview even if your experience is missing one of the requirements.

The real danger, especially for the applicant coming in from outside the federal government, is that you might assume that an unfamiliar term such as "certification and accreditation" is just a generic description of the process of putting into place a robust plan to manage information technology security threats. In actuality, Certification and Accreditation (C&A) usually is capitalized (it was *not* in this actual job announcement) and refers to a very formalized process within the federal government of identifying, prioritizing, and putting into place appropriate controls for all of the potential risks associated with bringing a new system or network into production. Although different federal agencies may follow different standards and processes (look into the Defense Information Technology Security Certification and Accreditation Process [DITSCAP], the National Information Assurance Certification and Accreditation Process [NIACAP], and the National Industrial Security Program [NISP]), it is generally safe to say that agencies as a general rule have fairly formalized requirements in this area.

The ideal approach, of course, would be to speak with someone in a similar technical environment to ensure that you fully understand the requirements. Don't hesitate to use any technical contacts you have to look over the job announcement with you if you see any terms that you are not 100 percent certain you understand. As with any position, you can also call the Point of Contact provided with the announcement to better understand what the agency is looking for.

Frequently Asked Questions About IT Federal Resumes

This chapter assumes that you already know the basics of putting together your federal resume (see Parts 1 and 2) and you have done the job analysis (see Chapter 12) to identify the key knowledge, skills, abilities, and experience you need to highlight to be fully qualified for the target positions. Here then are some recommendations and answers to common questions about putting together a really effective IT resume.

Remember that every IT job seeker's specific experience and situation will be different, and this, plus the specifics of the job you are applying for, needs to be taken into account in the final format, organization, and content of your resume. So take these as good rules of thumb, but also feel free to apply a different strategy if it makes sense for your particular situation.

Table 15.4: Frequently Asked Questions (FAQs)
for IT Federal Resumes

IT Resume FAQ	Rule of Thumb
Where should I put my certification?	Certifications are as important for federal IT positions as they are increasingly in private industry. Don't bury them on the last page (unless you have to, as in a Resumix resume). These belong near the top of the first page. See Figure 15.1, which places these after the Profile and any Clearance you may have.
Where should I put my clearance(s)?	Security clearances are tremendously important in the current job environment. If you have or have ever had a clearance, you should note this right after your Profile. Include dates and whether the clearance is still current. Even the fact that you have an expired clearance could be an asset in that the hiring manager might feel you would pass a new background investigation.
Where and how should I list all of the hardware/software I have worked with?	This is a tough one and it really depends on just how hands-on the target position is and whether you have really impressive achievements that will take up lots of real estate on the first page of the resume. The rule of thumb here: If you are very hands-on in your position—a system administrator, software developer, or systems integrator—you should probably provide a categorized list of your key technical skill areas at the bottom of page 1. If you currently work more as a project manager or supervisor, devote the first page more to your expertise section and accomplishments and save the technical skills for the last page.

Wipe out all the outdated technologies from your resume. Nothing looks more dated than including references to Wang, Windows for Workgroups, and COBOL (unless, of course, you are actually applying for a COBOL position if there is one still lurking out there somewhere). Even "client/server" at this point sounds pretty out-of-date in a web-centric world.

One more note: Avoid the obvious. Don't drill down to the point that you are listing every single version of software you have ever used or every printer you ever touched. Suffice it to say that you have worked on Tektronix printers, Cisco routers, or Dell servers. You can always mention specific models in your achievements or KSAs, but don't trivialize your experience by listing everything you ever touched. |

(continued)

(continued)

IT Resume FAQ	Rule of Thumb
	Also, do not include applications, programming languages, or systems that you just studied in college or training courses (although it is okay to include these if you specifically mention the fact that this was through academic study only).
I am a contractor to a specific federal agency. How do I indicate that in my resume?	Be very careful here. As a contractor, you need to carefully list your employer as your contracting firm. Never imply that you worked for an agency if you were not a federal employee. Instead, include the agency's name either in your job description ("Provided contracted system administration support for XYZ Agency…") and/or in your job accomplishments. A neat way that works in some circumstances is to provide a general job description first and then show key customers and projects (see Figure 15.1).
What is the best way to describe my current and past positions?	See Figures 15.1 and 15.2 for two completely different resume formats. There are two key ideas to consider. First of all, start by explaining something about the company or organization you work for. Instead of just providing your employer's name, include at least a one-line description of what the firm or agency does. At some level, you can ride on the coattails of your employer. Including the fact that your employer is an "industry-leading provider of…" or "serves over 10,000 clients…" will enhance your personal role. Next, be sure to provide some idea of the scope and responsibilities of each position. Although accomplishments are very important, it is still important to answer the question, "What do I do?" Include numbers. If you managed an IT budget, for example, say so and provide the amount. The same applies to any projects that you describe.
How do I select and then properly describe my accomplishments?	The most important rule of thumb is to name every accomplishment. If the project never really had a formal name, make one up. Instead of just saying that you implemented a tracking system for all system changes, at least call it a System Change Log (capitalized). Instead of just saying that you implemented a process to deploy system patches, call it an Enterprise Patch Management System. This gives the impression that you developed something of lasting importance (which you probably did).

IT Resume FAQ	Rule of Thumb
	As far as selecting the accomplishments, do not worry that every accomplishment has to be prize winning. The key is to look for specific milestones and ways that you improved your current working environment. These could be as significant as designing and implementing a new system or as concrete as developing a Standard Operating Procedure (SOP), representing your group at a conference, or researching and recommending a new product. Whenever possible, include *numbers* (numbers of systems or users, cost of a new system, percent improvement in system uptime, and so on).
Should I include *all* of my IT training courses?	That depends on how long you have been in the workforce and how many training courses you have. If you are new to the IT workforce and have only a few training courses, include every one! If you have been around for a while and have lots and lots of training courses, include only those in the last 10 years and pick out of those the ones that are the most impressive and most applicable to the job you are applying for. If there is a certain course you know they are looking for, include it regardless of how long ago it was.
How many courses should I include?	Never more than 10 to 15, and consider the final length of the resume.
Do I have to write a new resume for each position I apply to?	No. Go through the position analysis presented in Chapter 11 and make sure that you have a clear reference somewhere in your resume to every one of the final key requirements for the position. After that, look through the job position description, pick out five to eight of the phrases used in the job description, and try to insert these someplace in your resume. Don't be too obvious—vary them a little. Once you have a really solid resume, this should take no more than 15 to 20 minutes.
Do I have to spell out really common IT terms?	Yes. Even spell out Information Technology (IT) the first time you use it. Never assume that your reader understands any acronym. Beyond this, it is critically important that you start by explaining any system or project in a clear, simple fashion that any reasonably informed reader could understand. Even if the target hiring manager is an expert, he or she will be impressed that you understand the technology well enough to explain it to a lay reader.

(continued)

(continued)

IT Resume FAQ	Rule of Thumb
What do I do if my job is classified?	First of all, follow the classification guidelines provided by the institution or agency that you serve. Remember that the hiring agency is not as interested in the specifics as it is in the key skills and experiences you have developed. It is perfectly acceptable, in fact in some cases mandatory, to show the name of your agency or organization as CLASSIFIED, and then to provide only a generalized, high-level description of your job duties. Coupled with your security classification, this will be interpreted as an asset.

Focusing on Your IT Career

Remember that there is no substitute for experience and qualifications. Although an effective IT resume is a great tool to assist you in getting the positions and career to which you aspire, hiring managers inside and outside the government ultimately are looking for well-qualified and experienced employees. Consider that carefully as you evaluate and pursue both academic training and job opportunities. Getting a firm grounding in your field is paramount, and nothing will make you stand out more than good, solid experience in the key functions of your trade. Beyond that, a formal education is the best bet for future promotion potential. To get to senior positions inside or outside Information Technology, nothing beats a college education.

IT Customer Services People Skills and Other Soft Skills in Addition to Technical Skills

Many of the vacancy announcements will require both technical skills and soft skills that focus on customer services, advising management, user support, team lead and user software training. These people skills are critical for an outstanding IT Specialist in whatever specialization you are seeking and at all grade levels in government.

Required Core Competencies for Most IT Positions

Candidates must possess at least one year of specialized experience at or equivalent to the next lower grade in the federal service.

Specialized experience is experience that is directly related to the position and has equipped the applicant with the particular knowledge, skills, and abilities (KSAs) to successfully perform the duties of the position, to include experience in applying and interpreting IT theories, principles, concepts, practices, knowledge management, and customer service support to IT clients.

You must have IT-related experience demonstrating each of the following four competencies.

USAJOBS vacancy announcements are requesting that IT specialists cover both technical skills and basic competencies to demonstrate their ability to perform technical work and work with customers, details, problem solving, and oral communications. Be sure to cover these skills in your project details.

Attention to Detail

Is thorough when performing work and conscientious about attending to detail.

Following is an example that demonstrates detail-oriented work style and services:

> --Led user acceptance testing group in creating testing plans and testing scenarios. Analyzed and defined customer workflow and process requirements. Created technical specifications to provide the programmers with specific instructions to complete the development work.

Customer Service

Works with clients and customers (that is, any individuals who use or receive the services or products that your work unit produces, including the general public, individuals who work in the agency, other agencies, or organizations outside the government) to assess their needs, provide information or assistance, resolve their problems, or satisfy their expectations; knows about available products and services; and is committed to providing quality products and services.

The best way to demonstrate your abilities in customer service is to add an accomplishment statement:

> --Created first-ever new-hire training policies and procedures for IT department. Created a standard reference guide and a quick-reference handbook for managers to update current IT standards. Provided new-hire training to 11 technical coordinators, including train-the-trainer.

Oral Communication

Expresses information (for example, ideas or facts) to individuals or groups effectively, taking into account the audience and nature of the information (for example, technical, sensitive, controversial); makes clear and convincing oral presentations; listens to others, attends to nonverbal cues, and responds appropriately.

Following is an example of advising and providing technical assistance and recommendations to customers and users:

> --INTERVIEWED RETAIL STORE AND DISTRICT MANAGERS: Obtained reports design information based on sales, personnel, and operations data in order to produce new Sales Reporting System. Determined additional information needed for decision-making in hiring, scheduling, and cost control for overhead. Advised on tracking systems for inventory and purchase plans.

Problem Solving

Identifies problems; determines accuracy and relevance of information; uses sound judgment to generate and evaluate alternatives, and to make recommendations.

Following is an example of problem solving you might add into your resume:

--SYSTEMS TESTING: Designed and developed an automated testing feature that was not part of the original requirements but became a very important part of the development lifecycle of this project. RESULTS: This proved to be a monumental time savings for the overall project, transforming what could have been months of testing into additional time we then utilized by adding more user-recommended features to the program.

IT Specialist Core Competencies

These core competencies are important for every IT specialist position. Be sure to cover these in your project or duties descriptions.

Top Ten List of Accomplishments and Projects

In order to write a federal resume that will include your best projects, make a list of your Top Ten Accomplishments or Projects before you start to write your resume. That way you will have content and examples to use for the resume, the questionnaire, and even the interview. Figure 15.1 is a sample of a Top Ten Projects list.

TOP TEN IT PROJECT LIST

Systems Analyst/Application Programmer   06/2003–01/2010

As lead developer on the Efficient Item Assortment project, managed all aspects of the requirements gathering; discussions with customers; operational, functional, and technical specifications; and project management of all tasks to ensure maximum utilization of resources of all teams.

Designed custom reports to identify program defects and track resolutions. Followed agile software-development methodology. Developed custom scripts to create installs for multiple languages using Visual Build Professional.

Completed a user interface rewrite of Efficient Item Assortment application.

Led team that analyzed retail business rules and processes and translated them into a list of functional requirements used to develop a software solution to automate these processes.

Created functional specifications for the Documentation and Quality Assurance teams to create help files and test plans; created in parallel with the actual coding of the project. Prototyped the Graphical User Interface (GUI) to users.

Designed and developed an automated testing feature that was not part of the original requirements but became a very important part of the development lifecycle of this project. RESULTS: This proved to be a monumental time savings for the overall project, transforming what could have been months of testing into additional time we then utilized by adding more user-recommended features to the program.

Systems Analyst/Application Programmer   01/1993–Present

Analyzed, documented, and developed a Point of Sale Order Entry System using Microsoft Visual Basic 6.0 and Microsoft Access. Created functional specifications that outlined the program's features and included screenshots of the new order-entry system. Continually updated specifications to reflect "new" functionality.

Analyzed, designed, and developed a Sales Reporting system using raw point-of-sale data from Army/Air Force Exchange Services and Navy Exchange Services, to provide various sales reports for manufacturers and marketing firms selling products to the military.

Team member in the development of the Point-of-Sale Order-Entry and Sales Reporting System for the Navy Exchange stores. Designed, documented, and developed a sales commission calculation and tracking program used to automate commission payments to 250+ sales associates supporting sales to the military.

Created technical specifications to provide the programmers with specific instructions to complete the development work. Created an interface to the customer's accounting software to enable them to import sales and customer data directly into the software.

Figure 15.1: Top Ten Projects list.

KNOWLEDGE, SKILLS, ABILITIES AND CORE COMPETENCIES:

In addition to the Basic Requirements above, the following KSAs/Competencies have been identified as critical for successful job performance. These KSAs/Competencies were used to develop the occupational assessment questions presented for your response.

1. Technology Management: Keeps up-to-date on technological developments; makes effective use of technology to achieve results; ensures access to and security of technology systems.

2. Customer Service: Anticipates and meets the needs of both internal and external customers. Delivers high-quality products and services; is committed to continuous improvement.

3. Problem Solving: Identifies and analyzes problems; weighs relevance and accuracy of information; generates and evaluates alternative solutions; makes recommendations.

4. Attention to Detail: Is thorough and precise when accomplishing a task with concern for all aspects of the job involved; double-checks the accuracy of information and work products to provide consistently accurate and high-quality work.

5. Written Communication: Writes in a clear, concise, organized, and convincing manner for the intended audience.

6. Oral Communication: Makes clear and convincing oral presentations; listens effectively; clarifies information as needed.

Sample Federal Resumes for IT Positions

Here are two fairly different examples of effective IT resumes. Note that although there are several must-haves for any federal resume, you still have a lot of latitude in how you present the information. The most important point to remember is to carefully read the job announcement. Read every line and make sure that you have not omitted any required detail. Plus, be sure to have the resume in the format requested.

Target Vacancy Announcement

This is the position that the federal resume is targeting. The keywords are listed here and included in the federal resume. The Specialized Experience has to be covered in the resume in order to show that you are Best Qualified for the position.

TARGET POSITION: IT Specialist, Systems Analyst, GS-2210-13/14

Internal Revenue Service Mission: WHAT IS THE MODERNIZATION INFORMATION TECHNOLOGY AND SECURITY SERVICES DIVISION? The mission of Modernization Information Technology & Security Services (MITS Services) is to provide leadership in the delivery of **information technology solutions** that anticipate and meet **enterprise-wide needs** by empowering employees to deliver **customer-centered, value-creating systems,** products, services, and support.

Major Duties:

As an Information Technology Specialist (System Analysis) your specific assignments may include the following:

- Assisting with or **translating IRS business rules and processes** into requirements.

- Assisting in or **identifying and specifying business requirements.**

- Meeting and consulting with customers to **refine functional requirements.**

- Possibly **drafting systems** or **operational specifications** with a team.

- Assisting **application developers in translating requirements into programming specifications.**

- Working with application developers to **isolate and solve design problems** encountered during testing and implementation stages.

- Analyzing functional problems and developing innovative solutions.

- **Analyzing and enhancing software tests** and procedures.

BASIC REQUIREMENTS: To be minimally qualified for the GS-14, you must meet the basic requirements below. At least one year of specialized experience equivalent to the next lower grade level of the normal line of progression of this position in the federal government.

Specialized experience is experience that is related to the work of this position and has provided you with the competencies required for successful job performance. Qualifying experience is experience that demonstrated accomplishment of computer project assignments that required a wide range of knowledge of computer requirements and techniques pertinent to the position to be filled. This knowledge is generally demonstrated by assignments where the applicant **analyzed a number of alternative approaches in the process of advising management concerning major aspects of ADP system design,** such as what **system interrelationships** must be considered, or what operating mode, system software, and/or equipment configuration is most appropriate for a given project.

Keywords and Skills

1. Information Technology solutions

2. Enterprise-wide needs

3. Customer-centered, value-creating systems

4. Translate business rules and processes; operational specifications

5. Identify and specify business requirements

6. Analyze and refine functional requirements

7. Translate requirements into programming specifications with application developers

8. Isolate and solve design problems

9. Analyze and enhance software tests

10. Analyze alternative approaches; advise management on major aspects of ADP system

11. System interrelationships

USAJOBS Project-Based Federal Resumes

Each paragraph in the resume in Figure 15.2 is a separate IT project. The all-cap keyword headlines are keywords from the announcement, so the resume experiences match the requirements needed in this new position.

The resume in Figure 15.3 is done in Outline Format and lists duties and project details—including budgets. Titles of employers and agencies have been deleted for privacy.

Target Job: IT Specialist, Systems Analyst, GS-2210-13/14.
Private industry seeking first federal position.
This resume combines duties and projects. Each paragraph in this resume is a separate IT project. The all-cap keyword headlines are keywords from the announcement, so that the resume experiences match the requirements needed in this new position.
Targeted, written, and designed by Rich Westfield, Certified Federal Resume Writer.

William C. Venters
2555 Vanilla Drive
Dallas, TX 75006
Mobile: 666-666-6666
Email: wcventers@hotmail.com

WORK EXPERIENCE

PROFESSIONAL PROFILE:

An accomplished, highly motivated Systems Analyst and Application Developer with 20+ years of progressively responsible experience planning, analyzing, developing, and implementing highly visible, cost-effective business system solutions at the enterprise level. Experience ranges from requirements analysis through design, development, and operational support. Outstanding analytical, problem solving, and communication skills.

JDA Software	**6/2003 - 1/2010**
Irving, Texas US	
	Salary: $110,000 USD Per Year
	Hours per week: 40

Systems Analyst / Application Programmer
APPLICATIONS DEVELOPMENT: As lead developer on the Efficient Item Assortment project, managed all aspects of the requirements gathering; discussions with customers; operational, functional, and technical specifications; and project management of all tasks to ensure maximum utilization of resources of all teams.

DESIGNED EFFICIENT REPORTS: Designed, developed, and maintained the application using Visual Basic, Visual C++, and C#.
Designed and developed automated simulation and testing with random data generation to build and test the application data using flat file and SQL Server and Oracle database environments.
Designed custom reports to identify program defects and track resolutions. Followed agile software development methodology.
Developed custom scripts to create installs for multiple languages using Visual Build Professional.

DESIGNED FRIENDLY USER INTERFACE AND PROVIDED SUPPORT: Completed a user interface rewrite of Efficient Item Assortment application. Ensured specifications were understood, code was unit tested, change tracking occurred, deployments were timely, and quality assurance issues were addressed. Directed ongoing support and maintenance of the system consisting of a team of business analysts and developers through the entire system development lifecycle.

TEAM LEAD, SYSTEMS ANALYSIS: Led team that analyzed retail business rules and processes and translated them into a list of functional requirements used to develop a software solution to automate these processes. Met with stakeholders to review requirements; modified or added additional requirements based on business needs. Created functional specifications for the Documentation and Quality Assurance teams to create help files and test plans; created in parallel with the actual coding of the project. Prototyped the Graphical User Interface (GUI) to users; made changes to the functional specifications based on user suggestions.

TECHNICAL SPECIFICATIONS: Created technical specifications to outline specific instructions as to which development tools to use, recommend which third-party software or components to incorporate, and define any incremental builds that would be given to the quality assurance team to begin testing individual components.
RESULTS: Major retailer clients implemented updated Efficient Item Assortment software for improved inventory control, faster analysis capabilities, and reports that were meaningful for buyers and store managers.

(continued)

Figure 15.2: Sample USAJOBS project-based resume.

(continued)

SYSTEMS TESTING: Worked on multiple client projects simultaneously, supplying functional specifications, test plans, guidance to team developers, and statuses to project managers. Developed and managed quality assurance test plans and testing resources to ensure complete and timely quality assurance testing of the system. Designed and developed an automated testing feature that was not part of the original requirements but became a very important part of the development lifecycle of this project. RESULTS: This proved to be a monumental time savings for the overall project, transforming what could have been months of testing into additional time we then utilized by adding more user-recommended features to the program. (Contact Supervisor: Yes, Supervisor's Name: John Smith, CEO, Supervisor's Phone: (987) 666-6666)

PC Services   **1/2006 - Present**
Carrollton, Texas US

                                                          Hours per week: 15

Systems Analyst / Application Programmer

REQUIREMENTS COLLECTION AND ANALYSIS: Analyzed, documented, and developed a point-of-sale order-entry system using Microsoft Visual Basic 6.0 and Microsoft Access. Served on requirements development team and provided detailed evaluation of proposed customer solution. Documented actionable, measurable, testable business needs and opportunities; defined to a level of detail sufficient for system design. Created functional specifications that outlined the program's features and included screen shots of the new order-entry system. Continually updated specifications to reflect new functionality.

INTERVIEWED RETAIL STORE AND DISTRICT MANAGERS: Obtained reports design information based on sales, personnel, and operations data in order to produce new sales reporting system. Determined additional information needed for decision-making in hiring, scheduling, and cost control for overhead. Advised on tracking systems for inventory and purchase plans.

DESIGNED NEW SALES REPORTING SYSTEM. Analyzed, designed, and developed a sales reporting system using raw point-of-sale data from Army/Air Force Exchange Services and Navy Exchange Services, to provide various sales reports for Manufacturers and Marketing firms selling products to the military. Reports include Sell Through, Summary, and Exception reporting. Validated test results against requirements traceability matrix. Facilitated joint application development sessions to explore business needs and requirements. Evaluated the impact of proposed requirements on existing operations and interfaces with Navy business systems.

APPLICATIONS DEVELOPMENT: Team member in the development of the point-of-sale order-entry and sales reporting system for the Navy Exchange stores. Designed, documented, and developed a sales commission calculation and tracking program used to automate commission payments to 250+ sales associates supporting sales to the military. Led user acceptance testing group in creating testing plans and testing scenarios. Analyzed and defined customer workflow and process requirements. Created technical specifications to provide the programmers with specific instructions to complete the development work. Created an interface to the customer's accounting software to be able to import sales and customer data directly into the software, thereby reducing the amount of time spent getting sales data transferred and ensuring data integrity, thereby eliminating the possibility of data-entry errors.

PROJECT MANAGEMENT: Develop project plans and schedules using Microsoft Project; define project goals and objectives; identify tasks, risks, and timelines for completion. Monitor the implementation of the project schedule, along with operating controls to ensure that there is accurate, objective information on performance and the mechanisms to implement recovery actions if necessary. Perform cost-benefit analysis to determine the feasibility of applications-development investments. Collect extensive data related to cost and operational impact, including advantages and disadvantages of proposed plan. Continuously evaluate and improve projects, processes, and services for effectiveness and efficiency.

	United States Air Force **Dallas, Texas US**	**1/1998 - 12/2002** **Hours per week: 50**

Defensive Aerial Gunner
Honorable Discharge

EDUCATION

University Of Texas
Dallas, Texas US
110 credits completed - 12/2007
Major: Computer Science

JOB RELATED TRAINING

TECHNICAL SKILLS
Server Windows Server 2003, Microsoft Virtual Server, VMware workstation and Software SQL Server v. 2005, Oracle 9i

Application Visual C#, WPF, ASP.net, XML, Visual C++ v. 6.0, Visual Basic v. 6.0, Visual Software Build Professional, Visual Source Safe v. 6.0, InstallShield v. 6.0, JavaScript

Target Job: IT Specialist, Management Information Systems, GS-2210-14.
Department of Defense federal to federal career progression resume.
Outline Format with duties and project details, including budgets. Titles of employers and agencies are deleted for privacy.
Targeted, written, and designed by Sandy Keppley, Certified Federal Resume Writer.

JOHN ERICKSON, PMP
10 Soft Landing Court
Townsend, AR 12345
Home Phone: xxx-xxx-xxxx
Work Phone: xxx-xxx-xxxx
Email: xxxxx@xxxxxx

US Citizen
Veterans' Preference: N/A
OPM/DEU Consideration: Yes
Highest Previous Grade: GS-2210-13
Security Clearance: Top Secret/SCI

PROFESSIONAL PROFILE

Career Information Technology professional Joint Chiefs of Staff (JCS) member in direct support of the Chairman, JCS. Proven Information Technology professional with demonstrated ability to manage multifaceted, DoD enterprise wide and JCS internal/external complex IT programs.

Demonstrated ability to analyze information technology needs, offer cost-effective solutions, and manage implementation efforts that meet program, resource, and time requirements.

Proven leadership skills in managing and motivating teams to achieve objectives. Excellent communication skills, including proficiency at writing reports and project documentation, and superior ability to interact with individuals at all levels of technical expertise. Well-organized and efficient. Detail-oriented with high quality standards. Experienced, focused support, analysis of JCS needs. Complete JCS projects, meeting deadlines and exceeding expectations.

Certified Project Management Professional (PMP). Certified Lean Six Sigma Green Belt. Certified IT Infrastructure Library (ITIL), v.3. Top Secret/SCI clearance. Top Honors Graduate/Top 5% Signal Officer Basic Course, Ft. Gordon, GA, 1992.

WORK EXPERIENCE

JOB EXPERIENCE #1

INFORMATION MANAGEMENT EXPERTISE in high-level business and customer processes, applications, systems, and security techniques in direct support to the Chairman of the JS. MANAGE INFORMATION SYSTEMS, customer requirements, helpdesk management network operations, and desktop

---

Figure 15.3: Sample USAJOBS project-based resume.

computer hardware and software problem identification and resolution; PLAN JS CUSTOMER SUPPORT piece of enterprise-wide initiatives. Develop CLEAR PROJECT TASKS AND MILESTONES, and assess performance measures.

PROJECT PLANNING involving hardware, software, and network systems integration, deployment of new technology hardware and software capabilities, network infrastructure operational development and implementation, and host-based security. DEVELOP PROPOSALS for new systems or modification to existing hardware, software, network, and information systems configurations to determine operability and effectiveness. REVIEW AND EVALUATE existing desktop and network hardware, software efficiency and effectiveness. DEVELOP WRITTEN RECOMMENDATIONS, technical guidance, and support to meet user and organizational needs and requirements. Prepare and MANAGE PROCUREMENT REQUIREMENTS; write technical requirements. Specify requirements; assess proposals; coordinate with contracting officers and evaluation committees. DEVELOP AND PRESENT FORMAL REPORTS.

QUALITY ASSURANCE for management, evaluation, development, selection, or installation of approved new or modified services or operating structures. APPLY STANDARDS, GUIDELINES, DIRECTIVES, AND REGULATIONS. Manage plans based on costs, documentation, specifications, timelines, and resource utilization. Perform and document analysis studies. DEVELOP ANNUAL UPGRADE STRATEGY FOR hardware and software environments. Manage budget submissions. Manage operations and maintenance, design, implementation, modification, and upgrade of server and client systems.

COMMUNICATION SKILLS as an experienced leader and manager. Extremely proficient in both ORAL AND WRITTEN COMMUNICATION. Manage (JCS) customer requirements and supervise (JS) technical support staff. PROVIDE ORAL AND WRITTEN TECHNICAL GUIDANCE and expert direction in problem identification and resolution.

JOB EXPERIENCE #2

PROJECT IMPLEMENTATION MANAGER on a wide range of complex DoD enterprise-wide information technology projects to include Defense Agencies Branch, Programs and Implementation Division. Directed project staffs in executing DISA IT program plans and objectives. Prepared, monitored, and implemented project timelines using Microsoft Project software. Obtained equipment through acquisition process: employed cost justifications, submitted bids, and acquired systems within budget limits. Visited project sites to perform quality control, conducted meetings and ensured client satisfaction. Exceeded customer and agency timeline expectations by completing many projects ahead

(continued)

(continued)

of schedule. Consulted with DoD agencies and DISA internal/external clients to DEFINE AND ANALYZE FUNCTIONAL REQUIREMENTS and translated into technical specifications on the client's Service Request Form (SRF).

- **NEW INITIATIVE: LEAN SIX SIGMA—SERVICE REQUEST FORM (SRF) IMPROVEMENT**
  As Implementation Project Manager, I successfully completed customer's SRF and delivery to the Business Office to ultimately deliver a Letter Estimate (LE) to the customer that contained the customer solution, summary of requirements, estimated costs, project approach and timeline, and implementation plan. I developed a leaner, more time-efficient process oriented toward greater customer satisfaction. This initiative facilitated an improved SERVICE LEVEL MANAGEMENT, ensuring that agreed services were delivered effectively and efficiently with maximum customer satisfaction.

- **HOST BASED SECURITY SYSTEM (HBSS) SHORTEN**
  Implementation Project Manager, Mandated IAW CTO 07-12, FRAGO 13, and INFOCON 3 to install HBSS application on all DoD Windows-based systems. Completion date: 30 Oct 2009. Project ongoing and ahead of schedule. Anticipate full IOC 30 July 2009. Project is now completed.

  Estimated Implementation Costs: $ 894,130.56
  Estimated Annual Recurring Costs: $86,236.04
  ANTICIPATED TANGIBLE/INTANGIBLE SAVINGS: Cost and man hours due to completions three months ahead of schedule.

PROVIDED EXPERT TECHNICAL ADVICE on complex issues involving integration and configuration of computer hardware and software. SERVED AS SUBJECT-MATTER EXPERT IN CONFIGURATION MANAGEMENT, SOFTWARE SERVICES CAPABILITIES, AND OPERATIONS, providing in-depth briefings at high-level DISA meetings. Assembled, researched, analyzed, and reported on information to improve IT systems, indicating specific recommendations for enhancements. Served as functional and technical expert for DISA products and services. Provided advice and guidance on technical problems and issues to project staff.

LED AND DIRECTED PROJECT STAFF in the implementation of critical DoD enterprise-wide and DISA IT projects. Led numerous IT professionals with responsibilities in operating systems and customer support to ensure mission-related activities are effectively planned, coordinated, and executed. Communicated to team the overall organizational mission, specific details of assignments, work product requirements, project work plans, and individual and team project deadlines. Developed goals and implemented processes to effectively meet and exceed mission objectives. Monitored implementation and completion of work, and evaluated performance and work quality to ensure smooth and efficient operations.

PROVIDED OUTSTANDING AND HIGH-QUALITY CUSTOMER SERVICE to DoD community and DISA internal/external customers. Worked closely with customers to identify and analyze new information systems requirements, operational problems, and quantitative and qualitative performance issues. Provided timely, efficient, and courteous service.

DEMONSTRATED EFFECTIVE ORAL COMMUNICATION SKILLS, developing collaborative relationships with customers, IT professionals, and external personnel. Conducted regularly scheduled Blue Team meetings to monitor and facilitate pre-implementation activities, ensuring successful completion of SRF and delivery to Business Office, proper pricing of requirements, and completion of customer LE, ultimately resulting in a Service Level Agreement (SLA). Participated in top-level briefings to discuss customer requirements and organizational problems; informed management of scheduling, costing, scope creep, and delays in projects that appear to jeopardize required timeline. Discussed impacts on project with senior leadership.

PREPARE A VARIETY OF COMPLEX WRITTEN MATERIALS AND REPORTS. Researched, gathered, compiled, and analyzed data; created project management briefings and reports, budgets, functional statements, organization charts, and resource plans for senior-level approval. Developed and executed project schedules and implementation plans. Ensured all documents were thorough, accurate, and timely.

JOB EXPERIENCE #3

Selected as Acting Branch Chief, Information Management Support Branch, facilitating accomplishment of organizational goals. Developed computer-based IT-assisted information-dissemination goals for DTS-W. Provided technical leadership across broad spectrum of telecommunications, IT, information management, and customer relationship management issues. Served as project manager, special projects coordinator, and technical liaison for key mission activities; collaborated with high-ranking officials throughout DoD, federal agencies, and private industry. Led meetings with DTS-W end users and vendors; ensured all contracts were managed in compliance with contract terms.

(continued)

(continued)

KEY PROJECTS AND ACCOMPLISHMENTS

- Provided project management and oversight for installation and modernization of integrated services digital network of 66 billing account codes and 3,000+ telephony stations.

- Played major role in development, implementation, and maintenance of DTS-W's World Wide Web site. Described by superiors as "customer focused...an exceptional job of managing conversion of the DTS-W website from HTML to MS FrontPage."

- Lead Account Manager of special committee providing value-added service for DoD accounts in National Capital Region. Managed installation of T1 circuits at Pentagon and Rosslyn, resulting in improved LAN workflow and reduced cost and time delays.

JOB EXPERIENCE #4

Successfully completed internship, earning repeated promotions as Telecommunications Specialist. Performed as technical advisor in designing, developing, testing, and evaluating procedures and/or methodologies used to design and install sophisticated electronic/electrical equipment. Performed complex evaluations of procedures, techniques, models, and systems. Initiated solutions with vendor technicians and in-house staff. Coordinated operation of organization's telecommunications network.

PROFESSIONAL TRAINING

Immersion Seminar, Public Speaking, Dale Carnegie Institute, 2009
DISA Lean Six Sigma Green Belt, 2008
Project Management Professional (PMP), 2008
IT Infrastructure Library (ITIL), ITIL Foundation Version 3, 2008
Leadership Development III, 2007
Leadership Development II, 2006
Microsoft Project 2000 (Level I & II), 2005
Leadership Development I, 2004
Aspiring Leaders, 2004
STAR Customer Service, 2002

EDUCATION

Master of Science, Strayer University, Alexandria, VA. Major: Computer Information Systems. GPA: 3.8; Honors Graduate.

Bachelor of Science, Rowan University, Glassboro, NJ. Major: Management Information Systems. GPA: 2.5.

LICENSURES AND CERTIFICATIONS

Certification—IT Infrastructure Library (ITIL), v.3, 01/2009
Certification—DISA Lean Six Sigma Green Belt, 12/2008
Certification—Project Management Professional (PMP), 01/2008
Certificate—Directorate of Information Management (DOIM), 1997
Certificate—US Army Signal School, Signal Officers Basic Course (SOBC), 1998
Certificate—Information Resource Management,
Army Material Engineering College, (AMEC), Rock Island, IL, 1997

Summary

To review and keep it simple, study the vacancy announcement carefully for the top critical skills. Make sure you are qualified for the position and present your relevant qualifications clearly. Write about your projects and accomplishments. And be sure to include customer services, problem solving, and meeting customer needs for IT services and projects.

CHAPTER 16

Contract Specialist and Acquisition Specialist Resumes

By Sandra Lee Keppley

Today more than ever, the federal government must ensure that it spends money wisely and eliminates waste and abuse of taxpayer dollars.

The Office of Federal Procurement Policy (OFPP) in the Office of Management and Budget plays a central role in shaping the policies and practices federal agencies use to acquire goods and services needed to carry out their responsibilities. OFPP was established by Congress in 1974 to provide overall direction for government-wide procurement policies, regulations, and procedures and to promote economy, efficiency, and effectiveness in acquisition processes. OFPP is headed by an administrator who is appointed by the president and confirmed by the Senate.

OFPP Background

The Clinger-Cohen Act, issued in February 1996, amended the Office of Federal Procurement Policy (OFPP) Act to require that the administrator of OFPP establish qualification requirements, including educational requirements, for positions at civilian agencies in the GS-1102 series (see 41 U.S.C. 433). Five years earlier, Congress had established requirements for 1,102 positions in defense agencies through the Defense Acquisition Workforce Improvement Act (see 10 U.S.C. 1724, 1732). The Clinger-Cohen language stipulates that qualification requirements established by OFPP shall be comparable to the DAWIA requirements. In June 1997, the U.S. Office of Personnel Management (OPM) published a qualification standard imposing requirements established by OFPP pursuant to Clinger-Cohen. In September 1997, OFPP established career management, education, and training requirement for contracting personnel in civilian executive agencies.

The OFPP published Policy Letter 05-01, dated April 14, 2005, "Developing and Managing the Acquisition Workforce." The letter established a government-wide framework for creating a federal acquisition workforce with the skills necessary to deliver best-value supplies and services.

A major focus of the OFPP policy is directed toward the development of a capable and competent workforce. As is true for all federal agencies developing core competencies to address skills gaps related to mission-critical occupations, the OFPP is fostering the development of core competencies in conjunction with DoD and OPM for use in defense and civilian agencies.

In January 2006, federal agencies were advised of the deployment of the Federal Acquisition Certification Program. The program is intended to standardize education, training, and experience requirements for contracting professionals, thus improving workforce competencies and increasing career opportunities. The program is akin to the DoD program requirements and is administered by each agency.

The federal certification in contracting is not mandatory for all GS-1102s; however, members of the workforce issued new Contracting Officer (CO) warrants on or after January 1, 2007, regardless of GS series, must be certified at an appropriate level to support their warrant obligations.

The following letters provide additional information on the contract specialist and acquisitions positions in government that may be of interest to you:

- Letter published by the Executive Office of the President, Office of Management and Budget, dated January 20, 2006, Subject: "The Federal Acquisition Certification in Contracting Program" (www.whitehouse.gov/sites/default/files/omb/procurement/acq_wk/fac_contracting_program.pdf).

- Letter published by the Executive Office of the President, Office of Management and Budget, dated April 25, 2007, Subject: "Federal Acquisition Certification for Program and Project Managers" (www.whitehouse.gov/sites/default/files/omb/procurement/workforce/fed_acq_cert_042507.pdf)

The Federal Acquisition Institute provides an example of acquisition competencies within specific occupational career fields—the essential acquisition competencies required for federal architectural/engineering employees (see www.fai.gov/acm/aecomp.asp). Many engineers are now dually trained as Acquisition Specialists, enabling them to manage contractors and contracts, and accomplish lifecycle management of engineering projects. The vacancy announcements often state that you may have dual responsibilities in your engineering/technical field, as well as acquisitions management. These competencies detail the knowledge, skills, and abilities needed to acquire and manage architectural/engineering services for an agency.

Finally, the Office of Personnel Management's website provides extensive information relative to educational requirements, exceptions, waivers, and qualifications: www.opm.gov/qualifications/standards/IORs/gs1100/1102QAs.htm

Skills for Contracting and Acquisition Experts

What skill sets do contracting experts in federal agencies need to demonstrate? The following sections list these skills by candidate type.

Federal Employees Seeking Positions in the Contracting Series

You need to know the technical skills of contracting, as well as the transferable business management and communications skills required to negotiate and monitor large-scale service and product provision contracts. It will help if you can show that you have done investigative work as well as detailed studies, collection, analysis, and dissemination of information in your present job or in recent jobs. You also need to demonstrate that you have studied business at the associate or bachelor's degree level. Include this information in your resume and in your Knowledge, Skills, and Abilities accomplishments in the resume.

Military Members with Contracting Experience Considering Federal Jobs in Contracting

Good news! If you are about to exit the military service and have professional contracting experience, you might qualify for the GS-1102 series in the federal government based on your experience and expertise gained in the military, even if you have not completed a college degree and even if you do not have 24 semester hours in business. This is a relatively new waiver procedure based on the fact that federal agencies are hurting for qualified professionals with experience.

Competencies Needed for Contract Specialists in Government

Here are the most important competencies for government contract specialists, who purchase billions of dollars of goods and services every year in order to provide government employees and military personnel with the support they need. These competencies are important for your federal resume, your accomplishments, and your structured interview.

- **Computer literacy:** Some agencies use more complex computerized contract writing software than others; however, the bottom line is that contract specialists are "administratively independent" in the 21st century and do not have contract clerks to type up lengthy contracts for them, as in the old days.

- **Ability to work independently:** Along with the new administrative independence comes more professional independence.

- **Quality assurance:** Continual review of the Statement of Work against the services being provided. Attention to detail is critical.

- **Problem solving and follow-up:** Answering questions concerning performance, expectations, timing, and cooperation with government employees. Problem solving with performance, statement of work questions, and change order requests.

- **Customer service:** Continual communication with project managers and contract officer technical representatives. Constant communication via e-mail and telephone to ensure products and services are delivered on time and on budget.

- **Negotiation skills:** The ability to represent the government for the best value in terms of product, delivery, and price; the skill in analyzing the vendor's ability to perform and meet the statement of work that was negotiated.

- **Teamwork:** Working in combination with project managers, employees, and supervisors.

- **Creativity:** As daily problems occur, contract specialists resolve them with contractors and other government employees to keep projects going for the good of the project and the government's investment.

Examples of the Types of Contracts Negotiated and Managed

Quoting from the online version of the GS-1102 series standards, contracting work in the federal government includes the following specialty areas:

- **Supplies:** Commodities range from commercial off-the-shelf products, components, or spare parts; to unique items requiring fabrication to specification.

- **Services:** Services include professional or nonprofessional, such as research for a specified level of effort, field engineering work requiring specialized equipment, the delivery of a series of lectures, or provision of janitorial services to perform specific tasks in specific locations. When contracting for services, competition may be based on both price and technical considerations.

- **Construction:** This includes construction of public buildings and repair or alteration of building structures, hospitals, prisons, mints, dams, bridges, power plants, irrigation systems, highways, roads, trails, and other real property. Construction contracts have a variety of special requirements that must be followed.

- **Computers and Telecommunications:** Computer acquisition with supporting software, maintenance, and services is governed by a separate statute and special regulations. In computer and telecommunications contracting, competition is based on both price and technical considerations.

- **Research and Development:** Research and development contractors are selected primarily for technical considerations, although a thorough evaluation and comparison of all relevant business, price, and technical factors are required for meaningful source selection. Technical evaluations are directed both to the proposal itself and to the contractor's capabilities in relation to it.

- **Major Systems:** Major systems are the combination of elements—such as hardware, software, or construction—that will function together to produce the capabilities required to fulfill a mission need. Major systems-acquisition programs are directed at and critical to fulfilling an agency mission; entail the allocation of relatively large resources; and warrant special management attention. Major systems are designated as such by the agency head according to a variety of criteria established by the Office of Management and Budget and by the individual agency. Examples of large procurements, some of which are designated as major systems and are subject to major systems acquisitions policies and procedures, are federal office buildings; hospitals; prisons; power-generating plants; dams; energy demonstration programs; transportation systems; ship, aircraft, or missile systems; space systems; and ADP systems designated as major systems.

Two Sample Federal Resumes for Contract Specialist Series

This section presents two sample resumes for the Contract Specialist series. Figure 16.1 is for a federal employee changing occupational series from Agricultural Marketing Specialist to Contract Specialist. There are similar skills in her current series. She is an expert study analyst, manager, negotiator, and program/contract analyst. Her current position is very unique but has similar skills to those needed in the Contract series.

Figure 16.2 is for a government contractor real estate professional seeking a change to the Contract Specialist series. The skills for real estate contracts are similar to federal contracts, including pre-award, post-award, contract management, and negotiation skills.

Both sample federal resumes include the KSAs in the resume, along with the keywords from the Specialized Experience and Duties sections. They are written in the Outline Format, which will be easy to copy and paste into the USAJOBS resume builder.

Target Job: Contract Specialist, GS-1102-12.
Career change—federal to federal resume.
Targeted, written, and designed by Dottie Hendricks, Certified Federal Resume Writer (CFRW).
Occupational Standards: www.opm.gov/fedclass/gs1102.pdf

SASHA HENRY
10404 D Street, NW
Washington, DC 20004
Day Phone: (444) 444-4444
Email: shenry1010@gmail.com

WORK EXPERIENCE	US Department of Agriculture, Foreign Agriculture Service Washington , DC US	11/2004 - Present

Grade Level: GS-12
Salary: 77,368 USD Per Year
Hours per week: 40

AGRICULTURAL MARKETING SPECIALIST, 1146
REVIEW, ADMINISTER, AND CLOSE FOOD AID AGREEMENTS
Demonstrate knowledge of Federal Acquisition Regulations and contract laws to perform reviews of agreement language and logistics and monetization reports submitted by Private Voluntary Organizations for the Office of Capacity Building and Development food assistance programs, including Food for Progress and Food for Education. Review budgets; compare reports to determine success of program.

• My role is combating world hunger. As an Agricultural Marketing Specialist, I helped enable the USDA to implement a $2.9 million food processing agreement with Zambia. I read the agreement language, closed the deal, reviewed report logs, and checked audits. I ensured proper shipping costs and fair prices. Despite logistical challenges and potential fraud, my awareness of details and procedures ensured that there were no major commodity losses.
• RESULT: The USDA food program successfully functioned in areas frequently plagued by hunger.

ANALYZE POST-AWARD AND CONTRACTS FOR FOREIGN FOOD SERVICE
Review and analyze Reports of Independent Auditors on Internal Control over Financial Reporting, Compliance, and other matters based on an audit of financial statements performed in accordance with Government Auditing Standards to determine if there were any reportable conditions. Determine and resolve cases where there are findings on Federal Award and Question Costs; report on status of the previous year's findings and resolution.

• I helped desperately poor people in the Third World. I supervised multiple agreements that funded micro- and mini-entrepreneurs through FINCA (Foundation for International Community Assistance). I negotiated and implemented deals to help fund family farms that needed to boost agricultural production. Funds also went to HIV patients, including many women who were primary breadwinners and caring for infants.

ANALYZE ACQUISITION PLANS
Monitor and evaluate data to ensure that all objectives and criteria for measuring progress have been met, including amounts sold, distributed, bartered, lost or destroyed; budget, audit, reporting, and tax requirements, along with the results of the program. Provide success stories – written and pictures – to Public Affairs of unexpected outcomes for a program. The information is forwarded to Congress for a yearly report and snippets are posted on the FAS's website.

ANALYZE CONTRACT PRICE / COST DATA AND PROCUREMENT ACTIONS
As the lead for government-to-government food aid agreements, analyze data submitted by the governments of specific countries and Private Voluntary Organizations (PVOs) designated by the program. Review agreements for completeness and accuracy in keeping with the program's closure regulations. In addition, review tax certifications, lists of equipment valued at more than $5,000 purchased in host countries, and how assets will be disposed.

DESCRIPTION AND ACCOMPLISHMENTS CONTINUED IN ADDITIONAL INFORMATION.
(Contact Supervisor: Yes, Supervisor's Name: Bernie Kenneth, Supervisor's Phone: (202) 999-9999)

US Department of Agriculture, Foreign	10/2009 - 3/2010

Figure 16.1: Resume for federal-to-federal career changer.

Agriculture Service
Washington, DC US

Grade Level: GS-12
Salary: 77,368 USD Per Year
Hours per week: 40

Executive Leadership Program Detail, 1146
Selected as the first Foreign Agricultural Service (FAS) employee for the Executive Leadership Program (ELP), offered at the USDA Graduate School. The ELP is an intensive nine-month leadership-development program designed to develop future public service leaders through assessment, experiential learning, and individual activity opportunities. Successfully graduated in June 2010.

ACCOMPLISHMENTS:
• Managed oversight of project funding for marketing plans submitted by three agricultural trade associations. Conducted and reviewed marketing plans, budgets, special money evaluations, and applicant's brand component to determine if the co-operator was in compliance with program's requirements. Compared current to previous years marketing performance and budget. RESULTS: Recommended new policies to support economic considerations for AMS services.

• Contributed to a background piece for the Raisin Administrative Committee in preparation for Secretary Vilsack's visit to Japan in April 2010. Participated in meetings with industry groups, industry board meetings, and internal training sessions with the Office of Trade Programs (OTP) staff. Assisted in coordinating the annual U.S. Agricultural Export Development Council (USAEDC) conference.
(Contact Supervisor: Yes, Supervisor's Name: Lily Staehl, Supervisor's Phone: (202) 444-4444)

USDA FAS
Washington, DC US

11/2004 - 11/2008

Grade Level: GS-9
Salary: 55,000 USD Per Year
Hours per week: 40

Agricultural Marketing Specialist, 1146
KNOWLEDGE OF THE FEDERAL ACQUISITION REGULATION
Evaluated and monitored active grant agreements and closed food aid agreements, ensuring grantee compliance with terms and applicable laws and regulations. Prepared final evaluations which illustrated that program had achieved objectives.

COST/PRICE ANALYSIS
Analyze cost/price of products distributed and stored by the PVO. Request full written explanations. Determine the price of the commodity based on reasonable, competitive price within 10-15% of world market and local market prices. Review deposits, including dates and interest on disbursements provided in both local currency and U.S. dollar equivalent.

PLAN AND NEGOTIATE MULTI-YEAR CONTRACTS AND AGREEMENTS
Reviewed, evaluated, and scored/ranked proposals in order to arrive at the final number of project plans to receive funding during fiscal year. Evaluated a complex set of criteria to determine and document a score and a letter grade for each proposal based on data that included budget constraints, past performance, and other organizations' programming in the country.

DEVELOPED BRIEFING MATERIALS AND REPORTS
Met with Branch Chief, Deputy Director, and/or Director to determine the successful bidders. Presented approval and rejection letters and all appropriate backup material to support decisions. Translated results of the briefing into the agreements.
(Contact Supervisor: Yes, Supervisor's Name: Duffie Day, Supervisor's Phone: (202) 333-3333)

EDUCATION

George Washington University

Washington, DC US
Some College Coursework Completed
Major: Graduate Courses, Information System Technology

(continued)

(continued)

Strayer University
Washington, DC US
Bachelor's Degree
Major: Computer Information Systems

Strayer University
Washington, DC US
Bachelor's Degree
Major: Business Administration

JOB RELATED TRAINING

USDA Graduate School, Executive Leadership Program, Washington, DC, 06/2010
Con 100 – Federal Acquisition Institute – 04/2010
Project Management – 09/2008
Data Collection & Analysis – 08/2008

ADDITIONAL INFORMATION

WORK EXPERIENCE CONTINUED:

AGRICULTURAL MARKETING SPECIALIST, GS1146 12 11/2004 – Present
United States Department of Agriculture 40 hours/week

INTERVIEW AND NEGOTIATE WITH STAKEHOLDERS
Collaborate with and contact stakeholders in PVOs and foreign governments and within the department to assemble information related to completing the closeout process. Review program reports, compile data, and assess extent to which program goals are attained, commitments fulfilled, and budgetary limits observed. Respond to questions via phone and e-mail or hard copy. Interact with PVOs and Embassies, and with USAID if country does not have an embassy.

DOCUMENT REVIEW FOR COMPLIANCE
Evaluate documents and proposals for compliance with specifications and purchase descriptions. Review applicable clauses in contracting document notes provided by third-party accounting firms conforming to the OMB's A-133 requirements concerning nonprofit organizations receiving more than $500,000 in federal awards in a year to determine whether notes apply to USDA grant food aid programs.

ANALYZE POST-AWARD AND CONTRACTS FOR FOREIGN FOOD SERVICE
Review and analyze Reports of Independent Auditors on Internal Control over Financial Reporting, Compliance, and other matters based on an audit of financial statements performed in accordance with Government Auditing Standards to determine if there were any reportable conditions. Determine and resolve cases where there are findings on Federal Award and Question Costs; report on status of the previous year's findings and resolution. Prepare letter to be signed by Division Director requesting documentation concerning the resolution, if finding involves a questioned cost, to file an official claim. The letter may request a meeting with the organization to discuss audit findings. In most cases, because there are findings unrelated to USDA programs or none at all, no action is warranted. Occasionally, a suspension or debarment is warranted.

INTERVIEW AND NEGOTIATE WITH STAKEHOLDERS
Collaborate with and contact stakeholders in PVOs and foreign governments and within the department to assemble information related to completing the closeout process. Review program reports, compile data, and assess extent to which program goals are attained, commitments fulfilled, and budgetary limits observed. Respond to questions via phone and e-mail or hard copy. Interact with PVOs and Embassies, and with USAID if country does not have an embassy.

WRITE COMPLIANCE NARRATIVES
Prepare reports, letters, and various documents including a comprehensive 5- to 10-page evaluation of each program's effectiveness detailing whether the program's objectives were met. Prepare a 3-page Evaluation and Compliance Checklist detailing commodity losses, commodity distribution, budgetary allocations, and monetization program data followed by a 1-page financial analysis Excel document which provides details on how the PVO has spent proceeds (called monetization) from the sale of the commodity and cash provided for Commodity Credit Corporation (CCC).

NEGOTIATE AND RECOMMEND CLOSE-OUT SETTLEMENTS

Lead analyst and negotiator if discrepancies are found. If criteria are met, I initiate letter stating that PVO has fulfilled their obligation for administering the program. This letter may include a request to return cash from monetization proceeds or request a reimbursement for outstanding expenses. If criteria are not met, I initiate an issue letter providing an analytical summary of any monetary disputes identified in connection with expenditure under an agreement. The letter includes citations in the agreement or regulations for each issue identified, and instructs the PVO what to do if they disagree with FAS's position. I then issue final close-out letter request upon completion of all steps.

SUMMARY OF QUALIFICATIONS:

-- Six years federal government experience as an Agricultural Marketing Specialist progressively earning responsibility and promotions.

-- Knowledge of Federal Contracting regulations and procedures, including Federal Acquisition Regulations and USDA regulations.

-- Proficient in Microsoft Office software and USDA systems including Food Aid Database (FAD) and the Unified Export Strategy (UES) Database, Federal Audit Clearinghouse Database.

COMPUTER PROFICIENCY:
MS Office Suite, Food Aid Database (FAD) and United Export Strategy (UES) Database, Federal Audit Clearinghouse Database

AWARDS:
2009-2010: Selected as the first Foreign Agricultural Service (FAS) employee for the Executive Leadership Program (ELP), offered at the USDA Graduate School.
Honorary Award, Foreign Agricultural Service Outstanding Cross-Agency Team, 2009

PROFESSIONAL AFFILIATIONS:
Heartland Hospice, current volunteer since 03/2010
USDA, Toastmasters Club, Club 3294, District 27, member since 03/2005
Board Member, Ottley Music School, member since 01/1999

SPECIALIZED EXPERIENCE:

Specialized Experience at the GS-12 level: One year specialized experience at the GS-11 level. Specialized experience is defined as experience applying **federal contract regulations** and procedures to federal acquisitions from inception to post-award for goods and services to include unique equipment and IT services. Experience working to assure that small businesses are utilized to meet the requirements of the **Federal Acquisition Regulations.** Experience **negotiating** the modification of **solicitation and/or contract terms,** conditions, or funding arrangements, as required.

HOW YOU WILL BE EVALUATED:

You will be evaluated to determine if you meet the minimum qualifications required; and on the extent to which your application shows that you possess the knowledge, skills, and abilities associated with this position as defined below. When describing your knowledge, skills, and abilities, please be sure to give examples and explain how often you used these skills, the complexity of the knowledge you possessed, the level of the people you interacted with, the sensitivity of the issues you handled, etc.

1. Knowledge of and experience applying **contract laws, regulations**, and procedures applicable to **federal acquisitions** from inception, to **post-award, and procurement** of unique equipment, IT services, Architect-Engineering, and Construction contracts.

(continued)

(continued)

2. Knowledge of and experience with a range of contract types, methods of contracting, and experience with source selection to plan appropriate strategies to procure complex requirements, and to conduct negotiations in the **pre-award and post-award phases of contracting.**

3. Knowledge of and experience applying the **Federal Acquisition Regulations (FAR)** and experience in the review and development of **Acquisition Plans,** determinations and findings, sole-source justifications, and source selection plans, as well as the ability to plan procurement strategies and participate in all stages of the procurement cycle, i.e., pre-award, source selection, **contract negotiation**, and administration). Please provide specific examples.

4. Knowledge of and experience with **cost/price analysis** techniques (i.e., analyze cost and pricing data and contract proposals) and to evaluate the offers for responsibility and realism.

Keyword List for the Outline Format Federal Resume

1. Federal contract laws and regulations
2. Post-award and procurement analysis
3. Pre-award and post-award phases of contracting
4. Federal Acquisitions Regulations (FAR)
5. Acquisition plans
6. Contract negotiation
7. Cost/price analysis

Target Job: Contract Specialist, GS-1102-9.
Government contractor to federal resume.
Targeted, written, and designed by Brian Wolak, Certified Federal Resume Writer (CFRW).

JOHNNY WESTFIELD
111 Manchester Drive
Boston, MA 22202
Day Phone: (444) 444-4444
Email: jwestfield11@gmail.com

WORK EXPERIENCE

CACI, Inc.	1/2009 - Present
Boston, MA US	

Salary: 40,000 USD Per Year
Hours per week: 40

REALTY TECHNICIAN
Contracted to General Services Administration
CONTRACT MANAGEMENT: Administer realty contracts with a broad and diverse range of government agencies to perform contract management, close outs, and terminations, including Social Security Administration, U.S Customs and Border Protection, Agricultural Marketing Services, Animal and Plant Health Inspection Service, Internal Revenue Service, Bureau of Indian Affairs, and Fish and Wildlife Service.

CONTRACT ADMINISTRATION: Support 15 contracting officers, 30 project managers, and over 300 projects. Manage paperwork, organize files, and provide general support while performing daily responsibilities. Knowledgeable of contractor and vendor performance parameters, and the need for clear, concise performance-based statements and measurements.

• Created new procedures that reduced contract processing time and enabled the swift identification of key documents among thousands to be reviewed. Drafted checklists to aid in the review process.

CONTRACT CLOSE OUTS: Process 7 to 10 contract close outs per month. Perform notification procedures to building service centers over the phone and in writing. Partner with contract officer. Correct documents as necessary. Create new agreements. Quality check documents to bill out correctly. Ensure that all paperwork, terms, steps, and procedures are complete so that contract is completed with absolute accuracy and integrity.

• Slashed processing time of close out procedures from months to hours. Suggested and helped implement personnel realignment so that key individuals now communicate critical steps, information, and updates. Devised inspection criteria to reduce processing time; errors are now spotted in minutes, and missing information is easy to procure.

PREPARE DOCUMENTS: Prepare new lease files and serve as the control point for new project requirements. Prepare award letters to contracting officer, Lessor, agency, and Federal Protective Services.
• Reduced Lessor billing time for contracts from months to days by suggesting and helping implement better inter-departmental relationship alignments. Able to produce contracts with few to no errors so that work is conducted up front, during process, instead of after. Created simultaneous processing procedures to speed up the schedule.

CONTRACT AWARDS: Maintain electronic copies of request-for-space documents and prepare lease file folders for project managers. Perform quality control of lease documents at award phase to enable the kick off of lease billing and rents.

(continued)

Figure 16.2: Resume for government contractor real estate professional transitioning to Contract Specialist series.

(continued)

CONTRACT TERMINATIONS: Process 5 to 6 contract terminations per month. Analyze contracts. Create termination documents to send out. Notify Lessor. Exercise rights for government. Send out letters with 60-, 90-, and 120-day notice. Create changes to lease contracts and send out contract modifications. Cancel billing to avoid incorrect charges.

++ DUTIES CONTINUED IN ADDITIONAL INFORMATION (Contact Supervisor: Yes, Supervisor's Name: Zia Warhol, Supervisor's Phone: (617) 444-4444)

Appraisal Group, Inc. **Waltham, MA US**	**1/2005 - 1/2009** **Salary: 65,000 USD Per Year** **Hours per week: 40**

Real Estate Appraiser
SUMMARY: Served as licensed residential real estate appraiser for numerous major banks and mortgage brokers. Appraised 20 homes per month while performing calculations, conducting research, writing reports, assembling information, and rendering conclusions.

ANALYSIS AND RESEARCH: Conducted field investigations of real estate properties to assign dollar value for home sales purposes. Performed in-person, empirical analysis of building type, improvements, construction quality, condition, and depreciation factors. Researched legal records for title and property information. Procured comparable property records for comparisons and the determination of accurate assessment value.

FINANCIAL ANALYSIS: Created appraisal reports with values, measurements, and statistics. Generated calculations based on numerous factors, including income records, operating costs, replacement estimates, building valuations, and cost estimators.

KEY ACCOMPLISHMENT:
- Managed all financial operations of a successful appraisal company, including accounts receivable, accounts payable, bookkeeping, and inflow.
(Contact Supervisor: Yes, Supervisor's Name: Self, Supervisor's Phone: (617) 444-4444)

County Assessor **Cambridge, MA US**	**1/2004 - 1/2005** **Salary: 36,000 USD Per Year** **Hours per week: 40**

REAL PROPERTY APPRAISER
INFORMATION COLLECTION: Collected market data, statistics, photographs, records, financials, comparables, and other information for each home being appraised. Conducted telephone interviews to verify information. Strategically amassed data then processed and distilled into workable points and formulas to arrive at final valuations.
• Successfully negotiated with several communities to release prior sales history to the county, which enabled me to properly classify the homes and land to arrive at an equitable value for the homeowner and the county.
• Reclassified 7,000 properties so they could be appraised in the same manner as the state-appraised properties adjacent to them.

REPORT CREATION: Created final appraisal reports in which researched and processed data was entered for home sales purposes. Incorporated financials, comparisons, photos, and records. Composed summaries.

WRITING: Displayed excellent writing skills and ability to convey complex concepts and processes in easy-to-understand terms. Knowledgeable of grammar, spelling, capitalization, and punctuation to compose straightforward letters or memoranda.
(Contact Supervisor: Yes, Supervisor's Name: Randolph Roberts, Supervisor's Phone: (617) 444-4444)

Sunset Homes **Cambridge, MA US**	**1/2000 - 1/2003** **Salary: 60,000 USD Per Year** **Hours per week: 50**

Project Manager

SUMMARY: Served as project manager while overseeing construction activities related to architects, engineers, and trade workers to ensure adherence to deadlines and funding parameters. Kept projects on task, on time, and within budget, according to contract specifications. Integrated project management knowledge with leadership and interpersonal, financial, and communications skills.

ACQUISITION: Created advertisements for bids; then reviewed and selected the bid most suitable to the timeframe and budget. Researched the price of materials, labor cost, and overhead expenses to analyze the bids received. Understood the uniform building construction codes and the county building codes to determine if the contractors were adhering to laws, regulations, and contract parameters.

PROCUREMENT AND CONTRACT MANAGEMENT: Prepared purchase agreements, contracts, and leases to acquire the most cost-effective services and terms. Compared prices, discounts, delivery dates, and handling charges. Negotiated prices and services. Managed contracts and activities related to electrical, plumbing, HVAC, excavation, and masonry work.

BUSINESS MANAGEMENT AND BUDGET: Coordinated integral business components pertaining to purchasing, estimating, contracts, construction, and architecture.

INTERPRET REGULATIONS AND TECHNICAL MATERIAL: Reviewed legal documentation to ensure that projects complied with state, government, and local building codes. Identified staffing requirements based on technical materials and documentation.

COMMUNICATION: Disseminated information by using telephone, mail services, websites, and e-mail. Communicated daily with wide range of individuals. Expressed ideas confidently in results-oriented manner. Actively listened to uncover unspoken needs. Provided constant status updates to supervisor and coworkers.

INTERPERSONAL SKILLS: Applied goals-oriented focus on all tasks and interactions to build and extend excellent relationships. Promoted positive interactions by adopting helpful, can-do attitude. Communicated with clients to determine needs and maintain complete and accurate records and files.
(Contact Supervisor: Yes, Supervisor's Name: Courtney Taylor, Supervisor's Phone: (617) 444-4444)

EDUCATION

Boston College
Boston, MA US
Bachelor's Degree - 5/2003
Major: Finance
GPA: 3.5 out of 4.0

ADDITIONAL INFORMATION

WORK EXPERIENCE (CONTINUED)

Realty Technician, 1/2009 – Present
CACI, Inc.
Boston, MA

ANALYZE FACTS AND CONDITIONS: Prepare and analyze contract data from procurement systems to create and maintain aging contract termination list. Serve as subject-matter expert with respect to close outs and terminations. Perceive positive or negative implications of contractual agreements and communicate findings to contract officers.

PROFILE

Tireless, analytical, expert professional with contract, real estate, and appraising experience. Constantly seeking ways to improve processes and optimize efficiencies. Take charge of initiatives with minimal guidance and complete all assignments ahead of schedule while exceeding expectations. Continually seeking new opportunities to broaden skills and knowledge while devoting maximum effort to all assigned tasks. Deconstruct complex activities into simpler, more manageable components. Able to perceive the larger picture while recommending and helping implement departmental or procedural alignments to reduce labor/time while ensuring accuracy.

PERFORMANCE AWARDS

+ Rated 5 (Outstanding) out of 5, Midyear Performance Review, General Service Administration, 5/2010
+ Rated 4 (Highly Successful) out of 5, Yearly Performance Review, General Service Administration, 10/2009

SPECIALIZED EXPERIENCE FOR GS-9

To qualify for the GS-9, you must have one year of specialized experience equivalent to at least the GS-7 grade level; OR two years of progressively higher-level graduate education OR masters OR equivalent graduate degree or LL.B. or J.D. Specialized experience is described as demonstrated experience: (1) reviewing **contracting or procurement actions** to determine that **proper specifications/purchase descriptions** are included in **solicitation documents**, and (2) **evaluating bids or proposals** for **compliance with specifications/purchase descriptions** and applicable clauses; OR comparable experience.

KSAs:

- Specialized experience must have provided a knowledge of **contracting laws, regulations,** principles, and procedures, contracts and provisions, and **methods of contracting**; knowledge of the principles, concepts, and techniques of procurement.

- Knowledge of basic **acquisition procedures** to carry out development assignments involving use of standard procedures and techniques.

- Knowledge and skill to draw conclusions and **make recommendations** by analyzing facts and conditions, and making comparison of prices, discounts, delivery dates, or handling charges.

- Knowledge of arithmetic **pricing practices** used in business (e.g., discounts and warranties) sufficient to compare prices on recurring types of procurements.

- Knowledge and skill to apply guideline material by reading and **interpreting procurement regulations and technical material**, and translating the guidance into specific actions, e.g., assisting in the preparation of solicitation documents.

Keywords:

1. Contracting or procurement actions
2. Proper specifications / purchase descriptions
3. Solicitation documents
4. Evaluating bids or proposals
5. Compliance with specifications/purchase descriptions
6. Contracting laws and regulations
7. Methods of contracting
8. Acquisition procedures
9. Make recommendations
10. Pricing practices
11. Interpreting procurement regulations and technical material

Summary

As you develop your Contract Specialist federal resume, think about your business acumen: your ability to manage contract dollars, monitor performance, manage information, negotiate changes, resolve problems, and keep the customer happy. You could make a "deal list" or "contract list" and add these contract negotiations to your federal resume as your accomplishments. Your ability to be expert with the types of contract "vehicles" for government will improve your performance and resourcefulness in achieving your government customer purchasing and contract objectives. The more you learn, the more you can grow your career in this professional job series.

CHAPTER 17

Management Assistant and Administrative Work Experience

With Hiring Reform and KSAs in the resume, including accomplishments in the resume will be mandatory to get referred or interviewed for a promotion in government or a first-time federal position. The following examples of Work Experience sections for three case studies for administrative professionals are written with accomplishments and without.

Some job seekers have trouble coming up with accomplishments for administrative tasks, so I wanted you to see how the resume looks with accomplishments and without. If you can come up with some examples that demonstrate your skill as an administrative assistant, it can help you stand out and get referred to a supervisor.

The challenge of writing your Work Experience/Duties sections will be to think of your duties and accomplishments differently. The entire culture of writing your resume has changed.

With separate KSA narratives eliminated, the HR specialists and supervisors will be looking for something in the resume that will give them an indication that you will solve problems in the office, improve efficiencies, give outstanding support to customers, train coworkers in new systems, and be resourceful in meeting the office objectives.

Ways to Remember Your Accomplishments

Think about things you have done in your job that are "above and beyond" your daily duties. Think of and remember accomplishments or new ideas that you have implemented—even without recognition by your supervisor or coworkers. These are examples of things you have done that improved the office operation, made your work faster to produce each day, and improved the quality of the work.

Here are questions to help you remember your work accomplishments:

- What has been most challenging about your job?
- What did you do most in your job?
- What problems did you solve?
- What do you really do in this job?
- Who is your biggest customer, or who do you talk to the most?
- Who is your most popular and problematic customer?

- Did you do anything that really made a difference in the office?
- Did you ever set up a new system that saved time or money for the office?
- Is your job critical for meeting the mission of your office?

Here are some of the most powerful keywords for accomplishments:

- Improved
- Changed
- Implemented
- Created
- Designed

Read Chapter 7, "Plain-Language Writing Lessons," and learn some language that you can use to stand out with your accomplishments.

Write Your Accomplishments with Numbers and Percentages

Accomplishments and KSAs should be written with quantifiable numbers. You will be proving your knowledge, skills, and abilities with specific accomplishments and the numbers or percentages will prove that you have success in a certain area.

Here are some examples of accomplishment statements that you might be able to customize to your situation by adding relevant numbers:

___(#) years of extensive experience in _____ and _____.

Won _____(#) awards for _____.

Trained/Supervised _____(#) full-time and _____(#) part-time employees.

Recommended by _____ (a number of notable people) as a _____ (something good that they said about you) for excellent _____ (an accomplishment or skill).

Supervised a staff of _____(#)

Recruited _____ (#) staff members in _____ (period of time), increasing overall production.

Purchased _____ (# of products) in _____ (period of time).

Exceeded organizational goals in _____(#) years/months/days.

Provided administrative and other support to _____(#) (senior managers, program managers, analysts, team members, contractors).

You can also write your accomplishments using percentages:

> Recognized as a leader in the office, using strong skills to affect a/an _____%
> increase in team/coworker production.
>
> Streamlined _____ (office procedure), decreasing hours spent on task by
> _____(%).
>
> Used extensive _____ (several skills) skills to increase customer/member
> base by _____(%).
>
> Financed _____(%) of tuition/education/own business.
>
> Graduated within the top _____(%) of class.
>
> Contributed to the success of the office mission as a result of new, more efficient processes
> which saved approximately _____(%) daily time.
>
> Resolved customer relations issues, increasing customer satisfaction by _____(%).
>
> Eliminated _____ (a customer or office problem), increasing productivity by
> _____(%).
>
> Upgraded _____ (an industry tool), resulting in _____ (%)
> increase in effectiveness.

Management Assistant Federal Resume Case Study

The following case study includes two samples of how *not* to write your federal resume. The Big Block and Bullet formats, better known as the laundry list, are favorite formats from the days before hiring reform.

The Outline Format with buckets of skills—small paragraphs and keywords—should also include accomplishments so that it will be easier for the HR specialist and the supervisor to read.

This first sample is really impressive. The first two versions of the resume are very boring and nothing stands out. But the third and fourth are fascinating. Look at this administrative accomplishment in both Iraq and Afghanistan:

> DIRECT, COORDINATE, AND MONITOR ADMINISTRATIVE FUNCTIONS AND ACTIVITIES for the Unit Equipping and Readiness Division (FDU) of Army G-8 (3-Star General), in support of soldiers in Afghanistan and Iraq. Coordinate U.S. Army staff actions among FDU, the Office of the Deputy Chief of Staff, Army G-8, and other U.S. Department of Defense offices.
>
> Designed and improved filing and recordkeeping system for personnel files for 350 contractors in 10 sites in Iraq and Afghanistan.

The Work Experience section has to prove the following six skills or KSAs:

DIRECT AND COORDINATE ADMINISTRATIVE FUNCTIONS AND ACTIVITIES

DEMONSTRATE KNOWLEDGE OF TRAVEL PROGRAM PROCEDURES AND PRACTICES

ADVANCED SKILL WITH OFFICE AUTOMATION SOFTWARE

SKILLED IN SCHEDULING AND COORDINATING WORK

MANAGED PURCHASES

OUTSTANDING ORAL AND WRITTEN COMMUNICATOR

Big Block Without Accomplishments

Following is an example of the Big Block format without accomplishments. This format is hard to read.

MANAGEMENT ASSISTANT   11/2008 - Present
CACI, Contractor for
U.S. Department of Defense, Arlington, VA 20310
40+ hours/week, Salary: $40,000/year

Direct, coordinate, and monitor administration for the Unit Equipping and Readiness Division (FDU) of Army G-8 (3-Star General), in support of soldiers in Afghanistan and Iraq. Coordinate U.S. Army staff actions among FDU, the Office of the Deputy Chief of Staff, Army G-8, and other U.S. Department of Defense offices. Maintain filing system and recordkeeping, manage administrative information and confidential personnel files, and assist in timely completion of evaluation reports and performance reviews, ensuring adherence to policy on records and reports control. Prioritize and meet time-sensitive deadlines. Manage administrative support in scheduling, planning, and arranging events and travel. Review, create, and process travel orders and claims. Utilize Defense Travel System (DTS) for travel Authorizations/Orders, vouchers, and other travel documents. Provide staff with information papers, read-ahead correspondence, trip books, slides, and speeches needed for travel and meetings. Proficient in the use of Microsoft Office suite; prepare correspondence, memoranda, briefing materials, and action and information papers using Word; create and maintain Excel spreadsheets to track personnel information and activities, to perform budget and financial tasks, and to maintain and provide database reports; utilize PowerPoint to prepare slides and presentations for groups of varied sizes. Determine integration of different types of software. Experienced with HTML, Internet navigation, and management of various other databases and federal software programs. Schedule and plan the calendar for Division Chief and track daily work schedule and responsibilities for FDU. SET ORGANIZATIONAL GOALS; use Headquarters of Department of the Army (HQDA) Tracking System to track timely completion of the division's tasks and actions.

Bullet Format (Laundry List)

Here's the same information in the Bullet format, which is also hard to read.

MANAGEMENT ASSISTANT   11/2008 - Present
CACI, Contractor for
U.S. Department of Defense, Arlington, VA 20310
40+ hours/ week, Salary: $40,000/year

- Direct, coordinate, and monitor administration for the Unit Equipping and Readiness Division (FDU) of Army G-8 (3-Star General), in support of soldiers in Afghanistan and Iraq.
- Coordinate U.S. Army staff actions among FDU, the Office of the Deputy Chief of Staff, Army G-8, and other U.S. Department of Defense offices.
- Maintain filing system and recordkeeping, manage administrative information and confidential personnel files, and assist in timely completion of evaluation reports and performance reviews, ensuring adherence to policy on records and reports control.
- Prioritize and meet time-sensitive deadlines.
- Manage administrative support in scheduling, planning, and arranging events and travel. Review, create, and process travel orders and claims.
- Utilize Defense Travel System (DTS) for travel Authorizations/Orders, vouchers, and other travel documents.
- Provide staff with information papers, read-ahead correspondence, trip books, slides, and speeches needed for travel and meetings.
- Proficient in the use of Microsoft Office suite; prepare correspondence, memoranda, briefing materials, and action and information papers using Word.
- Create and maintain Excel spreadsheets to track personnel information and activities, to perform budget and financial tasks, and to maintain and provide database reports.
- Utilize PowerPoint to prepare slides and presentations for groups of varied sizes. Determine integration of different types of software.
- Experienced with HTML, Internet navigation, and management of various other databases and federal software programs.
- Schedule and plan the calendar for Division Chief and track daily work schedule and responsibilities for FDU.
- Set organizational goals for Headquarters of Department of the Army (HQDA) Tracking System to track timely completion of the division's tasks and actions.
- Schedule and coordinate teleconferences involving the coordination of time sensitive international settings requiring specific and varied operational equipment and trained personnel to provide required security and ensure operational effectiveness.
- Monitor and track via spreadsheets the status of Division computer and IT equipment by name, serial number, service tag numbers, and make/model.
- Prepare accurate, clear, concise, and timely correspondence, reports and documents; provide correct instructions, information and guidance.
- Research regulations and draft reports on diverse themes involving program accomplishments and recommend further study and analysis to ensure effective decision-making.
- Communicate with military and civilian leaders at all organizational levels up to and including 2 Star Generals as well as groups of military and civilian contracting staff with widely divergent backgrounds, interests, and points of view.
- Handle high volume of inquiries from internal and external stakeholders. Maintain strict confidentiality with sensitive and privileged information.

Outline Format Without Accomplishments

The following example is easier to read than the Bullet Format (laundry list) because it uses the Outline Format and the all-cap keyword headings. This section will just fit into the USAJOBS resume Duties section's 3,000 character limit.

(2,917 characters)

MANAGEMENT ASSISTANT   11/2008 - Present
CACI, Contractor for
U.S. Department of Defense, Arlington, VA 20310
40+ hours/ week, Salary: $40,000/year

DIRECT, COORDINATE, AND MONITOR ADMINISTRATIVE FUNCTIONS AND ACTIVITIES for the Unit Equipping and Readiness Division (FDU) of Army G-8 (3-Star General), in support of soldiers in Afghanistan and Iraq. Coordinate U.S. Army staff actions among FDU, the Office of the Deputy Chief of Staff, Army G-8, and other U.S. Department of Defense offices. Maintain filing system and recordkeeping, manage administrative information and confidential personnel files, assist in timely completion of evaluation reports and performance reviews, ensuring adherence to policy on records and reports control. Prioritize and meet time-sensitive deadlines.

DEMONSTRATE KNOWLEDGE OF ADMINISTRATIVE PROCEDURES AND PRACTICES; manage administrative support in scheduling, planning, and arranging events and travel. Review, create, and process travel orders and claims. Utilize Defense Travel System (DTS) for travel Authorizations/Orders, vouchers, and other travel documents. Provide staff with information papers, read-ahead correspondence, trip books, slides, and speeches needed for travel and meetings. Reserve facilities; schedule meetings, seminars, and special events within and outside the Pentagon which are conducted in-person, via video, and by telephone. Prepare materials and briefing books for participants.

POSSESS ADVANCED KNOWLEDGE AND SKILL IN THE USE OF OFFICE AUTOMATION SOFTWARE, proficient in the use of Microsoft Office suite; prepare correspondence, memoranda, briefing materials, and action and information papers using Word; create and maintain Excel spreadsheets to track personnel information and activities, to perform budget and financial tasks, and to maintain and provide database reports. Experienced with HTML, Internet navigation, and management of various other databases and federal software programs.

SKILLED IN SCHEDULING AND COORDINATING WORK and integrating planning efforts across work units. Manage calendar for Division Chief and track daily work schedule and responsibilities for FDU. SET ORGANIZATIONAL GOALS; use Headquarters of Department of the Army (HQDA) Tracking System to track timely completion of the division's tasks and actions.

OUTSTANDING ORAL AND WRITTEN COMMUNICATOR. Prepare accurate, clear, concise, and timely correspondence, reports, and documents; provide correct instructions, information, and guidance. Review, edit, and proofread all written information and action papers, memoranda, and forms. Ensure that procedural compliance, style, composition, and typing are correct.

COMMUNICATE EFFECTIVELY with military and civilian leaders at all organizational levels up to and including 2-Star Generals as well as groups of military and civilian contracting staff with widely divergent backgrounds, interests, and points of view. Handle high volume of inquiries from internal and external stakeholders. Maintain strict confidentiality with sensitive and privileged information.

Outline Format with KSAs in the Resume

This Work Experience section is just under 3,000 characters and places equal emphasis on the accomplishments. The USAJOBS resume builder will allow only 3,000 characters for each job block.

(2,933 characters)

MANAGEMENT ASSISTANT   11/2008 - Present
Quantum Research International, Contractor for
U.S. Department of Defense, Arlington, VA 20310
40+ hours/ week, Salary: $40,000/year

DIRECT, COORDINATE, AND MONITOR ADMINISTRATIVE FUNCTIONS AND ACTIVITIES for the Unit Equipping and Readiness Division (FDU) of Army G-8 (3-Star General), in support of soldiers in Afghanistan and Iraq. Coordinate U.S. Army staff actions among FDU, the Office of the Deputy Chief of Staff, Army G-8, and other U.S. Department of Defense offices.

- Designed an improved filing and recordkeeping system for personnel files for 350 contractors in 10 sites in Iraq and Afghanistan..
- Set up the first tracking systems for education and training courses for new hires and reassigned staff in changing locations. Implemented a more efficient system to track vendor invoices and payments for more than $2.5 million per year.

DEMONSTRATE KNOWLEDGE OF TRAVEL PROGRAM PROCEDURES AND PRACTICES. Utilize Defense Travel System (DTS) for travel Authorizations/Orders, vouchers, and other travel documents.

- Improved travel management services for more than 350 contractors who traveled extensively throughout Afghanistan, Iraq, and the U.S. locations. In 2009, booked more than 2,400 airline tickets and countless travel plans for Overseas support services.

POSSESS ADVANCED KNOWLEDGE AND SKILL IN THE USE OF OFFICE AUTOMATION SOFTWARE. Create and maintain Excel spreadsheets to track personnel information and activities, and to perform budget and financial tasks.

- For instance, with only 48 hours' notice before a major presentation in Iraq before senior-level officers, I updated a complex 75-slide PowerPoint with the most up-to-date stats, talking points, and 20-page briefing book for an emergency travel event.

SKILLED IN SCHEDULING AND COORDINATING WORK and integrating planning efforts across work units. Manage calendar for Division Chief.

- Planned a major emergency teleconference event with 3 time zones in consideration with 24 hours' notice attended by media, senior officers, and staff. Created press plan, wrote e-mail announcement, advised senior officers, and reviewed talking points. The event was successful and met the mission of the media event.

MANAGED PURCHASES. Monitor and track via spreadsheets the status of division computer and IT equipment. Research regulations related to funding issues; assist in determining vendor options for purchases.

- In 2009, the organization purchased 150 laptops, 75 BlackBerries, and other IT equipment for travel, onsite, and headquarters. Maintained detailed spreadsheet of products, costs, and whereabouts of equipment throughout the world.

COMMUNICATE EFFECTIVELY with military and civilian leaders at all organizational levels up to and including 2-Star Generals as well as groups of military and civilian contracting staff.

- Write more than 50 e-mails per day for all levels of communication—senior officers, senior civilian managers, contractors, field personnel, vendors, and coworkers. Expert in regulations, report formats, and knowledge of content to represent the mission.

Correspondence Analyst Federal Resume Case Study

This Work Experience section is written in three formats. The first format is a plain Outline Format with buckets of skills. The second format is the same buckets of skills with some routine accomplishments at the end. The third format is Outline Format with buckets of skills plus more jazzy accomplishments, such as one about the administrative support during the Underwear Bomber litigation. These accomplishments not only prove the applicant's knowledge, skills, and abilities, but the resume is also interesting to read.

UTILIZED SKILL IN ORAL AND WRITTEN COMMUNICATION to obtain and provide information, guidance, and instructions; prepare correspondence, reports, and other documents. Coordinated the creation, clearance, and distribution of written communication and responses on behalf of the former DHS Secretary and other senior leaders.

- Handled complex correspondence for 6 months concerning the Underwear Bomber from multiple law-enforcement agencies. Prioritized critical actions.

The third version is the best to present to federal human resources and hiring managers.

Keywords, KSAs, and skills to feature in the resume:

- Coordinated and monitored administrative functions and activities
- Demonstrated skill in use of office automation software
- Utilized skill in oral and written communication
- Communicated with individuals and groups representing widely divergent backgrounds
- Set goals, planned strategies

Outline Format Without Accomplishments

The first format is the Outline Format that features the duties and skills to support the five areas that are of most importance for this job seeker's next position.

(2,729 characters)

CORRESPONDENCE ANALYST/MANAGEMENT ANALYST, GS-9 05/2007 - 08/2008
U.S. Department of Homeland Security (DHS), Office of the Secretary
Washington, D.C. 20528
40+ hours/week, $46,000 Salary/year

COORDINATED AND MONITORED ADMINISTRATIVE FUNCTIONS AND ACTIVITIES in the Office of the Secretary as a federal employee from 09/2007 to 09/2008, and as a contractor from 05/2007 to 09/2007. Managed time and attendance and payroll records of more than 50 staff within the 4 divisions. Acted as point of contact with DHS Mail Room Staff; helped manage the handling of incoming mail and provided suspense files for return responses from DHS senior leaders.

DEMONSTRATED SKILL IN USE OF OFFICE AUTOMATION SOFTWARE in addition to proficiency in Microsoft Office suite, used computer database system called Intranet Quorum (IQ) to maintain specific and unique information and complex tracking of individual items of written correspondence. Used WEBTA Time and Attendance software to track and account for payroll among more than 50 staff.

UTILIZED SKILL IN ORAL AND WRITTEN COMMUNICATION to obtain and provide information, guidance, instructions; prepare correspondence, reports and other documents. Coordinated the creation, clearance, and distribution of written communication and responses on behalf of the former DHS secretary and other senior leaders. Handled and coordinated outbound correspondence, and observed policies in preparing written responses in a timely manner.

COMMUNICATED WITH INDIVIDUALS AND GROUPS REPRESENTING WIDELY DIVERGENT BACKGROUNDS, interests, and points of view. Professionally collaborated with individuals in 11 divisions of DHS. Maintained ongoing interaction with multiple governmental and non-governmental vendors. Developed solid working relationships with colleagues, maintenance, custodial, building engineers, and emergency management personnel.

SET GOALS, PLANNED STRATEGIES, scheduled and coordinated work, and integrated planning efforts to meet organizational goals. Assisted in directing numerous ongoing financial tasks involving budgets, departmental programs, personnel, operations, and facilities, in support of more than 50 staff people in the Office of the Secretary. Tracked correspondence in a multitude of reports; assisted in delegating correspondence to various staff to respond; observed and monitored strict guidelines, protocol, and timeliness regarding responses. Managed a federal government credit card. Assisted in launching "DHScovery," the online professional educational development program for staff throughout DHS. Served as Content/Training Manager; assisted in coordinating the preservation and records management of Professional Development accomplishments for a staff of 50.

Outline Format with General Accomplishments at the End of the Resume

The second format is in the Outline Format with general accomplishments. The accomplishments are listed at the end of the Work Experience section. These accomplishments are not focused toward one particular skill.

(2,969 characters)

CORRESPONDENCE ANALYST/MANAGEMENT ANALYST, GS-9   05/2007 - 08/2008
U.S. Department of Homeland Security (DHS), Office of the Secretary

COORDINATED AND MONITORED ADMINISTRATIVE FUNCTIONS AND ACTIVITIES in the Office of the Secretary as a federal employee from 09/2007 to 09/2008, and as a contractor from 05/2007 to 09/2007. Managed time and attendance and payroll records of more than 50 staff within the 4 divisions. Acted as point of contact with DHS Mail Room Staff; helped manage the handling of incoming mail and provided suspense files for return responses from DHS senior leaders.

DEMONSTRATED SKILL IN USE OF OFFICE AUTOMATION SOFTWARE in addition to proficiency in Microsoft Office suite; used computer database system called Intranet Quorum (IQ) to maintain specific and unique information and complex tracking of individual items of written correspondence. Used WEBTA Time and Attendance software to track and account for payroll among more than 50 staff.

UTILIZED SKILL IN ORAL AND WRITTEN COMMUNICATION to obtain and provide information, guidance, and instructions; prepare correspondence, reports, and other documents. Coordinated the creation, clearance, and distribution of written communication and responses on behalf of the former DHS Secretary and other senior leaders. Interacted with and responded to Transportation Security Administration (TSA) personnel about TSA policies and complaints from the general public.

COMMUNICATED WITH INDIVIDUALS AND GROUPS REPRESENTING WIDELY DIVERGENT BACKGROUNDS, interests, and points of view. Professionally collaborated with individuals in 11 divisions of DHS. Maintained ongoing interaction with multiple governmental and non-governmental vendors. Developed solid working relationships with colleagues, maintenance, custodial, building engineers, and emergency management personnel.

SET GOALS, PLANNED STRATEGIES, scheduled and coordinated work, and integrated planning efforts to meet organizational goals. Assisted in directing numerous ongoing financial tasks involving budgets, departmental programs, personnel, operations, and facilities, in support of more than 50 staff people in the Office of the Secretary. Managed a federal government credit card. Assisted in launching "DHScovery," the online professional educational development program for staff throughout DHS.

ACCOMPLISHMENTS:
- Manage time and attendance and payroll records of more than 50 staff within the 4 divisions. Acted as point of contact with DHS Mail Room Staff.
- Received, reviewed, and prioritized more than 2,500 items of mail per day for DHS senior leaders.
- Primary point of contact for purchasing of supplies supporting 45 professional and admin staff. Managed contracts for custodial, repairs, and maintenance.
- Coordinated a multi-facility carpet-cleaning project.
- Proficient with Microsoft Office suite, database system, and Intranet Quorum (IQ) to maintain complex tracking of individual items of written correspondence.

Outline Format with KSAs in the Resume

The third version is a good format for KSAs in the resume. The resume includes both Outline Format with keywords and accomplishments that could support KSAs for the position.

At 2,706 characters, the third version is still under the 3,000-character limit, but proves from the Accomplishment Record that this person is innovative, supports the mission, communicates very well, uses computer skills proficiently, and acts on critical correspondence for the Secretary's office and program managers at DHS.

CORRESPONDENCE ANALYST/MANAGEMENT ANALYST, GS-9   05/2007 - present
U.S. Department of Homeland Security (DHS), Office of the Secretary

COORDINATED AND MONITORED ADMINISTRATIVE FUNCTIONS AND ACTIVITIES in the Office of the Secretary as a Federal employee from 09/2007 to present, contractor from 05/2007 to 09/2007.
- Manage time and attendance and payroll records of more than 50 staff within the 4 divisions. Acted as point of contact with DHS Mail Room Staff.
- Received, reviewed, and prioritized more than 2,500 items of mail per day.
- Primary point of contact for purchasing of supplies supporting 45 professional and admin staff. Managed contracts for custodial, repairs, and maintenance. Monitored contracts and review costs.
- Coordinated a multi-facility carpet-cleaning project.

UTILIZED SKILL IN ORAL AND WRITTEN COMMUNICATION to obtain and provide information, guidance, and instructions; prepare correspondence, reports, and other documents. Coordinated the creation, clearance, and distribution of written communication and responses on behalf of the former DHS Secretary and other senior leaders.
- Handled complex correspondence for 6 months concerning the Underwear Bomber from multiple law-enforcement agencies. Prioritized critical actions.

DEMONSTRATED SKILL IN USE OF OFFICE AUTOMATION SOFTWARE
- Proficient with Microsoft Office suite, database system, and Intranet Quorum (IQ) to maintain complex tracking of individual items of written correspondence.
- Used WEBTA Time and Attendance software to track and account for payroll for 50 staff.

UTILIZED SKILL IN ORAL AND WRITTEN COMMUNICATION to obtain and provide information, guidance, and instructions; prepare correspondence, reports, and other documents. Coordinated the creation, clearance, and distribution of written communication and responses on behalf of the former DHS Secretary and other senior leaders.
- Handled complex correspondence for 6 months concerning the Underwear Bomber from multiple law-enforcement agencies. Prioritized critical actions.

COMMUNICATED WITH INDIVIDUALS AND GROUPS REPRESENTING WIDELY DIVERGENT BACKGROUNDS, interests, and points of view.
- Professionally collaborated with individuals in 11 divisions of DHS. Maintained ongoing interaction with multiple governmental and non-governmental vendors.
- Developed solid working relationships with colleagues, maintenance, custodial, building engineers, and emergency management personnel.

SET GOALS, PLANNED STRATEGIES, scheduled and coordinated work, and integrated planning efforts to meet organizational goals.
- Assisted in launching "DHScovery," the online professional educational development program for staff throughout DHS.
- Served as Content/Training Manager; assisted in coordinating the preservation and records management of Professional Development accomplishments for a staff of 50.
- Supported Congressional testimony by the Secretary which could impact changes to governing statutes, regulations, policies, and guidance on a variety of subjects affecting the administration and substance of critical, departmental programs.

Administrative/Staff Assistant Federal Resume Case Study

This Work Experience section is written in several formats. You can see three versions here. The first one is the Outline Format with the plain buckets of information. The second one is a long format with everything the person does with detailed accomplishments. This one will be great to prep for an interview. The third format is edited to 3,000 characters.

This administrative federal resume is interesting because she supported an SES executive during the Gulf Crisis:

EXECUTIVE ASSISTANT TO THE ASSISTANT DEPUTY ADMINISTRATOR (ADA), Associate Director of PPQ/EDP: Planned and managed administrative procedures, procedures and regulations, operational plans, and program evaluation. Planned, prioritized, and coordinated administrative operations and workload with emergency program clerical, secretarial, and administrative personnel to ensure quality and accuracy, and meet deadlines. Directly supported an SES-level executive.

- Supported the director's plans and actions during the Gulf Crisis in New Orleans. The director traveled to the Gulf and cooperated with Bureau of Land Management and Dept. of Interior directors in implementing plans to support emergency services to support both plants and animals affected by the oil crisis.

Keywords, KSAs, and skills to feature in the resume:

- Executive Assistant to the Assistant Deputy Administrator (ADA)
- File & Data Management
- Managed and scheduled travel and conferences
- Budgeting
- Liaison
- Communications Management
- Policy & Procedure Development
- Personnel Support

Outline Format Without Accomplishments

The first example is in the Outline Format with keywords. It does focus on the keywords and KSAs for the announcement, but it does not include the accomplishments to prove the expertise.

(2,781 characters)

STAFF ASSISTANT, GS-0303-8, 5/2008 to Present
Office of the Assistant Deputy Administrator
APHIS, Plant Protection and Quarantine, Emergency & Domestic Programs (PPQ/EDP)
Annual Salary: $27.75/hour; 40 Hours/week

EXECUTIVE ASSISTANT TO THE ASSISTANT DEPUTY ADMINISTRATOR (ADA), Associate Director of PPQ/EDP: Planned and managed administrative procedures, procedures and regulations, operational plans, and program evaluation. Planned, prioritized, and coordinated administrative operations and workload with emergency program clerical, secretarial, and administrative personnel to ensure quality and accuracy, and meet deadlines. Directly supported an SES-level executive.

FILE & DATA MANAGEMENT: Maintained subject-matter files. Researched, extracted, and compiled data for supervisors and staff. Received, reviewed, summarized, and ensured the accuracy of preliminary and final reports. Compiled and summarized data in tables, charts, reports, or other formats for oral and PowerPoint presentations. Maintained special records for program staff. Established new files to improve the efficient operation of the office.

MANAGED AND SCHEDULED TRAVEL AND CONFERENCES for the Administrator and staff using GovTrip. Booked rooms for conferences. Completed meeting notes. Prepared monthly travel reports.

BUDGETING: Tracked and managed staff expenditures using PCMS. Assisted in developing the unit's annual budget using current and historical budget data. Entered T&A data in Star Web.

LIAISON between staff, PPQ Deputy Administrator, Regional and field offices, government agencies, external organizations, and the public. Responded to Congressional inquiries. Provided technical advice and information to callers and visitors. Used discretion and independent judgment when handling sensitive or confidential information. Troubleshot and resolved operational and administrative problems.

COMMUNICATIONS MANAGEMENT: Utilized knowledge of agency communications policies and procedures to review, prioritize, and disseminate correspondence, reports, memoranda, and other materials to the ADA and staff. Conducted research to provide background and subject-matter information to support speaking engagements or the development of special reports. Maintained a computerized correspondence log. Reviewed program manuals for accuracy.

POLICY & PROCEDURE DEVELOPMENT: Utilized extensive knowledge of administrative concepts and practices to recommend changes and improvements in administrative policies, procedures, and office practices. Ensured the smooth and accurate development of work and timely flow of information. Provided guidance and training to administrative support staff.

PERSONNEL SUPPORT: Verified, entered, and updated SF-52 forms in the Personnel Action Tracking System (PATS).

Outline Format and KSAs in the Resume

The second example includes accomplishments as well as the Outline Format with keywords. This version is longer than the 3,000 characters allowed in the USAJOBS resume builder. The additional text will have to be copied into the Additional Information field.

(4,663 characters)

STAFF ASSISTANT, GS-0303-8, 5/2008 to Present
Office of the Assistant Deputy Administrator
APHIS, Plant Protection and Quarantine, Emergency & Domestic Programs (PPQ/EDP)
Annual Salary: $27.75/hour; 40 Hours/week

EXECUTIVE ASSISTANT TO THE ASSISTANT DEPUTY ADMINISTRATOR (ADA), Associate Director of
PPQ/EDP: Planned and managed administrative procedures, procedures and regulations, operational plans and
program evaluation. Planned, prioritized, and coordinated administrative operations and workload with emergency
program clerical, secretarial, and administrative personnel to ensure quality and accuracy, and meet deadlines.
Directly supported an SES-level executive.

- Supported the director's plans and actions during the Gulf Crisis in New Orleans. The Director traveled to
  the Gulf and cooperated with Bureau of Land Management and Dept. of Interior directors in implementing
  plans to support emergency services to support both plants and animals affected by the oil crisis.
- Demonstrated knowledge of administrative concepts and practices to recommend changes and
  improvements in administrative policies, procedures, and office practices. Improved administrative
  workflow to support busy mission projects and emergency situations throughout the U.S. for plants and
  animals.

FILE & DATA MANAGEMENT: Maintained subject-matter files. Researched, extracted, and compiled data for
supervisors and staff. Received, reviewed, summarized, and ensured the accuracy of preliminary and final reports.
Compiled and summarized data in tables, charts, reports, or other formats for oral and PowerPoint presentations.
Maintained special records for program staff. Established new files to improve the efficient operation of the office.

- Established an alphabetical color-coded project filing system for the ADA's office. Centralized files within
  EDP for easy access by more than 25 internal staff.
- Set-up a chronological filing system for travel, purchase cards, and phone records. Improved efficiency for
  travel invoice research, problem-solving for employees and managers.
- Implemented and updated the personnel filing system for 45 employees to improve accessibility to
  employee files. Improved information management for research personnel questions concerning training,
  retirement, promotions, and documents.

MANAGED AND SCHEDULED TRAVEL AND CONFERENCES for the Administrator and staff using GovTrip.
Booked rooms for conferences. Completed meeting notes. Coordinated materials. Prepared monthly travel reports.
- Planned and coordinated a major annual conference for APHIS in San Diego, CA, in 2009. More than 100
  agency and industry professionals attended for a 2-day meeting with the objective of communicating about
  veterinary, equine, and emergency preparedness.

BUDGETING: Tracked and managed staff expenditures using PCMS. Assisted in developing the unit's annual
budget using current and historical budget data. Entered T&A data in Star Web.
- Skilled in budget management for 3 program managers. With extensive travel in 2009 to support Gulf Oil
  Crisis, the budget management was more critical than ever. Monitored and prepared monthly reports to
  monitor travel and emergency services budget.

PERSONNEL SUPPORT: Verified, entered, and updated SF-52 forms in the Personnel Action Tracking System
(PATS). LIAISON between staff, PPQ Deputy Administrator, regional and field offices, government agencies,
external organizations, and the public. Responded to Congressional inquiries. Provided technical advice and
information to callers and visitors.
- Expertise in researching and resolving personnel questions and problems. Emphasis has been on retirement
  support, researching documentation and information to support employees with decision-making regarding
  retirement, and succession planning. More than 60% of managers at APHIS are at retirement age and are
  considering retirement within 2 years. New recruit support to provide training and orientation.

COMMUNICATIONS MANAGEMENT: Utilized knowledge of agency communications policies and procedures
to review, prioritize, and disseminate correspondence, reports, memoranda, and other materials to the ADA and

(continued)

(continued)

staff. Conducted research to provide background and subject-matter information to support speaking engagements or the development of special reports. Maintained a computerized correspondence log. Reviewed program manuals for accuracy.

- Write more than 50 e-mails per day; write communication regarding conferences, speeches, and talking points. Prioritize correspondence and act on emergency and critical communications. Knowledge of mission, format, and regulations to write responses independently.

Outline Format and KSAs in the Resume

The third version is under 3,000 characters, so there will be no continuation. The shorter version should be used if the applicant has several positions where the resume might be longer than five pages. The shorter version still includes the Outline Format, keywords, and accomplishments.

(2,722 characters)

STAFF ASSISTANT, GS-0303-8, 5/2008 to Present
Office of the Assistant Deputy Administrator
APHIS, Plant Protection and Quarantine, Emergency & Domestic Programs (PPQ/EDP)

EXECUTIVE ASSISTANT TO THE ASSISTANT DEPUTY ADMINISTRATOR (ADA), Associate Director of PPQ/EDP: Planned and managed administrative procedures, procedures and regulations, operational plans, and program evaluation. Directly supported an SES-level executive.
- Supported the director's plans and actions during the Gulf Crisis in New Orleans. The Director traveled to the Gulf and cooperated with Bureau of Land Management and Dept. of Interior directors in implementing plans to support emergency services to support both plants and animals affected by the oil crisis. Improved administrative workflow to support busy mission projects and emergency situations.

FILE & DATA MANAGEMENT: Researched, extracted, and compiled data for supervisors and staff.
- Established an alphabetical color-coded project filing system for the ADA's office. Centralized files within EDP for easy access by more than 25 internal staff.
- Set up a chronological filing system for travel, purchase cards, and phone records. Improved efficiency for travel invoice research, problem-solving for employees and managers.
- Implemented and updated the personnel filing system for 45 employees to improve accessibility.

MANAGED AND SCHEDULED TRAVEL AND CONFERENCES for the Administrator and staff using GovTrip.
- Planned and coordinated a major annual conference for APHIS in San Diego, CA, in 2009. More than 100 agency and industry professionals attended a two-day meeting with the objective of communicating about veterinary, equine, and emergency preparedness.

BUDGETING: Tracked and managed staff expenditures using PCMS. Assisted in developing the unit's annual budget using current and historical budget data. Entered T&A data in Star Web.
- Skilled in budget management for three program managers. With extensive travel in 2009 to support the Gulf Oil Crisis, budget management was more critical than ever. Monitored and prepared monthly reports.

PERSONNEL SUPPORT: Verified, entered, and updated SF-52 forms in the Personnel Action Tracking System (PATS). LIAISON between staff, PPQ Deputy Administrator, regional and field offices, government agencies, external organizations, and the public.
- Emphasis has been on retirement support, researching documentation and information to support employees with decision-making regarding retirement, succession planning. More than 60% of managers at APHIS are at retirement age and are considering retirement within 2 years.

COMMUNICATIONS MANAGEMENT: Conducted research to provide background and subject-matter information to support speaking engagements or the development of special reports. Write more than 50 e-mails per day; write communication regarding conferences, speeches, and talking points. Prioritize correspondence on emergency and critical communications. Knowledge of mission and regulations to write responses independently.

Summary

As you write your administrative federal resume, strive to cover your basic skills as well as a few accomplishments that will help your resume stand out and grab the attention of both the HR specialist and the supervisor. If you are working on an interesting project, program, or mission, mention the mission that you are supporting. If your supervisors or program analysts are involved in a complex project, *you* are also involved in that project as their administrative support specialist. The mission, objectives, and programs will make your administrative tasks come alive and demonstrate that you have great administrative, communications, liaison, and writing skills. Additionally, it will prove that you work hard to make your supervisors look great.

CHAPTER 18

Management and Program Analyst Resumes

The Management and Program Analyst position is the least well known to private-industry applicants and possibly the most prevalent management position in government. Many current federal employees strive to move into the Management Analyst occupational series so that they can be promoted to higher grade levels, work on projects that will improve and enhance government services to the American public, and have diverse and challenging work. You will see in this chapter that the Management Analyst positions are all different, and you will need to read each vacancy announcement to determine whether you are qualified for a particular position. Some positions are very technical, requiring subject-matter knowledge; others are general and require basic skills in program or management analysis, writing, and oral communications skills.

According to Ligaya J. Fernandez, Senior Research Analyst for the Office of Policy and Evaluation at the U.S. Merit Systems Protection Board:

The Management and Program Analyst positions are very important in government…yes, these positions are critical in government. The government does not provide products to the public. The government provides services. These services are based on programs that government policymakers have determined the American public needs and wants, and so they pass laws to make sure that these services are provided to the people. Once the laws are passed, the executive branch of government implements them. Management and Program Analysts are involved in the process of passing and implementing the laws…they actually do the analytical work required, from which important decisions are made.

Decisions are based on information. Information (or data) has to be gathered, organized, and analyzed. And Management and Program Analysts do the gathering, the organizing, and the analyzing of information so that decisions can be made. Many are involved in program funding; and so many program analyst jobs require an understanding of financial management.

*Once a law is passed and implemented, the government also needs to know if the program is working the way Congress said it should work. They need to know if the program is cost-effective or if improvements are needed. Answers to these and other questions are very important to the policymakers. And the people who are assigned the task of answering questions like these are the **Management and Program Analysts.** They gather essential information, organize and study it, analyze it, and then make recommendations to government officials by way of formal reports.*

The requirements for, and responsibilities of, a Management and Program Analyst differ from job to job depending on grade, organization, location, etc. Reading the vacancy announcement very carefully is key to understanding what the job is all about. Some will require specialized subject-matter knowledge; but generally, they don't. What is required is knowledge and skill that would enable them to perform analytical and evaluative work regarding the agency's operation or management of its programs.

The basic qualification needed for these types of jobs is the knowledge of the theories, function, and processes of management so that analysts can identify problems and recommend solutions. (And so, there really is no specific education required for these jobs, although coursework that includes math, statistics, economics, accounting, and finance is very helpful.) These types of jobs also require knowledge of the different analytical tools and evaluative techniques needed to analyze qualitative and quantitative data.

In sum…I would say the importance of this series is this: Important government program decisions are made based on what Management and Program Analysts recommend, so candidates for these jobs better be good!

Read Ligaya Fernandez's and other Management Analyst Reports at www.mspb.gov. Read their excellent and informative reports and newsletters to view excellent Civil Service public policy writing, qualitative and quantitative analysis, recommendations, and solutions.

The Management and Program Analyst, According to OPM

We have heard from a government expert and Senior Personnel Policy Analyst from www.mspb.gov about how important the Management and Program Analyst is in terms of keeping the "wheels of government" rolling and on track. So now let's examine the actual basic position description for this critical government employee.

 Note: Management Analysts are also usually known as Project Managers.

The following is from OPM's USAJOBS website (www.usajobs.gov):

Management and Program Analysis Series include positions which primarily serve as analysts and advisors to management on the evaluation of the effectiveness of government programs and operations or the productivity and efficiency of the management of federal agencies or both. Positions in this series require knowledge of: the substantive nature of agency programs and activities; agency missions, policies, and objectives; management principles and processes; and the analytical and evaluative methods and techniques for assessing program development or execution and improving organizational effectiveness and efficiency. Some positions also require an understanding of basic budgetary and financial management principles and techniques as they relate to long-range planning of programs and objectives. The work requires skill in: application of fact finding and investigative techniques; oral and written communications; and development of presentations and reports.

Some Management Analyst positions are very technical and specific to the agency mission, where the Analyst would also serve as senior expert, subject-matter expert, advisor, and consultant to senior executives. Other Management Analyst positions are more general in description without requiring subject-matter expertise. These positions offer opportunity for career changers who are not subject-matter experts in the mission of the organization.

A Selection of Management Analyst Job Announcements

Here are three excerpts from Management Analyst announcements. Each position is similar in terms of skills, but the area of specialization is different—Immigration, Veterans Health Administration, and International Securities. Each federal agency will hire Management Analysts to analyze, evaluate, and give recommendations for change and improvement for their agency or office programs.

Program & Management Analyst Position—Immigration, Headquarters' Intra-Agency Coordination & Protocol Division

U.S. Citizenship and Immigration Services, Department of Homeland Security, GS-0343-13/14

<u>**U.S. Citizenship and Immigration Services**</u> secures America's promise as a nation of immigrants by providing accurate and useful information to our customers, granting immigration and citizenship benefits, promoting an awareness and understanding of citizenship, and ensuring the integrity of our immigration system.

Every day, the Management and Program Analysts:

- Implement, coordinate, and/or analyze a variety of management programs.

- Prepare and/or provide briefings and presentations.

- Develop and/or evaluate policies.

As **Management and Program Analyst** in the Headquarters' Intra-Agency Coordination & Protocol Division, your duties and responsibilities will include:

- Developing guidance and processes for USCIS-wide engagement with external stakeholders.

- Managing and tracking engagement conducted by the agency using applicable tools and resources.

- Supporting the planning and execution of all high-profile events and public USCIS initiatives.

- Developing written guidance and processes for defining internal communication and coordination protocols within the agency.

- Developing processes for implementation of an effective feedback loop.

- Coordinating and tracking agency participation in national, regional, and international events and working closely with the DHS Speaker's Bureau.

- Leading in planning and executing high-profile events and public USCIS initiatives.

Figure 18.1: Management Analyst job announcement—Homeland Security.

Program & Management Analyst Position—Veterans Health Administration, National Office of Compliance

Dept. of Veterans Affairs, Veterans Health Administration, GS-0343-11/12

Major Duties and Responsibilities:

This position is located within the National Office of Compliance within the Office of Patient Care Services of VA Medical Centers in various locations throughout the United States. The National Office of Compliance is a new transformational program whose primary purpose is to assist medical centers in aligning their processes and practices with regulations and standards. This assistance will provide on-site assessment, consultation, education, and action plan development. The National Office of Compliance will work synergistically with all VHA departments including the Office of Nursing Service, Infection Control, Logistics, Systems Redesign, Quality Management, Patient Safety, and others.

Program Analysts provide oversight and education of administrative policies, programs, and operations for the Regional and National Office of Compliance and its affiliates with regard to the integration and adherence to Program and Process Compliance. Duties include, but are not limited to, the following:

- Handle issues related to program assessment and prepare communication to all levels of the healthcare system;

- Act as a liaison regarding communication with persons and groups within and outside the Regional and National Office of Compliance;

- Analyze and evaluate designs, studies, proposals, ideas, and best practices submitted by field facilities;

- Work with an interdisciplinary, structured performance improvement model to ensure customers and stakeholders are satisfied in a high-quality, cost-efficient, and schedule-compliant manner;

- Collaborate with team members in the study of system interactions and relations to people, information, equipment, and material to predict the best results to be obtained;

- Collaborate with and support the Regional and National Office of Compliance and facilitate Strategic Planning, Performance Measures, and Utilization Management Programs with emphasis on Access, Value, Efficiency, and Performance Improvement goals;

- Identify and develop action plans and work with educational and redesign specialists to develop and implement training programs for a diverse group of employees;

- Collect data and coordinate reports, projects, and initiatives related to customer service and access.

Figure 18.2: Management Analyst job announcement—Veterans Affairs.

Program & Management Analyst Position—Securities in Office of International Affairs

Securities and Exchange Commission, SK-343-11

As a Program Analyst in the Office of International Affairs, you will provide program management, research, and logistical coordination associated with the administration of the technical assistance function. You will also assist with the regulatory policy, comparative law and regulation, and enforcement functions as needed.

- Organize and provide logistical support for OIA and Commission technical assistance training programs for foreign securities regulators.

- Assist in formulating training programs, including providing insights and analysis of methods for streamlining and improving program execution.

- Evaluate work processes and make recommendations for effective organizational changes.

- Assist in the regulatory policy and comparative law and regulation functions, including helping to organize and provide support for OIA and Commission meetings with foreign securities regulators.

- Assist in implementing management policies and controls related to tracking, filing, and as needed, responding to correspondence and other information relevant to OIA technical assistance and other office programs as needed.

- Analyze and prepare reports and manuals and gather data relevant to implementing management policies and controls with respect to office files.

- Assist with procurement, budget, and expense reports related to execution of technical assistance training programs and meetings relating to regulatory policy and comparative law and regulation.

- Use qualitative and quantitative methods and techniques to analyze and measure the effectiveness, efficiency, and productivity of organizational programs and operations.

- Perform liaison duties in support of program and meeting planning process.

- Participate in developing and implementing long- and short-range plans, procedures, and policies relating to the organization's administrative needs.

Figure 18.3: Management Analyst job announcement—SEC.

A Significant Management Analyst Skill: Qualitative and Quantitative Analysis

Many job seekers will find this terminology in vacancy announcements. A recent workshop attendee at the Drug Enforcement Administration asked me in a course, "What does an announcement mean when they ask for experience in qualitative and quantitative methods?" This is a good question. I see this in many announcements. Think about when you measure qualitative and qualitative numbers about a program, budget, or office performance.

1. Knowledge of qualitative and quantitative methods for analyzing workload trends and survey data; assessing and improving complex management processes and systems, and program effectiveness.

A Management Analyst designs and conducts quantitative and qualitative analyses to evaluate and report on cost/benefit matters, financial issues, and organizational performance. The differences in qualitative and quantitative analyses are in the way data or information is collected in conducting a study. Simply stated, it is a difference between the use of numbers and words when conducting a study or evaluation. Quantitative analysis involves the utilization of questionnaires, tests, and existing databases. Qualitative analysis employs observations, interviews, and focus groups.

Collecting information using quantitative techniques is typically used to evaluate obvious behavior, and this methodology permits comparison and replication. And in most instances, it is believed that the reliability and validity of a study may be determined more objectively than when using qualitative techniques.

Utilizing qualitative methodologies to conduct an evaluation permits the consideration of concepts that were not part of the predetermined subject areas. Therefore, using qualitative techniques in conducting a study can be more exploratory in nature.

In summary, if you are applying for any kind of analyst or technician position, it would be very good to mention the type of qualitative and quantitative skills you have and the types of information you have analyzed.

Create a Project Map of Your Accomplishments and Projects That Match the Top-Level Skills

Most program and management analysts in government manage multiple projects in their jobs. The best way to write an impressive management analyst federal resume is to write about the projects you have managed. You can follow the Project Map in Table 18.1 to create a project list that answers the following six critical skills for a management analyst. You could prove your competencies with examples. You can use a project list in the Duties section of your federal resume. With USAJOBS, you can include your project list in the Additional Information section.

Table 18.1: Project Map

KSA or Special Qualification	Project Examples
1. Quantitative and qualitative analysis	
2. Improving operations for more efficiency and effectiveness	
3. Recommending solutions; acting as an advisor or consultant	

(continued)

(continued)

KSA or Special Qualification	Project Examples
4. Project management skills	
5. Writing and verbal communications	
6. Customer services/contract management	

Use Projects and Accomplishments to Prove Your Top-Level Skills

Expand your project map into narrative descriptions of your projects and analytical tasks. Define your projects and accomplishments with quantifiable numbers for excellent, impressive, on-target content for your resume. The projects or stories will be useful for interview preparation as well because most federal interviews are now behavior-based and require specific examples or stories as answers (see Chapter 27 for more on preparing for behavior-based interviews).

Here is a highly effective project outline that you can use to build your own project list:

Title of the project (or story):

Your role, name of task, project description, and date:

Budget (if this is appropriate):

Challenge/situation:

Observations, challenge, and description:

Recommendations, solutions, and actions:

Results—how did things improve?

Top 10 List of Program Analyst Accomplishments

Following are examples of both long and short project descriptions that include the critical skills of a Management Analyst. These projects involve Lead Six Sigma activity studies, studies resulting in new data, test management, research analysis, analysis and solutions to improve a safety program, analysis of post-award contracts, analysis of technical data sets, and process improvement studies.

HISTORICAL LANDSCAPE RESEARCHER/ANALYST, GLEN ECHO PARK

Project Leader / Lead Researcher for Glen Echo Park in Maryland, which was first opened as an educational park in 1891. Glen Echo is a 22-acre National Park Service site currently being used as an amusement park, dance hall, and venue for classes. Objective is to better inform management of assets and resources. Analyzed resources in compliance with Section 110 requirements of the National Historic Preservation Act. The major challenge was being liaison between the Park Service and the nonprofit organization currently renting space at the park for dance events, classes, and children's programs. During the project, consulted on environmental assessment, extending a bike path through the park.

Actions: Organized the information into the format required for the Cultural Landscape Inventory (CLI).

Results: Discovered the Joy Jigger ride, an original patent, as well as 20 other previously unseen amusement park patents. Produced a 100-page report, which includes photographs, text, archival drawings, maps, chronology of dates, and patent index. I made recommendations on several significant issues of historic integrity and contributions to the local cultural landscape.

ANALYZED AND MANAGED COMMUNICATIONS CONTRACT—SAVED MONEY

Chaired a Sole Source Selection Board for a 3-year, $3 million communication contract. I led the board in setting the policies for all ongoing advertising, brand identity, marketing programs, and evaluating effectiveness of advertising, outreach, and communication marketing and contract staffing. When I became the chairman, four vendors were known for their interest in the contract, but I felt that their skills and professionalism levels would not meet our objectives. I requested changes in the statement of work and reductions in the contract fees. We use a large amount of communication resources, social media/web/print/exhibits, and we needed the required skill sets from the contractors.

I drafted and evaluated the contract procedures. I directed the cross-disciplinary team in evaluation of the proposal.

Results: I was instrumental in a 65% reduction in our contract costs by identifying new contract skills and recommending new techniques for improving the processes of communications contractors.

TEST MANAGER FOR DEFENSE TRAVEL SYSTEM—DEVELOPED MORE EFFICIENT SYSTEMS

Test Manager for Defense Travel System, an enterprise automated travel management system first established in 2007 throughout DOD. I consult with managers concerning staff performance, reports, and customer services. Log and track major problems to ensure that solutions were implemented and information was disseminated quickly to users. Oversee and direct 15 testing contractors managing the updates, programming, and researching problems. The challenges are that the updates are monthly and with more than 2 million Department of Defense users worldwide. New problems appear with each update.

Results: As a result of close logging and tracking problems, errors were reduced from 15,000 logged errors in 2007 when the system was new, to 1,234 errors logged in 2010. Dramatically improved efficient updating of the software with no time down for updates.

(continued)

Figure 18.4: Long accomplishments.

(continued)

EVALUATE SOLUTIONS TO IMPROVE CONTRACTOR SAFETY PROGRAM. As Team Leader, tasked to evaluate and develop solutions for common issues to drive the improvement of a contractor safety program; organized multidisciplinary teams to identify and address key safety issues with contractors and the onsite staff. Developed and presented a training program to increase the awareness of safety in areas where metrics showed an increase in repeated incidents.

Results: Reduced recordable events by 23% at sites where the training program had been implemented. The results drove an acceptance-to-apply process by other project teams.

QUANTITATIVE AND QUALITATIVE ANALYSIS: Managed six Ph.D. AT&T Bell Labs technical staff in the analytical techniques and tools needed to evaluate data sets on international telecommunication technology and usage patterns for base protection and market-share-growth activities. Applied analytical and evaluative methods and techniques for assessing program and project development or execution and improving organizational effectiveness and efficiency. Employed understanding of strategic planning and product management principles and techniques. Applied fact-finding and investigative techniques. Led data analysis efforts to categorize client base and create programs matching client base need. Provided technical sales and account management services. Performed simple and complex network designs, recommendations, and proposals.

Results: Instrumental in the negotiation and agreement of a Nabisco National Letter of Agency for utilizing only AT&T for all long-distance services for the entire company.

LEAD PROCESS IMPROVEMENTS: Implemented Lean process improvement methods that significantly reduced project costs, lowered staff resource requirements, and thus improved the project management process and performance results. Projects under my control have included construction and supervising the work of professional/technical personnel assigned to projects. Completed project scope, schedules, and cost estimates and provided professional engineering expertise on technical areas and design changes. Applied engineering skills, knowledge, and abilities in project design, construction, geotechnical, and environmental areas.

Results: Identified and completed several Lean Energy projects to achieve the cost savings of $650K pilot facility. This resulted in adding drive to the projects' sustainability.

IMPLEMENTED CHANGE TO IMPROVE CUSTOMER SERVICES that positively impacted design of the employee Call Center, employee on-boarding/off-boarding processes, and background check review. Analyzed and updated domestic and international relocation processes.

CONDUCTED STUDIES; DEVELOPED AND MONITORED THE EXECUTION AND REPORTING OF PERFORMANCE DATA for strategic HC and HR projects and initiatives. Applied knowledge of analytical tools and techniques to analyze and evaluate effectiveness; recommended improvements.

US 1-9 COMPLIANCE AND AUDIT: Spearheaded automation of I–9 Employment Verification form through E-Verify, which streamlined the process and ensured compliance with federal regulations and contract requirements.

PROMOTED SMART CARD TECHNOLOGY to improve the effectiveness and efficiency of agency-wide business activities. Created the business case, working capital fund justification, program management plan, governance framework, and charter for the Smart Card Program Management Office.

Figure 18.5: Short accomplishments.

Sample Behavior-Based Interview Questions

Here are examples of the types of questions you might be asked in a behavioral interview where you can talk about your Analyst accomplishments:

- Can you describe a time when you needed to analyze employee performance and workload in order to improve performance and productivity?

- Can you describe a time when you had to improve productivity with available staff and needed to give recommendations to improve staff performance?

- Can you give an example of a situation where you discovered an imbalance in workload of employees and had to resolve this problem?

See Chapter 27 for more on behavioral interviews.

Federal Employees Seeking Career Change with Career Ladder Management Analyst Positions

The Management Analyst series is an excellent choice for career development and new challenge. Because these positions vary among agencies and offices, you can write your current resume featuring your projects and skills that are similar to what is described in this chapter. Changing careers to a Management Analyst position will involve analyzing the top skills needed in the target position and highlighting those same skills in your job.

Transitioning from Specific Positions

Here are some tips for transitioning from specific positions:

- If you are currently an **Administrative Assistant,** you would write about your special projects, database development, research, problem solving, setting up more efficient systems, and giving recommendations to the supervisor to improve operations.

- If you are currently a **Lead Accounting Technician,** GS-8, and hope to change series and move up a grade, you would emphasize your problem solving, special projects, research and analysis, consulting, and advising customers about more efficient methods of accounting information management and special reports, including spreadsheets.

- If you are currently a **Housing Management Specialist,** GS-12, and would like to move into the Management Analyst series at a GS-12 or GS-13 level, you would want to emphasize your projects, partnerships with agencies, consulting services to housing entities, problem solving, analysis of programs, skills in spreadsheet design, and briefings written and given on housing topics. The focus of the project is on the analytical skills, not the content of housing.

Changing Levels

Changing careers at the GS-9 or GS-11 level is easier than at the higher grade levels because usually the qualifications for the positions are more general, such as this one:

> One year of specialized experience that equipped the applicant with the particular knowledge, skills, and abilities to perform successfully the duties of the position, and that is typically in or related to the work of the position to be filled. This experience must be equivalent to the GS-9 level in the federal government. Examples of such experience may include: analyzing the effectiveness of programs; analyzing the efficiency of operations; participating in studies to increase efficiency; preparing work plans and reports based on existing procedures or observations of activities; preparing materials for workflow and operational analyses, studies of costs, or equipment utilization; reviewing operational plans and current and incoming work projects; making recommendations for improving work methods; advising on the adequacy of budgets; and determining the need for work standards and control systems.

More Hints for Writing a Management and Program Analyst Resume

Here are some more tips to keep in mind as you write your resume.

Research the Mission of the Office or Agency

Considering the mission of the office or agency will help you write more compellingly. Research the challenges of the agency or office to consider its analysis and project priorities. For instance, if you are applying to FEMA, you should know that problem solving, efficient operations, and working under pressure are critical competencies. If you are applying to TSA, think about fast-changing priorities, media reports, emergencies, and threats that might affect your writing and programs.

Add the Numbers and Quantify Your Information

In order to write a "qualitatively correct" Management Analyst resume, you will need numbers to demonstrate that you can track information, demonstrate results, prove performance and efficiency, and present data. Because Management Analysis is all about information management, your resume should demonstrate these skills at the basic resume writing level.

How Does Your Private-Sector Job Involve Management Analyst Skills?

Just because your private-industry job title is not "Management Analyst" does not mean you couldn't qualify for a Management Analyst position in government. The following are the private-sector occupations that match the public-sector Management and Program Analyst job:

- Advertising Director
- Business Analyst
- Business Process Engineer
- Category Analyst
- Configuration Analyst

- Database Administrator
- Marketing Analyst, Market Researcher
- Operations Manager
- Program Analyst
- Program Manager
- Programmer Analyst (playing down the IT part of your work)
- Project Manager
- Quality Systems Administrator
- Research Analyst
- Sales Executive (focus on marketing, analysis, and program management)
- Strategic Analyst
- Systems Analyst
- Web Project Engineer
- Writer-Editor

A Sample Management and Program Analyst Resume

Triple Series—Chiropractic Practice Owner Seeking Administrative Management/Policy, 0301, Management and Program Analysis, (0343), Medical/Health, 0601.
Target Jobs: GS 11–15 positions.
Outline Format federal resume with keywords in all caps.
Targeted, written, and designed by Sandra Lee Keppley, Certified Federal Job Search Trainer and Senior Certified Federal Resume Writer.

Strategy: Utilized typical KSA and specialized experience requirements for these occupations at the grade level being pursued (11–15). Both work experience and accomplishments are included in the Outline Format resume to highlight requirements and are inclusive of pertinent keywords. Client possessed differing occupational experiences requiring focus in like competencies between occupations being pursued.

 Note: It's important to identify publications attributed to you for scientific or engineering-type work experience.

Keywords and Skills for Three Occupational Series
Administrative Management/Policy, 0301
- Skill in presenting information and negotiating resolutions
- Ability to analyze and evaluate complex issues
- Knowledge of budgetary principles, practices, laws, and regulations
- Ability to lead and direct others

Management and Program Analysis, 0343

- Development of long-range goals, objectives, strategies, and multilayered transition implementation plans.

- Application of analytical and evaluative methods techniques to assess program development.

- Projects lifecycle/cost benefit analysis of projects and analyzes the economic impact on programs.

- Leads cost-effectiveness studies across coordinating centers' operations and administrative programs.

Medical and Health, 0601

- The Medical Center Director has overall responsibility for planning, organizing, directing, coordinating, and controlling medical, administrative, and supporting operations of a health-care facility.

- Administers medical care and treatment, or a consolidated medical and veterans' benefits facility for a large geographic area.

- Develops and implements a comprehensive health-care delivery system tailored to the needs of the veteran patient population served.

- Establishes and maintains effective and harmonious relationships with local communities; veterans' organizations; civic, professional, and other similar organizations; and with other hospitals.

Donald S. Fountain, CE
704 S. Delaware Ave.
Fairview, NC 21224
Day Phone: 444-444-4444
Email: donaldsfountain@yahoo.com

WORK EXPERIENCE   Fairview Chiropractic Center   4/1998 - Present
Fairview, NC US

Salary: 150,000 USD Per Year
Hours per week: 40

CLINIC DIRECTOR, CHIROPRACTOR
HEALTHCARE ADMINISTRATOR / CLINIC DIRECTOR: Program
and administrative manager. Responsible for planning, business
development, performance, operations facilities management, and
marketing. Formulate, implement guidance, and apply new methods and
procedures. Manage multiple doctors, rehabilitation therapists, massage
therapist, marketing specialist, bookkeeper, office manager, related staff,
and numerous contract suppliers.

*Profitable multifunction wellness center utilizing chiropractic, multiple
doctors, nutrition, physiotherapy, massage, rehabilitation, decompression
traction, cold laser, and durable medical equipment.
*Developed Chiropractic Educational Ambassador Program for North
Carolina Chiropractic Association

LOCAL AND STATEWIDE LEADERSHIP IN CHIROPRACTIC
PUBLIC AFFAIRS: Develop statewide doctor, legislator, healthcare
influencer public health educational programs. Assume local and
statewide leadership positions within the North Carolina Chiropractic
Association as district president, state treasurer, and current state
secretary, Public Awareness Committee Chairman, committee member
legislative and insurance relations.

*Instrumental in securing key NC legislation favorable to chiropractic
(copay equality).
*Planned and developed Legislative Educational Ambassador Program for
use by NC chiropractors to educate NC state legislators on the role of
chiropractic in today's healthcare model and influence favorable
chiropractic legislation in NC.

SPECIALIZED PUBLIC HEALTH PROGRAM MANAGEMENT:
Apply knowledge of health organizational, operational, and programmatic
concepts and practices applied by public, private, or nonprofit agencies
and organizations. Develop policy, identify interventions and mechanisms,
and initiate research activities.

*Created and delivered a Durable Medical Equipment Training Program
for NC chiropractors sponsored by the North Carolina Chiropractic
Association to train DCs on ethical, compliant integration of advanced

(continued)

Figure 18.6: Management and Program Analyst resume.

(continued)

pain management medical technology in chiropractic practices.

HEALTHCARE ANALYST: Conceptualize, design, document, and manage health programs or projects. Employ administrative or analytical methods and techniques. Analyze effectiveness of programs and functions. Develop and introduce new technologies and approaches and increase availability and use of proven interventions to reduce mortality, morbidity of spinal disease–related health conditions. Conceive, plan, and oversee implementation and evaluation of complex chronic spinal disease–focused strategies, projects, and programs.

*Orchestrated ongoing annual chiropractic/neurosurgeon symposium as area president to increase mutual understanding of respective professions.

HEALTHCARE TRAINING SPECIALIST: Develop and deliver statewide healthcare provider training program on integrating advanced pain management technology into their practices. (Contact Supervisor: Yes, Supervisor's Name: Self)

Arrowhead Chiropractic Clinics   **1/1997 - 4/1998**
Atlanta, GA US

Salary: 35,000 USD Per Year
Hours per week: 40

CLINIC DIRECTOR
PUBLIC HEALTH PROGRAM MANAGEMENT: Responsible for running all aspects of high-volume chiropractic clinic treating all types of musculoskeletal injuries with a special focus on the needs of acute and chronic spinal pain syndromes.

PATIENT TREATMENT: Responsibilities included patient treatment, practice building, insurance management, public relations, community marketing, community education, and staff training. Routinely applied knowledge of organizational, operational, and programmatic concepts and practices applied by public, private, or nonprofit agencies and organizations engaged in public health or other health-related activities. Developed policy, identified interventions and mechanisms, and initiated research activities. Formulated health practice goals and objectives and coordinated with state and local agencies.

RESEARCH AND ANALYSIS: Conducted background studies or analysis to carry out internal policy development. Accomplished work related to the conceptualization, design, documentation, and management of health programs or projects. Employed administrative or analytical methods and techniques within a health organization and related program functions. Analyzed and evaluated effectiveness of programs and functions.

KNOWLEDGE OF A SPECIALIZED PUBLIC HEALTH PROGRAM: Developed and introduced new technologies and approaches and increase availability and use of proven interventions to reduce mortality, morbidity, and the spread of spinal diseases. Conceived, planned, and oversaw implementation and evaluation of complex spinal disease–focused strategies, projects, and programs at local and state level.

ORAL AND WRITTEN COMMUNICATIONS: Served as expert and coordinator in providing intellectual leadership and focus to initiate dialogue relative to health practice, technology, legislative strategy, and approaches. Gathered and conveyed information, made oral presentations, and prepared reports, correspondence, and other written materials. Exceptional skill in interpersonal relations and team interaction. Competent and confident leader and collaborator. Met and communicated with others such as neurosurgeons, business executives, newspaper reporters, and legislators, and engaged with colleagues on technical and politically sensitive issues and to identify needs and key issues related to healthcare.

ACCOMPLISHMENT(S):
*Learned, integrated, and led staff in all aspects of patient care protocols, office procedures, insurance processes, and best practices for high-volume chiropractic clinics.
*Led and managed support staff in all aspects of patient care, office management, insurance management, and community education programs.
*Implemented office work task specialization with addition of x-ray technicians and electrodiagnostic in-office testing.
(Contact Supervisor: Yes, Supervisor's Name: W. Reilly, DC, Supervisor's Phone: (717) 777-7777)

AT&T   **10/1989 - 1/1993**
Atlanta, GA US

                                            Salary: 130,000 USD Per Year
                                            Hours per week: 40

District Manager
Product Manager, Software Defined Network International (SDN-I), 1990-1992, Supervisor Name: Diana Callahan, Telephone Number (210) 821-4105, Hours Worked: 40, Salary Earned $60,000

Product Manager, SDN-Domestic & Software Defined Data Network (SDDN), 1989-1990, Supervisor Name: Sue Thomas, Telephone Number (210) 888-8888, Hours Worked: 40, Salary Earned $50,000

PROGRAM AND PROJECT MANAGEMENT SKILL: Managed $250 million in Client Base accounts in extremely competitive environment. Coordinated and synthesized account and sales data to interpret composite production results. Advised, developed, coordinated, and carried out company policies, procedures, and plans. Reviewed, analyzed, and reported program accomplishments. Managed staff of 12 managers to develop competitive pricing proposal for largest Fortune 100 customers throughout the world. Negotiated with customers and internal corporate AT&T business managers for limited resourcing. Analyzed RFPs, led bid preparation team, negotiated contracts, and followed through with Federal

(continued)

(continued)

Government Tariff filings. As product manager, managed profit and loss on $500 million annual revenue stream and lifecycle management of AT&T premiere private networking product. Developed first service product plan and product teams leading to SDN-International tariff restructures and feature enhancements.

QUANTITATIVE AND QUALITATIVE ANALYSIS: Applied analytical and evaluative methods and techniques for assessing program and project development or execution and improving organizational effectiveness and efficiency. Employed understanding of strategic planning and product management principles and techniques. Applied fact-finding and investigative techniques.

DATA ANALYSIS: Led data analysis efforts to categorize client base and create programs matching client base need. Managed six Ph.D. AT&T Bell Labs technical staff in the analytical techniques and tools needed to evaluate data sets on international telecommunication technology and usage patterns for base protection and market-share growth activities. Provided technical sales and account management services. Performed simple and complex network designs, recommendations, and proposals. Instrumental in the negotiation and agreement of a Nabisco National Letter of Agency for utilizing only AT&T for all long-distance services for the entire company.

TECHNOLOGY SKILL: Analyzed management information requirements to develop program or administrative reporting systems, including systems specifications, data gathering and analytical techniques, and systems evaluation methodology.

DUTIES AND ACCOMPLISHMENTS CONTINUED IN ADDITIONAL INFORMATION.

EDUCATION

University of Maryland
Baltimore, MD US
Doctorate
Major: Chiropractic
Honors: cum laude

University of Delaware
Dover, DE US
Master's Degree
Major: Business Administration
GPA: 3.4 out of 4.0

University of Maryland
College Park, MD US
Bachelor's Degree
Major: Management / Marketing
GPA: 3.4 out of 4.0

JOB RELATED TRAINING

CERTIFICATIONS:

Certified Chiropractic Sports Physician – 2008
Fellow International Academy Medical Acupuncture – 2007
Kennedy Decompression Technique Certificate – 2009

PROFESSIONAL LICENSING:

National Board of Chiropractic Examiners Licensure in:
Part I, II, III, & IV and Physiotherapy Licensure
State Licenses: NC, GA, and PA, NJ
Board eligible 45+ States
Board Certified Chiropractic Sports Physician
Board Certified Licensed Acupuncturist

POST-GRADUATE TRAINING (PARTIAL LISTING):

Negotiation Strategies
Business Function Marketing
Information Technology Management
Lumbar Spine Symposium – Treating spinal disorders
Treatment of Difficult Conditions of the Extremities
Advanced Principles of Lower Extremity evaluation and management
Advanced Principles of TMJ, Ribs, Shoulder Girdle Evaluation & Management
Advanced Principles of Upper Extremity Evaluation & Management
Advanced Principles of Foot Mechanics and Gait, Evaluation and Management
Physical Therapy Credential – NYCC
Chiropractic Treatment of Sports Injuries
Treating Myofascial Disorders of the Upper Extremities
Whiplash Case Management
Documenting Spinal Pain Syndromes

ADDITIONAL INFORMATION

WORK EXPERIENCE CONTINUED:

Fairview Chiropractic Center, Fairview, NC, 1998 to present
Clinic and Administrative Director

ORAL AND WRITTEN COMMUNICATION: Serve as expert in providing intellectual leadership to initiate dialogue relative to health practice, technology, and approaches. Gather and convey information, make oral presentations, and prepare reports, correspondence, and other written materials. Exceptional skill in interpersonal relations and team interaction. Competent and confident leader and collaborator on technical and politically sensitive issues and to identify needs and key issues related to healthcare.

AT&T, 1982-1993
District Manager, International Virtual Telecommunications Network

(continued)

(continued)

Services 1992-1993

COMMUNICATIONS SKILLS: Demonstrated exceptional communication skills. Wrote AT&T corporate strategic business and communication plans and contract proposals. Developed presentations and reports for self and higher-level executives. Used business development and relationship management skills to identify market needs and structured business plans. Represented AT&T in negotiations with Canada, Mexico, UK, Japan, Australia, and other countries.

ACCOMPLISHMENT(S):
*Product Manager of the Year from pool of 30 product managers, 1991.
*AT&T Orchestration Award, 1990, Management Award

+++++++++++

CAREER ACCOMPLISHMENTS:

HEALTHCARE MANAGEMENT AND LEGISLATIVE ACCOMPLISHMENTS:
*Planned and developed Legislative Educational Ambassador Program for use by NC chiropractors to educate NC state legislators on the role of chiropractic in today's healthcare model and influence favorable chiropractic legislation in NC.

* Played leading role within the North Carolina Chiropractic Association by being elected to local and state leadership positions directly affecting the practice of chiropractic in NC.

*Orchestrated ongoing annual chiropractic/neurosurgeon symposium as area president to increase mutual understanding of respective professions.

*Lead integration of western NC chiropractors into county-government-run pro bono medical program, Project Access, as area president.

*Played continuous leadership role in NC chiropractics since 2001 as area president, state treasurer, state executive board secretary, Public Awareness Chair, member Legislative and Insurance relations committees.

*Instrumental in securing key NC legislation favorable to chiropractic (copay equality).

BUSINESS / TECHNOLOGY / QUALITY ASSURANCE ACCOMPLISHMENTS:

*Recipient of 1990 AT&T Bell Labs Architecture Award for SDDN.
*Shared patent for technical development; defined customer needs set for SDDN data networking platform.
* 1991 nominee for AT&T Engineering Quality Award.
*Consistently Rated "Far Exceeds" in Product Management Positions
*Evaluated as "Two Step Promotion Potential" to vice president level in

last assignment as district manager.

PROFESSIONAL AWARDS:
2007 Distinguished Service Award – North Carolina Chiropractic Association
1991 AT&T Orchestration Award – Top Product Manager
1990 AT&T Bell Labs Architecture Award

COMMUNITY ASSOCIATIONS:
Food for Fairview – Food Bank – Board Member
A.C. Reynolds High School Team Chiropractor for Football / Baseball / Basketball / Softball / Track, 1997 to 2009
N.C. Fitness & Sports Foundation – Board Member – past
Fairview Community Center – Committee Member – past
Kiwanis Club of Fairview & Asheville – past
A.C. Reynolds High School Senior Project Mentor Program
A.C. Reynolds High School – Regular presenter, Health Class
Fairview Business Association – Member
Community Health & Wellness Lectures – over 200 provided

Donald S. Fountain, CE
704 S. Delaware Ave.
Fairview, NC 21224
Day Phone: 444-444-4444
Email: donaldsfountain@yahoo.com

Office of Human Resources
Mr. Aaron Jones
Branch Chief, Special Emphasis Programs and Recruitment
200 Constitution Avenue, NW
Washington, DC 20210

Dear Mr. Jones,

I am submitting my federal resume for consideration for positions within the Management and Administrative Occupational Family. Specifically, I am interested in being considered for Program Manager and/or Management Analyst–type positions.

I am an experienced professional with outstanding business management, program management, and diversified healthcare skill. During my tenure with AT&T, I advanced from managing a $6 million sales account to $500 million Profit & Loss business manager in a fiercely competitive environment in a Fortune 5 corporation. Regularly created and delivered presentations to audiences of more than 200 executives of the largest corporate U.S. businesses. As a chiropractic professional, I have delivered more than 200 health, wellness, and safety-related talks in the western North Carolina area in the last 11 years. I managed staff ranging from 15 direct to 50 employees in a matrix management environment. Finally, I opened a chiropractic clinic in 1998 that was profitable within 30 days and grew to $500K in five years and $1,000,000 in nine years. Serving as statewide chiropractic leader with roles in the North Carolina Chiropractic Association since 2002, I was elected to state district president (twice), board treasurer, and currently am executive board secretary.

I am qualified for the following positions at the 11/12/13 grade level:
- Program Manager, GS-0301
- Management Analyst, GS-343

My relevant qualifications include

- Broad-based knowledge of business and organizational management, chiropractic, chiropractic management, healthcare management, product/project management, marketing, business strategies, and sales.
- Outstanding administrative management skills; i.e., budget management, human resources, contract management, procurement, inventory control, facility management, safety and security
- Adept with analyzing and applying laws, rules, and regulations.
- Well-developed quantitative and qualitative analytical problem-solving skills.
- Ability to multitask with changing marketplace demands, accommodating complex internal and external business drivers while adapting plans and priorities to successfully meet business needs.

I would be an asset to your organization because of the following skills:
- Strong strategic and tactical thinker.
- Outstanding written and oral communication skills.
- Strong team leader and organization builder.
- Results driven leader—top results and top personal performer.

I would like to apply my leadership and administrative management skills, technical ability, and exceptional ability to collaborate and meet and deal with others in a position within your agency to support your organizational goals and objectives.

Thank you for your time and consideration.

Sincerely,

Donald S. Fountain, CE

Figure 18.7: Introductory cover letter for Program Analyst.

Summary

Follow the advice of the HR specialist: "Your resume should explain the nature of experience, accomplishments, education, and training opportunities that best illustrate how, to what degree, and with what impact you have applied/used each of the knowledges, skills, and abilities needed for successful performance in this position. Your description may include examples of accomplishments, problems resolved, risks/threats averted, or processes improved as a result of your efforts."

Consider the supervisor who is hiring, think about his or her programs and challenges, and determine how you could contribute to analyzing the performance and results of the program. Write about your successes in the past, be specific, and add numbers.

CHAPTER 19

Administrative Officer Federal Resumes

Administrative officers manage the operations, supervise staff, plan the workforce, review performance, ensure efficiency, implement new initiatives and regulations, communicate with internal/external customers, brief senior people, write and prepare quantitative and qualitative reports, purchase items, direct contractors, manage the budget, and solve problems. The administrative officer spends at least 50 percent of his or her day on operations and about 50 percent on special projects, improvements, problems, and new program initiatives.

With Hiring Reform and KSAs in the Resume

Your resume must have more emphasis on the big picture of meeting the mission, performance, new programs, and problem solving. A top-notch administrative officer can juggle 10 plates in the air and get things done with finesse and people skills—and political savvy, too!

Think Executive Core Qualifications

The goal of most GS-11 or GS-12 administrative officers is to get promoted to a GS-13 at the minimum. The way to get promoted is to think ECQs. Study, print, and post the Leadership Map (see Figure 19.1) in your cube or office and work toward these leadership competencies in your projects and leadership opportunities.

Following are some thought-provoking questions for the admin officer based on the ECQs:

- Have you helped to lead change in your organization?
- Do you lead people?
- Do you demonstrate your business acumen when you are managing the budget to meet your office objectives?
- Do you work to achieve results when you are analyzing performance?
- Do you work with other agencies in collaboration to achieve your operational goals?

If you said *yes* to these, you are on your way to a great set of ECQs (for later).

Your Accomplishments Will Get You Recognized and Promoted

Since this job is a 50/50 federal resume (Duties versus Accomplishments), the Accomplishments have to stand out. In this job you have a lot of duties. But the performance of your regular duties will not get you to GS-13. If you look back on your original vacancy announcement, your position description, or the OPM's Classification Standard, you will see that you are a master of operations—the juggler.

Source: Office of Personnel Management.

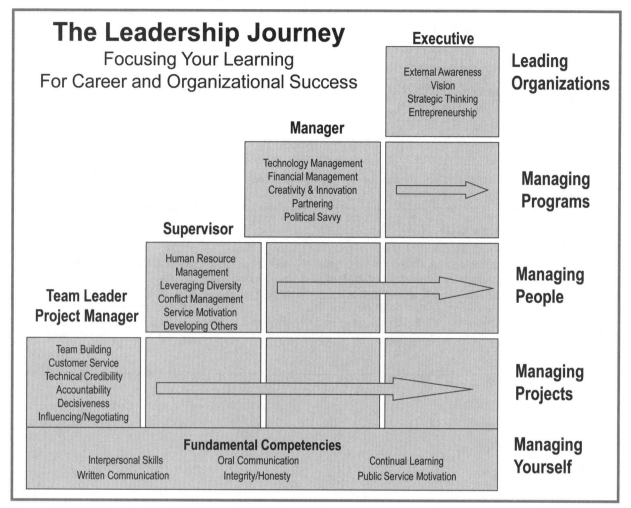

Figure 19.1: The Leadership Map.

Administrative Officer Federal Resume Case Study

Mark White is moving up. He has made a difference in every position and he can prove it with accomplishments. He is a hard worker, obviously, but he can prove results by adding quantifiable numbers, recognitions, examples, and new ideas:

- $4 million renovation on time and on budget.

- Senior civilian…diligent dedication.

- Improved training completion rate for all VA employees within four months from 40 percent to 95 percent of all staff having completed mandatory annual training.

- Initiated face-to-face contact with 100 percent of staff to inform of training requirements, follow up to see that training was conducted, and offer assistance to complete online training requirements.

Mark White was eventually promoted to a GS-1(3) Administrative Officer. I am sure his supervisor is thrilled to have him on board for whatever challenges are in store for that office. Mark will continue to work on projects and accomplishments that demonstrate his expertise and leadership and keep writing them down. He is on his way to SES—next stop GS-14, and then maybe a CDP program. But the accomplishments will make the difference (see Figure 19.2).

Job Analysis and Keywords

Target Job: Administrative Officer, GS-0341-12, Dept. of the U.S. Army, Army Corps of Engineers. Federal to federal resume.
Researched, analyzed, and written by Lex Levin, Certified Federal Resume Writer (CFRW).

Specialized Experience:

Specialized Experience is defined as at least one year of demonstrated experience in the same or similar work in difficulty and complexity to at least the next lower grade or level that equipped the applicant with the particular knowledge, skills, and abilities to successfully perform the duties of the position, and that is typically in or related to the work of the position to be filled. To be creditable, your specialized experience must demonstrate administrative officer, budget manager, supervisor, staff trainer, project leader, researcher, and analyst.

Keywords
- Supervisor/Trainer/Teamlead
- Facilities Coordinator
- Budget Management
- Program Implementation
- Briefings, Reports
- Efficiency and Effectiveness

ACCOMPLISHMENT RECORD
Top Ten List of Accomplishments

MARK JEREMY WHITE

WORK EXPERIENCE

XX/20XX to Present
ADMINISTRATIVE OFFICER, GS-0341-11
REGIONAL LEGAL SERVICE OFFICE

1. Oversaw and completed $4.1 million renovation of facilities on time and on budget.
2. Named Senior Civilian of the Quarter, October–December 20XX, "for exceptional performance of duty while serving as Administrative Officer," "…for diligent dedication to ensuring the seamless integration and execution of iBets (budget and accounting) and SLDCADA (electronic time keeping) systems…," allowing for full and timely accounting and obligation of all FY20XX budget dollars, and improving the working environment in offices throughout the region.

XX/20XX to XX/20XX
PROGRAM SPECIALIST, GS-0301-09
VA HEALTH CARE SYSTEM
Improved training completion rate for all VA employees within four months from 40 percent to 95 percent of all staff having completed mandatory annual training.

3. Initiated use of Microsoft Live Meeting to share training dates, subject matter, and location. Used Live Meeting to conduct training for offsite employees.
4. Initiated face-to-face contact with 100 percent of staff to inform of training requirements, following up to see that training was conducted and offering assistance to complete online training requirements.
5. Provided systematic instruction to all staff on how to complete online National Mandated training; initiated process with Microsoft Live Meeting to inform all staff members of training dates, subject matter, and location.
6. Created a tasker tracking system utilizing Microsoft Calendar to track and assigned all taskers for the entire Information Technology service, enabling effective monitoring of and faster completion of taskers.

XX/20XX to XX/20XX
PROGRAM MANAGER
COMMANDER, TACTICAL GROUP

7. Analyzed, monitored, and effected changes for military and civilian manpower allocations, requirements, and authorizations. Compiled, organized, and analyzed manpower data to develop statistical and narrative data to justify changes and/or recommendations. Effectively advocated and defended recommendations to senior leadership.

8. Trained and oversaw manpower duties for 160 air traffic controllers in the Pacific Naval Surface Commands. Reviewed and recommended manpower changes that identified and categorized shortfall and potential offsets for the Warfare Enterprises and Provider/Enablers during Program Reviews (PRs) and the Program Objective Memorandum (POM) process.

9. Created and implemented initiatives and concepts of Amphibious Air Traffic Control guidance for SURFORCE Training Manual. Successfully coordinated and managed the operation of the Manpower personnel and Amphibious Air Traffic Control Center Training Course for COMNAVSURFOR Area of Responsibility (AOR) attended by a number of Senior Enlisted Managers and Naval Officials.

XX/20XX to XX/20XX
SENIOR ENLISTED ADVISOR
MILITARY ENTRANCE PROCESSING STATION

10. As Security Manager, planned, coordinated, and scheduled the installation of a $76,000 security system for a 27,000+-s.f. facility. Brought the entire building in compliance with the anti-terrorism guidelines for stand-alone federal buildings. Helped control access to the building for security purposes. Ensured that facility met Inspector General's inspection requirements. Improved process for staff checking in and out of the organization from seven days to one day.

Figure 19.2: Administrative Officer accomplishment record.

MARK JEREMY WHITE

123 Any Street
Town, State 12345
Contact Phone: (555) 123-4567
Work Phone: (555) 234-5678
Email Address: sample@aol.com

U.S. Citizen
Veterans' preference: 10-point honorably discharged U.S. Navy veteran
SSN: XXX-XX-XXXX
Highest Federal rank: GS-0341-11 (current)

Objective: Job Announcement Number TBD
Job Title, Series, and Grade: Administrative Officer, GS-0341-12
Agency: Department of the Navy

WORK EXPERIENCE

XX/20XX to Present; 50 hours per week; **ADMINISTRATIVE OFFICER;** GS-0341-11; last promoted XX/XX/20XX; permanent employee; not on a temporary promotion; REGIONAL LEGAL SERVICE OFFICE, City, State; CDR John Johnson, 555-222-3333; may contact supervisor.

MANAGE AND ENSURE TIMELY AND EFFECTIVE IMPLEMENTATION OF FULL RANGE OF ADMINISTRATIVE SERVICES AND PROGRAMS for 45 employees, including workforce planning, human resources, budget, training, facilities, records management, security, and administrative support.
- Named Senior Civilian of the Quarter, October–December 20XX, "for exceptional performance of duty while serving as Administrative Officer."
- Appointed as Approving/Certifying Official for Government Credit Purchase Card Program.
- Appointed as Authorizing Official for Defense Travel System.

PLAN, DEVELOP, EXECUTE, AND MONITOR $1.5 MILLION BUDGET; monitor and track budget execution, ensure all expenditures are consistent with plan; identify and resolve discrepancies.
- Received Time-Off & Performance Award, September 20XX, "for diligent dedication" in ensuring seamless systems integration and execution, for proper accounting and obligation of all FYXX budget dollars, and for improving working environments in offices throughout the XXX region.

SKILLFULLY TRAIN, MANAGE, AND SUPERVISE 7 civilian and military subordinates; mentor them to exceed expectations and meet organizational goals; assign and monitor work; exercise full personnel authority, including hiring, training, leave approval, and discipline. Analyze and evaluate workforce needs. Make recommendations for increase and reallocation of staff, consistent with organizational goals.

OVERSEE AND MANAGE FACILITIES consisting of XX,XXX-s.f. historic facility and grounds, including condition, rehabilitation, and all related services. Manage upgrades, energy use and efficiency, and safety and security consistent with master plan, community design, zoning, and environmental standards. SECURITY MANAGER with Top Secret clearance. Oversee and direct administrative training and distribution of support personnel within the command.
- Oversaw and completed $4.1 million renovation of facilities on time and on budget.

PREPARE WRITTEN NARRATIVE AND NUMERIC REPORTS, analyses, policies, procedures, and recommendations used by senior management for decision making. Use the full range of MS Office, including Word, Excel, PowerPoint, and Outlook.

USE EXPERT KNOWLEDGE OF FEDERAL LAWS AND REGULATIONS impacting administrative services and programs to provide advice and guidance to managers and employees. Monitor new and

Figure 19.3: Administrative Officer resume.

proposed legislation and case decisions, identify potential impact, and make recommendations for needed adjustments in operations.

CURRENTLY PURSUING MASTER'S DEGREE IN PUBLIC ADMINISTRATION. Estimated completion date: September 20XX.

XX/20XX to XX/20XX; 40 hours per week; **PROGRAM SPECIALIST;** GS-0301-09; last promoted Not Specified; permanent employee; not on a temporary promotion; VA HEALTH CARE SYSTEM, City, State; Mary Jameson, 555-666-7777, may contact.

PERFORMED ESSENTIAL TRAINING SYSTEM ADMINISTRATIVE DUTIES, including training users/employees, advocating for systems utilization, preparing reports, changing/resetting passwords, adding users, unlocking accounts, troubleshooting problems, and more. System Administrator Learning Management System (LMS) for local facility service and region duties; LMS Domain Manager; Service Training Coordinator for Information Technology Service. Monitored service staff member compliance with training requirements and other identified performance measures.

KEY ACCOMPLISHMENTS:
- Improved training completion rate for all VA employees within four months from 40 percent to 95 percent of all staff having completed mandatory annual training.
- Initiated use of Microsoft Live Meeting to share training dates, subject matter, and location. Used Live Meeting to conduct training for offsite employees.
- Initiated face-to-face contact with 100 percent of staff to inform of training requirements, follow up to see that training was conducted, and offer assistance to complete online training requirements.
- Provided systematic instruction to all staff on how to complete online National Mandated training; initiated process with Microsoft Live Meeting to inform all staff members of training dates, subject matter, and location.
- Created a tasker tracking system utilizing Microsoft Calendar to track and assigned all taskers for the entire Information Technology service, enabling effective monitoring of and faster completion of taskers.

IMPROVED EFFICIENCY AND PRODUCTIVITY in administrative support activities. Planned and implemented improvement projects. Used qualitative and quantitative techniques to identify, analyze, and make recommendations to resolve work problems.

PERFORMED ADMINISTRATIVE WORK in personnel, budgeting and financial management, travel, equipment procurement and contracting, property management, and supply, using knowledge of the organization, programs, and functions of the Medical Center.

FORMULATED, PRESENTED, EXECUTED, AND ANALYZED ORGANIZATION BUDGETS. Participated in developing the annual budget formulation and the execution process. Performed cost-benefit analyses and statement of work documentation for labor contract purchases. Used NASA SEWP contract to obtain quotes and make procurement decisions.

OVERSAW ALL HUMAN RESOURCES MANAGEMENT FOR IT DEPARTMENT; created and processed position descriptions and recruitment actions, reviewed resumes for consideration and related activities; prepared all personnel actions for processing, ensuring appropriateness of actions and documentation.

PROVIDED EXPERT IT ADMINISTRATIVE SUPPORT for the department; administered Learning Management System (LMS); interfaced with HR, IT, and other departments; recognized expert in maximizing technology to improve efficiency and effectiveness. As Communication Specialist, oversaw and monitored XXX+ pagers and XXX+ cell phones for authorized staff. As Government Credit Traveler Card Coordinator, processed and monitored government credit card issuance and usage by all authorized staff.

(continued)

(continued)

XX/20XX to XX/20XX; 40 hours per week; **SENIOR SUPPORT ANALYST;** $50,000 per annum; last promoted Not Specified; permanent employee; not on a temporary promotion; U.S. NAVY OFFICE, City, State; Jack Brown, 555-333-4444, may contact.

SENIOR ANALYST in support of the XXXX TRAINING GROUP for Training Operational Readiness Information Services (TORIS) at Naval Station XXX XXXX.

COMPILED, MAINTAINED, VERIFIED, AND INTERPRETED DATA. Collected and managed data, devised metrics, and analyzed trends. Identified potential technical and management problems, drew conclusions, and devised solutions.

RECOMMENDED IMPROVEMENTS in training, afloat assessments, data capture, and certification processes. Drafted reports for higher-level review.

USED STRONG ORAL AND WRITTEN COMMUNICATION SKILLS to develop and maintain effective relationships with customers and coworkers. Created presentations.

SERVED AS FLEET LIAISON to ensure smooth and timely data flow from afloat installs of TORIS/Training Figure of Merit (TFOM)-Afloat; and with ATG staff regarding applications within the ATG TORIS Enterprise.

CONDUCTED TRAINING AND TROUBLESHOOTING with ATG and ship personnel in use of the TORIS within the ATG Enterprise. This training data collection system informed superiors of training status of individuals across departments and provided a snapshot of real-time training strengths and weaknesses related to war-fighting capabilities of each department of the ship.

XX/20XX to XX/20XX; 60 hours per week; **SENIOR ENLISTED ADVISOR;** $60,000 per annum; last promoted Not Specified; permanent employee; not on a temporary promotion; XXX MILITARY ENTRANCE PROCESSING STATION, City, State; LDCR Martinson, 555-888-9999; may contact.

SUPERVISED 45 MILITARY AND CIVILIAN CLERICAL, ADMINISTRATIVE, AND SUPPLY SUPPORT PERSONNEL. Planned, prepared, and revised work schedules and duty assignments according to budget allotments, customer needs, employee capabilities, problems, and workloads. Verified completeness and accuracy of work. Monitored and effected changes for military and civilian manpower allocations, requirements, and authorization for United States Military Entrance Processing Command.

- As Security Manager, planned, coordinated, and scheduled the installation of a $76,000 security system for a 27,000+-s.f. facility. Brought the entire building in compliance with the anti-terrorism guidelines for standalone federal buildings. Helped control access to the building for security control purposes. Ensured that facility met Inspector General's inspection requirements. Improved process for staff checking in and out of the organization from seven days to one day.

TRAINING OFFICER: Developed, modified, and updated training materials in accordance with United States Military Entrance Processing Command regulations. Employed a variety of instructional techniques and formats such as role playing, simulation, team exercises, group discussions, videos, and lectures. Scheduled classes based on availability of classrooms, equipment, and instructors.

CONTRACTING OFFICER REPRESENTATIVE: Managed three government support contracts valued at $3 million. Verified contractor adherence to technical requirements and in accordance with contract terms, conditions, and specifications. Performed monthly quality-assurance inspections and submitted monthly reports.

PROPERTY AND FACILITY OPERATIONS MANAGER: Ensured the day-to-day upkeep of a XX,XXX-s.f. facility. Inspected grounds, facilities, and equipment routinely to determine necessity of repairs or maintenance. Investigated complaints, disturbances, and violations; resolved problems; followed management rules and regulations. Planned, scheduled, and coordinated general maintenance, major repairs, remodeling, and construction projects.

SERVED AS LIAISON AND ADVISOR TO CIVILIAN AND MILITARY COMMANDERS. Performed morning processing brief. Consulted with supervisors and other personnel to resolve problems, such as equipment performance, output quality, and work schedules. Advised executive-level officials and dealt with high-level officials of other organizations.

RESOLVED EMPLOYEE COMPLAINTS AND GRIEVANCES. Effected minor disciplinary actions (e.g. warnings or oral admonishments) involving subordinates. Supported Affirmative Employment Program and Equal Employment Opportunity (EEO) in all personnel management activities. Identified and approved developmental and training needs for employees, providing or arranging for needed development training.

XX/20XX to XX/20XX; 60 hours per week; **PROGRAM MANAGER;** $60,000 per annum; last promoted Not Specified; permanent employee; not on a temporary promotion; COMMANDER, TACTICAL GROUP XXX, City, State; Bill Major, 555-444-6666, may contact.

TRAINED AND OVERSAW MANPOWER DUTIES for 160 AIR TRAFFIC CONTROLLERS.

PROVIDED POLICY GUIDANCE TO SUBORDINATE AND FLEET COMMANDS in the interpretation of directives and guidelines regarding assigned shore and fleet manpower management programs. This includes Manual of Navy Total Force Manpower Policies and Procedures (OPNAVINST 1000.16 Series), Total Force Manpower Management System Program Objectives Memorandum (POM)/ Program Review (PR), and Fleet Manpower Document (FMD) review.

RESEARCHED AND ANALYZED MANPOWER ISSUES utilizing Total Force Manpower Management System (TFMMS) database and applied knowledge in the preparation of manpower inquires, briefs, and other related documentation and correspondence.

Analyzed, monitored, and effected changes for military and civilian manpower allocations, requirements, and authorizations for Pacific Naval Surface Commands. Compiled, organized, and analyzed manpower data to develop statistical and narrative data to justify changes and/or recommendations. Effectively advocated and defended recommendations to senior leadership.

- Reviewed and recommended manpower changes that identified and categorized shortfall and potential offsets for the Warfare Enterprises and Provider/Enablers during Program Reviews and Program Objective Memorandum process.
- Reviewed Required Operational Capability/Projected Operating Environment instructions, Draft Ship and Fleet Manpower Documents, and submitted updates to be implemented using the Total Force Manpower Management System, Micro Manpower Change Application system.
- Reviewed, analyzed, updated, created, and maintained Activity Manpower Documents, Organizational Change Requests, and Billet Change Requests (BCR) under the provisions of OPNAVINST 1000.16 Series.
- Monitored and updated Activity Manpower Documents to ensure COMNAVSURFOR workforce aligned with Warfare Enterprise.

CURRICULUM DEVELOPMENT: Created and implemented initiatives and concepts of Amphibious Air Traffic Control guidance for SURFORCE Training Manual. Successfully coordinated and managed the operation of the Manpower personnel and Amphibious Air Traffic Control Center Training Course for COMNAVSURFOR Area of Responsibility (AOR) attended by a number of Senior Enlisted Managers and Naval Officials.

QUALITY ASSURANCE: Completed onboard quality assurance evaluations biennially and provided assist visits as necessary.

(continued)

(continued)

PROCURED EQUIPMENT: Reviewed requirements and initiated appropriate requests for equipment upgrades and changes. Thoroughly researched assigned projects providing a logical, cost-effective solution within budgetary constraints and within consideration of higher authority. Instrumental in the early installation of the SPN-35C Precision Approach Radar System on four of six Amphibious Assault ships.

REVIEWED AND PROCESSED AWARDS and staff Air Traffic Control Specialist certificate revocation/reinstatement requests. Assisted in the training and interim qualifications of AATCC Teams prior to deployment.

SERVED AS COMNAVSURFOR's representative for air traffic control issues in meetings. Coordinated, wrote, and developed COMNAVSURFOR instructions on amphibious air traffic control procedures. Corresponded with subordinate activities and higher-echelon commands regarding manpower and management issues to include OPNAV and NAVMAC. Effected communication with subordinate activities regarding manpower and management issues to include COMTACGRU ONE, COMNAVSURFOR, OPNAV, and NAVMAC.

SUBJECT MATTER EXPERT and Model Manager for the Amphibious Ships Air Traffic Control Manual. Revised and updated training instructions/manuals. Updated Personnel Qualifications Standards. Authored Advanced Amphibious Air Traffic Control training scenarios for simulating training environment using real-time equipment and computer-generated training scenarios.

KEY ACCOMPLISHMENTS:
- As CNSF voting member on CNO's ATC Executive Steering Committee, proposed and helped implement much-needed ATC equipment upgrades and ships' space design improvements.
- As Fleet Project Team member for Precision Approach Landing Systems (PALS), helped expedite the test, evaluation, and installation program for SPN-35C PALS.

EDUCATION

MASTER'S IN PUBLIC ADMINISTRATION, XXX University, City, State, degree expected XX/20XX.

BACHELOR OF SCIENCE in Business Administration, 20XX, XXX University, City, State.

TRAINING

- Completed Navy Correspondence Manual and Contemporary Navy Writing course, 20XX.
- Completed Administrative Officers Workshop, 20XX.
- Completed Lean Six Sigma Champion Training, 20XX.
- Federal Budgeting. GS Graduate School, City, State, 20XX.
- Civilian Personnel Management Academy Course, Commander Navy Region XXXX, Human Resource Office, City, State, 20XX.
- Lead Defense Travel Administrator, City, State, 20XX.
- Chief Petty Officer Leadership, Naval Aviation Schools Command, City, State, XX/20XX.
- Tasked-Based Curriculum Development, Naval Air Technical Training Center, City, State, XX/20XX.
- Naval Technical Training Center, XXX Station, City, State, XX/19XX.
- Physical Training Instructor Class F2. Naval Air Station XXX, State, XX/19XX.
- Fundamentals of Total Quality Leadership Training, Expeditionary Warfare Training Group Pacific, XXX Base, City, State, XX/19XX.
- Navy leader Development Program Leading Petty Officer, Expeditionary Warfare Training Group XXX, XXX Base, City, State, XX/19XX.
- Administration and Operation of Shipboard 3-M Systems Shipboard Training Enhancement Program, Fleet Training Center, City, State, XX/19XX.
- General Shipboard Fire Fighting, Fleet Training Center, City, State, XX/19XX.

APPRAISALS & AWARDS

- SELECTED SENIOR CIVILIAN OF THE QUARTER, and received Time Off and Performance Award, XX/20XX, "…for diligent dedication to ensuring the seamless integration and execution of iBets (budget and accounting) and SLDCADA (electronic timekeeping) systems…" allowing for full and timely accounting and obligation of all FY20XX budget dollars and improving the working environment in offices throughout the region.
- DEFENSE MERITORIOUS SERVICE MEDAL, 20XX.
- NAVY AND MARINE CORPS COMMENDATION MEDAL, 20XX AND 20XX.
- NAVY AND MARINE CORPS ACHIEVEMENT MEDAL, 20XX, 19XX, AND 19XX.

MILITARY SERVICE INFORMATION

- U.S. Navy Active Duty: XX/19XX to XX/20XX
- Honorable Discharge
- Retirement Rank: XX. Date: XX/XX/20XX

PROFESSIONAL PROFILE

- 20-plus-year U.S. Navy veteran with extensive experience in successful project and program management and analysis.
- Substantial knowledge of and hands-on application of management practices, theories, and techniques in both military and civilian contexts.
- Strong track record of analyzing and evaluating organizational needs and producing, conducting, and coordinating effective studies and project analyses.
- Skilled in evaluating program effectiveness; formulating, advocating, and justifying programmatic and process improvements to senior staff; and implementing recommendations.
- Subject-matter expert in federal administrative laws and regulations, including HR, training, workforce needs assessment, and budget analysis.
- Work independently and exercise own judgment to interpret and resolve ambiguous and conflicting policy and regulations, and to plan and carry out assignments.
- Very strong oral and written communication skills.
- Develop, maintain, and grow effective cross-cutting inter-agency working relationships.
- Currently pursuing Master's degree in Public Administration.

MARK JEREMY WHITE
123 Any Street
Town, State 12345
Contact Phone: (555) 123-4567
Work Phone: (555) 234-5678
Email Address: sample@aol.com

October 14, 2011

Navy HRSC Southwest
Human Resources Service Center Southwest
525 B Street, Suite 600
San Diego, CA 32101-4418
USA

Dear Ms. Howard:

Enclosed is my application responding to Vacancy Announcement #SW0-0341-12-P5822589-UDE, Administrative Officer.

I have enclosed my federal resume, which highlights my professional accomplishments over the last decade.

I can offer the Resources, Requirements, and Assessments Department of the Naval Special Warfare Command proven management and program analysis expertise, together with a master's degree in public administration, a Bachelor of Science degree in business administration, plus strong executive leadership experience in the following areas:

- **Critical thinking, analysis, and problem-solving**—Experienced short- and long-term project and program analyst with extensive experience in using evaluative and technical skills to analyze and optimize complex operations quickly and decisively.
- **Subject matter expert in federal administrative laws, regulations, and policies**—Assisted in and led the supervision and administration of essential naval operations. Analyzed and evaluated organizational needs; conducted effective studies; developed, advocated, and implemented process improvements; and fostered inter-agency partnerships.
- **Leadership**—20 years with the U.S. Navy as a highly effective, successful, decorated Non-Commissioned Officer and project leader with substantial knowledge of and hands-on application of management practices, theories, and techniques in both the military and civilian contexts.

I would like to have the opportunity to offer my extensive experience to the Naval Special Warfare Command. I look forward to the opportunity to meet in person for an interview.

Thank you for your consideration of my application materials.

Sincerely,

Mark J. White

Enclosures: Federal Resume

Figure 19.4: Cover letter for Administrative Officer position.

Summary

The administrative officer federal resume should read like the resume of an operations manager or general manager of a business or operation. The administrative officer makes sure that the operation runs smoothly, solves problems, leads people, and improves efficiency every day. Your federal resume will be successful if you can prove your general management skills and abilities with your operational improvements. This federal position has room for advancement to a GS-15. The person whose resume is shown in this chapter was hired into the government and is serving there today.

CHAPTER 20

General Engineer and Project Manager Resumes

Engineers are in demand in government. The 0800 (Engineer), 0340 (Program Manager), and 1101 (Project Manager) series are popular for all kinds of engineers from private industry and government contracting. Since 2008, the engineers that are gravitating to government jobs are mechanical (usually moving toward DOD research and development), civil engineers, structural engineers, construction engineers, and project managers from all sectors, including information technology, manufacturing, and construction.

Although many jobs may be advertised on the USAJOBS website, there may be additional job announcements on individual agency websites (for example, the Navy's civilian HR site at https:// chart.donhr.navy.mil—accept the Temporary Security Certificate). These websites may advertise "open continuous" positions that offer hiring authorities a pool of candidates to interview when a position is available. Interviewees may be selected based on keywords related to the position. It helps to network through neighbors, colleagues, societies (such as SAE and AMS) to find out when these positions become available and the related keywords. As you learn of keywords, include them into your resume to improve the chances of being selected for other positions.

If you are selected for an interview, become familiar with the type of interview that will be conducted. Many agencies have a standardized interview process. In one type of interview, a candidate may be given a list of questions prior to the interview. During the interview, the candidate answers the list of questions to a panel of interviewers. The panel cannot acknowledge the candidate and will wait until the end to ask questions. Become familiar with the type of interview and practice with family and friends.

The General Engineer, According to OPM

If you are writing an engineer specialization federal resume, the Position Classification Standard should be your first stop. This standard clearly defines each engineer specialization with specialized knowledge, skills, and abilities that you must cover in your federal resume.

Job Family Position Classification Standard for Professional Work in the Engineering and Architecture Group, 0800

This JFS covers the following occupational series:

Series		Series	
General Engineering	0801	Computer Engineering	0854
Safety Engineering	0803	Electronics Engineering	0855
Fire Protection Engineering	0804	Bioengineering and Biomedical Engineering	0858
Materials Engineering	0806	Aerospace Engineering	0861
Landscape Architecture	0807	Naval Architecture	0871
Architecture	0808	Mining Engineering	0880
Civil Engineering	0810	Petroleum Engineering	0881
Environmental Engineering	0819	Agricultural Engineering	0890
Mechanical Engineering	0830	Chemical Engineering	0893
Nuclear Engineering	0840	Industrial Engineering	0896
Electrical Engineering	0850		

Job Family Position Classification Standard for Professional Work in the Engineering and Architecture Group, 0800

The following is taken from the Classification Standard for Safety Engineer (www.opm.gov/fedclass/gs0800P.pdf). This describes the position in government. Your federal resume should reflect these skills, as well as projects that demonstrate your skills. This series covers positions managing, supervising, leading, and/or performing professional engineering and scientific work involving safety, health, and environmental issues anticipating, dealing with, eliminating, or controlling hazardous conditions, exposures, and practices. These hazards may result from human error, equipment, or machine operation and may lead to injuries or damage to property or the environment.

SAFETY ENGINEERING, 0803	Qualification Standard
Series Definition	This series covers positions managing, supervising, leading, and/or performing professional engineering and scientific work involving safety, health, and environmental issues anticipating, dealing with, eliminating, or controlling hazardous conditions, exposures, and practices. These hazards may result from human error, equipment, or machine operation and may lead to injuries or damage to property or the environment. This series requires a functional classification code.
Titling	The basic title for this occupation is Safety Engineer.
Occupational Information	**General Occupational Information** Safety engineering work involves the generation and/or application of theories, principles, practical concepts, systems, and processes related to: the science of safety engineering, engineering design, and the traditional engineering science disciplines (e.g., civil, mechanical, electrical, and chemical); design standards and codes relevant to safety engineering practices and methods; physical science disciplines, advanced mathematics, and economics; critical inquiry, problem solving, and scientific methodology; safety related elements of ergonomics, psychology, and physiology; and safety principles, standards, practices, and analytical techniques. Safety engineers identify, analyze, and control hazardous conditions, exposures, and practices. They apply their knowledge of psychological and physiological factors to design and/or evaluate safety features and controls compensating for the possibility of human errors in the operation of machinery and equipment. This work frequently includes analyzing materials, structures, safety codes, legal requirements, and operations; advising on safety requirements, including the economic impact of alternative solutions; and conducting accident investigations and inspections or reviews of facilities, plans, and equipment. Within the federal government, professional safety engineering work is performed in a wide variety

SAFETY ENGINEERING, 0803	**Qualification Standard**
	of environments such as health research, energy generation, construction and facilities management, industrial and manufacturing operations, recreation, and transportation.

Engineer positions are very specific and your federal resume should match the Classification Standard, as well as the vacancy announcement description.

A Significant Government Engineer Skill: Acquisition Management

Many engineers are now dual trained as Acquisition Specialists/Systems Engineering so that they can manage contractors, contracts, and lifecycle management of engineering projects. The vacancy announcements will state that you may have dual responsibilities in your engineering/technical field, as well as acquisitions management.

You can gain training in Acquisition Management through courses toward your DAWIA Certificate at various levels of certification. In addition, many colleges offer advanced degree programs in Systems Engineering. Generally, although not always, the technical engineering disciplines are limited to the GS-13 level with few GS-14 technical engineering positions available. To advance beyond this level, experience in Acquisition Management and/or Systems Engineering is desired.

The following vacancy announcement describes the Materials Engineer position with Acquisition as a secondary title, which will be a secondary job responsibility. This engineer will eventually become certified in the Defense Acquisition Workforce Investment Act (DAWIA). This Materials Engineer will be managing contractors, monitoring contracts for performance management, communicating about change orders, and ensuring that the government is receiving cost-effective quality and efficient services from contractors.

The acquisitions training can usually be developed after you are hired into a position like this one. You can read the announcement to see whether you need to have the Acquisitions Certification before you are hired, or whether you can complete the training certification within one year of your hire.

Job Title: MATERIALS ENGINEER (ACQUISITION)

Department: Department of the Navy

Agency: Navy Field Offices

Sub Agency: This announcement covers Navy and Marine Corps positions.

Job Announcement Number: DON0806-HQ

All positions are covered under the Defense Acquisition Workforce Improvement Act (DAWIA) and require additional education, training and experience. If you possess DAWIA

(continued)

(continued)

Certification, please indicate your Certification Level and Career Field information in your resume.

Applicants not certified may still apply and be selected for DAWIA positions, but must achieve certification within 24 months of appointment. Certification requirements may be viewed at http://www.dau.mil/catalog/.

Some DAWIA positions may be designated as Critical Acquisition Positions (CAPs). In addition to DAWIA certification requirements, individuals selected for CAPS must also be a member of the Acquisition Corps at the time of selection and sign a three-year tenure agreement prior to assuming the position. If you are an Acquisition Corps member, please indicate your membership in your resume. Acquisition Corps requirements may be viewed at http://acquisition.navy.mil/navyaos/content/view/full/117.

Warrant authority above the small purchase threshold may be required.

The selection of an annuitant is subject to the Department of Defense and Department of the Navy policy on the employment of annuitants. Policy information may be found at https://www.donhr.navy.mil/NSPSdocs/ASN_MRA.pdf.

DAWIA positions at the GS-14 and GS-15 level or equivalent require the selectee to sign a tenure agreement to remain in that position for at least 3 years.

*** SPECIAL NOTICE TO APPLICANTS ***

The Duncan Hunter National Defense Authorization Act (NDAA) FY 2009 provides that the Secretary of Defense can designate acquisition positions within the Department of Defense as shortage positions and recruit and appoint highly qualified persons to those positions. This announcement is open to accept resumes from candidates interested in helping the Department of the Navy meet our mission requirements for the acquisition of systems, equipment and facilities.

The following Defense Acquisition Workforce Improvement Act (DAWIA) Career Fields are included within the authority:

A. Auditing

B. Business, Cost Estimating, Financial Management (BCEFM)

C. Contracting

D. Facilities Engineering

E. Information Technology

F. Life Cycle Logistics

G. Production, Quality and Manufacturing

H. Program Management

I. Quality Control and Assurance

J. Science and Technology Management

K. Systems Planning, Research, Development, Engineering and Testing

L. Test and Evaluation

Create a Project List of Your Engineering Accomplishments and Projects

Most engineers manage multiple projects in their jobs. The best way to write an impressive engineer federal resume is to write about the projects you have managed. You can follow the project map in Table 20.1 to create a project list. You can use a project list to prove your knowledge, skills, and abilities in your federal resume.

The projects and accomplishments will be listed within your Work Experience sections. The projects will demonstrate your knowledge, skills, and abilities and hopefully will impress the human resources reviewer and the supervisor. Your unique projects will help your resume stand out from your competition.

Table 20.1: Project List

	Project Details
Your role	Project Manager, General Engineer, Owner's Representative, Design Engineer
Name of project	Was there a name for your project?
City, state, country, and year	So the reader will know where in the world you were.
Scope of work	In three sentences, include numbers such as square footage, miles, numbers, and any way to quantify the scope of the project for the supervisor.
Budget	Add if appropriate; this can be very informative.
Challenge of the project	This will show your ability to overcome obstacles, perform special innovations, meet challenges, and solve problems. This section could get you hired for being an engineering/project manager genius.
Results	Was it completed on time and on budget? Was the customer happy?

Use Projects and Accomplishments to Prove Your KSAs and Specialized Experience

Expand your project map into narrative descriptions of your projects and analytical tasks. Define your projects and accomplishments with quantifiable numbers for excellent, impressive, on-target content for your resume. The projects or stories will be useful for interview preparation as well because most federal interviews are now behavior-based and require specific examples or stories as answers. (See Chapter 27 for more on behavioral interviewing.)

Sample Project Descriptions

Following are examples of project descriptions that include the critical skills of a PE and Project Manager:

OWNER'S REPRESENTATIVE. ENVIRONMENT, HEALTH AND SAFETY (EHS) CAPITAL PROJECTS. Led interdisciplinary teams in the successful execution of major construction, engineering and Environment, Health & Safety (EHS) capital projects.

- Initiated a design/build "fast track" approach on a strategic $2.5M project to prevent the impact of a contaminant plume on a regional water-supply system. Managed the engineering design, all contract negotiations, and construction of a 1.5-mile discharge pipeline/ barrier well system; and the startup of a groundwater recovery/treament facility. Managed the project team to meet all expedited schedule requirements. The project startup allowed water-supply wells to continue their operation and therefore prevented significant potential cost/fines to the company operating division. The company received a letter of thanks from the city for its proactive approach and expedited solution.

LEAD PROJECT MANAGER. As Lead Project/Program Manager of a business consolidation program, relied heavily on that knowledge and experience for the renovations of 55 administration/manufacturing facilities. Carefully reviewed each project's scope and plan to determine areas requiring compliance with the overall corporate policy, guidance documents, and/or related decisions.

- Established a consistent project management process comprised of a standard schedule, budget and other project documents pertaining to a $35M multi-facility site remediation program, together with 15 different consultant/contractor teams. Resulted in 5% reduction in annual project management costs and a 15% improved on-time acheivement of key milestones.

Target Job: Project Manager, GS-1101-12, Dept. of the U.S. Army, Army Corps of Engineers.
Resume Format: Outline Format federal resume.
Government Contractor, Civil Engineer, Project Manager Seeking Usage Position.
Researched, analyzed, compiled, drafted, and finalized by Jim Dalton, Certified Federal Resume Writer and Coach (CFRWC).

Specialized Experience:

Specialized Experience is defined as at least one year of demonstrated experience in the same or similar work in difficulty and complexity to at least the next lower grade or level that equipped the applicant with the particular knowledge, skills, and abilities to successfully perform the duties of the position, and that is typically in or related to the work of the position to be filled. To be creditable, your specialized experience must demonstrate project management or project leadership with the planning, design, or construction of various projects.

Duties:

1. • **Lead multidisciplinary project teams** from planning, design, cost engineering, real estate, contracting, and construction from initial studies through design and construction. 2. 3. 4.

5. • **Develop, analyze, and maintain project schedules,** prepare fiscal-year budget requests, brief public and upper management and respond to internal and external data calls. 6.

• **Balance project requirements and meeting mandated obligation milestones** against internal and external challenges of resourcing and prioritization of workload. 7.

• **Prepare, review, approve, and fund Scopes of Work.** Prepare meeting agendas and meeting minutes.

8. • **Attend and lead meetings** with in-house design staff, external consultants, sponsors, and partners.

KEYWORDS

1. Lead multidisciplinary project teams
2. Planning, design, cost engineering
3. Real estate, contracting, and construction
4. Studies through design and construction
5. Develop, analyze, and maintain project schedules
6. Prepare fiscal-year budget requests
7. Balance project requirements and meeting mandated obligation milestones
8. Attend and lead meetings

Ronald F. Zimble

22288 Comanche Trail
Cleveland, OH 45410
(410) 888-8888 HOME
(410) 888-8888 WORK
Email: rzimble@hotmail.com

WORK EXPERIENCE	**Halliburton, Inc.** **Dayton, OH US**	**8/2006 - 2/2010**

Salary: 111,000 USD Per Year
Hours per week: 40

PROJECT MANAGER / PROFESSIONAL ENGINEER
PROJECT MANAGER AND PROFESSIONAL ENGINEER / PMP

OWNER'S REPRESENTATIVE. ENVIRONMENT, HEALTH AND SAFETY (EHS) CAPITAL PROJECTS. Led interdisciplinary teams in the successful execution of major construction, engineering and Environment, Health & Safety (EHS) capital projects.

• Structured a company team; formed a joint partnership with the U.S. Environmental Protection Agency (EPA) and an industry group for developing Lean–EHS and Lean–Energy Toolkits. Subsequently integrated the toolkits into Lean training to drive additional value-added projects.

• Saved $757K by managing pilot program to integrate EHS into the Lean function. Projects received annual Halliburton corporation award and were featured in the Halliburton 2007 Maintainability Report.

• Prevented major environmental damage and saved company from significant costs and fines. Initiated a design/build "fast-track" approach on a strategic $2.5M project to prevent containment plume from impacting water system. Managed the engineering design, all contract negotiations, and construction of a 1.5-mile discharge pipeline/barrier well system and the startup of a groundwater recovery/treatment facility. Met all deadlines as project manager. Avoided fines by enabling water-supply wells to continue operations. The company received a letter of thanks from the city for its proactive approach and expedited solution.

STAKEHOLDER LIAISON AND PROJECT MANAGER. Managed all planning, engineering design, construction, and permit considerations. Applied methods learned from PMP training and hands-on experience to develop stakeholder relationships, prepare effective project plans, coordinate project communications, and manage projects through their entire lifecycle span from inception through execution and initiation.

SUBJECT-MATTER EXPERT FOR ANALYZING PROGRAM AND/OR PROJECT PROCESSES. Developed a standard process for the company's facility renovation and Haliburton capital projects. Then initiated a Project Management Processes Manual (PMPM) which comprised the standard project management processes, plus also addressed how to manage multiple projects simultaneously. Initiated a "turnkey" approach to expedite the design and construction of strategic engineering projects to protect company assets. For example, led a project team in the construction of a 2km discharge pipeline and barrier well/treatment system.

+++++ MORE PROJECT DETAILS CONTINUED IN ADDITIONAL INFORMATION (Contact Supervisor: Yes, Supervisor's Name: Mark Stringer, Engineering Manager, Supervisor's Phone: (412) 444-4444)

	Halliburton, Inc. **Dayton, OH US**	**8/1998 - 8/2006**

Salary: 89,000 USD Per Year
Hours per week: 40

Figture 20.1: Engineer and Project Manager resume.

CIVIL ENGINEER (CE)
SUCCESSFUL MINORITY BUSINESS ENTERPRISE (MBE) ENGINEERING
CONSULTANT. Developed the criteria, selected qualified firms, completed
contract documents, managed work, and reported the current status to the
management team.

CONTRACTOR SAFETY PROGRAM MANAGER
As Team Leader, tasked to evaluate and develop solutions for common issues to
drive the improvement of a contractor safety program; organized multidiscipline
teams to identify and address key safety issues with contractors and the onsite
staff. Developed and presented a training program to increase the awareness of
safety in areas where metrics showed an increase in repeated incidents.

• Reduced recordable events by 23% at sites where the training program had
been implemented. The results drove an acceptance-to-apply process by other
project teams.

LEAD PROCESS IMPROVEMENTS
Reduced project costs, lowered staff resource requirements, and improved the
management process and performance results by implementing LEAN process. I
have controlled construction projects and supervised the work of
professional/technical personnel. Completed project scope, schedules, and cost
estimates and provided professional engineering expertise on technical areas and
design changes. Applied engineering skills, knowledge, and abilities in project
design, construction, geotechnical, and environmental areas.

• Identified and completed several Lean-Energy projects to save $650K. This
resulted in adding drive to the projects' sustainability.

NEGOTIATED AND ADMINISTERED CONTRACTS. Negotiated and administered all
contracts; and monitored project schedules, budgets, and key stakeholder
metrics for work at each site. Analyzed cost reports, approved project invoices,
and evaluated change orders with each project team. Met all expedited project
schedules, budgets, and key metrics required by each group of stakeholders.
Facilities were located throughout North America. This effort therefore required a
careful review of applicable corporate policy, EHS, and other government
regulations.

• Developed and managed program to complete renovation of a 4.5M-sq.-ft. site
with 55 manufacturing facilities. Managed more than 20 consultant/contractor
teams in support of $1.2B business acquisition. Saved $75K from planned costs.
(Contact Supervisor: Yes, Supervisor's Name: John Smith, Supervisor's Phone:
(412) 444-4444)

EDUCATION

University of Maryland
College Park, MD US
Bachelor's Degree
Major: Civil Engineering
Minor: Structural Engineering, Construction Management, Environmental
Engineering
GPA: 3.8 out of 4.0

University of Maryland
College Park, MD US
Some College Coursework Completed
Relevant Coursework, Licensures, and Certifications:
Advanced Soil Mechanics, Foundation Engineering, Engineering Geology

**PROFESSIONAL
PUBLICATIONS**

"Lean-Energy Toolkit" - US EPA Publication; October, 2007 (contributor/co-
author)

"Industrial Facility Deactivation/Renovation: A Proactive Approach for Reducing

(continued)

(continued)

Costs and Liabilities" Remediation (the journal of environmental technology and techniques), Fall 1986 (co-author)

"Environmental Project Management Using Fast-Track Methods to Save Time and Money"; Remediation, Summer 1995 (co-author)

ADDITIONAL INFORMATION

WORK EXPERIENCE CONTINUED

Project Manager/Professional Engineer
Halliburton Inc., August 2006 – February 2009

MANAGED MULTIPLE PROJECT TEAMS. Provided weekly status reports to stakeholders pertaining to each project's ongoing status comprising the monitoring of milestones including cost, schedule, and compliance, along with design/construction specifications. Consistently improved project performance results with key metrics – on-time completion (schedule), completion within budget (cost), and product consistency/quality.

LEAD PROJECT MANAGER. As Lead Project/Program Manager of a business consolidation program, relied heavily upon that knowledge and experience for the renovations of 55 administration/manufacturing facilities. Carefully reviewed each project's scope and plan to determine areas requiring compliance with the overall corporate policy, guidance documents, and/or related decisions.

• Improved contractor safety program by evaluating and developing solutions for common issues. Organized multidiscipline teams to identify and address key safety issues with contractors and on-site staff. Developed and presented training program to increase safety awareness in troubled areas.
Established a consistent project management process comprised of a standard schedule, budget, and other project documents pertaining to a $35M multi-facility site remediation program, together with 15 different consultant/contractor teams. Resulted in 5% reduction in annual project management costs and a 15% improved on-time achievement of key milestones.

CERTIFICATES/LICENSES
Advanced Project Management Certificate; University of Maryland, College Park, 2009
Lean Manager, 2007
Certified Lead ISO 14001 Auditor, 2006
Malcolm Baldridge Examiner, 2004
Registered Project Management Professional (PMP), PMP #29110, 2000
Registered Environmental Manager (REM); REM #7968, 1996
Registered Professional Engineer (PE); PE #51880, 1988

PROFESSIONAL SOCIETIES
National Society of Professional Engineers
Project Management Institute
Cleveland Engineering Society
American Society of Civil Engineers
National Registry of Environmental Professionals
Society of Manufacturing Engineers with Lean and Green Council

SPECIAL AWARDS AND RECOGNITION
Achievement Award; Halliburton Corporation, 2007
Engineer of the Month; Halliburton Corporation, 1992
Dean's List; Drexel University; GPA: 3.8

Letter of Commendation: Jim Smart; General Manager, Halliburton Electric Division
"Ron has been an important part of our strategic facility integration program. As Program Manager he has led multiple project teams on several important projects. He also initiated several innovative concepts that expedited project completions and generated an estimated cost savings of $750,000 to date."

Letter of Commendation: Steve Kavanaugh, Operations Manager, Halliburton Inc.
"We received excellent support throughout the entire site renovation project from

Ron. His thoroughness and effective control of the project schedule, costs, and onsite contractors were outstanding. His project management and engineering skills provided us with a savings of $177,000 at this site. These savings helped us lower project costs from $533,000 to $356,000, a savings of 33% against our original budget estimate."

Summary

The Engineer federal resume should match the classification standard and the vacancy announcement, and should include specific details of projects in order to get Best Qualified and Referred and engage the supervisor's interest in interviewing you. Be specific.

CHAPTER 21

Human Resources Management Positions

By Susan Custard

One of the most challenging and rewarding occupations in the federal government can be found in human resources management (HRM). HRM continues to find itself challenged by new demands and requirements from management to strategically assist the organization in improved performance. While earlier changes had been tied to specific functional changes, the new direction and challenge facing HRM is the need to be strategic, integrated, and aligned with agency goals and objectives.

The evolving nature of HR work calls for HR leaders and staff to continuously evaluate their skills. The changes to the occupation can easily be identified in the evolving work environment, and in the competencies required to successfully perform the work. Whether you are a current practitioner or looking to enter the field, this period of change is a good time to evaluate your own career plans, assess the value you bring to the organization and the occupation, decide whether this is work you want to do, and begin to look at new opportunities in the field.

While HR has been shifting over the last decade, the nature of the change was focused on automation, streamlining, standardization, and most critically, evolving client expectations. The world of HR is now focused on talent management workforce planning and integration of products and services. Additionally, there are significant external changes, for example, OPM's and President Obama's hiring reform. Hiring reform calls for a successful integration of workforce planning, automation, and changes in staffing strategies and tactics to ensure the U.S. government has the workforce needed for the future.

Along with these changes, management expectations are now focused on HR's changing role in being strategic, which can be defined as leading the organization in meeting business goals and objectives through effective utilization of human capital. Talent management strategies and workforce planning have become the first iteration of "strategic HR," and allow the agency to address significant HR issues proactively. For example, effective talent management and workforce planning may alleviate a skills shortage or identify new skills critical to agency performance. Use of these tools can position both the HR office and the agency to effectively address these challenges before missions are impacted or additional needs arise for use of flexibilities.

HR employees seeking to further their careers need to clearly articulate their value to the organization in providing service to management and employees that meets strategic goals and objectives. Of critical importance to HR specialists seeking a successful HR career is experience in more than one

HR function. As HR specialists look for positions with different agencies, they should consider organizations with a strong commitment and resource dedicated to HR development, including allowing for functional rotations within HR, as well as details and assignments to business units to enhance or develop your business acumen.

Of critical note to both HR managers and specialists is the opinion held by many senior federal managers that HR can't deliver. For example, an executive was recently heard to say to an HR manager, "Workforce planning and talent management are great, but until you can deliver quality candidates on time, don't bother us with this stuff." A recent survey of chief human capital officers by the Partnership for Public Service indicated that HR personnel aren't necessarily capable of carrying out hiring reform or other critical HR work. Forty-six percent of 68 CHCOs surveyed reported that their HR staffs lack the skills necessary to successfully implement new federal hiring practices.

So, of all the skills needed, which is most critical? HR specialists need to be able to *analyze* situations and data, present risk-based options, and design solutions that are based on best practices. Too often in the past, HR staff have relied on anecdotes to inform HR policy and practice, or the old and reliable "we've always done it that way" approach. HR practitioners of the future will need to be able to analyze situations and scenarios, research, identify trends, and develop fact-based solutions.

As hiring reform and other HR initiatives take place, HR managers and staff must develop and maintain a flexible skill set that will allow them to address short- and long-term agency needs, using every flexibility available.

Necessary Competencies and Skills

The amount of change and the challenges facing HR leaders and practitioners call for HR staff to ensure they have the competencies and skills needed to provide world-class services. With the strategic focus now expected of HR, there are many initiatives underway throughout the federal government to support HR employees (and those seeking to enter the occupation). For example, there has been significant direction from the Chief Human Capital Officer's (CHCO) Council regarding the competencies required of HR staff to be effective in a field that is ambiguous at best. For example, the CHCO Council recently sponsored a competency and skills assessment for all GS-201 (Human Resources Management) positions throughout the federal government.

In order to prepare for positions within the new HR paradigm of strategically focused, customer-oriented service to managers and employees, HR employees and "wannabes" should be focused on developing or enhancing their competencies as described in the following list:

1. **Classification:** Knowledge of classification concepts, principles, and practices related to structuring organizations and positions and determining the appropriate pay system, occupational grouping, title, and pay level of positions.

2. **Compensation:** Knowledge of compensation concepts, principles, and practices, including pay and leave administration and compensation flexibilities.

3. **Employee Benefits:** Knowledge of HR concepts, principles, and practices related to retirement, insurance, injury compensation, and other employee benefits programs.

4. **Talent Management:** Knowledge of employee development concepts, principles, and practices related to planning, evaluating, and administering training, organizational development, and career-development initiatives.

5. **Employee Relations:** Knowledge of laws, rules, case law, regulations, principles, and practices related to employee conduct, performance, and dispute resolution.

6. **HR Information Systems:** Knowledge of HR management concepts, principles, and practices related to identifying and analyzing HR processes, translating functional requirements into technical requirements, and delivering and maintaining HR information systems.

7. **Labor Relations:** Knowledge of laws, rules, regulations, case law, principles, and practices related to negotiating and administering labor agreements.

8. **Performance Management:** Knowledge of performance management concepts, principles, and practices related to planning, monitoring, rating, and rewarding employee performance.

9. **Talent Acquisition:** Knowledge of HR concepts, principles, and practices related to identifying, attracting, and selecting individuals and placing them into positions to address changing organizational needs.

And, as discussed previously, HR specialists must deliver products and services that are *integrated;* the days of passing managers around the HR functional areas for different services are over. Many organizations are creating "business partners" or other HR positions that are responsible for clearly understanding the business needs of specific organizations, combined with leveraging a broad HR knowledge set to design solutions for management's HR challenges that are comprehensive and aligned with HR flexibilities and agency goals and objectives.

In addition to the technical competencies listed above, OPM has identified key "soft skills" that HR specialists need to be effective in the new world of HR. The new HR is focused on a less regulatory or bureaucratic approach, and is changing to a consultant, client-centric delivery model. At the full performance level (GS-12), HR staff should highlight experiences that will develop or enhance their skills in the following areas:

Attention to detail	Creative thinking
Change management	Customer service
Decision making	Flexibility
Influencing and negotiating	Integrity and honesty
Interpersonal skills	Oral communication
Planning and evaluation	Problem solving
Reasoning	Risk management
Self-management	Tolerance for stress
Teamwork	

Applying for HR Jobs

So—what does this mean to you if you are interested in an HR career?

To begin with, you need to develop a clear emphasis on developing both the technical and "soft" skills in the preceding lists in order to further your career. And, most importantly, you need to be able to articulate these skills in a well-developed application. HR people, who should be among the best at self-marketing through the application process, are generally among the poorest in the government. How can you coach and mentor applicants through the selection process, giving them feedback on improving their applications, without taking your own advice?

As you decide to apply to pursue other HR opportunities by applying to vacancies, you need to develop a marketing plan that will ensure that you address the technical expertise required, combined with clear descriptions or evidence of your possession of the required competencies. Your marketing plan needs to incorporate three aspects of the application process:

- **Self-assessment:** Complete a self-assessment of your competencies, and determine your strengths and weaknesses. This might involve getting feedback from management, customers, peers, or others who can provide you with an honest and direct assessment of your skills.

- **Resume and KSAs:** Develop an effective resume and KSA responses that reflect your technical competence and demonstrate your ability to effectively consult (provide options to management) and assess risk.

- **Interviews:** Be prepared for an intensive, behaviorally based interview process for any position you apply for. The interview is where you'll have your best opportunity to show you are part of the new HR.

Resume Development: Your Personal Marketing Tool

Follow the steps in Part 1 to develop your resume. Additionally, once you have a completed resume, get lots of feedback. You might have forgotten a key experience, or a peer or manager might be able to point out critical strengths to build into your resume. Finally, review your resume against each job announcement to ensure that you are addressing the specific competencies required for that position.

See the HR Management resume at the end of this chapter for a place to get started.

Putting It All Together: Writing KSAs in the CCAR Format

While it's anticipated that KSAs are going away, that doesn't mean the end to creating narratives to support your self-assessment for various vacancies. To write effective narratives for the HR Specialist or Assistant job, follow the advice outlined in Chapter 9. That chapter outlines the "CCAR" format, a special template OPM recommends for SES candidates who are writing their KSA statements (known as Executive Core Qualifications, or ECQs). "CCAR" stands for *Context* (what work environment were you in?), *Challenge and Actions* (what was the problem you faced and what did you do to resolve it?), and *Result* (how did your actions improve the situation?). The underlying theme of the CCAR format is that specific examples or stories that illustrate problems you've resolved, cases you've handled, actions you've taken, and accomplishments you've achieved will always make you stand out above applicants who merely state that their experience has provided them with the needed KSAs.

As you work with the factor-level descriptions in the HR classification standards, write down the accomplishments that illustrate your knowledge and your ability to perform the tasks the standards call for. What guidelines do you use? If you can't apply them directly, do you interpret them? If you do, how does your interpretation affect the quality of service you deliver? Can you write a paragraph about a work assignment you've had that required you to interpret unclear guidance? With a little practice, you'll soon be giving examples of problems you've solved instead of just telling the job rater, "My job requires me to interpret a variety of guidance that is not always clear."

Eight Emerging KSAs for the HR Career Field

As more agencies transition toward the "new role" model of HR management, new KSAs will begin to be used in vacancy announcements. Although no one can predict exactly how these KSAs will be worded, the following suggested KSAs begin to capture the changes and competencies needed in the new HR. When reviewing these proposed KSAs, you should challenge yourself with developing draft responses, which may assist you in your self-assessment, and identifying those areas where you need skill development or enhancement.

- How HR management and development contributes to the agency's ability to reach its strategic goals and objectives.
- How HR professionals collaborate with managers to design and implement strategic approaches to overall agency objectives.
- How HR professionals develop and recommend options best suited to particular missions, labor markets, and work technologies.
- How HR organizations invent and adapt their processes and programs to the agency's mission.
- How HR professionals provide advice about the latest practices and developments that might help achieve mission results and maintain a strong performance culture for the workforce.
- How HR organizations integrate methods and options from different HR functions to streamline operations and make them more relevant to clients and customers.
- How HR professionals work across multiple functions to tailor solutions to various HR challenges.
- How HR information systems development is used to affect management's and employees' expectations about timely, quality service; for example, using the Internet to educate the workforce about HR programs and options.

As you develop your narratives, be aware that in the future, many HR candidates will be called on to illustrate how they have played one or more of these roles in their own HR organizations. Look for opportunities within the context of your current job to lead change, and you will automatically become a stronger candidate for the "new role" HR job of the future.

Interviewing: Practice Makes Perfect

Based on the preceding sections, you should be prepared for a competency or behavior-based interview. In a behavioral interview, the interviewer will ask you questions in which you will demonstrate your behavior in a given situation. You can't get enough practice in preparing for an interview, so choose your questions and start talking! Here are some sample questions to challenge you.

Customer Focus:

Describe a time when you found yourself in a position where you had to "recover" with clients—how did you handle it, and were you successful?

Business Acumen:

How do you go about developing the required knowledge of the business of your service organization(s)? How does your level of knowledge impact your ability to provide advice and service?

Working as a Member of a Team:

What are your team-player qualities? Give examples.

Integrity and Trust:

Have you ever been asked to violate a policy or procedure to get something for a client?

Priority Setting:

If you have competing client priorities, what do you do?

Other:

Of the four functions that this job encompasses (classification, compensation, staffing, and recruitment), which would you rate yourself highest in and why?

If you had a chance to create a work environment in which you would be most successful, what would it be?

What is your most significant accomplishment in the world of HR?

How would you go about developing and implementing a knowledge transfer plan?

What do you know about our position classification program? Why do you want to be a part of it? What do you think will be the biggest challenge in doing the work?

What do you know about our position management program?

What do you know about our overall HR program? How do you think you can add value?

HR is undergoing significant change. On a scale of one to ten, how would you assess your ability to manage change? Why?

Using the same scale, how would your boss assess your ability to manage change? Why?

How have you added value to your job over time?

How do you feel that you can contribute to an environment of teamwork?

What did you do to make your last job interesting and more challenging?

Tell us about a suggestion you made on the job to improve how things worked. What was the result?

Sample HR Management Resume

Following is a sample resume for an HR assistant position.

Target Job: Human Resources Assistant, GS-0203-07, from current position as Human Resources Benefits Administrator.
Resume Format: Electronic federal resume.
Private industry to federal career transition.

VICTORIA E. MORRIS
1010 D Street, NE
Washington, DC 20002
Victoria.morris@fda.gov
Home: 222 222-2222   Work: 222 222-2222

PROFESSIONAL PROFILE

Dedicated, customer-service-oriented Human Resources professional with 16 years of federal government experience and expertise in federal staffing and recruitment, automated systems management, and administration.

Knowledgeable of full range of automated human resources tools, including USAJOBS, QuickHire, and USA Staffing.

Demonstrated analytical skills and proven ability to develop effective vacancy announcements and targeted recruitment strategies to meet customer requirements.

Outstanding oral communication skills; professional manner.

EMPLOYMENT HISTORY:

DEPARTMENT OF HEALTH AND HUMAN SERVICES   Nov. 1998 to Present
Office of the Secretary, Washington, D.C.

HUMAN RESOURCES SPECIALIST (GS-201-12)   Oct. 2010 to Present
Food & Drug Administration (FDA), Center for Food Safety and Applied Nutrition
Washington, DC 20350
Hours per week: 40, Salary per year: $82,359
Supervisor, Eric Edwards (301) 444-4444, May contact

PROVIDED HIGH-QUALITY FEDERAL STAFFING AND CLASSIFICATION SERVICES.
As senior Human Resources Specialist, manage day-to-day human resource operations within the Recruitment, Hiring, and Staffing Center. Expert in merit employment, pay demonstration, delegating, examining student employment, and researching internal policies in accordance with OPM and HHS compliance.

IMPLEMENTED REVISED PROGRAM OPERATIONS AND AUTOMATED RECRUITMENT SYSTEMS. Participated in extensive reviews of revised program operations and new program projections in utilizing organizational development and workforce strategic planning. Methodologies consisted of major management objectives, program goals, priorities and current/anticipated workloads, and resource requirements.

Figure 21.1: Sample Human Resources Assistant resume.

- Advised on the redesign of the recruitment process to effectively implement new authorities and enhancements in program structures.

- Member of Assessment Development Team implementing USA Staffing recruitment system; department converted from QuickHire to USA Staffing system in November 2010.

SUPERVISED AND PROVIDED MANAGER SUPPORT on recruitment for 5 managers within a 5,000-person agency. Ensured requests were completed and deadlines were met. Trained and mentored staff; delegated tasks.

ANALYZED AND CONSULTED ON HUMAN RESOURCES ISSUES WITH CUSTOMERS. Provided timely, accurate, and professional responses in the areas of recruitment, placement, position management, pay administration, employee/labor relations, employee performance evaluations, individual development plans, disciplinary actions, incentive awards, employee services, and benefits. Reviewed standard operating procedures, OPM regulations, and multiple policy revisions to render recommendations and commentary on the impact of the agency's mission and goals.

HUMAN RESOURCES SPECIALIST (GS-201-12)   Oct. 2005 to Dec. 2009
Food and Drug Administration (FDA), Center for Tobacco Products
Washington, DC 20350
Hours per week: 40, Salary per year: $80,000
Supervisor: Richard Edwards (301) 333-3333, May contact

DEMONSTRATED KNOWLEDGE OF RECRUITMENT, SELECTION, AND PLACEMENT; developed crediting plans and job analysis through collaboration with managers and field personnel under Title 5, Title 38, Title 42, and special hiring authorities. Received applications for manual cases and conducted evaluation of applicant's eligibility through ranking and rating to prepare selection certificate based on qualifications, experience, and education. Subsequent to selection of candidates, made job offer to applicants, established salaries, and entered on-duty dates.

ADEPT IN UTILIZING RECRUITMENT AUTOMATION AND INFORMATION SYSTEMS; Served as super user and resident expert in the function of automated human resource systems such as QuickHire for recruitment and staffing, and QuickClass for position classification. Comprehensive working knowledge of automated HR systems enhancements such as EWITS, PAWS, E-OPFs, RHRC Work log, and IMPACT. Employed E-Induction program to prepare job offer letters; advise applicants of orientation process, reporting date, and website link for completion of employment forms. Processed multiple personnel actions with EHRP software for non-recruitment actions, including details, reassignments, promotions, new hires, and termination of appointments.

- Expert in staffing; identified as a QuickHire super user.
- Served on the assessment development team for USA Staffing.

UTILIZED PRINCIPLES, PRACTICES, AND TECHNIQUES of federal classification principles, concepts, and practices. Encompassed classification and recruitment

(continued)

(continued)

processes for congressionally authorized positions, evaluating positions. On daily basis, established pay setting for GS scheduled employees as well as relocation bonuses, retention allowances, and superior qualifications under specific guidelines for above the minimum pay (ATM).

ABILITY TO DRIVE PROCESS IMPROVEMENT; coordinated with employee/labor relations branch to research and provide background information in arbitration awards, settlement agreements, and grievances. Consistently provided advisory and consultation services to clients regarding staffing complement, recruitment alternatives, incentives, relocation, awards, retention, and special hiring authorities to provide information to managerial staff to improve decision-making function. Anticipated future needs of clients and provided marketing tools and strategies to enhance customer service. Communicated through monthly meetings on issues and conceptual methodologies employed to improve and accomplish agency mission.

- Participated in work groups in the development of flexi workplace policies and procedures, which was instituted and implemented by the Rockville Human Resources Center, Department of Health and Human Services, in 2005.

EFFECTIVE COMMUNICATOR ORALLY AND IN WRITING. Routinely responded to technical and complex inquiries relative to payroll, compensation, promotions, reassignments, recruitment processes, and more. Developed vacancy announcements for posting on USAJOBS and XI QuickHire systems. Maintained monthly status reports reconciling actions processed, timetable, and final results.

HUMAN RESOURCES SPECIALIST (GS-201-11)   July 2003 to Oct. 2005
Recruitment Center
Washington, D.C. 20350
Hours per week: 40, Salary per year: $55,000
Supervisor: Nancy Peterson (301) 444-4444, May contact

KNOWLEDGEABLE IN HUMAN RESOURCES LAWS, REGULATIONS, RULES, AND RESEARCH; provided a variety of personnel management services and management advisory functions in the areas of position classification, wage administration, recruitment and placement, and organizational design. Demonstrated extensive knowledge in and ability to research rules and regulations in the Code of Federal Regulations, OPM regulations, Merit Promotion rules, Veterans' Preference Guides, and Union Agreements.

UTILIZED FEDERAL AUTOMATED SYSTEMS including QuickHire and web-based software that performs external placement and recruitment work.

EDUCATION:

Bachelor of Arts in Human Resources, Columbia Union College, Takoma Park, MD, 2002

PROFESSIONAL TRAINING:
USA Staffing—2010
QuickHire—2003
Basic Staffing & Placement—2003
DEU Certification—2003
EHRP—2001
Position Classification for Administrative Staff—2001

AWARD
Outstanding Performance Appraisal—2003

COMPUTER SKILLS
Microsoft Word, Excel, Outlook, PowerPoint, Access
USAJOBS, EHRP, QuickHire, EWITS, PAWS, E-OPFs, RHRC Work log, IMPACT. and
Travel Management System

Summary

The HR occupation and work environment are consistently evolving. In order to continue to advance your HR career, you should focus on developing the critical technical and "soft skills" required, with a special emphasis on understanding how the broad use of all HR functions together can contribute to your organization's success. With these skills in hand and an effective marketing campaign, your success in finding new and challenging positions in the HR field will be assured.

Part 6

Special Federal Job Seeker Strategies: Executives, Military and Spouses, PPP/BRAC, and Schedule A

CHAPTER 22

Senior Executive Service, Executive Core Qualifications

Updated by Diane Hudson-Burns and Susan Custard

In an effort to develop a corps of executive managers with the talent, foresight, and flexibility required to lead a soon-to-be-reformed federal service through a new era, Congress, through enactment of the 1978 Civil Service Reform Act, created the Senior Executive Service (SES). Congress envisioned the SES as a cadre of exceptional leaders recruited from the top levels of government and private industry, who would move among agencies and share their broad background and experience to create new efficiencies and innovations government-wide.

Managerial experience gained solely in the federal government is no longer the most important criterion for gaining a senior position in an agency, nor would the Best Qualified new leader necessarily be the career civil servant who spent his or her entire career in one agency. A corporate c-level executive could write an SES application with the best leadership accomplishments and be seriously considered for an SES leadership position. It is remarkable that unlike virtually all other governments around the world, high-level professional positions within the United States government still remain open to those who have gained their experience outside the federal civil service.

A Profile of the SES

The SES has changed in many ways during the past 30-plus years, but it is still the leadership cadre of the federal service. Of the 6,800 members of the SES, 88 percent are career civil servants. The remainder are noncareer appointments (usually political) or appointments for a limited term. Almost half of SES positions are based in the Washington, D.C., metropolitan area. The composition of the SES reflects various federal agencies' functional requirements. Forty-five percent are in administrative or management fields. Another 12 percent provide legal services. Engineering, science/math, and other fields each account for 12 to 14 percent. Twenty-six percent of the SES are women, and nearly 14 percent are minorities.

A Word About the SES Selection Process

The Office of Personnel Management convenes Qualifications Review Boards (QRBs). The QRB is made up of volunteer SES executives currently in government for a two-week period. They review the applications that come to OPM. They provide an independent peer review of candidates proposed for initial career appointment to the SES. The candidate cannot be appointed to the SES until the QRB certifies his or her executive qualifications. The QRB review is the critical last step in the SES selection process. By focusing attention on executive qualifications, the QRB helps ensure that technical skills do not outweigh leadership expertise in the selection of new senior executives.

QRBs provide a critical, independent peer review of a candidate's executive qualifications to be a member of the SES. This objective review ensures that the government is hiring executives with the leadership qualifications needed in today's environment, especially the ability to lead in times of change.

OPM draws on SES members to serve on QRBs and to advise on QRB policy and procedures. The board normally consists of three SES members, each from a different agency. A majority of board members must be SES career appointees. QRB members cannot review candidates from their own agencies.

After the agency completes its merit staffing process and makes a selection, the agency requests QRB certification of the selectee's executive qualifications. OPM administers the QRBs, which meet every Tuesday and Friday. A QRB reviews each case and either approves or disapproves the candidate's executive qualifications. If approved, the agency may proceed with the appointment. Disapprovals are usually due to the candidate not meeting the executive qualifications requirements or not adequately addressing his or her qualifications in terms of the five ECQs. The entire QRB certification process is usually completed in less than two weeks.

The first word of "Senior Executive Service" is appropriate: It *is* a senior service, with 50 percent of its membership eligible for retirement in the next five years. Retirement remains the primary method of attrition in the SES.

Jeffrey Zeintz, Federal Chief Performance Officer and Deputy Director for Management, Office of Management and Budget (OMB), wrote on February 18, 2011, that the retiring Senior Executive Service executives will be "taking with them significant knowledge and expertise. In addition, through the biennial allocation process, a number of agencies have or may receive new SES spaces to meet future needs or address legislative changes, increasing the urgency to build deep and diverse pipelines of talent. Given this confluence of daunting demographic challenges, agencies will have to pursue multiple approaches, coupling active recruitment of current staff with talent channels outside their agencies and government."

The Office of Personnel Management and a new pilot group have broadened the use of a resume-based SES hiring model with ECQs combined in the federal resume, along with Technical Qualifications and templates to modernize the application format. Agencies are determining what SES application format will work for their agency, but the five-page SES ECQ federal resume is the latest format being requested for SES positions.

The Office of Personnel Management revised the Executive Core Qualifications (known as ECQs, listed later in this chapter), which are the five main rating factors used to evaluate an SES candidate's "corporate perspective." OPM has recently updated the "leadership competencies" that define the ECQs; this minor change is the only change seen in the ECQs since their inception.

The ECQs are defined in Tables 22.1 and 22.2. Each ECQ definition has been modified to provide a clear explanation of the ECQ's requirements. The most significant changes in the ECQs are the addition of the "fundamental competencies," which are considered as an inherent part of the skills of each ECQ. Additionally, the competencies for several ECQs have changed. Leading People has changed, with the addition of Developing Others as a competency; many of the other ECQ competencies have been moved into the fundamental competencies, including Interpersonal Skills (Building Coalitions and Communication), Written Communication (Building Coalitions and Communication), and Continual Learning (Leading Change), as well as the addition of Public Service Motivation.

Fundamental Competencies: These competencies are the foundation for success in each of the Executive Core Qualifications:

- Interpersonal Skills
- Oral Communication
- Continual Learning
- Written Communication
- Integrity/Honesty
- Public Service Motivation

Table 22.1: Executive Core Qualifications

Leading Change	Leading People	Results Driven	Business Acumen	Building Coalitions/ Communication
		Definitions		
This core qualification involves the ability to bring about strategic change, both within and outside the organization, to meet organizational goals. Inherent to this ECQ is the ability to establish an organizational vision and to implement it in a continuously changing environment.	This core qualification involves the ability to lead people toward meeting the organization's vision, mission, and goals. Inherent to this ECQ is the ability to provide an inclusive workplace that fosters the development of others, facilitates cooperation and teamwork, and supports constructive resolution of conflicts.	This core qualification involves the ability to meet organizational goals and customer expectations. Inherent to this ECQ is the ability to make decisions that produce high-quality results by applying technical knowledge, analyzing problems, and calculating risks.	This core qualification involves the ability to manage human, financial, and information resources strategically.	This core qualification involves the ability to build coalitions internally and with other federal agencies, state and local governments, nonprofit and private-sector organizations, foreign governments, or international organizations to achieve common goals.
		Competencies		
Creativity and Innovation External Awareness Flexibility Resilience Strategic Thinking Vision	Conflict Management Leveraging Diversity Developing Others Team Building	Accountability Customer Service Decisiveness Entrepreneurship Problem Solving Technical Credibility	Financial Management Human Capital Management Technology Management	Partnering Political Savvy Influencing/Negotiating

Table 22.2: Executive Core Qualifications and Competency Definitions

ECQ 1: Leading Change

	Definition: This core qualification involves the ability to bring about strategic change, both within and outside the organization, to meet organizational goals. Inherent to this ECQ is the ability to establish an organizational vision and to implement it in a continuously changing environment.

Competencies

Creativity and Innovation	Develops new insights into situations; questions conventional approaches; encourages new ideas and innovations; designs and implements new or cutting-edge programs/processes.
External Awareness	Understands and keeps up-to-date on local, national, and international policies and trends that affect the organization and shape stakeholders' views; is aware of the organization's impact on the external environment.
Flexibility	Is open to change and new information; rapidly adapts to new information, changing conditions, or unexpected obstacles.
Resilience	Deals effectively with pressure; remains optimistic and persistent, even under adversity. Recovers quickly from setbacks.
Strategic Thinking	Formulates objectives and priorities, and implements plans consistent with the long-term interests of the organization in a global environment. Capitalizes on opportunities and manages risks.
Vision	Takes a long-term view and builds a shared vision with others; acts as a catalyst for organizational change. Influences others to translate vision into action.

ECQ 2: Leading People

	Definition: This core qualification involves the ability to lead people toward meeting the organization's vision, mission, and goals. Inherent to this ECQ is the ability to provide an inclusive workplace that fosters the development of others, facilitates cooperation and teamwork, and supports constructive resolution of conflicts.

(continued)

(continued)

	Competencies
Conflict Management	Encourages creative tension and differences of opinions. Anticipates and takes steps to prevent counterproductive confrontations. Manages and resolves conflicts and disagreements in a constructive manner.
Leveraging Diversity	Fosters an inclusive workplace where diversity and individual differences are valued and leveraged to achieve the vision and mission of the organization.
Developing Others	Develops the ability of others to perform and contribute to the organization by providing ongoing feedback and by providing opportunities to learn through formal and informal methods.
Team Building	Inspires and fosters team commitment, spirit, pride, and trust. Facilitates cooperation and motivates team members to accomplish group goals.

ECQ 3: Results Driven

Definition: This core qualification involves the ability to meet organizational goals and customer expectations. Inherent to this ECQ is the ability to make decisions that produce high-quality results by applying technical knowledge, analyzing problems, and calculating risks.

	Competencies
Accountability	Holds self and others accountable for measurable, high-quality, timely, and cost-effective results. Determines objectives, sets priorities, and delegates work. Accepts responsibility for mistakes. Complies with established control systems and rules.
Customer Service	Anticipates and meets the needs of both internal and external customers. Delivers high-quality products and services; is committed to continuous improvement.
Decisiveness	Makes well-informed, effective, and timely decisions, even when data are limited or solutions produce unpleasant consequences; perceives the impact and implications of decisions.
Entrepreneurship	Positions the organization for future success by identifying new opportunities; builds the organization by developing or improving products or services. Takes calculated risks to accomplish organizational objectives.
Problem Solving	Identifies and analyzes problems; weighs relevance and accuracy of information; generates and evaluates alternative solutions; makes recommendations.

| Technical Credibility | Understands and appropriately applies principles, procedures, requirements, regulations, and policies related to specialized expertise. |

ECQ 4: Business Acumen

Definition: This core qualification involves the ability to manage human, financial, and information resources strategically.

Competencies

Financial Management	Understands the organization's financial processes. Prepares, justifies, and administers the program budget. Oversees procurement and contracting to achieve desired results. Monitors expenditures and uses cost-benefit thinking to set priorities.
Human Capital Management	Builds and manages workforce based on organizational goals, budget considerations, and staffing needs. Ensures that employees are appropriately recruited, selected, appraised, and rewarded; takes action to address performance problems. Manages a multisector workforce and a variety of work situations.
Technology Management	Keeps up-to-date on technological developments. Makes effective use of technology to achieve results. Ensures access to and security of technology systems.

ECQ 5: Building Coalitions/Communication

Definition: This core qualification involves the ability to build coalitions internally and with other federal agencies, state and local governments, nonprofit and private-sector organizations, foreign governments, or international organizations to achieve common goals.

Competencies

Partnering	Develops networks and builds alliances; collaborates across boundaries to build strategic relationships and achieve common goals.
Political Savvy	Identifies the internal and external politics that impact the work of the organization. Perceives organizational and political reality and acts accordingly.
Influencing/Negotiating	Persuades others; builds consensus through give and take; gains cooperation from others to obtain information and accomplish goals.

(continued)

(continued)

Fundamental Competencies

Definition: These competencies are the foundation for success in each of the Executive Core Qualifications.

Competencies	
Interpersonal Skills	Treats others with courtesy, sensitivity, and respect. Considers and responds appropriately to the needs and feelings of different people in different situations.
Oral Communication	Makes clear and convincing oral presentations. Listens effectively; clarifies information as needed.
Integrity/Honesty	Behaves in an honest, fair, and ethical manner. Shows consistency in words and actions. Models high standards of ethics.
Written Communication	Writes in a clear, concise, organized, and convincing manner for the intended audience.
Continual Learning	Assesses and recognizes own strengths and weaknesses; pursues self-development.
Public Service Motivation	Shows a commitment to serve the public. Ensures that actions meet public needs; aligns organizational objectives and practices with public interests.

The Changing Competition for SES Positions

Competition for SES positions will become more intense in the next five years. It is not unusual for HR professionals to report receiving 100 to 150 applications for each SES announcement. Not only are numerous baby boomers seeking the promotions that will cap careers that began in the late 1960s, but agencies reduced the number of SES positions during the mid-to-late 1990s as a result of the National Partnership for Reinventing Government—the successor to the National Performance Review.

Most SES reductions were achieved by cuts in the Department of Defense (closures of major installations resulted in many workforce cuts) or by eliminating positions that were on the books but had not been filled. In other instances, agencies eliminated one position only to create another—redesigning jobs to align with "reinvention" initiatives. Such restructuring, however, tended to be at the margins of the SES. Most executive positions lead core agency programs that would require statutory changes to modify or eliminate. In an era of divided government, such changes are difficult to effect.

Who Should Apply?

In most cases, new SES members rise through career-development ladders within single agencies or departments. They might serve within different agency components during their careers, but the federal service generally still adheres to the principle of advancement within a profession. A new SES manager in the Environmental Protection Agency's water program, for example, is more likely to come from within that program than from any other program in the EPA. Although most agencies have SES attorneys, an immigration law attorney is unlikely to transfer into an SES position in the antitrust division at the Department of Justice. Demonstrating relevant skills is the surest route to entering the SES, and that is usually done most credibly at the agency where the position will be filled.

There is no substitute for substantial experience. Entrants who rise through career ranks to the SES frequently have 15, 20, or even 30 years of experience, most of which was gained within their own agencies. They typically have at least a college education, and frequently possess graduate degrees and other forms of professional development training. Many will be identified and nurtured—or mentored—through their agency's SES candidate-development programs or through other well-recognized channels, such as the Federal Executive Institute. Their experiences will include broadening through a number of detail assignments at other agencies. Nearly all successful SES applicants will have a succession of outstanding performance evaluations and demonstrate a record of developing other people to ensure that their organizations continue to work well in their successors' hands. In addition to this sustained superior performance, it usually helps to have pulled one or two major projects out of the fire under emergency or adverse circumstances.

An important dimension of an SES application, as with most federal positions, responds to the question, "What have you done lately?" Federal human capital officers and selecting officials are looking for progressively responsible performance at or near the level for which one is applying. Typically, the SES applicant will be able to describe five to seven years of experience at the GS- or GM-15 level.

Successful SES applicants must demonstrate an ability to think at least two bureaucratic levels above the advertised position. An SES appointment usually requires the approval of an agency head and the Office of Personnel Management, so a Senior Executive applicant must be able to speak that executive's language.

An SES opening in any agency signals some organizational change—maybe an experienced executive is retiring or agency leaders are creating a new position to address a perceived problem. Knowing the agency and its needs is critically important. You can strengthen your SES application if you know what the agency leadership believes its problems to be and can demonstrate that you have the experience to tackle those issues. You need not be an insider to gain familiarity with an agency's mission and requirements; however, you bear the burden of demonstrating that experience and knowledge you gained elsewhere provides enough background for you to perform effectively.

Finally, senior executives at or above the SES job level being filled usually rate SES applicants. You will be a stronger candidate if these executives already know you and are familiar with your significant accomplishments, and if you effectively represent these accomplishments in your ECQ statements.

If the preceding description fits you, consider applying for the SES. Vacancies for SES positions are listed on the www.USAJOBS.gov website. The vacancy list is updated regularly. Many individual agencies also advertise SES positions on their websites.

Requirements for Successful Applicants: Remember the Basics

As you begin to develop your SES package, keep in mind that regardless of the federal agency to which you apply, staffing an executive position is much more complex than staffing other types of federal jobs. Because of the high visibility and broad impact to the agency, nearly all SES selections require agency-level approval. Before you can even hope to get an interview, your application must survive the initial and secondary screening phases it will pass through in the agency's HR office.

One seasoned HR professional who has staffed many SES jobs and has reviewed hundreds of applications offers the following advice to those applying from both within and outside the government.

Read and Follow the Instructions

Follow the application instructions. As obvious as this might seem, an appalling number of applicants are eliminated at the initial screening phase because they simply fail to submit the required documents.

"We received 55 applications for our agency's SES General Counsel position last year," our HR professional reports. "Of those 55, over half were eliminated because they did not submit proof that they were licensed to practice before a state bar—even though the announcement stated clearly that applicants who did not submit such documentation would receive no further consideration."

If you're an attorney applicant with many years of service, you might think such a requirement is unnecessary, or perhaps even nitpicky: After all, you've worked as a civil-service attorney for 30 years. Surely the personnel office "knows" you're licensed to practice before a state bar. Or, at worst, if it doesn't have record of this, surely the personnel office will call you or your agency's personnel office and ask for it. Remember this: Forty to sixty candidates are applying for only one job. It is an enormous task for the HR specialist to review these applications and whittle them down to a manageable number of candidates for senior managers to interview. If you fail to include the information required in the vacancy notice, it is an easy way for him or her to disqualify you from further consideration. Don't let this be you. Follow the application instructions to the letter.

Make the Length "Just Right"

Think Goldilocks. Or maybe Procrustes (the mythological host who adjusted his guests to the size of the bed). Make sure the length and substance of each document in the package is neither too long nor too short. "Internal applicants tend to submit way too much information," our HR advisor says. "They've been with the government a long time and think they have to include everything they've done since they were a GS-5." On the contrary, statements should describe experience that is directly relevant and closely focused to the job requirements. "On the other hand," our advisor continues, "external candidates tend to submit only one-page resumes, often with no cover letter, and seem to feel we are lucky to get even that."

The SES selection process, a very daunting one even for internal candidates who are familiar with lengthy staffing procedures, is often incomprehensible to external candidates. "The government loses a lot of good talent because of the process," our advisor notes, "they simply get frustrated and go away. OPM is working on streamlining the process, so we hope it will get better." In the meantime, external candidates must take the time to describe their experiences in-depth and explain how they relate to the vacant position. Otherwise, HR professionals simply will not have enough information to determine that an external candidate is highly qualified for the job.

Balance the Strengths and Weaknesses of Your Background

Both internal and external candidates need to balance the inherent strengths and weaknesses of coming from either a federal or private-sector background. To be effective as a senior leader in an SES position requires a mix of both worlds: Candidates must know the internal workings of government systems—how the bureaucracy works—but they also must have the ability to bring new ideas and approaches to the agency.

What Does the SES Announcement Require?

The normal SES package contains a cover letter, a strong federal resume (study Parts 1 and 2 of this book), special statements addressing as many as three sets of technical and managerial factors listed in the vacancy notice, and most importantly, statements showing that the candidate possesses the five Executive Core Qualifications (ECQs) established by OPM—the managerial skills that are the prerequisites for entry into the SES. Unless the resume and the statements demonstrate that you possess the Executive Core Qualifications, even exceptional technical qualifications will not be enough to develop a successful SES application.

As a reminder, from Table 22.1, the five Executive Core Qualifications (ECQs) are as follows:

- Leading Change
- Leading People
- Results Driven
- Business Acumen
- Building Coalitions/Communication

In addition to the five ECQs, each agency can define both mandatory and desirable technical qualifications for any SES position advertised. These qualifications vary according to the position. For example, an applicant for Assistant Administrator of the Federal Aviation Administration for airway facilities must be able to demonstrate professional knowledge of the design and engineering of radio navigational systems. Firsthand flying experience using this system might strengthen those qualifications, but that would be a desirable, rather than a mandatory, technical requirement.

Nearly one-third of SES applications are rejected for not describing the advertised qualifications for the position. Of the remaining two-thirds, the quality of the ECQ statements determines who will be grouped among the Well Qualified, and ultimately, who will gain interviews for the position. It is not unusual for agencies to report a final list of only 3 to 12 Well Qualified candidates from a pool of 60 applicants. With competition this intense, your core qualifications statements must stand above the crowd.

Are All ECQs Created Equal?

A frequently asked question we receive from SES candidates is, are some ECQs more important than others? In a recent government-wide survey, OPM asked career senior executives how the ECQs ranked in order of importance to their current federal jobs. The majority responded as follows:

1. Leading People
2. Building Coalitions/Communication
3. Results Driven
4. Leading Change
5. Technical Competence (based on your Mandatory Technical Qualifications Narratives)
6. Business Acumen

These results confirm that communications and "people skills" continue to be the most important characteristics required of senior leaders in the federal service. The survey went on to conclude that Business Acumen was also emerging as a more desirable characteristic of future government leaders.

The core qualifications demand more than managerial experience. A candidate must demonstrate keen business acumen, the ability to foresee and overcome challenges to successfully lead change, and the ability to gain others' support and cooperation to reach results. It is not enough to discuss the duties of positions you have held or to make conclusive statements that you have managed large staffs or held jobs that gave you these abilities. You must provide concrete examples of the problems you faced, how you solved them, and how your effort improved the organization. As one personnel officer responsible for SES positions commented, "I want to know not merely what the applicant claims to have done; I need to know when and where it was done to make the case credible." In short, to be a successful SES applicant, you must master the art of writing powerful ECQs. Let's get started!

Resume-Based SES Application Packages: The Five-Page SES/ECQ Resume (Senior Executive Service/Executive Core Qualifications)

The Office of Personnel Management (OPM) conducted a pilot of innovative methods for SES selection in 2008, including a streamlined resume-based hiring process and an applicant accomplishment record. Federal agencies now have a choice in filling specific vacancies through any of the three processes:

1. Traditional SES resume (about five pages) and set of ECQ narrative essays (10 pages maximum) with required Technical Qualifications narrative essays (two pages each), for an approximate application package of 20 pages.

2. The new five-page SES resume-based method with ECQs addressed within the body of the resume.

3. The new Accomplishment Record, a one-page narrative essay focused on one leadership competency identified from an ECQ.

Each federal agency will determine which application process to use, and each federal vacancy announcement posted for SES positions will specifically indicate which format is required by that agency for the posted position. Therefore, it is critical to read each vacancy announcement thoroughly before applying for positions. Applicants may now be required to create two or three types of SES application packages and the associated required documents.

No matter the application format used, the focus is still on the 28 Leadership Competencies identified by OPM:

- **Leading Change:** Creativity & Innovation, External Awareness, Flexibility, Resilience, Strategic Thinking, Vision

- **Leading People:** Conflict Management, Leveraging Diversity, Developing Others, and Team Building

- **Results Driven:** Accountability, Customer Service, Decisiveness, Entrepreneurship, Problem Solving, and Technical Credibility

- **Business Acumen:** Financial Management, Human Capital Management, and Technology Management

- **Building Coalitions:** Partnering, Political Savvy, Influencing/Negotiating

- **Cross-cutting Fundamental Competencies:** Interpersonal Skills, Oral Communications, Integrity/Honesty, Written Communication, Continual Learning, and Public Service Motivation

The QRB is seeking demonstrated strong executive experience for initial career SES appointments.

Combined with the SES resume, ECQs (in any of the three identified formats), and scoring from a structured interview, candidates are selected for SES based on demonstrated evidence of executive experience.

The Resume-Based Application Method (Five-Page SES/ECQ Resume)

Crafting a five-page resume for an executive can be a challenge when covering 20 years of experience. And, with the use of the five-page SES/ECQ resume, the task can be even more challenging, by making you try to boil down some 20 pages of resume and ECQ narratives previously created for traditional SES application packages into a coherent five-page document that tells your story of senior leadership by covering all of the 28 leadership competencies, but not actually identifying the ECQ categories.

To best prepare the five-page SES/ECQ resume, it is strongly recommended that you fully develop your CCAR (Context, Challenge, Actions, Result) narratives for the five ECQs and then shrink the stories into short, five-to-eight-line bullets/short paragraphs. Then, as you build the resume, include the short bullets in the appropriate time frame. You may not be able to use the full CCAR format in each bullet or short paragraph in the five-page SES/ECQ resume; so rather, focus on the accomplishment and the result. Remember, the evaluators are looking for demonstrated evidence of your ECQs and the leadership competencies woven throughout the entire five pages.

Accomplishment Record Narrative Method

The other format that an SES applicant might see on a vacancy announcement is the Accomplishment Record Narrative. These are one-page narrative statements based on an identified leadership competency from one of the ECQs. The announcement will specifically indicate how many essays to write and which leadership competencies to address. The stories should be written in the CCAR format, describing a specific story and result.

If you have previously written an ECQ narrative, you can most likely extract some stories from your "library" of stories for use in the Accomplishment Record narrative.

Important points to keep in mind:

- Each agency will now select a method for SES applicants to use to apply for open positions. As an applicant, read an announcement carefully and in its entirety before preparing the required SES resume and ECQs format.

- You may need more than one resume package if you are going to apply for many SES positions at varied agencies.

- No matter the application method (traditional resume and ECQ narratives or resume-based application), prepare your top ten list of accomplishments and develop your ECQ stories from that list. The exercise of developing your list of leadership initiatives is excellent preparation for developing the SES resumes and/or ECQ narratives, for use in the interview process, and even in networking.

Job Analysis/Keywords and Executive Leadership Competencies

Target Job: Executive Director, ES-0343-00, EPA.
Federal to Senior Executive Service.
Researched, analyzed, compiled, and finalized by Diane Hudson Burns, Certified Federal Job Coach and Trainer.

Specialized Experience

As a basic requirement for entry into the SES, applicants must provide evidence of progressively responsible leadership experience that is indicative of senior executive level management capability and directly related to the skills and abilities outlined under Technical Qualifications and Executive Core Qualifications listed below. Typically, experience of this nature will have been gained at or above the GS-15 grade level in the federal service or its equivalent in the private sector.

DUTIES

This position serves as the Executive Director with administrative oversight for Information Sharing for the Office of Chief Information Officer (OCIO). Provides Information Sharing **direction** and **leadership** and establishes and carries out the program to provide for the effective and efficient use of IT systems and programs. Establishes and coordinates the transition of the agency's **Information Sharing Architecture (ISA),** including **performance metrics, business functions,** data assets, systems and technologies that are interoperable not only with other Federal Departments and Agencies, but with state, local, tribal, and private sector **Data Reference Models (DRMs).** Agency **spokesperson.**

Provides **leadership vision** and **implementation** for national information sharing programs. Provides **leadership** and acts as the **pioneer** in developing theories, practices and strategies for program requirements to ensure.

Develops the **tools** and incentives necessary at the **institutional, leadership, and workforce levels** to **collaborate** and **share knowledge,** expertise, and information. The incumbent creates and/or identifies new practices, theories, and strategies for the presentation, discovery, and delivery of information and data to enable **information sharing** between various levels of government. Expertise in advancing **information search, discovery, retrieval, dissemination, and pervasive connectivity** through common metadata, tagging, security marketing, and network.

Develops advanced search and retrieval protocols for information repositories; establishes governance mechanisms; develops information security policies; develops information sharing communication programs to create awareness of a responsibility to provide culture.

(continued)

(continued)

EXECUTIVE CORE QUALIFICATIONS AND TECHNICAL QUALIFICATIONS (Leadership-oriented Knowledge, Skills, and Abilities)

To meet the minimum qualification requirements for this position, you must show in your resume that you possess the five Executive Core Qualifications (ECQs) and the Technical Qualifications (TQs) listed below. We recommend that your resume emphasize your level of responsibilities, the scope and complexity of the programs managed, and your program accomplishments, including the results of your actions.

The application process used to recruit for this position is RESUME-ONLY, although you should not address the ECQs or TQs separately, evidence of each must be clearly reflected in your resume. Any information in excess of 5 pages WILL NOT be considered.

Executive Core Qualifications (Leadership Competencies)

ECQ 1 - **LEADING CHANGE**: This core qualification involves the ability to bring about **strategic change,** both **within and outside the organization**, to meet organizational goals. Inherent to this ECQ is the ability to establish an organizational **vision** and to **implement** it in a **continuously changing environment.**

ECQ 2 - **LEADING PEOPLE**: This core qualification involves the ability to **lead people** toward meeting the organization's **vision, mission, and goals**. Inherent to this ECQ is the ability to provide an **inclusive workplace** that fosters the **development of others**, facilitates **cooperation** and **teamwork**, and supports **constructive resolution of conflicts**.

ECQ 3 - **RESULTS DRIVEN**: This core qualification involves the ability to meet **organizational goals** and **customer expectations**. Inherent to this ECQ is the ability to **make decisions** that produce high-quality results by applying **technical knowledge, analyzing problems**, and **calculating risks**.

ECQ 4 - **BUSINESS ACUMEN**: This core qualification involves the ability to **manage human, financial, and information resources** strategically.

ECQ 5 - **BUILDING COALITIONS:** This core qualification involves the ability to **build coalitions** internally and with other **Federal agencies, State and local governments, nonprofit** and **private sector organizations, foreign governments,** or **international organizations** to achieve common goals.

Technical Qualification(s) – Mandatory

TQ 1. In-depth knowledge of **Information Sharing** issues within the federal government, other governmental agencies, state, local, and private industry.

TQ 2. Excellent technical expertise in one or more technical disciplines relevant to the **Information Sharing** environment and **architecture across components**.

Keywords and Leadership Competencies

- Direction
- Leadership
- Information Sharing Architecture (ISA)
- Performance metrics
- Business functions
- Data Reference Models (DRMs)
- Spokesperson
- Vision
- Implementation
- Pioneer
- Develop tools to collaborate and share knowledge
- Institutional, leadership, and workforce levels
- Information search, discovery, retrieval, dissemination, and pervasive connectivity
- Develop advanced search and retrieval protocols for information repositories
- Leading change; strategic change; within and outside the organization; continuously changing environment
- Leading people; mission; inclusive workplace; development of others; cooperation; teamwork; constructive resolution of conflicts
- Results driven; organizational goals; customer expectations; make decisions; technical knowledge; analyzing problems; calculating risks
- Business acumen; manage human, financial, and information resources
- Building coalitions; federal agencies; state, local, foreign governments; nonprofit, private sector, international organizations
- Architecture across components

The sample SES/ECQ resume in Figure 22.1 is formatted for e-mailing, snail-mailing, or hand delivery. The Office of Personnel Management's guidelines indicate to not use the headers for the Executive Core Qualifications (Leading Change, Leading People, Results Driven, Business Acumen, or Building Coalitions) in the resume; however, we identified the ECQs in the resume as a sample.

This document may require use of different Key Leadership Achievements for varied announcements because the competencies may change based on the series applied for or the Technical Qualifications. Each resume that is submitted for a specific announcement needs to be adjusted to meet the new keywords and identified competencies.

JOYCE C. MYLES

1234 Canyon Dr.
Los Angeles, CA 55555

jcmyles@yahoo.com
(555) 555-5555 (c)

Citizenship: U.S. Citizen
Social Security Number: XXX-XX-XXXX
Veteran Status: N/A
Highest Federal Grade: GS-343-15
Announcement # USA-789 | Executive Director

EXECUTIVE PROFILE

Senior leader and Subject Matter Expert with 17 years of experience creating and delivering innovative and cutting-edge Information Sharing and e-Government operations and programs. Provide leadership vision, direction, and administration for the efficient and effective use of IT systems and programs. Broad, deep, executive knowledge of federal IT needs and requirements. Architect agency-wide strategic action plans, draft policies and procedures, and oversee execution to meet Congressional and White House directives. Develop, nurture, and leverage new joint partnerships, and collaborate with federal, state, local and private-industry stakeholders to improve access to crucial information. Improve data quality to support strategic and tactical decision-making. Provide significant input into enterprise architecture, IT investment reviews, and IT security policies. Extensive experience in senior-level project management.

EXECUTIVE EXPERIENCE

xx/xxxx - Present
DEPUTY DIRECTOR
Office of the Chief Information Officer (CIO)
Department of Transportation, Los Angeles, CA
Supervisor: John Thompson, (555) 555-5555, may contact

Hours per week: 40+
Rank: GS-343-15
Salary: $xxx/year

SCOPE OF LEADERSHIP:
Oversight leadership for carrying out critical e-Government and Information Sharing Program for the DOT. Align business strategy with IT to ensure operational excellence for the agency. Initiate and formulate program strategies including performance metrics, business functions, data assets, systems, and technologies that are interoperable with other federal agencies and state and local law enforcement Data Reference Models (DRM). Ensure compliance with congressional acts, executive orders, and directives. Initiate inter-agency partnerships and collaborate with executive officials on the status and future of information sharing.

Lead and supervise multidisciplinary web team in achieving web design, application development, database administration, and system administration goals. Participate in investment review boards to review major information technology investments. Administer $55 million budget.

Leverage service-oriented architecture to develop solutions that support information sharing goals and objectives. Conduct technical reviews of privacy impact assessments. Pioneered and developed new theories, practices, and strategies for Attribute Based Access Control Security-in-Depth and other measures to ensure secure information sharing. Catalyst for advancing information search, discovery, retrieval, dissemination, and pervasive connectivity through common metadata, tagging, security marketing, and network throughout the wider inter-agency community. Integrate privacy officials early on into the planning and execution phases of information sharing efforts.

Figure 22.1: Sample SES/ECQ resume.

System owner for the Intra-Agency Exchange Architecture / Infrastructure, a system designed to facilitate the publishing and dissemination of critical data from agencies to consumers (e.g., select information sharing systems, federal, state, local fusion centers and task forces).

Cultivate and expand federal, state, and local information sharing partnerships. Advise potential partners on and coordinate mandatory security requirements for information sharing. Perform public speaking for and brief senior state and local officials to describe agency process to improve information sharing. Meet with mission, technical, and privacy representatives to gain consensus on the sharing of additional data sources. Serve as the agency's spokesperson and represent the Executive Director at meetings and conferences. Discuss governance, law enforcement data, federated identity management, and future developments.

Chair the Industry Advisory Council to bring industry and government executives together to collaborate on information sharing issues of interest to the government.

KEY LEADERSHIP INITIATIVES AND ACCOMPLISHMENTS:
- Hired to execute the information sharing program and meet demanding timelines. Spearheaded initiative and led my team to deliver a 100% increase in the quantity of agency information shared with federal, state, local, and tribal law enforcement agencies, in response to continued high-level Congressional demands for enhanced inter-agency information sharing after 9/11. Navigated challenging turf battles, institutional inertia, and agency cultures; established governance framework for the program and developed tools and incentives at the institutional, leadership, and workforce levels including executive committee and working groups. Conceived a disciplined process to engage other agencies to establish information sharing partnerships. Exponentially increased the number of shareable information / records from 11 to more than 40 million. Initiated measures to improve the quality and quantity of shareable information in support of strategic and tactical operations, and established monthly dashboard to review progress, identify approaches to resolve obstacles. Led my team in accelerating the creation of more than 80 regional information sharing partnerships with 1,200 agencies across the nation. *(Results Driven)*

- Faced pending retirement of 10 senior managers just as the organization was beginning to support the new administration's priorities for open government. Resources were flat, probability for increased funds was dismal, and customer demands on my organization were increasing. Developed strategic plan, revamped human capital requirements, reorganized staff and separated functions to position groups to effectively manage increasing demand. Prioritized delivering new capabilities with existing resources. Used departures of senior staff as opportunity to recruit top technical talent to meet organizational goals. Redefined vacant positions to be more technical. Led team to successfully deliver technical applications to support the administration's goals of improved transparency. Lifted declining staff morale and secured their buy-in to work for change and deliver new agency-wide capabilities. *(Business Acumen)*

- Led a multidiscipline staff of 105 including federal employees and contractors managing highly visible departmental programs. Oversaw their work to design and manage content for the agency's website and support the Information Sharing Program. Resolved prior low morale and productivity, and poor quarterly scores, by conducting global review of staff and programs, conveying to staff how I envisioned the change, streamlining processes and responsibilities (personally taking over reporting responsibilities to allow staff to focus on meeting milestones prescribed by OMB), leveraging existing resources, realigning team members to quell conflicts, describing the strategy of how capabilities would be used within existing constraints, identifying additional training needed to improve performance, eliminating barriers to success, and modeling optimism. My staff focused on achieving the e-Government goals. After six months, my team delivered the first of many subsequent Green scores for status and progress in support of the President's Management Agenda goals. *(Leading People)*

- Administer a $55+ million budget and oversee budget allotments, execution reviews, and reallocation decisions for three different accounts. Resolved a $12 million shortfall by making hard funding decisions after

(continued)

(continued)

meeting with project managers to discuss impact and consequences. Defended my decisions to the senior leadership, who agreed with my justifications. Controlled costs through economical use of personnel and materials while striving for the maximum return on the taxpayer investment. *(Business Acumen)*

- Built coalition to facilitate creation of the Information Sharing Program. As lead, quickly solicited and built strong and effective relationships with senior officials from inter-agency components nationwide. Formed and chaired the Information Sharing (IS) Working Group to ensure execution of plans for information sharing as directed by the executive committee. Sat on the executive committee with SESers and delivered regular reports from the IS Working Group. Engaged support from executives of another lynchpin agency to bolster our ability to expand information sharing nationwide through their 600 district offices. Interviewed senior operations officials to document their organizations' specific information sharing protocols; created baseline document summarizing current information sharing efforts and opportunities for improvement that defined future activities of the working group. Led working group efforts to secure agreements to improve information sharing across agencies. Catalyst for increasing the number of information sharing partnerships from 10 to more than 85 covering more than 1,200 federal, state, local, and tribal agencies. Initiated expansion of the type of partnerships that could be established. The Committee expressed great admiration for the effectiveness of the working group, and I was awarded a letter of appreciation. *(Building Coalitions)*

- Demonstrated high political sensitivity in responding effectively and diplomatically to repeated inquiries from the Appropriations Subcommittee during two years about the scope, status, benefits, and goals of the e-Government program (15 individual initiatives in three broad portfolios) relative to the Department. Helped define success benchmarks for the Department regarding its participation in e-Government. *(Building Coalitions)*

xx/xxxx - xx/xxxx
OPERATIONS DIRECTOR, IT Division   Hours per week: 40+
U.S. Customs and Border Protection, Los Angeles, CA   Rank: GS-0343-15
Supervisor: John Smith, (555) 555-5555, may contact   Salary: $xxx

SCOPE OF LEADERSHIP:
Conceived, developed, and executed short- and long-term enterprise service and infrastructure management vision and strategic plan. Directed service delivery, change and configuration management, infrastructure operations, and customer support activities, and managed service agreements. Ensured readiness of classified networks and telecommunications 24x7, secure compartment information facilities, and Continuity of Operations locations. Supervised staff of 60. Administered $23 million budget.

KEY LEADERSHIP ACHIEVEMENTS:
- Led change initiative and reinvention of Directorate's expanding IT operations to meet high-level Congressional demands and respond to a significant backlog of customer support requests. Led comprehensive review of operations and identified four major systemic problems requiring global reform. Operated in a challenging environment, leveraged resources with no budget, improvised as needed, and introduced scaled economies reducing operational costs. Led staff in implementing my vision of improved operations and enterprise infrastructure services. Transformed program and introduced completely new procedures and policy for procuring or requesting services; introduced a process flow and ensured "human interaction" from the support desk, where none previously existed; changed the mindset and organizational culture by forming an effective team that reduced the backlog of customer service requests influencing service management; secured unclassified and classified data center space. Identified and documented requirements for secure compartment information facilities to serve 4,000 users. *(Leading Change)*

- After 9/11, the agency recruited aggressively and required facility build-outs to handle its projected new workforce (3,000+ personnel) to meet Congressional requirements. Oversaw that facility build-outs in our Directorate were accomplished expeditiously with minimal impact on daily operations. This goal was soon challenged by conflicts between my senior contractor and my first-level supervisor, and between my senior contractor and key stakeholder. I supported my contractor's correct assessment of the situation, and reassigned the contractor as my deputy to provide oversight leadership for a wide range of operations, as part of my team-building concept. Placed a new contractor in the facilities working group who had good working relationship with my deputy, and provided guidance to new contractor to "win the hearts and minds" of stakeholders. Continued to work closely with the team, resolve conflicts, and rally for consensus, even during a constant travel schedule. Removal of one of my contractors decreased much of the distraction, and the group became more focused. Morale improved and team development corrected scheduling issues. Facility build-out proceeded as scheduled, providing space for 3,000 expected new employees. *(Leading People)*

xx/xxxx - xx/xxxx
SENIOR SYSTEMS ANALYST, Office of the Chief Information Officer   Hours per week: 40
VETERANS ADMINISTRATION, Los Angeles, CA   Rank: GS-0334-14
Susan Smith, (555) 555-5555, may contact   Salary: $xxx

SCOPE OF LEADERSHIP:
Senior expert for innovative efforts to improve delivery of enterprise services in the Department. Identified strategic technologies and products that achieved cost savings and improved operational efficiencies. Reviewed emerging technologies for potential prototype and pilot implementation. Guided in development of strategic Information Technology plans.

KEY LEADERSHIP ACHIEVEMENTS:
- Delivered on time and under budget an external enterprise certificate authority that provided a mechanism for the department to conduct secure transactions with external trading partners. *(Results Driven)*

- Promoted Smart Card technology to improve the effectiveness and efficiency of agency-wide business activities. Created the business case, working capital fund justification, program management plan, governance framework, and charter for the Smart Card Program Management Office. *(Business Acumen)*

- Inserted standards to the agency's enterprise architecture for reuse. *(Business Acumen)*

EDUCATION
- MBA, University of Maryland, MD, xxxx
- BS, Public Administration, University of Maryland, MD, xxxx

CERTIFICATIONS
- Project Management Professional, Project Management Institute (xxxx)
- Information Assurance Certificate, National Defense University (xxxx)

PROFESSIONAL DEVELOPMENT
- Executive Potential Program, USDA Graduate School (xxxx)
- Supervisory Leadership Program (xxxx)

AWARDS
- Civilian of the Year (xxxx)
- Certificate of Achievement (xxxx)
- Outstanding Performance Ratings (xxxx – xxxx consecutively)

SECURITY CLEARANCE
- Active: Secret

Writing Executive Core Qualifications

Writing Executive Core Qualification statements is like writing KSAs for other types of federal jobs. Unlike the KSA statements, however, the ECQs are exactly the same government-wide. Consequently, the statements will be applicable to virtually any SES position for which you apply. Although writing and polishing the statements requires significant time and effort, your initial investment will pay off, particularly if you apply for more than one vacancy.

Writing ECQs is no different from any other writing challenge: Well-written material that keeps the reader's interest gets more attention than sleeper prose. Still, the challenge of consolidating 20 years of accomplishments into five pages is significant—especially if you have had too many successes to fit into the allotted space.

Basic Principles

Here are some basic principles that will help you write successful ECQ statements:

1. **The basics of effective writing still apply.** Use the active voice. Your responses must convey what you did and what difference it made. Avoid passive constructions and bureaucratic phrasing: Say "I decided and directed" instead of "I was given responsibility for."

2. **Demonstrate the application of your knowledge.** Whereas KSAs require you to state what you know (knowledge) and what you have done or can do (skills and abilities), Executive Core Qualifications require you to demonstrate effective *application* of what you know. Effective statements require more than an explanation of your personal growth. In each ECQ, describe the effects you and your work have had on other people, other organizations, and agency policies. If you have held a job that required interagency coordination, bring it to the evaluators' attention.

3. **Demonstrate executive performance.** This is not the place to write about how you gained your skills. Many of the KSA statements written for lower-level positions are effective because they show "progressive responsibility"—that is, they describe how increasingly complex work assignments prepared them for the next job up the ladder. The SES needs people who can demonstrate through what they have already done that they are in a position to take charge *now.* Well-qualified applicants must be able to describe how they used or obtained available resources to bring about significant changes or accomplishments while heading agency programs. In addition, OPM suggests explaining how recent education or training enhanced your skills in particular factors. If you mention education or training courses, detailed work assignments, or other skills-enhancement efforts, make the link specific and stress the recentness of the information or experience gained.

4. **What have you done for me lately?** The SES needs people who are ready to lead in today's environment. Use recent examples as much as possible. Examples within the past three years are fine, but if you have to go back more than five years, the achievement must be spectacular. If an applicant's responses to Executive Core Qualifications dwell on accomplishments at the GM-13 level, the description will be less favorably received than comparable accomplishments at the GM-15 level.

Helpful Hints for Developing ECQs

Executive Core Qualifications are most effective if they are consistent continuations of the resume and any other documents in the application package. They should summarize—concisely—a record that demonstrates that you are ready for SES responsibilities. Effective statements of the Executive Core Qualifications combine breadth of accomplishments, a record of supervising other people in the successful completion of substantial tasks, and a record of applying current skills and training to challenging circumstances.

In describing your achievements, try to give different examples for each of the ECQs. A candidate with a true likelihood of success will have numerous achievements in each category. As you sift through your experience, you must ask yourself, "Will this example be a better illustration of Leading People, Results Driven, or Building Coalitions/Communications?" Review the core qualifications as a group, sort through your resume and supporting notes, and make the hard choices about where your achievements best fit into the factors.

The samples in this chapter include the words "Context, Challenge, Actions, and Result." You can include these words in the text of your narratives if you choose. This storytelling outline approach can help the Quality Review Board members read your text more easily. Several SES recruiters have recommended that including the CCAR terms helps with readability if the flow is not interrupted.

Remember that most SES applications are reviewed by agency Executive Resources Boards, whose members are familiar with your accomplishments and the conditions facing the agency at the time. Your responses need to remind people of these achievements in a credible, consistent way.

5. **Be concise.** OPM seeks one to one-and-a-half pages for each qualifications statement. You are writing executive summaries, not autobiographies. If you need more than one page, make certain that every word is important to convey your full leadership abilities. As much as possible, avoid repetition and use different achievements for each of the ECQ statements.

6. **Be specific.** Use precise numbers to describe budget, personnel, dates (time frame), and other factors. Avoid the "various," "numerous," and "several" quantifiers that make people guess about how much. You need to show that you are familiar with the results and how they were achieved so that your reader can understand the environment you were working in and the significance of the accomplishment.

7. **Keep the resume builders in mind.** Some SES applications are copied and pasted into the USAJOBS builder now. You should read the character limits and instructions for submitting the USAJOBS federal resume, ECQs, and technical factors online.

Here's an example of a keyword Profile statement from a federal resume, which could be placed in the Additional Information field (see Chapter 5):

PROFILE:

Senior program manager with 20-year background creating and managing innovative, cost-effective, large-scale, and long-term programs. Extensive governmental reengineering and streamlining experience. Strong strategic sense with the ability to balance short-term priorities against long-term organizational mission and goals. Excellent communication, leadership, and negotiation skills. National network of professional contacts in and out of government.

Use OPM's Recommended Format

OPM recommends that SES applicants use a structured format to address each Executive Core Qualification factor. Using this format helps candidates focus the relevancy and impact of their own experiences on the five ECQs all agencies expect their senior leaders to bring to the table. The format is known by the acronym *CCAR,* which stands for

- Challenge
- Context
- Actions
- Result

Let's analyze the components of this format to learn the best way to write your ECQs.

Challenge

What was the specific problem you faced that needed to be resolved?

- The problem should have existed at a large organizational level, with agency-wide, government-wide, or national effects.
- Resolution of the problem should have required more than one individual's actions. Leadership means, at minimum, that you have the ability to get other people to follow when you set direction.

Context

Define the other factors or limitations (people, institutions, procedures) that made the challenge of executive caliber.

- The problem should require redefinition of goals, changes in conditions, or the need to persuade other people/organizations to comply with your changed direction.
- Be specific about factors that made the challenge substantial: resources, people, laws, regulations, deadlines, and complexity.

Actions

What did you do that made a difference?

- Express your achievement in a team environment, but focus on your leadership role with the team.

Result

What difference did it make?

- Performance and accountability are the key factors. Your participation must be seen as the critical factor in realizing some goal or action that someone else wanted and/or needed done.

As we take an in-depth look at the five ECQs, keep the CCAR format in mind. The format will prompt you to write about specific results instead of citing general information about job responsibilities.

The Anatomy of an ECQ

Now that you're familiar with the fundamentals of writing the ECQs, let's take an in-depth look at the five ECQs and the specific types of information you should include in the statements.

ECQ 1: Leading Change

Definition: This core qualification involves the ability to bring about strategic change, both within and outside the organization, to meet organizational goals. Inherent to this ECQ is the ability to establish an organizational vision and to implement it in a continuously changing environment.

Your Leading Change statement needs to articulate an understanding of the mission and vision of the organization that you have led. Think up the organizational ladder. Describe your achievements in terms of how the head of the agency would have seen the challenge and why it should have been considered important.

If you have participated in a major transformation of an organization—for example, taking a nuclear weapons program from a production focus to an environmental clean-up mission—this is the time to highlight your account of how you achieved the change.

Emphasize the continuity factor here. It is important to realize that sometimes missions change even when authorizing laws and regulations stay the same. Convey the scope of the challenge and describe your role in transforming the organization.

Subfactors of the Leading Change ECQ are the following:

- **Creativity/Innovation:** Have you implemented a new way to solve an old problem?
- **External Awareness:** What is or was happening outside your agency that affected your programs, or how did your agency's programs affect others and what did you do to improve the situation?
- **Flexibility:** Did you identify and work different options to reach a desired result? Was it possible to use one authority versus another to get around a longstanding problem?

- **Resilience:** Did you overcome obstacle after obstacle to change an agency policy, program, or operating procedure?
- **Strategic Thinking:** Did you develop and execute a long-range plan to improve the agency?
- **Vision:** Did you predict a cause-and-effect situation and then act to take advantage of changing circumstances? Or, did you propose and then implement a change?

The questions attached to each of these subfactors are not the only way to address the ECQs; they are just examples to get you thinking about how you can describe what you've done to lead a substantive change in your agency.

ECQ 2: Leading People

Definition: This core qualification involves the ability to lead people toward meeting the organization's vision, mission, and goals. Inherent to this ECQ is the ability to provide an inclusive workplace that fosters the development of others, facilitates cooperation and teamwork, and supports constructive resolution of conflicts.

Leading people includes supervisory responsibilities—but you should express these in terms of coaching, mentoring, and motivating for success. Stress good communication skills, the ability to convey instructions, the ability to delegate responsibilities, and your success in planning for the professional career development of your subordinates.

Working across organizations is vital. Your ability to reach out, gain the support of other organizations, integrate the working of other managers, and represent your organization is critical. Your description of this ECQ should signal the reader to expect a strong statement about coalition building in the fifth ECQ factor.

Workforce diversity is part of the Leading People factor. Government requires an ability to work with all races, creeds, genders, colors, religions, and nationalities. This factor should affirm a solid commitment to the professional development of women and minorities, describe affirmative employment achievements, and discuss overcoming challenges in this arena. Recruiting and retaining highly qualified people is one dimension of the presentation. Demonstrating your ability to train other team members who are highly regarded in the organization is also a big help.

Diversity also should highlight the need to integrate a complex range of professional skills. Scientific, human resources, legal, public affairs, and other talents need to be melded to achieve complex missions. If you are a mathematician, how did you get your public affairs office to understand the importance of what you accomplished? If your skill is legal, how did you develop a mastery of the technology that your agency uses?

Subfactors of the Leading People ECQ are the following:

- **Conflict Management:** Have you effectively resolved conflicts between working groups, either within or outside your organization? What happened to cause the conflict, and how did you resolve it?
- **Leveraging Diversity:** Have you used the diverse makeup of your staff to understand the perspective and needs of both your incumbent workforce and the customer base the agency is designed to serve?

- **New Leadership Characteristic—Developing Others:** Describe the steps or programs that you have managed in order to ensure that employees have the right skills at the right time, and in the right place.

- **Team Building:** Have you been able to foster trust and support among staff members to achieve a better program?

ECQ 3: Results Driven

Definition: This core qualification involves the ability to meet organizational goals and customer expectations. Inherent to this ECQ is the ability to make decisions that produce high-quality results by applying technical knowledge, analyzing problems, and calculating risks.

This factor relies on presenting strong numerical achievements. When possible, cite before-and-after data. In defining challenges, use performance indicators that were considered unsatisfactory (that is, things you had to change). When describing results, compare the differences and describe the resources that you brought to bear to make a difference.

You don't need to base changes solely on program results; they also can be brought about in terms of context. If your actions built alliances, strengthened relationships, or overcame resistance, that too is a result.

Mention successes during organizational changes—for example, sustaining productivity despite reduced resources. Mention policies and procedures you developed to incorporate new assignments while sustaining the organization's current productivity.

Describe methods you developed to define nonessential factors and reduce or eliminate bureaucracy while sustaining results. For example, if OSHA currently measures an agency's performance by how well it complies with rules, and you are successful in changing that approach to now measuring agencies in terms of reductions in accident rates or reductions in time lost due to illness and injury, you should highlight this change in focus here.

What changes or processes did you institute—for example, monitoring mechanisms—to identify future opportunities for improvement and to provide incentives to sustain improved performance? What measures did you take to correct performance problems that preceded your leadership?

Subfactors of the Results Driven ECQ are the following:

- **Accountability:** What did you do to ensure that performance or outcomes could be measured or quantified? What happened?

- **Customer Service:** How did you improve it?

- **Decisiveness:** Were you forced to make a difficult decision? How did you decide which option was best? What happened as a result of taking that approach versus another?

- **Entrepreneurship:** How have you shown your ability to make smart business decisions?

- **Problem Solving:** What was the problem and how did you resolve it? If various solutions were possible, don't forget to discuss why you used the approach you selected and why the outcome using this particular approach was superior.

- **Technical Credibility:** Why did this particular result work better than other alternatives? Did the solution help give customers confidence in your program or agency?

ECQ 4: Business Acumen

Definition: This core qualification involves the ability to manage human, financial, and information resources strategically. Highlight budget data, numbers of people, size of the constituency served, and methods of reducing costs/increasing efficiency here. You should also discuss your familiarity with procedures for establishing and justifying budgets, securing resources, and managing finances.

Demonstrate the effective use of information technology for your activities. The critical factors here are not the abilities to use word processors and spreadsheets, but to define System Development Life Cycle strategies and other factors associated with the acquisition and management of technology resources. The Executive Review Board must be able to see that you know how to apply information technology to the design and management of the organization that you will supervise.

If you have corrected major administrative weaknesses—financial management and accounting procedures, security deficiencies, or potential vulnerabilities of organizations—this is the place to discuss those achievements.

Subfactors of the Business Acumen ECQ are the following:

- **Financial Management:** Have you managed large program budgets to reach agency goals?
- **Human Resources:** Have you reorganized or restructured your human resources to better the organization and the services it provides to customers?
- **Technology Management:** How have you applied information technology to the design and management of your organization?

ECQ 5: Building Coalitions/Communication

Definition: This core qualification involves the ability to build coalitions internally and with other federal agencies, state and local governments, nonprofit and private-sector organizations, foreign governments, or international organizations to achieve common goals.

Just as the Leading People factor addresses your ability to communicate down the organizational chart, this one emphasizes your ability to reach out to other organizations. This factor should highlight your ability to work with nongovernmental organizations, the media, professional associations, and at least other substantial organizations within your agency.

Written and oral communications are both required here. The question should not focus on your ability to write, but on your ability to set direction for others who will draft the correspondence, memoranda, speeches, and other material.

Working on interagency committees and coordinating multi-agency policy development and reporting groups are examples of achievements that you should describe in this factor. Effecting change might require bringing other agencies' perspectives back to your organization and winning support for something that serves the public interest, even if it generates resistance within the agency.

This factor asks you to convey that you are in charge of an organization and that you can convince others that your agency's positions on critical issues are well based. If you have testified before Congress or other legislatures, have spoken to state and local governments, or have represented the U.S. on international working groups, these are the experiences to include here. Again, the focus needs to be on the results that were realized from your efforts.

Subfactors for the Building Coalitions/Communications ECQ are the following:

- **Influencing/negotiating:** How were you able to bring together two or more factions to reach a mutually acceptable resolution to a problem?
- **Partnering:** Have you been able to establish solid working relationships with groups that might have been at odds with your organization or agency?
- **Political savvy:** Were you able to broker a desired outcome or make your organization look good in the face of a potentially nasty outcome?

Grow an Accomplishments List

To develop stories related to the preceding ECQs and leadership competencies, begin by creating a list of your top ten or more senior-level accomplishments. Some of these accomplishments need to be oriented to the ECQs, so be certain to add accomplishments to your list that focus on the specific ECQs. An accomplishment that is not directly related to an ECQ may be an excellent story to meet the needs of a Technical Qualification requirement.

Once you have your list created, begin to tell the story in the CCAR format (Context, Challenge, Actions, Result). Following are two lists of accomplishments. Figure 22.2 is a simple list from a brainstorming session; Figure 22.3 is the brainstorming list for a different applicant and includes more detail—the stories are starting to develop.

TOP TEN ACCOMPLISHMENTS LIST (FOR EXECUTIVES)

1. *Manage the National Information Section of the Foreign Airport Assessment Program for my geographical area (covering some 20 countries).*
2. *Served as Acting Division Manager in the Transportation Security Administration's (TSA) Office of Security Regulation and Policy.*
3. *Developed and revised civil aviation security regulations, security programs and amendments to security programs, and guidance policies for industry.*
4. *Interpreted federal regulations and developed different training manuals for ground staff and security personnel on policies and procedures for airline security for six major air carriers.*
5. *Trained screeners in extraordinary security procedures designated by U.S. government requirements. My airline established a new screening company with fully qualified screeners meeting stringent security requirements.*
6. *Led numerous overseas/international air carrier inspections governed by the Foreign Airport Assessment Program (FAAP).*
7. *Oversaw the application of special security measures during an Orange Code at Frankfurt, Germany, and during a World Summit at the airport in Atlanta, Georgia.*
8. *In response to the attacks of 9/11, drafted and interpreted complicated emergency policies and standards for air carriers' security programs.*
9. *Reconfigured baggage x-ray screening procedures in foreign airports, introducing a third layer of security. Negotiated with senior airport officials to secure additional security guards.*
10. *Initial responder to the Atlanta, Georgia, World Summit bomb threat emergency. Coordinated with the air carrier, the government, and other officials to counter the threats.*

Figure 22.2: Simple list of accomplishments.

Longer List / Different Application

1. Led the effort to implement a new methodology for managing the federal workforce, referred to as the "Multi-Sector Workforce (MSW) initiative," to meet the Office of Management and Budget directive driven by the new administration (President's office), a highly visible initiative throughout the Department, the federal government, and outside interest groups, and a high-priority agenda item for the new President and administration. I created an innovative, effective, and repeatable process for in-sourcing, including a methodology and framework to include a new process for conducting Human Capital analysis, developing new in-sourcing guidelines, workforce planning and analysis, cost analysis, and budgeting. In addition, as a strategic thinker, I am anticipating that this initiative will be implemented government-wide; and therefore, I have commissioned a marketing and implementation team to create a full marketing plan of the MSW initiative for the department. ***(Leading Change)***

2. Introduced a revolutionary change initiative and reversed an 8-year negative hiring trend through Appropriations Committees. Envisioned a strategic plan to reverse use of overtime, up to 25%, which prevented the agency from hiring some of the most critical functions to unfunded mandates, putting a substantial strain on the agency's workforce. Designed a system for evaluating FTE requests that would lead to approval of the FTE requests from the Appropriations Committees. I won the support and buy-in of all levels of management at our agency to adopt the new FTE Scoring Methodology that I developed and delivered numerous briefings to the House and Senate Appropriations Committees to defend/discuss our FTE requests, gaining their confidence, which led to the approval of all our FTE requests that year. The FTE Scoring Methodology was fully implemented in FY 200x and all Agency FTE requests that were submitted in our FY Budget Submission were approved. The system proved successful in eliminating frivolous or unwarranted FTE requests and it also elevated all FTEs with bona fide agency-wide needs to the top of the approval list. For the first time in five years, the Agency was granted all FTEs requested. ***(Leading Change)***

3. I developed and implemented a new workforce planning program for the entire agency, which was approved by both the General Accountability Office (GAO) and the Office of Personnel Management (OPM). I designed and introduced a successful workforce planning program that incorporates succession planning, fiscal planning, and strategic planning for the agency. I developed competencies for all agency positions, instituted an agency-wide automated system (working with contractors) that analyzes skills and competencies, designed a training program to address skill gaps, and introduced Performance Improvement Plans. To implement these programs and ensure the future growth of the organization, I recruited and hired Presidential Management Interns (PMI) from career fairs; and then served as their mentor. ***(Leading people)***

4. As Acting Chief, I transformed the organization and received a customer service award. At my new Agency, I served as Acting Chief over the Small Purchase Division, supervising 40 employees. I stepped into chaos, high absenteeism, and high turnover with an unprecedented high number of customer complaints—with a mandate to fix the problems. I conducted a number of audits and skills surveys to identify gaps and issues. Based on the results, I set in motion a strategic plan with tactical elements to reverse the problems. As the acting supervisor for two years, I led my team in improving the customer service by 72% (post-survey results), upgraded several employees based on duties performed, ensured that all employees received certifications, and improved the processing of purchase orders from 40 to 7 days. I received a Customer Service Award for my leadership in transforming this office. ***(Leading People or Results Driven)***

Figure 22.3: More developed accomplishments.

5. Created a new organizational structure for the agency, leading to programmatic efficiency and effectiveness and reversing numerous Equal Opportunity complaints. Unfolded a strategic vision to analyze the entire organization, including organizational structures, missions, and function statements of all agency organizational entities. I gained approval from the agency head to put a moratorium on all organizational changes until the study was completed. I took a global review of how the agency was structured, grouping organizational entities by work functions and mission. My analysis revealed that the agency as a requisite needed a consistent structure and appropriate functional groupings and I proposed a new agency-wide organizational structure (that would result in consistency across all organizations). I designed a politically sensitive strategy and transformed the entire organizational structure, resulting in a drastic reduction of EEO complaints from employees (from 16 to 1), the elevation of numerous positions to appropriate grade levels, and a future plan for reducing grade levels that were incorrectly classified to higher levels. Also, I developed a communications plan for our stakeholders (Congress) explaining the new organizational changes. The organizational structure and full strategy that I proposed was approved by the agency, the Senate and House Appropriations Committees, the EEO Division, and the HR Division and was implemented in FYxx. **(Results Driven)**

6. Revitalized the HR Division and overhauled the compensation system. Led a study to determine the effectiveness of all HR programs to ensure that the agency is in the best position to hire and retain highly qualified employees. As I identified the agency's human capital challenges, I pinpointed that our HR department needed a new direction and strategy for training, compensations, performance management, and recruitment. I developed a new strategy that would prove successful in revitalizing the HR division. I recommended a complete overhaul of the agency's Statutory Rate (SR) Pay system (equivalent to the Executive Branch's SES system). The inconsistencies in the SR Pay and Compensation Program were questioned by Congress and the agency was forced to explain the merits of our SR system and how employees were selected for SR positions. I recommended a total revamp of the SR Pay and Compensation package, which included my recommendations for establishing a set of criteria for selecting candidates for the different types of SR positions, and that the pay levels be increased to be competitive with the Executive Branch (leading to fewer turnovers in our SR levels). All of my recommendations were accepted by the agency and the SR system is currently being overhauled to incorporate the recommendations. As I suggested, the agency requested Congress to allot our agency more SR slots, increase the pay levels to the maximum SES levels (without having a certified OPM performance system), and to also allow our agency to have most of the benefits as offered for the SES positions in the Executive Branch. Upon approval, I drafted the appropriate language in the Budget Request. **(Results Driven)**

7. Developed an agency-wide automated model, full-time employee staffing system for tracking, forecasting, and managing FTEs, which was adopted by other agencies. In the Full Conference Report on Appropriations, the House and Senate Appropriations Committee directed my agency to "not request any additional Full-time Employees (FTEs) for the General Administration Appropriation due to the continual under-utilization of current FTEs." Because of this concern, the House Appropriations Committees directed my agency to immediately transfer the FTE function from the Budget Office to my office, the Workforce Planning and Management Division. With the confidence of the Chair of the House Appropriations Committee and the agency head, I was challenged to turn around the FTE problem in the General Administration Appropriations. I met with the Information Technology group to discuss the types of financial reports that were available and I also met with the Director of Information Technology to discuss "Information Security." I discovered that our financial system did not par with our payroll system. After months of cleaning up data from the two systems and finally obtaining accurate financial and payroll data, I provided the details and a conceptual design for a new FTE Automated System that

(continued)

(continued)

would forecast FTE utilization for the year end, track FTEs automatically by nine appropriations, and provide bi-weekly FTE forecast reports for the agency. The agency was able to accurately improve FTE utilization by 85% in the first year and 100% the second year; we went from leaving 40 FTEs unused to zero in two years. I demonstrated the system to both the House and Senate Appropriations Staff, which led to a full write-up in the Full Conference Report on Appropriations of the success of the system. In addition, both the House and Senate Appropriations Committee suggested to other Legislative Branches to use my FTE system as a model. *(Business Acumen)*

8. Automated HR systems at AOC. In an effort to improve the efficiency of our HR programs, I worked closely with the HR director to conceptualize methods to automate HR program areas. Building these automated systems required me to facilitate numerous meetings with senior-level managers at my agency (to understand their system needs), with the CEO of AVUE to begin the development of the system, and with the HR specialists to gain their expertise in developing the system. The system was successful in automating our most critical HR services and resulted in a reduction of 5% of personnel in our HR offices, saving the agency over $450,000 in payroll costs. I was also asked to conceptually develop, test, write, and evaluate (within the AVUE system) the Skills Survey and serve as a senior expert in the development and evaluation of the new Personnel Action Request) system within AVUE. *(Business Acumen)*

9. Changed the grade structure for the 9 major jurisdictions at my agency. Most of my agency's work is conducted on Capitol Hill. However, the agency had classified some levels of work as "headquarters" and "field." Approximately 80% of our agency's workforce was wage-grade employees. The "headquarters" is designated as those organizational components that provide agency-wide administrative support to the "field" organizations. This distinction of duties became a concern to me as several managers were comparing grades between the headquarters and field offices and began requesting upgrades in some of their positions based simply on "if the position was considered a headquarters or field position." Because this organizational structure had been in place for over 30 years, I knew that this would be a politically charged issue to manage and correct. The issue was very sensitive as the findings could result in adverse impacts to grade levels for several levels of management. In addition, this review would require a fresh look at the classification of positions, the history behind the "headquarters/field" determination, and could possibly question the accuracy of how positions were classified. In order to gain the support and collaboration of the HRMD department and the managers, I formed a Working Group with representatives from HRMD, EEO, and Management from the Field and Headquarters offices. As a result of this study conducted by the working group, my agency implemented all recommendations from the Working Group, which included elevating several Directors to the GS-15 level, several managers to the SES-equivalent level, abolishing the term and organizational structure of "Headquarters and Field Offices," and creating new policy for establishing grade levels for all positions within the agency. I briefed and gained approval for all recommendations from the Senate and House Appropriations Committee. *(Building Coalitions)*

10. Wrote the first ever Workforce Planning Guide to be used by the agency with 21 associated institutes. Worked in coalition with all 21 institutes and shadowed an SES, serving as the driver of the concept of Workforce Planning. The Workforce Planning guide was introduced by GAO in a conference to all agencies on "Workforce Planning." Workforce Planning was in its infancy in 20xx and my agency was the first federal agency to publish a Workforce Planning guide as a model for use by other government Agencies. I briefed my work and the concept and Guide were adopted by several other agencies. *(Building Coalitions)*

Sample ECQ Statements

The following pages contain samples of core qualifications statements developed for various jobs. Some are actual statements taken verbatim from successful SES applicants. Others are composites of various statements. Study these samples to get an idea of how to compose your ECQs.

ECQ 1: LEADING CHANGE

Context: As the Program Director, I was subordinate to the Joint Contracting Command-Iraq/Afghanistan, providing overarching leadership for contracting support for 250,000 troops stationed in the Middle East. I provided executive oversight for over 7,500 contracts, valued at more than $950 million, for work including construction, vehicle maintenance, intelligence gathering, media services, and water bottling. My span of control included 12 Regional Contracting Centers located in Iraq and Afghanistan.

Immediately after assuming leadership responsibilities, I assessed the status and effectiveness of organizational operations. In my judgment, the organization was operating effectively in support of tactical operations. Army leadership in the region and at the Pentagon gave contracting forces high marks for customer service and responsiveness, indicating satisfaction with our support. This high-quality, yet tactical, support was indicative of outstanding "contingency" contracting.

I held discussions with my senior leader and the leader of Multi-National Forces Iraq to brief them on our current operational support and explain my strategic vision and action plan for future operations. At that time, he directed my organization to take on a more strategic focus—specifically to focus on improving the Iraqi and Afghani economies. His reasoning was that our contracted work created jobs, and if young men had jobs to support their families, they would be less likely to take money from, and operate with, extremist elements. I embraced the opportunity of making strategic contributions in the Middle East; but my organization was not immediately ready. My 12 regional centers, while operating well, were largely operating independently of each other, without any integrated focus or standardized procedures—capabilities critical to successful strategic operations.

Challenges: My vision was to transform the organization into one capable of taking on and achieving strategic Theater objectives, while still supporting tactical operations. To realize this vision, I faced numerous obstacles to affect major organizational changes in an environment of violence and fluidity. My operational objectives included transforming my organization's tactical focus to a broader strategic focus, creating capacity in the organization to take on increased work, enforcing federal procurement standards, and introducing hardware and software infrastructure changes across the enterprise to improve interoperability.

Actions: Time was of the essence; I took decisive action to implement the transformation. To begin, I challenged my staff to develop an action plan. I then briefed my senior leader and the Deputy Assistant Secretary for Procurement on my vision, my frontline assessment, the inputs of regional DoD and State Department leaders, and my plan of action to accomplish my objectives. I also revisited many combat leaders to explain my plan of action. This crucial step provided them situational awareness, engendered trust, and ensured their buy-in.

Next, to redirect focus, I brought my regional center leaders to Iraq and conveyed the need to transform our organization and my vision and plan of action, and sought their support and ideas for improvement. Interoperability and process improvements were advanced by the regional center leaders, discussed, and modifications were made to the action plan. I fundamentally changed infrastructure operations by standardizing regional center hardware, software, and reporting procedures. Doing so allowed me to receive and analyze data more rapidly. Regional center leaders made input to, and I agreed with, a common set of performance measures. This provided regional center leaders with timely, decision-quality data to assess progress toward tactical and strategic objectives and to assess their capacity constraints.

(continued)

Figure 22.4: Executive Core Qualifications: traditional 10-page version.

(continued)

I focused the regional center leaders on the need to enforce federal procurement processes across the enterprise. I told them the integrity and credibility of deployed procurement operations was on the line; that Congress and the public questioned our ability to make quality business decisions, while still supporting our mission. I set the standard high, explaining I would accept nothing less than quality work that met the standards set out by the Army. My transformed quality focus included a new quality review process, regular audits by legal experts, and weekly policy discussions with the Deputy Secretary.

Challenges and Actions: My regional leaders were generally supportive, yet some feared they would not always have capacity to perform tactical AND strategic operations. Workload could increase and decrease suddenly and dramatically at forward operating bases due to mission changes. ***Results:*** I approved a transformational initiative to normalize workload throughout the enterprise by electronically passing work between the regional centers as needed. This highly effective process had never been done in a wartime environment. Work-sharing among regional centers, regardless of their theater-of-operations, optimized enterprise operations and alleviated regional center leaders' capacity concerns. Electronic work sharing is now a standard practice.

My leadership inspired innovative and creative thinking among my leadership team. Solutions to important procedural challenges were addressed and solved—all with the focus of creating a well organized, well-oiled enterprise capable of taking on a greater leadership role in this theater-of-operations. With organizational transformation underway, I was able to shift my focus, and my discussions with senior leadership, to establishing my vision and action plans for future strategic operations.

Before transforming the focus of my organization, it was not capable of supporting broader strategic initiatives and economic development faltered; after the shift in operations and workloads across the regional centers, I began effectively executing procurement programs to improve/speed the process of economic recovery in Iraq and Afghanistan. I engaged with senior U.S. leaders throughout the region, and my senior leader, and began focusing on both supporting the troops AND strategic economic development. This shift in primary focus completely revamped my organization's role in the region: I supported nation building, laid the groundwork for NATO assumption of procurement responsibility in southern Afghanistan, designated economic safe zones, and increased the use of local small businesses, building trust among the Iraqi and Afghan businesspeople and public. Overall, I led and prepared my organization to deliver a wider range of services, with much broader impact at the national level. My ability to affect strategic change in the region was a direct result of my initiative, decisive action, and inspired leadership in transforming a well-running tactical operation into a strategic powerhouse.

ECQ 2: LEADING PEOPLE

Context: I led an organization of 115 contracting professionals (military and government civilians) responsible for 18,000 contract actions valued at $123 million; providing sole acquisition support for Fort Shafter Army Base and Headquarters Pacific Army, touching 15 military bases in the Pacific. With this volume of work, you would think I would have walked into a finely honed machine. I could not have been more wrong.

Challenges: There were "issues" with the contracting professionals. After I arrived, the organization underwent a Unit Compliance Inspection and received a marginal rating. The Inspector General found numerous errors. For files needing headquarters approval, my group had the worst metrics in the organization—an average of 16 major errors per file. The organization was in a state of disrepair; contracts were taking much longer than normal to complete, quality and throughput of contracts were poor, and there was a very high level of customer dissatisfaction. Professional pride was lacking: one member had recently been court-marshaled for inappropriate use of drugs and DUIs were at an all-time high. Additionally, staff members were held to low contract quality standards, and the organization had no contract quality review process in place.

Actions: My vision was to change attitude and improve performance. I laid out my vision to my leadership team and quickly created a program to improve morale, improve training, introduce standardization, and incorporate performance measurement.

Taking control, I took aggressive steps to reverse negative trends in morale. In my judgment, negative morale had a direct impact on the quality of our products and services. I invited experts to discuss drug and alcohol abuse; I created a multi-tier recognition program and formed an Awards Board, using performance metrics. As the leader, I provided final authority, but to maintain the integrity of the program, and to foster its impartiality, I did not participate. Next, to grow personnel development, improve training, and advance the quality of our contracting processes, I took decisive action to close the organization one morning per week for mandatory unit-level training. My decision met with initial contention at all levels, and I negotiated and persuaded upper leadership and functional managers to support my goals and objectives. Through conflict at the thought of losing valuable "work hours" for training, I eventually gained buy-in, convincing the leadership chain that training would, over time, improve organizational productivity. I sold my vision; improvements followed.

To introduce standardization and improve quality, I established a quality assurance/contract review function to ensure my team complied with Federal Acquisition Regulations. I set clear expectations and high standards; assigned the strongest midlevel professional in the organization to perform contract review duties; and introduced a team-building concept where I brought the unit together in special meetings and challenged each member to improve his/her personal goals and accountability, thus improving his/her performance. I invited outside agencies to inspect our contracting operations, monitor customer service levels, and review our metrics, rendering external opinions. Finally, I incorporated performance measurement. I developed an intranet-hosted metrics program that allowed each member to populate data fields upon the completion of tasks. Access to real-time metrics allowed me to identify and correct trends before they became problems, and access to these critical pieces of data empowered my leaders to take timely actions to correct deficiencies in their departments.

Contracting actions that supported the infrastructure of the entire life-support systems for thousands of people on numerous bases across the Pacific region were managed by my team. It was my responsibility to ensure my managers and team members were professionally developed and well motivated.

Challenges and Actions: During this time of implementing measures to turn around my team of professionals, I also discovered extreme conflict within the organization concerning one functional manager. He provided oversight management for the contract for the entire infrastructure of the base, his responsibilities directly impacting quality of life. He supervised 30 people and his area received more than 50% of the organization's customer complaints. His staff was frustrated. Consequently, there were numerous errors in his section. There was conflict among all of the functional managers due to this issue; and the ripple effect of dissatisfaction of working under or near this manager was growing. I dealt with the issue immediately. I confronted him with quality deficiencies and customer and employee

(continued)

(continued)

complaints. I explained that I valued his experience but changes in his leadership and functional performance needed to be made. I committed myself to his improvement, mentoring him on communication skills, adherence to standards, and developing and rewarding people. I was successful in growing this leader and avoiding further disruption. As the entire organizational transformation program was implemented and morale improved, his performance improved, and customer complaints in his section dropped.

Results: My actions to improve morale, training, standardization, and performance measurement inspired and motivated people, and I succeeded in developing a high-performing, cohesive team that excelled in delivering superior customer service. Organizational performance improved; quality errors dropped 92%. Morale improved significantly; the unit climate assessment rose 40 points, into the mid 80s; customer complaints dropped substantially; and my organizational awareness program resulted in two years of DUI-free driving—garnering us a gold certificate award. At the end of my two-year tenure, my personnel won seven corporate-level awards (HQ Pacific Air Force); and I personally I received acclaim from Pacific leadership for driving quality output.

ECQ 3: RESULTS DRIVEN

I have a distinguished record of navigating high-complexity issues and achieving substantive results across entire theaters of operation (U.S., Korea, the Pacific, and Iraq and Afghanistan).

Context: Supporting an Army base, I led a 1,000-person organization operating the base infrastructure, and all mission support for the Electronic Systems Center and a Research Laboratory. I led five operationally and professionally diverse organizations and provided oversight for personnel, construction, repair, and readiness budgets totaling $90+ million, supporting a population of 160,000 personnel in a 10-state region. Additionally, I was the On-Scene Director for the Disaster Control Unit, leading responses to real-world and simulated emergencies.

Post-Katrina evaluation of the Federal Emergency Management Agency's hurricane response caused changes to be made to align all federal agencies to one National Incident Management System. The Army's Incident Management System (AIMS) was created to mirror the National Incident Management Systems' emergency response structure. *Challenges:* As I led the transformation of emergency/disaster response at the military base to the new AIMS structure, I was challenged to align the old response organization and its people, processes, and structure to the new system. This involved reorganizing how medical, safety, law enforcement, fire, caregiver, and command and control units and personnel responded to emergencies, and were allocated and managed, to best target and maximize the response. The traditional Army incident response organization was installation focused; critical state and local relationships had not been developed to coordinate actions beyond the base perimeter; and response and management of multiple, concurrent emergencies was less effective than single-incident responses because the prime command and control practice was to lead at the scene. I revamped the process and built an organization with a broader focus that could handle multiple emergencies effectively.

Actions: I began building relationships with state and local agencies to provide broader community support. I presented a plan to the director of the state's Emergency Management Agency detailing a collaborative effort between my operations and their operations. I also visited the local Army National Guard to establish mutual support agreements for transportation, airlift, explosive ordinance, and biological/chemical support. I dispatched our medical experts to local hospitals to establish mutual emergency support agreements. I revised on-scene command and control by requiring "first responders" to assume command of the incident once they arrived. To prepare these midlevel leaders to lead during a wide range of emergencies, and to effectively communicate with the higher-level Emergency Operations Center (EOC), I worked closely with emergency response stakeholders to create realistic, multi-scenario training simulations involving situational awareness, task delegation, cordon control, and crowd management. During repeated exercises, first responder leadership and communication skills dramatically improved.

As the Emergency Operations Center Director, I funded and oversaw creation of a new installation control center, funded day-to-day operations, and directed the renovation of a new communications suite to ensure contact with first responders in the field. To support multi-agency interoperability, I provided state and local agencies with command and control stations. Additionally, I led several emergency operations simulations, which highlighted our weaknesses and vulnerabilities, allowing us to create and execute corrective action plans. The interim simulations provided valuable lessons in interagency and intergovernmental cooperation and coordination and culminated in a large-scale integrated disaster-control exercise with state and local agencies to test our operational readiness.

Results: I led the transformation of the base's emergency response apparatus from a traditional, locally focused disaster-control element to a nationally oriented emergency management machine, merging military, state, and local emergency-response agencies into one powerful emergency management operation capable of managing multiple events, while effectively coordinating response actions with many internal and external stakeholders. I reviewed exercise results with the state's Emergency Management Agency, Army Guard, and my leadership who praised our performance, acknowledged our readiness, and complemented me on establishing an AIMS-compliant EOC in just six months—37% ahead of schedule. My actions elevated my base to national-level compliance and provided a broader, more effective capability for the military. For actual and follow-on simulated emergency situations, I reduced the response time needed to establish multi-event command and control by approximately 15–30 minutes; a significant improvement in this critical, life-and-death, time-sensitive environment.

ECQ 4: BUSINESS ACUMEN

During my career, I provided leadership for large organizations, was accountable for executing multimillion-dollar budgets, and oversaw management of thousands of contracts valued at more than $1 billion. *Context:* For example, during my tenure leading a large organization with a procurement budget of $105 million and 95 staff supporting 25,000 contracts throughout the Pacific region—reaching from Hawaii to Japan and satellite offices as far south as Australia, including the Pacific Headquarters at my location—I introduced the vision of implementing Wide-Area Workflow (WAWF), a complete end-to-end processing of an invoice through to electronic payment, elevating the organization into the 21st century by replacing antiquated technology and introducing technology that would create efficiencies enterprise-wide.

Taking decisive action, I determined the need for and led my team in implementing a new WAWF application for electronic receipt, inspection, and acceptance of services performed at the headquarters base. WAWF is a Paperless Contracting application designed to eliminate paper from the receipts and acceptance process of the DOD contracting lifecycle by work-flowing an electronic vendor invoice through government receipt, inspection, and acceptance personnel. The invoice is then work-flowed to the Defense Finance and Accounting Service (DFAS) to make electronic payment to the vendor. My goals

(continued)

(continued)

included being the first contracting unit in the Army to operationally implement WAWF, to establish a technology challenge for my organization, reduce interest penalty payments, and decrease overall invoice processing time.

Challenges: There were many initial challenges brought to my attention. When my organization implemented Wide-Area Workflow, not all of the components were in place to allow full implementation, and the application was not web-based, although planned for in the future. I believed, however, that my goals could be achieved by implementing Wide-Area Workflow in its current form, a CD ROM-based software program, and to implement workaround solutions for the incomplete process elements. The major challenge was our inability to network directly to DFAS, creating the possibility the Army would need to print acceptance documents and send them to DFAS for payment. This would have negated the benefit of electronic processing. Also, vendors needed to be identified who were willing to try the new electronic process and absorb the cost of the software and training. *Actions:* By tapping internal IT resources and targeting vendors to absorb costs, the Army incurred zero costs, and no budget was required.

I established and coached a team to determine the feasibility of using WAWF and to prepare plans and briefings that would be used to seek approval to take on the project. Our team focused initially on civil engineering services because of the close operating relationship between civil engineering and our contracting organization, and because we could easily gather and train their Quality Assurance Personnel, who were then involved in receiving and accepting the services. I established a relationship with senior Defense Finance and Accounting Service leaders in the region to devise a solution regarding lack of network connectivity. My team crafted a workaround solution: we agreed to hand-carry a daily electronic file of receipts and acceptances to DFAS until WAWF became web-based, so they could make electronic payments. I briefed senior leadership within the Pacific region and DFAS leaders explaining the expected benefits to the Army and DFAS of moving forward quickly: reduced interest penalties and invoice processing time. This was also a "first-in-the-Army" project opportunity for my team. After receiving approval, I developed a cadre of contractors willing to work within our new process.

Results: After implementing Wide-Area Workflow, interest penalty payments reduced 38% overall, invoice processing time initially reduced ~60% for contracts in the project, settling around 80% when I left. Results of my initiative were briefed to my senior counterparts in the Pacific Theater during a leaders' conference. By the time I left my leadership position in the organization, other leaders were beginning to explore WAWF implementation. My headquarters' leadership lauded me and my organization for being the first to implement WAWF in the Army. Presently, the use of Wide-Area Workflow is mandatory for all contracts.

ECQ 5: COALITION BUILDING

Context: As the Program Director for Contracting, one of the Multi-National Forces-Iraq (MNF-I) senior leader's strategic objectives was to improve the Iraqi economy, and to create jobs for Iraqi men and women to increase goodwill and deter extremism. My actions to improve the economic situation in Iraq in support of MNF-I objectives took place in an environment of limited local infrastructure, no local trust of government or large business institutions, no effective banking system, and obstructionist elements of Iraqi society.

Challenges: The objective was to use our contracts to offer business opportunities, to counter employment by extremists. One challenge was to accomplish this in a climate of pervasive violence. I worked with vendors who literally risked their lives to work with me. Anti-Iraqi forces would watch as vendors left the base, would follow them home and intimidate them, and would sometimes kill them.

Actions: I began by holding an industry day in Baghdad in the international zone. I gained approval for an industry conference within our perimeter and I published the invitation on the website we used to solicit our requirements. Security was a big concern; I coordinated closely with the U.S. and Iraqi security forces to ensure we had a safe venue; consequently, security measures were increased. Close to 120 vendors attended. I set the agenda for the conference, much of the discussion centering on two ideas: establishing a "safe haven" where vendors could sell or manufacture their goods, and increasing the Iraqi vendor base.

Partnering with the Army Installation Manager to increase the size of a small "shopping" area that already existed on one of our major bases, I built and led a coalition to launch the creation of a "safe haven" for Iraqi companies to sell their goods and services. Approximately 40 vendors were allowed on the base to sell local items to our troops. I worked closely with the installation Department of Public Works (DPW) and installation command team to scope the construction needed to create space for up to 100 vendors, and I collaborated closely with the Multi-National Corp (MNC) staff to source the funding needed to complete the project. The coalition I built and led was highly effective in launching the safe haven project within weeks.

Next, I arranged a cross-functional team (members of my staff, the Iraqi government, MNC intelligence, and operations officers and security personnel) to begin the process of increasing our Iraqi vendor base. I worked with computer database experts and an Iraqi government economic development organization to organize a list of all contractors we were conducting business with in Iraq and a list of perspective contractors. This was a very sensitive project because the list of contractors was prone to becoming a target list for terrorists. Moreover, I had to assure Army leadership that using Iraqi contractors would not result in inferior services.

Finally, I developed a plan with the Multi-National Corps' operations element to use capacity and funding on one of their existing contracts to hire Iraqi expatriates to serve as our vendor development experts. I briefed the Multi-National Corps leader on this joint project and obtained his approval, including funding, to proceed. I worked with the Iraqi government to identify expatriates willing to be U.S. contractors who would identify and establish relationships with potential sources of supplies and services throughout Iraq. Each expert was assigned to one of my Regional Contracting Centers.

Results: By recruiting a corps of experts to identify and develop local small businesses, my efforts to award contracts to Iraqi vendors and lay the groundwork for building "safe haven" economic zones resulted in a threefold increase, from 25% to 75%, of contract awards to local Iraqi vendors within six months. These results were a direct consequence of my executive leadership and my ability to forge coalitions and strong working relationships in a diverse, multicultural, hostile, and high-stress environment. Moreover, I directly met Multi-National Forces-I and U.S. Central Command strategic theater objectives of improving the Iraqi economy, creating jobs for Iraqi men and women, increasing goodwill, and deterring extremism.

Describing Leadership

Congratulations! In following the preceding steps, you should now be in possession of a great set of Executive Core Qualifications. After you have read, proofread, and sought feedback on your ECQs, you should take a final step and ensure that your ECQ narratives describe your leadership accomplishments. One simple way to do this is to define and apply leadership vocabulary throughout your narrative. Here is a list to get you started. And as you identify new leadership terms, you should add them to your list.

Table 22.3: Leadership Terms

Accelerate	Discover	Leverage
Advance	Encourage	Manage
Advise	Energize	Mentor
Advocate	Enhance	Momentum
Agility	Envision	Optimize
Approve	Establish	Oversee
Build	Evaluate	Point the way
Coach	Expand	Promote
Complete	Expedite	Propel
Conceive	Exploit	Reinforce
Conduct	Forerunner	Reorganize
Control	Foresight	Represent
Coordinate	Formulate	Review
Create	Guide	Revise
Delegate	Influence	Streamline
Design	Initiate	Structure
Develop	Inspire	Train
Direct	Lead	

Summary

As you develop your specific application package for each SES job, review and study this chapter on writing the ECQs. Developing these statements is a challenging process, but it is supported by a formula that you can learn. Because mastering the ECQ statements is critical to qualifying for an SES job and being selected for an interview, the time you spend learning how to structure your statements is an investment that has the potential to pay huge dividends.

CHAPTER 23

Military to Federal Resume Conversions

By Diane Hudson Burns, FJSTC, CCMC, CPRW

The preparation and development of a federal resume for a service member is no different than it is for a nonmilitary member. The content of the resume needs to be in alignment with the duties and specialized experience noted on the federal job vacancy announcement.

Constructing a resume while still engaged in the military is an excellent strategy. When you are ready to retire or ETS, you will have a resume ready to "tweak" to meet specific announcements, and you will be ready to apply for open positions. If you wait until your retirement is upon you to prepare your resume, you may find that the job search takes many weeks or even months. So early preparation is best.

Military conversion resumes should look and "speak" the same as those of their civilian counterparts. However, after being in the military for many years, you may speak "military," using plenty of military acronyms and jargon. You will need to translate the military speak in the federal resume. Someone unfamiliar with military acronyms, ranks, and other jargon may not be able to determine whether your work experience is a good fit with the job posting and thus may screen out your resume. You may find yourself not qualifying for many positions.

 Note: For more samples and information for writing military federal resumes, refer to *Military to Federal Career Guide* by Kathryn Troutman.

Translating Military Speak to Civilian Speak

Service members have the added challenge of looking for civilian keywords that help their resumes qualify in the federal system, by thoroughly analyzing the job vacancy announcement Duties and Specialized Experience sections. Identify the minimum skills and experience required for a position and match that list with your personal list of accomplishments, skills, and competencies.

You will also need to spend extra time learning what your military terms, acronyms, and jargon translates into in the corporate/federal market. This may be a bit of a culture change, as you learn to integrate yourself into the corporate/industry/federal segment. As a service member, you will need to carefully translate your military rank, career history, job titles, military occupational specialties, career fields, and training courses. You can use your awards, training justifications, and performance rating justifications to glean accomplishments.

Note: If you are not yet nearing retirement, an excellent suggestion is to begin an accomplishments log. Keep a list of projects, accomplishments, awards, and duties (how many people you supervised, project scope, budgets, value of projects, award received, specialized training or certifications, and so on) so that when you are ready to prepare your resume, you have all of the information you might need in one place. If you are preparing your resume now, pull all of your military documents into one file, highlight major projects and accomplishments, and develop a list to use in the resume development process.

Translating Military Terms

Table 23.1 contains a few sample translations for military rank, responsibilities, and acronyms. Sometimes service members tell me that they don't know what an acronym means because they never spelled it out. If you don't know what it means, ask someone or look it up. Federal resumes need to have all acronyms spelled out at least once in the first reference. Each branch of service has its own set of acronyms for individual systems. Some acronyms might be the same, but the meaning is very different (PMA can mean President's Management Agenda or Pre-Market Approval; and a Captain in the Army is a junior officer and a Captain in the Navy is a senior officer).

Table 23.1: Translating Military Speak to Civilian Speak

Military Speak	Civilian Speak
	Rank
Senior Officer (Naval Commander, Army or Air Force Major and up)	Chief Executive, Administrator, Chief of Staff, Senior Executive/Vice President, Chief Administrator, CEO, COO, CFO, SES
Senior Enlisted (E-7 to E-9) or Junior Officer	Program/Project/Plant Director, Manager, or Coordinator
Enlisted (E-5 to E-6)	Team Leader, Training Manager, Instructor
	Responsibilities
Commanded	Directed, supervised, or guided
Provisioning Chief	Logistics management
Briefings	Presentations, seminars, or public speaking (communications)
	Acronyms and Terms
Battalion	250 personnel
ANOC	Advanced Noncommissioned Officers Course (Leadership and Administration Course)
COMSEC	Communications Security

(continued)

(continued)

Military Speak	Civilian Speak
ACofS	Assistant Chief of Staff
OCONUS	Outside Continental United States
PCS	Permanent Change of Station (a move or transfer)
PAC	Personnel Actions Center
AORS	Areas of Responsibility
ATRRS	Army Training Requirements and Resources System
Pathfinder	Army Intelligence Database System
SGT	Sergeant
CPT	(Captain: senior officer in the Navy; junior officer in the Army)

Keywords

Your military service probably spans varied experiences, advanced training and education, diverse leadership roles, and special awards. These experiences and accomplishments need to be translated into qualitative and quantitative sentences that are oriented to the competencies; knowledge, skills, and abilities; occupational questions; and other keywords found on a federal job vacancy announcement. A well-translated sentence can be very successful in describing years of leadership and management credentials.

Here is a sample translation for operations management (extracted from a resume written by a veteran):

Before:

> Support the 76th aircraft wing providing services to 12 carrier air wing squadrons and 32 reserve squadrons, supported commands, and a special project unit. Manage inventory and a budget.

After:

> Supervise a staff of 35 shop personnel providing maintenance services to 12 major customers and 32 tenant units encompassing 87 worldwide sites. Orchestrate logistical support and inventory requirements controlling a bench stock of 2,400 items. Execute a $60M operational budget.

The first sentence includes only three keywords (inventory, budget, and manage), and it is confusing to the reader. A civilian without any knowledge of aircraft wing, reserve squadrons, or supported commands will not fully comprehend the credentials behind the candidate. The sentence will be vague and complicated to a civilian recruiter. With some strong questioning and a thorough review of "what you actually do on the job," you can write a strong qualitative or quantitative sentence that shows the employer what you managed and what value you have to offer the organization.

The second sentence includes at least 11 keywords that fit a vacancy announcement and translates many military-specific terms: supervise, staff, shop, personnel, maintenance, services, customers, logistical, inventory, bench stock, and budget. Moreover, it describes for the reader how vast the needs are to coordinate logistical requirements for the 76th aircraft wing. Additionally, the second sentence captures the reader's attention with specific accomplishments and numbers. This translation is strong and factual.

Uncovering and Quantifying Accomplishments

The second sentence was derived from a line of questioning using the information provided in sentence one:

What is the 76th aircraft wing?

> 12 major customers and 32 smaller customers in 87 sites around the world.

Do you have a team to accomplish this support?

> Yes, I supervise 35 personnel.

Tell me about the inventory you control.

> Well, it is pretty big; I coordinate logistical support for the 87 sites with a bench stock of 2,400 items.

Tell me about your budget. Is it significant?

> Yes, $60M, which includes pricey aircraft maintenance parts.

This line of questioning helps unfold skills, accomplishments, and credentials that are otherwise lost in the military speak.

Also, remember that if you convert your paper copy (formatted resume) to an electronic Resumix version (for CPOL/Army applications), the Resumix system will not understand the military terms in the first sentence. Furthermore, the second sentence quantifies the military terms and adds keywords that are critical for a candidate seeking employment in logistics or supply discipline management.

Remember, this is only one sentence in a three- to five-page federal resume. Each sentence needs to carry its weight in order to match the skills required for a specific federal series. You might want to research private-industry job announcements as well as federal job announcements to learn how to properly translate military terms.

When a military sentence (full of military acronyms and military terms) is properly converted to a civilian-speak sentence, there is almost no recognition that the applicant is from the military. Private-industry employment specialists, recruiters, and hiring managers will be able to understand and appreciate your qualifications.

Here are some another examples of military translations.

Try to qualify and quantify accomplishments as often as possible:

> Directed an organization with 250 personnel, supervised 12 department managers, executed an operational budget of $3M, managed assets worth $70M, and significantly reduced a logistical backlog by 87%.

A short quantitative statement is successful in describing years of leadership.

And for more complex translations, try this method:

> Strategic Planner, Strategic Planning & Policy Directorate, U.S. Pacific Command, Camp Smith / equivalent to Strategic Planner and Advisor to CEO & VPs regarding multinational issues.

Or this:

> Deputy CIO for Data Management, Joint National Integration Center, Missile Defense Agency, Schriever Air Force Base / equivalent to Executive VP of Data Management / Technology of a large company advising the CIO.

In each of these examples, we translated not only individual military acronyms and terms, but also career experience and skill sets; we dug deep into each career history to identify those experiences and skills not directly related to the career field (perhaps you were designated as a recruiter for a year, were an event planner, or trained in IT—you just never know), as well as those skill sets directly related to your career field.

Service members who prepare early to exit or retire from military service can learn to write a successful civilian-language, skills-based federal resume; maneuver the federal application process; and land a second career with the federal government.

Focusing Your Resume

Often, military clients tell me that they can do anything: They are leaders and they have managed personnel, human resources, logistics, computer repairs and LANs, accounting and budgets, supply systems, commissary operations, aircraft maintenance, security requirements, instructors, health care…and the list goes on. Interestingly, they might perform many of these duties under the job title of Ammunition Specialist, Administrative Specialist, or Field Artillery Surveyor. Very often, the work completed on the job and the skills and training acquired are very different from the job title or occupational field.

Unfortunately, the federal resume system does not favor "jack-of-all-trades" resumes. In order for a candidate to be deemed Best Qualified, his or her federal resume must meet requirements for a position within a federal series. So, for example, one candidate told me he was an accountant and was seeking accounting positions based on his work with budgets in the military. However, he began to apply for different positions such as Force Protection Manager and Security Operations Manager. This client was not qualifying for any positions in the security series because his resume was focused toward accounting and auditing. He needed to rewrite his federal resume to incorporate security operations, focusing on his military background and highlighting specific accomplishments in both accounting and security. As a result, he began to qualify for jobs in the security series. He submitted two resumes into USAJOBS—one more focused on accounting and one more focused on security.

In order to focus your federal resume and target critical skills required in the federal vacancy announcements, you need to review the duties and qualifications in the vacancy announcements and highlight keywords, in the same manner that you develop keywords from your military language. Train yourself to highlight keywords in vacancy announcements and use the same words when you translate your background. For example, here is a sample section of a federal vacancy announcement for an Intelligence Specialist. The keywords are marked in bold.

Instructor experienced in one or more of the following **Counterintelligence (CI)** and **Human Intelligence (HUMINT)** disciplines: Department of Defense (DoD) **surveillance tactics, CI and/or HUMINT operations, tradecraft,** DoD CI **Counterespionage (CE) investigations,** and the employment of special **investigative** techniques. The selected applicant will **develop, update, and present classes** on the aforementioned subjects at various skill levels. He/She will also participate in **role-playing** practical exercises, and serve as an **operational mentor.**

Then be certain to use the keywords in your federal resume, while translating your military language and focusing on your key accomplishments. As you develop your federal resume, use small paragraphs and plenty of nouns, and outline the format using all caps to lead off on sentences starting each new paragraph.

Note: Each agency has different application and resume requirements; consequently, military candidates need to read the application procedures carefully for each agency to which they want to submit an application. Also, application procedures may change at a moment's notice, so reread application procedures at the time of submission and nomination.

Triple Series Sample Resume—Military Officer Seeking Senior Management Positions

Target Job: GS-11–13 positions: Administrative/Management, 0301; Policy/Program Management, 0341; Management/Program Analysis, 0343.
Resume Format: Outline Format federal resume with keywords in all caps.
Targeted, written, and designed by Sandra Lee Keppley, Certified Federal Job Search Trainer and Senior Certified Federal Resume Writer.

Strategy: Utilized typical KSA and specialized experience requirements for these occupations at the grade level being pursued (11–13). Both work experience and accomplishments are included in the Outline Format resume to highlight requirements and are inclusive of pertinent keywords. Client possessed differing occupational experiences requiring focus in like competencies between occupations being pursued.

Keywords and Skills for Three Occupational Series
Administrative Management, 0301

- Skill in presenting information and negotiating resolutions
- Ability to analyze and evaluate complex issues
- Knowledge of budgetary principles, practices, laws, and regulations
- Ability to lead and direct others

Management and Program Analysis, 0343

- Development of long-range goals, objectives, strategies and multilayered transition implementation plans
- Application of analytical and evaluative methods techniques to assess program development
- Projects life cycle/cost benefit analysis of projects and analyzes the economic impact on programs
- Leads cost-effectiveness studies across coordinating centers' operations and administrative programs

Policy/Program Management, 0341

- Knowledge of concepts, procedures, and techniques related to policy development, implementation, application, and evaluation
- Ability to conduct research and compile data into effective written and oral presentations, including briefings and policy papers relating to security operations
- Ability to plan, organize, and conduct research into problems that involve major areas of uncertainty in approach, methodology, or interpretation to identify courses of action
- Ability to work with senior-level staff for coordination and liaison purposes
- Ability to independently plan and lead projects and activities, and evaluate and recommend significant changes in policies and procedures

Samuel Jackson
2524 Smith Ave
Sunset Way, California 12345
Day Phone: (617) 444-4444
Email: samj1010@yahoo.com

WORK EXPERIENCE

MacDill Air Force Base
Tampa, FL US

3/2009 - Present

Salary: LTC USD Per Year
Hours per week: 40

CHIEF OF PERSONNEL MANAGEMENT POLICY
SENIOR ADMINISTRATIVE OPERATIONS OFFICER responsible for directing, overseeing, and facilitating timely execution of critical operational and administrative programs for a 50,000+-person organization. Assist senior management by providing guidance, recommendations, and senior-level representation for programs managed.

ACCOMPLISHMENTS:
• Boosted Commander's personnel management authorities over his organization through role in rewriting Department of Defense Personnel Policy.
• Contributed to 25% increase in personnel retention by leading effort to extend key compensation incentives through the Office of the Secretary of Defense.
• Increased unit efficiency through management and supervision of over 500 personnel as Army Element Commander.

ANALYZE OPERATIONAL PROGRAM PRIORITIES, OBJECTIVES, AND RESOURCES. Determine degree of compliance with programs and instructions. Suggest approaches for addressing programmatic issues. Work with program staff and senior program managers to identify best means and approaches to integrate programs and resources and to link operational programs and strategic direction.

PERFORM QUANTATIVE AND QUALITATIVE ANALYSIS as an expert analyst evaluating effectiveness of programs or operations and productivity and efficiency of management. Implement, coordinate, and oversee a variety of complex management programs impacting the agency's activities.

PLAN AND MANAGE STUDIES: Plan and conduct broad and in-depth special studies. Analyze findings and make recommendations on substantive operating programs applying knowledge of qualitative and quantitative analytical techniques along with knowledge of the mission, organization, and work processes of the programs and the relationships of administrative support activities. Recommend policy and develop procedures for operational program development and results-oriented performance measures.

ANALYZE HUMAN RESOURCES ADEQUACY. Provide independent and objective analysis and evaluation of human resource adequacy, utilization, and program performance. Develop recommendations on resource adequacy. Provide complex briefings to leadership on critical program issues and provide options for solutions to problems.

LEADER AND HUMAN RESOURCES MANAGER directing work through subordinate supervisors. Exercise delegated supervisory authority in the establishment and issuance of technical and administrative guidance. Plan and assign work, advise on program goals and objectives, make decisions on work problems, and organize and monitor flow of work to achieve effective results within a complex environment.

IMPROVE OPERATIONAL EFFICIENCIES: Determine operational priorities and adjust staff assignments to ensure compliance with suspense requirements.

(Contact Supervisor: Yes, Supervisor's Name: Col. Mary Johnson, Supervisor's Phone: (666) 666-6666)

U.S. Army
Baghdad, Iraq

12/2007 - 3/2009

Salary: 97,000 USD Per Year
Hours per week: 40

Figure 23.1: Sample military conversion resume.

DEPUTY TRAINING CHIEF AND SENIOR ADVISOR
ADMINISTRATIVE OPERATIONS OFFICER as Deputy Commander of a 150+-person organization, and principal military advisor to an Iraqi Army General Officer for logistics, personnel, and communications for an 18,000-person organization. Achieved mission by connecting people, supplies, and equipment. Planned, provided leadership, and carried out difficult and complex assignments and developed new methods, approaches, and procedures. Prioritized, acquired and administered human, financial, material, and information resources.

ACCOMPLISHMENTS:
• Boosted protection of personnel and saved countless lives by advising Iraqi counterparts while fielding 300+ combat vehicles, with a value above $31 million.
• Increased personnel morale and unit efficiency by overseeing planning and construction of $15M Iraqi Army Headquarters facility.
• Improved unit readiness and morale by supervising $3M renovation of U.S. Army base camp.
• Boosted personnel protection and unit readiness by supervising turn-in of 33 U.S. vehicles with value above $17M and fielding of 45 U.S. vehicles with a value over $50M.

U.S. MILITARY INTERMEDIARY: As intermediary, acquired trust of Iraqi counterparts and conventional U.S. military organizations in accomplishing the overall mission. Used new technology to enhance decision making. Applied management principles and monitored mission performance. Provided resources and support to ensure key strategies and results were achieved. Improved effectiveness and held people accountable for achieving their goals.

PROJECT MANAGER skilled in project management concepts, principles, methods, and practices. Managed aspects of project planning, execution, and close-out of one or more projects. Utilized performance management and measurement methods, tools, and techniques. Developed detailed project plans and schedules. Gathered and facilitated definition of project scope and requirements.

STAFFING ANALYSIS: Determined staffing requirements/employee discipline(s) and formed project team(s). Monitored project milestones and critical dates to identify potential jeopardy of project schedule. Conducted formal review at project completion to confirm acceptance and satisfaction. Provided continuing work direction and leadership, including scheduling, assignment of work, and review of project efforts. Applied doctrinal concepts and procedures necessary to effectively assimilate diverse mission elements across varying environments to meet situational requirements and appreciated the tight linkages between people, process, and technology.

CONTINUED IN ADDITIONAL INFORMATION (Contact Supervisor: Yes, Supervisor's Name: COL Jeffrey Zigler, Supervisor's Phone: 001 10 272 2222)

U.S. Army	**12/2007 - 3/2009**
Baghdad, Iraq	
	Salary: 80,000 USD Per Year
	Hours per week: 40

INFORMATION MAANGEMENT CHIEF
INFORMATION MANAGEMENT CHIEF developing strategies and plans to address all aspects of classified communications related to special operations in support of Homeland Defense initiatives. Worked with users to develop a comprehensive project plan, budget requirements, task descriptions, and work breakdown structure, and to accomplish program/project requirements and mission objectives.

DESIGNED PROJECT AND CONTRACTURAL METHODOLOGIES. Developed project or contractual methodologies, and monitored sub-operating units to ensure deliverable milestones are achieved. Prepared statements of work and participated in contract negotiations. Managed entire life-cycle management process from development to implementation; i.e. managing the project or contract, developing the technical approach, monitoring and overseeing project and contractors, to include adherence to cost and schedule, coordinating all government activities, serving on technical committees, and maintaining contractual activities afterwards. Group management informed on all significant acts of project or contract activity.

PERFORMED QUANTATIVE AND QUALITATIVE ANALYSIS as an expert analyst evaluating effectiveness of programs or operations and productivity and efficiency of

(continued)

(continued)

management. Implemented, coordinated, and oversaw a variety of complex management programs, i.e., evaluating data, information, and trends to identify improvements to policies, procedures, and technology.

PLANNED STUDIES. Planned and conducted broad and in-depth special studies. Analyzed findings and made recommendations on substantive operating programs applying knowledge of qualitative and quantitative analytical techniques along with knowledge of the mission, organization, and work processes of the programs and the relationships of administrative support activities. Recommended policy and developed procedures for operational program development and results-oriented performance measures. Provided independent and objective analysis and evaluation of human and financial resource utilization and program performance. Developed recommendations on resource adequacy. Provided complex briefings to leadership on critical program issues and provided options for solutions to problems.

ACCOMPLISHMENTS:
• Recognized for singlehandedly evaluating and suggesting a change to the directorate's manpower numbers, which resulted in a 50% increase in personnel.
• Established a classified communications system, which resulted in the successful receipt, distribution, and transmittal of thousands of highly critical and sensitive pieces of information.
• Managed a government services contract in excess of $1.5M, which greatly increased office efficiency.
• Introduced two unique concepts to the organization, which attained CEO approval and greatly increased the organizational leadership span of control.

CONTINUED IN ADDITIONAL INFORMATION

U.S. Army   **4/2005 - 8/2007**
where, where US

                                                Salary: 92,000 USD Per Year
                                                Hours per week: 40

MATERIAL REQUIREMENT ANALYST AND STRATEGIC PLANNER
PROJECT MANAGEMENT skilled in project management concepts, principles, methods, and practices. Responsible for managing all aspects of project planning, execution, and close-out of one or more projects. Utilized performance management and measurement methods, tools, and techniques. Developed detailed project plans and schedules. Gathered and facilitated the definition of project scope and requirements.

DETERMINED STAFFING REQUIREMENTS: Determined staffing requirements/employee discipline(s) and formed project team(s). Monitored project milestones and critical dates to identify potential jeopardy of project schedule. Conducted formal review at project completion to confirm acceptance and satisfaction. Provided continuing work direction and leadership, including scheduling, assignment of work, and review of project efforts. Applied doctrinal concepts and procedures necessary to effectively assimilate diverse mission elements across varying environments to meet situational requirements and appreciated the tight linkages between people, process, and technology. Responsible for reviewing and validating classified operational material requirements for special operations equipment.

STRTEGIC PLANNER: As Strategic Planner, responsible for internal and DOD wargame scenarios all Services and Combatant Commands used as part of their modeling processes, i.e., computer wargames, conducted in an effort to justify resources (money, manpower, etc.).

KNOWLEDGE OF ACQUISITION PRINCIPLES AND PROCESSES: Graduate of the Basic Acquisition Course. Knowledgeable of contract administration policies and procedures, Federal procurement contract administration and techniques, policies, and principles of application derived from governing laws, regulations, directives, manuals, and agency supplements. Understand the importance of maintaining uniform management controls over the prime contractor's performance and to provide direction and leadership as a post-award representative.

ACCOMPLISHMENTS:
• Chaired eight unique 14-person cross-functional teams responsible for identifying and fielding equipment to personnel engaged in combat, which resulted in the delivery of combat-critical material to personnel in combat.
• Played a key role in the fielding of 333 Mine Resistant Ambush Protected vehicles with a value in excess of $400M to our forces in Iraq and Afghanistan, which

contributed to increased personnel protection and combat readiness.
• Lead author of a DOD classified Irregular Warfare planning scenario and briefed the plan at a DOD conference.
• Assisted in assessing Special Operations war fighting contributions, which eventually led to an increased force structure of 13,000 personnel.
• Served as the Department of Defense (DOD) lead for a classified Irregular Warfare planning scenario, which became the DOD standard for wargame scenarios.

U.S. Army **city, state US**	**6/2002 - 6/2005**
	Salary: 80,000 USD Per Year **Hours per week: 40**

INFORMATION MANAGEMENT CHIEF
INFORMATION MANAGEMENT CHIEF developing strategies and plans to address all aspects of classified communications related to special operations in support of Homeland Defense initiatives. Worked with users to develop a comprehensive project plan, budget requirements, task descriptions, and work breakdown structure, and to accomplish program/project requirements and mission objectives. Developed project or contractual methodologies, and monitored sub-operating units to ensure deliverable milestones are achieved. Prepared statements of work and participated in contract negotiations. Managed entire life-cycle management process from development to implementation; i.e., managing the project or contract, developing the technical approach, monitoring and overseeing project and contractors, to include adherence to cost and schedule, coordinating all government activities, serving on technical committees, and maintaining contractual activities afterwards. Group management informed on all significant acts of project or contract activity.

PERFORMED QUANTATIVE AND QUALITATIVE ANALYSIS as an expert analyst evaluating effectiveness of programs or operations and productivity and efficiency of management. Implemented, coordinated, and oversaw a variety of complex management programs, i.e., evaluating data, information, and trends to identify improvements to policies, procedures, and technology. Planned and conducted broad and in-depth special studies. Analyzed findings and made recommendations on substantive operating programs applying knowledge of qualitative and quantitative analytical techniques along with knowledge of the mission, organization, and work processes of the programs and the relationships of administrative support activities. Recommended policy and develop procedures for operational program development and results-oriented performance measures. Provided independent and objective analysis and evaluation of human and financial resource utilization and program performance. Developed recommendations on resource adequacy.

ACCOMPLISHMENTS:
• Recognized for singlehandedly evaluating and suggesting a change to the directorate's manpower numbers, which resulted in a 50% increase in personnel.
• Established a classified communications system, which resulted in the successful receipt, distribution, and transmittal of thousands of highly critical and sensitive pieces of information.
• Managed a government services contract in excess of $1.5M, which greatly increased office efficiency.
• Introduced two unique concepts to the organization, which attained CEO approval and greatly increased the organizational leadership span of control.

U.S. Army **where, where US**	**1/2001 - 6/2002**
	Salary: 75,000 USD Per Year **Hours per week: 40**

Director of Operations
Managed the operations and training for a 450-person elite unit, consisting of 24 separate elements.
• Supervised the planning and execution of numerous training exercises throughout the world, which validated unit combat readiness.
• Developed a plan for the reception, integration, and training validation for an 83-person National Guard company mobilized for the global war on terrorism.

(continued)

(continued)

EDUCATION

Naval Post Graduate School

Monterey, California US
Master's Degree
Major: Defense Analysis

Concordia College
Boston, MA US
Bachelor's Degree
Major: Political Science and History
Honors: cum laude

JOB RELATED TRAINING

Project Management Professional (PMP), Pending July 2011 Completion Date
Command and General Staff College
Joint Forces Staff College
Basic Acquisition Course
Combined Arms and Services Staff School
Indonesian Basic Military Language Course
United States Air Force Military Air Command Airlift Planners Course

ADDITIONAL INFORMATION

PROFESSIONAL PROFILE:

United States Army Officer with 20 years of experience in managing international and domestic operations with emphasis on leadership, planning, and security coupled with an education in defense analysis and political science. Areas of operations expertise and experience include project management, strategic planning, quantitative and qualitative analysis, budget administration, human resources management, training, safety and security compliance, supply and logistics, and maintenance. Strong leader with outstanding communication skill, both orally and in writing. Proficiency in negotiation, collaboration, and conflict resolution.

Active TS/SCI Security Clearance
Willing to Relocate

WORK HISTORY CONTINUED:

UNITED STATES ARMY, Deputy Training Chief and Senior Advisor, December 2007 – March 2009
THREAT ANALYST ensuring proper threat or enemy analysis was conducted in support of hundreds of combat operations. Conducted analysis of and operationalized analysis to counter threat analysis. Advised Iraqi counterparts on basic threat analysis Intelligence Preparation of the Battlefield. Applied proficient knowledge of intelligence information systems, indications, and warnings.

COMMUNICATED ORALLY AND IN WRITING with a wide variety of individuals and able to handle sensitive, difficult situations with tact and discretion. Promoted a free flow of information and communication (upward, downward, and across) as well as collaboration and teamwork across organizational boundaries.

UNITED STATES ARMY, Material Requirements Analyst and Strategic Planner, April 2005 – August 2007

COMMUNICATION SKILLS, orally and in writing, are excellent. Possess interpersonal skills to meet and deal effectively with representatives of private sector or with other government experts and managers in order to procure unique and often unprecedented services. Provide expert technical leadership, staff coordination, and consultation in the contracting area, including responsibility for directing the formulation of guidelines and providing contracting policy guidance. Responded to constructive feedback to improve processes, products, and services. Developed solid relationships with customers through regular contact in order to understand needs and expectations.

The military to federal resume has to be understandable to a nonmilitary human resources specialist who will be the first reviewer. The sample in the Outline Format includes paragraph headings that are clear and easy to understand. The descriptions are more technical and specific to his military leadership experience. Attention to detail and focusing the resume and accomplishments can make the difference in a veteran's federal resume and result in getting referred and interviewed.

Summary

The military to federal resume examples illustrate some of the methods you can use to convert military experience into a federal resume. Remember to frame your experience in terms that are familiar to the federal human resources rater and the qualifications standards. Follow these rules and you will be well on your way to developing a winning military-translation federal resume that qualifies you for federal positions.

CHAPTER 24

Military Spouses and Federal Employment

In her article "First Lady Thanks Military Families at Homecoming" on MilSpouse.com, Vivian Greentree talks about a visit First Lady Michelle Obama made to champion military families. The article starts with this reference to the first lady's speech.

> When the first lady of the United States visited Naval Station Norfolk on July 31, 2010, for a homecoming ceremony, she made it a point to honor the sacrifices of the families at home.
>
> "We must all remember that when our troops are deployed, their families are left behind and faced with an entirely different set of duties," Michelle Obama told a crowd of 500 sailors and their families, who were celebrating the return of the USS Eisenhower Carrier Strike Group and the USNS Comfort. "If you have the opportunity, just reach out and simply say thank you—sometimes that goes a long way—say thank you to the spouses and the children of our military members and thank them for their sacrifice because it is real and it is powerful."

There are many federal employment opportunities available to military spouses that provide for attainment and retention of federal jobs. Unfortunately, not all spouses are aware of these opportunities. The intent of this chapter is to provide an awareness of military spouse employment and preferences.

Military Spouse Employment Preference (MSP)

The MSP provides employment opportunities for military spouses and applies to spouses of active-duty military members of the U.S. Armed Forces, including the Coast Guard, who relocate to accompany their sponsor on a permanent change of station (PCS) move. The program is intended to lessen the career interruption of spouses who relocate with their military sponsors. MSP is a Department of Defense (DOD) program. Therefore, it applies only to DOD vacancies.

The MSP applies only if

- The spouse was married to the military sponsor prior to the reporting date to the new assignment.
- The relocation was based on PCS move and not for separation or retirement.
- The vacancy is within the commuting area of the sponsor's permanent new duty station.
- The spouse is among the Best Qualified group and is within reach for selection.

Note: Ensure you know what documentation you will need to submit when applying for career opportunities in the federal government.

There are two main types of federal employment opportunities within the DOD to which MSP applies:

Civil Service or Appropriated Fund (AF) Vacancies

- Filled through the human resources office on military installations. Spouse preference is available for positions at grades GS-15 and below or equivalent wage-grade positions, with some exclusions.
- To use MSP, spouses must create an application within the applicable resume building website, i.e., CPOL.
- Spouses must have an appointability or eligibility in the civil service system (current or previous work experience in the federal government [AF or NAF] or military service).
- Spouses must register for MSP and apply for Program "S," the Priority Placement Program (PPP) for military spouses. This is the only way you can apply and exercise your military spouse preference for an AF position within CONUS. You can apply for the "S" Program through the local civilian human resources office.
- Required documentation must be submitted:
  - Copy of sponsor's PCS orders
  - Copy of Standard Form 50 (if you have prior federal employment experience) or your DD Form 214 (if you are a former service member)
  - Copy of your most recent performance appraisal (if you are a current or former federal employee)
  - Other documents, such as college transcripts or licenses, as required for the position

Non-appropriated Fund Vacancies

- Filled by the NAF Human Resources Office on your military installation.
- MSP applies to NAF positions at grades NF-3 and below (or equivalent grade levels).
- NAF positions include jobs at military exchanges, recreation facilities, restaurants, and other NAF activities.
- To use MSP, spouses must file an application with the installation NAF Human Resources Office.
- Spouses must provide a copy of sponsor's PCS orders.
- Spouses must submit a written statement requesting MSP or complete a form provided by the NAF office.

Noncompetitive Appointments for Spouses of Certain Members of the Armed Forces

The purpose of this type of appointment from Executive Order 13473 of September 25, 2008, is to provide for expedited recruitment and selection of military spouses for appointment to positions in the competitive service of the federal civil service. This is part of the effort of the United States to recruit and retain in military service skilled and experienced members of the armed forces and to recognize and honor their service.

Eligibility:

- Spouse of a member of the armed forces serving on active duty, to include members of the National Guard and Reserves on active duty, who have orders specifying permanent change of station (not for training)
- Spouse of a 100% disabled service member injured while on active duty
- Unmarried widow or widower of a service member killed while on active duty

General Hiring Provisions:

- Spouses will have two years from the date the PCS orders are issued to obtain federal employment.
- Spouses of relocating service members are limited to one appointment under this authority per PCS order. (There is no limit on the number of appointments a spouse of a 100% disabled veteran or the widow of a deceased service member may receive.)

The noncompetitive appointment is limited to the geographic area of the PCS or the surrounding commuting area. (This limitation may be waived if no federal agency exists in the geographic area.)

Spouses can find out about federal job opportunities by going to the Office of Personnel Management's USAJOBS site (www.usajobs.gov). Spouses may also check websites of specific agencies for employment opportunities.

This new hiring authority is not limited to specific positions or grade levels; however, spouses have to meet the same requirements as other applicants, including qualification requirements. It is the responsibility of the applicant to request consideration for employment under this authority as a military spouse.

The use of this hiring authority is discretionary with managers. It does not mean spouses will get a hiring preference, nor does it create an entitlement to federal jobs over other qualified applicants.

During the application process, be sure to do the following:

- Identify yourself as a person with noncompetitive appointment eligibility within USAJOBS.
- Find required documentation; i.e., marriage certificate, military orders authorizing the spouse in conjunction with assigning the service member to a certain post.
- Make your appointment eligibility stand out first and foremost on your resume.
- Use USAJOBS to find federal jobs that provide for consideration of your noncompetitive appointment eligibility.

- Work closely with your Family Support Office/Employment Readiness Office. Attend available TAP classes.
- Take responsibility for your career!

2010 Military Spouse Intern Program

The 2010 National Defense Authorization Act, Section 564, authorized a pilot program to secure internships for military spouses with federal agencies. DOD will reimburse federal agencies for first-year salary, benefits, and training costs if an eligible military spouse is appointed to a permanent position offering training and career progression. Ideally, the positions will be those common across the federal government to accommodate the constant geographic relocation of a spouse.

 Note: Be sure to submit a complete application and highlight preference/programs you are eligible to compete for.

Derived Veterans' Preference

Eligibility:

- Spouse of a disabled veteran who is unable to work because of a service-connected disability.
- Mother of a veteran who died or is permanently disabled while on active duty during a war, campaign, or expedition.
- Unmarried widow or widower of a veteran who died while on active duty during a war, campaign, or expedition.

Benefit:

- Adds 10 points to earned score under competitive examination.

Filing Your Application as a Military Spouse

When applying for federal employment, be sure to clearly articulate preference/programs under which you are eligible to compete. A sample military spouse resume follows.

Military Spouse Seeking Readiness Counselor Position at Fleet and Family Support Center, Rota, Spain

Target Job: Work and Family Life Specialist, GS-0101-9.
Resume Format: Outline Format federal resume with keywords in all caps.
Edited and advised in writing by Lisa Casillas, Work & Family Life Specialist and Certified Federal Job Search Trainer.

ANLECTA L. KENNEY
PSC 999 Box 11, FPO, AE, 09634
666.666.666 or 666.6666
Email: anlectakenney@ymail.com

Spouse Preference:

Spouse Preference: N/A, Family Member of U.S.N. Active Duty
Eligible for Consideration under Executive Order 13473, September 11, 2009,
Non-competitive Appointment for Certain Military Spouses
Eligible for consideration for the 2010 Military Spouse Intern Program

WORK EXPERIENCE   **Highlights of Qualifications**   **9/2010 - Present**
                       FPO, AE US

• Provided adult education, instruction, and training at University of West Florida, and increased operational readiness.
• Coordinated and supervised first Annual Northwest Florida Districts High School Speech Tournament.
• Community liaison: Established a network for the University of West Florida and N.A.S. Pensacola.
• President's Award for Leadership and Diversity, University of West Florida (2008).

Fleet and Family Support   **8/2010 - Present**
FPO, AE US

                                      Hours per week: 20

Volunteer
• INFORMATION AND REFERRAL: Identified and clarified issues or concerns and determined appropriate referral services for military members, retirees, and family members. Ensured customer service and satisfaction.

• CUSTOMER SERVICE: Primary contact for department and ensured and delivered services to customers including educating clients on resources offered at Fleet and Family Support Center (FFSC), such as Relocation Services and Career Resource Development.

• MARKETING: Gathered data for Fleet and Family Support Center and updated information for department calendar and for NAVSTA Rota advertisement.

• DATA GATHERING: Utilized Microsoft Office software to compile and report information and statistics for use at the installation. Utilized Fleet and Family Support Center P-Drive in order to insert client registration information.
(Contact Supervisor: Yes, Supervisor's Name: Lisa Casillas, Supervisor's Phone: 972-727-3232)

Figure 24.1: Sample resume for a military spouse.

University of West Florida
Pensacola, Florida US

8/2008 - 5/2010

Salary: 10.25 USD Per Hour
Hours per week: 30

Graduate Assistant Coach
• EDUCATION / INSTRUCTION / TRAINING: Trained, coached, and counseled 15 students one-on-one in the area of speech delivery and self-development. Educated diverse groups through seminars and workshops. Evaluated students on regional and national levels for collegiate speech competitions; instructed students on areas for improvement. Reviewed and evaluated students' written work and performance through evaluation of students' findings and conclusions in speeches and performances. Instructed students to communicate effectively orally and in writing. Trained and educated a staff of 5 individuals for presenting information to a variety of audiences.

• COACHED / IDENTIFIED AND CLARIFIED ISSUES with training structure and determined appropriate alternative routes to more effective coaching techniques. Tailored practice sessions to meet the specific needs of students in order to meet goals both long and short term. Supervised student learning outcomes by coaching students and evaluating their improvement.
-- Over 5,000 hours of coaching students in effective writing and presentation skills. Adapted to students' needs in order to effectively identify concerns and reach solutions. Demonstrated flexibility and adaptability.

• MADE RECOMMENDATIONS for University of West Florida Forensics Team. Community liaison for team; supervised a variety of matters concerning community relations. Advised and consulted with Director of Forensics and staff to develop a proper reward system for students to be recognized for their efforts. Recommended and developed an instructional DVD for volunteer judges.
--Made recommendations to Director on tools for attracting new recruits to the university. Generated new concepts for promotion: Created promotional DVDs; coordinated external events on campus to recruit on-campus students.

• PRIORITIZED CONCERNS AND PROBLEMS as Coordinator and director for the first Annual High School Speech Competition; hosted over 30 students in three counties. Completed pre-arrangements: Delegated tasks, created press releases, compiled information, and created tournament schedule. Coordinated workshops, presentations, and seminars at the university campus and in local high schools.
--Coordinated with Director of Forensics with national and regional travel plans for approximately 10 students. Counseled and advised students on prioritizing concerns for personal matters in addition to career-centered goals in order to enhance their stability and self-sufficiency.

Position Description Continues 1 of 2 (Contact Supervisor: Yes, Supervisor's Name: Dr. Brendan Kelly, Supervisor's Phone: (850) 474-2323)

University of West Florida
Pensacola, Florida US

8/2008 - 5/2010

Salary: 10.25 USD Per Hour
Hours per week: 30

Graduate Assistant Coach
Position Description Continues 2 of 2

• PLANNING AND IMPLEMENTATION: Contributed to the planning phase and implementation phase of Novice Nationals 2009 and Florida Intercollegiate Forensics Association State Championships 2010. Completed tournament logistics of contestant entries, rooms, ballots, and awards. Coordinated efforts for university speech and debate showcases. Implemented a high school partnership program, providing outsource services to teachers and students within three school districts.

--Coordinated and supervised First Annual Northwest Florida Districts High School Speech Tournament.
--Developed high school speech presentations and speech competition, which resulted in increased awareness of university program in three school districts.
--Community liaison: Established a network for the University of West Florida and N.A.S. Pensacola.

(continued)

(continued)

• INCREASED OPERATIONAL READINESS through evaluations and interpretation of data received from the students' performance. Established objectives, procedures, and plans that would help students to meet both long-range and short-range goals for performance, delivery, and preparation.

• ADVOCACY: Initiated and implemented strategies for university Speech and Debate team; advocated for the team's presence in Northwest Florida. Worked closely with local high schools and developed timelines and an overall plan to attain recruitment objectives and goals. Created a workshop and seminar manual for future outreach recruitment. Built and sustained positive relationships with N.A.S. Pensacola; recruited 20 military personnel volunteers for regional and national speech tournaments.

Pensacola Junior College **Pensacola, Florida US**	**1/2010 - 5/2010** **Salary: 21.00 USD Per Hour** **Hours per week: 4**

Adjunct Instructor
• EDUCATION INSTRUCTION: Instructed 25 students in basic speech, listening, and interpersonal skills. Developed curricula and examinations for students in the area of public speaking and interpersonal communication. Utilized communication theories, principles, and techniques to develop strategies and models for student improvement. Established educational objectives for students in accordance with national policies for students to exceed in both long- and short-range public speaking goals.

• EDUCATIONAL EVALUATIONS AND ASSESSMENTS: Evaluated students and interpreted data for students to improve on speech development. Assessed students in the area of presentation, verbal and nonverbal signals, and context of speech. Determined students' success or failure of class based on established criteria.

• COMPILED DATA AND REPORTED INFORMATION to supervisor as determined appropriate for biweekly and semester updates. Compiled students' overall information and input into college grading system.

• PRIORITIZED CONCERNS AND PROBLEMS: Advised students as a nonclinical consultant on a wide variety of concerns. Identified issues and concerns with students' plans or goals and clarified problems. Determined recommendations for students' needs and improvement, and then tailored their plans to meet their specific needs. (Contact Supervisor: Yes, Supervisor's Name: Thom Botsford, Supervisor's Phone: (850) 474-1400)

University of West Florida **Pensacola, Florida US**	**8/2009 - 1/2010** **Salary: 26.00 USD Per Hour** **Hours per week: 8**

Graduate Teaching Assistant
• EDUCATION INSTRUCTION: Instructed 26 foreign-language-speaking students on English as a Second Language (ESL). Developed curricula and administered tests for students in the area of listening, speaking, and pronunciation in English. Utilized communication theories, principles, and techniques to develop diverse methods for student improvement. Established educational objectives for students in accordance with national policies for students both long and short range.

• ESTABLISHED OBJECTIVES AND PROCEDURES through educational evaluations and assessments. Supervised and assessed students in the area of pronunciation, speaking, and listening skills. Determined students' success or failure of class based on established criteria.

• COMPILED DATA AND REPORTED INFORMATION progress to supervisors. Identified and clarified issues and concerns and determined recommendations for students' needs and improvement. (Contact Supervisor: Yes, Supervisor's Name: Elena Moore, Supervisor's Phone: (850) 474-2974)

EDUCATION

University of West Florida
Pensacola, Florida US
Master's Degree - 8/2010
Major: Master of Science, Public Administration

Relevant Coursework, Licensures, and Certifications:
• Financial Management, University of West Florida, 1.5 Sem. (2009)
• Public Budgeting, University of West Florida, 3.0 Sem. (2009)
• Public Service Human Resources Management, University of West Florida, 3.0. Sem (2009)
• Conflict Management & Resolution, University of West Florida, 3 Sem. (2009)
• Marketing Management, University of West Florida, 3 Sem. (2008)

University of West Florida
Pensacola, Florida US
Bachelor's Degree - 5/2008
Major: Bachelor of Arts, Organizational Communications
Relevant Coursework, Licensures, and Certifications:
• Understanding Relations, University of West Florida, 3 Sem. (2008)

Accomplishments:
• Leadership Communications (Project Car-A-Van) - raised funds to purchase 15-passenger van for Ronald McDonald House of Northwest Florida (2006).
• Health Communications (Project KidCare) - Worked with Florida KidCare to raise awareness of medical insurance to families of lower socioeconomic status (2008).

Woodham High School
Pensacola, Florida US
High School or equivalent - 5/2004

JOB RELATED TRAINING

Communication Leadership Skills, Certificate, University of West Florida (2008)

COMPUTER SKILLS:
Typing Speed 60 wpm. Proficient in Microsoft Office programs, Windows Movie Maker, Final Cut Pro, and iMovie.

ADDITIONAL INFORMATION

HONORS AND AWARDS:

Outstanding Graduate Student Award, University of West Florida (2010)
Recipient of Letter of Appreciation from Commanding Officer for Volunteer Service, N.A.S. Pensacola (2009)
President's Award for Leadership and Diversity, University of West Florida (2008)
Four-time National Finalist: 2008 Pi Kappa Delta National Speech and Debate Championship Finalist (2008)
Top 24 collegiate speaker in the United States in multiple categories, National Forensic Association (2008)
Volunteer Shining Star Award, Ronald McDonald House of Northwest Florida (2007)

Summary

Military spouses are dedicated to supporting their spouse and family, but they are also career-minded. The best positions are those federal civil service jobs that require a detailed federal resume that is targeted toward a particular occupational series. The sample in this book demonstrates the volunteer work, education, and leadership of a dedicated spouse. Her career can follow her spouse's career if she can begin her federal career.

CHAPTER 25

Base Realignment and Closure Act (BRAC) and Priority Placement Program (PPP) Federal Resume Writing

This chapter is written for current Department of Defense employees whose jobs are eliminated, BRACced, or RIFFed (Reduction in Force) and who will be given priority rights to other vacant positions in the Defense Department (and other federal agencies). It is dedicated to the DOD employee who needs to write a comprehensive federal resume for the Priority Placement Panel, who will review your resume and give you recommendations for positions in other DOD agencies. The goal is to focus your resume toward specific occupational series or PPP Codes so that it is clear what your specialized skills are and what positions you are seeking.

This PPP federal resume is different from the one-occupational-series federal resume that we show elsewhere in this book. This federal resume should be more flexible so that you can compete and demonstrate skills for more than one occupational series.

The success story in this chapter of a real DOD employee who was RIFFed includes strategies for success with PPP. This success story landed a position that was lateral and changed his occupational series. His PPP federal resume made the difference. It detailed his skills in several PPP codes, which also demonstrated the occupational standards for three series.

The bottom line is that your PPP federal resume needs to demonstrate specialized skills in two or three occupational series so that your PPP counselor and panelist can help you land a new federal position that will be competitive and utilize your experience and qualifications.

PPP Strategy Story: GS-11, Electronics Technician/IT Specialist

This Electronics Technician needed to change his occupational series in order to land a position in the Ft. Knox area, which was hiring. The resume was written toward three occupational series. He successfully landed a PPP offer that changed his series to IT Specialist. While it was lateral move, there is more career growth opportunity in his new position. He will continue his career at Ft. Knox in this new field of work.

The successful PPP federal employee writes:

> *I finally received a valid PPP offer to Fort Knox. I did receive an offer for GS-11-2210 Customer Support. Looks like I will be able to finish my career here in the Louisville area.*

The Beginning

His journey began by sending us a letter:

> *I believe that you are aware NSWC is closing due to BRAC and that Fort Knox is hiring. I need to have my resume tailored for series 2210 Customer Support, 0332 Computer Operations, and 0391 Telecommunications Series. I'm currently an Electronics Technician 0856/0802. I was told by personnel at Fort Knox to focus on the 2210 Customer Support Series, but I need to qualify for all of these series.*

During the PPP Application Process

I met Tim in Louisville in a federal resume writing workshop. I taught the employees at Pt. Hueneme Naval Warfare Center how to write a competitive federal resume for USAJOBS or the PPP. Tim had been working steadily on his resume, trying to write down his most important projects and skills so that he could land a new career position either through the PPP or online with USAJOBS. When he learned that Ft. Knox would be interested only if his resume could prove his IT specialist skills, he worked on his resume more toward that series.

> *I had to tweak my resume after your workshop, only because I could not remember all duties performed over my 21-year career here.*

Working with the PPP

Tim had an additional struggle with his federal resume. He had to bring the HR specialist to prove that he had been performing IT specialist work in addition to his Electronics Technician duties. Tim was a major advocate for his skills in his resume and built his case that he has been performing IT specialist responsibilities. This strategy worked for Tim.

> *In my opinion, one has to convince his or her PPP coordinator that they are well qualified for the positions they are applying for. In writing my resume, I actually had to bring our HR person down to my working area and physically show her what a military ruggedized computer is before they would qualify me for the 2210 position.*

Next Job, 2210

Tim's new position description (PD) says "varies," but he is happy to be employed as an IT specialist at the grade level that is lateral to his last position. He will be flexible and I am sure he will be successful at Ft. Knox.

> *I'm not sure exactly what I will be doing as my new PD says "VARIES" everywhere. As you know by reading my resume, I'm currently an Electronics Technician, computer hardware side. I will try to do what is asked of me at Fort Knox.*

What Advice Would You Give to Others Who Are BRACCed or Downsized?

Tim was proactive in getting HR to see that he had been performing IT specialist tasks and then writing it down on paper. Without the federal resume demonstrating the IT specialist work, he would never have landed the Ft. Knox position.

> *I would reiterate to folks to be proactive, to make changes to their resumes whether they write it or have it written. It's hard to remember everything one does over the years in one or two sittings/ e-mails. Try to tailor the resume to the job announcement. I entered PPP in May and did not get a hit until August, changing my resume several times in that time frame after reading a job announcement and then remembering, "Hey I did that at one time or another." Thank you and your team for all of the help.*

Tim's actual federal resume for PPP is here in this chapter. This resume was focused toward three occupational series for the PPP. It worked: He was hired!

The Importance of PPP Codes

Become familiar with Chapter 10 of the *PPP Operations Manual*. The codes in this manual equal the Classification Standards. You can talk to your PPP counselor about how these codes should be covered in your federal resume. The sample resume in this chapter covered three of the PPP codes and three Occupational standard series.

Table 25.1: Excerpt from Chapter 10, Option Codes PPP Operations Manual, July 1998

Series	Series Title	Option Code	Option Title
343	Management and Program Analyst	ACQ	Systems Acquisition
		COZ	Cost Analyst
		FMS	Foreign Military Sales
		IMG	Information Management Specialist
		MAL	Manpower
		MBR	Manpower/Budget (Resource) Management
		MOB	Mobilization
		REC	Reports/Forms/Files
		ORG	Organization and Mission
		STI	Statistical Analysis

Series	Series Title	Option Code	Option Title
		TEV	Tests and Evaluation
344	Management Clerical and Assistance (GS-5 and above only)	MAL	Manpower
		REC	Reports/Forms/Files
		WOC	Work Measurement
		SPR	Systems Programmer
		MBR	Manpower/Budget (Resources) Management
346	Logistics Management (GS-12 and above only)	ACQ	Systems Acquisition
		ALS	Automation of Logistics Systems
		AIB	Aircraft
		FAC	Facilities
		FMS	Foreign Military Sales
		AUD	Automotive
		CEL	Communications-Electronics
		ILS	Integrated Logistics
		MIB	Missile
		MOB	Mobilization
		NUA	Nuclear
		ORB	Ordnance

Federal Employee Changing Job Series with DOD Priority Placement Program

Targeting 2210 Series. Common organizational or functional titles for positions in this specialty:

- Technical support specialist
- Customer support specialist
- Help desk representative
- Maintenance specialist

2210: Work that involves the planning and delivery of customer support services, including installation, configuration, troubleshooting, customer assistance, and/or training, in response to customer requirements.

Duties

Functions commonly performed by employees in this specialty may include

- **Diagnosing and resolving problems** in response to customer-reported incidents
- Researching, evaluating, and providing feedback on **problematic trends** and patterns in customer support requirements
- Developing and maintaining **problem tracking and resolution databases**
- Installing, configuring, troubleshooting, and **maintaining customer hardware and software**
- Developing and managing customer service performance requirements
- Developing **customer support policies,** procedures, and standards
- Providing customer training
- Ensuring the rigorous application of **information security**/information assurance policies, principles, and practices in the **delivery of customer support services**

Other Occupational Series of Interest

0332: This series includes positions the paramount duties of which involve operating or supervising the operation of the controls of the digital computer system. Also included are positions involving the operation of peripheral equipment when (a) such equipment is used directly in support of computer operations; and (b) the operation of such equipment is directly related to acquiring the knowledge and skills needed in operating the control console of a computer system. Positions in this series require a knowledge of the functions of the various computer features and the skill to read, interpret, and correctly respond to information in the form in which it is transmitted through the computer system.

0391: This occupation includes positions that involve (1) technical and analytical work pertaining to the planning, development, acquisition, testing, integration, installation, utilization, or modification of telecommunications systems, facilities, services, and procedures; (2) managerial and staff work in the planning, implementation, or program management of telecommunications programs, systems, and services or; (3) line supervision over communications operations, when such work includes responsibility for management functions such as planning, recommending changes, and determining organizational structure, staffing, training, and budgetary requirements.

Keywords and Skills

1. Diagnosing and resolving problems
2. Researching, evaluating problematic trends
3. Problem tracking and resolution databases
4. Maintain customer hardware and software
5. Customer service performance requirements
6. Customer support policies
7. Customer training
8. Information security/information assurance

Target Job: IT Specialist, Customer Services GS-2210-11; Career Change from Electronics Technician—requiring a desk audit.

2210 Customer Support; 0332 Computer Operations; 0391 Telecommunications Series; Currently an Electronics Technician 0856/0802.

PPP federal resume with triple occupational series with keywords and accomplishments.

Resume format: USAJOBS Federal Resume focusing three occupational series.

Targeted, written, and designed by Marcie Barnard, Certified Federal Resume Writer.

Timothy B. Smith
8607 Clifford Ave
Louisville, KY 40219
Contact Phone: (502) 888-8888
Work Phone: (502) 888-8888
DSN Phone: 888-8888
Email Address: timothy.smith@navy.mil

WORK EXPERIENCE	**Naval Surface Warfare Center Port Hueneme Louisville Detachment Louisville, KY US**	**4/1997 - Present**
		Grade Level: GS -11 **Hours per week: 40**

Electronics Technician, 0856/0802
Maintain and support electronic and computer systems and workload forecasting for the Electronic/Engineering Laboratory.

COMPUTER CUSTOMER SUPPORT: Configure portable personal computers. Performed installation of four peripheral component interconnect (PCI) circuit cards, two synchro, and two Naval Tactical Data System (NTDS) Type E Low Level Serial (LLS) and Type A Fast Parallel in each. Perform installation and configuration of Windows XP operating system on each portable personal computer.

ELECTRONIC TECHNICIAN: Support the acquisition and engineering efforts within the Mark 34 Gun Weapons System (GWS) Division. Plan, organize, and execute projects in development. Independently accomplish work assignments on systems and subsystems requiring solutions of both design and operational discrepancies. Coordinate with other technical personnel, both within and outside the immediate work group, to resolve difficult problems and to be a resource for the task group. Serve as Hazmat coordinator.

RESOLVE CONTROVERSIAL OR NOVEL PROBLEMS: Extensive knowledge of the MK 160 Gun Computer System (GCS) and MK 46 Optical Sight System. Valuable technical source for operational, maintenance, system integration, and engineering lab support. High-level understanding of state-of-the-art hardware and software applications. Define systems actions, security principles, and methods and procedures for documenting resolutions. Update problem resolution databases. Perform troubleshooting and data analysis. Use communicative methods and techniques in order to receive, respond to, and ensure complete resolution of any inquiry. Document actions taken and provide needed guidance or training to customers to prevent recurrences. Resolve complex problems.

HARDWARE/SOFTWARE INSTALLATION: Technical support in the installation, alignment, operation, maintenance, and system integration test site performance. Install, test, and assembled ordalts/conversion kits on equipment such as the Mark (MK) 46 Optical Sight System (OSS), SDC/GMP, and the AN-UYK-44 at land-based sites and aboard Navy vessels. All various tasks involve assembling, installing, testing, troubleshooting, performing pretest, post-test, and complete final operational check-out of systems and subsystems and, in some cases, fabricating for proper fit and performance. Perform power and continuity checks on all electronic and electrical equipment and lock out power in accordance with safety practices. Modify the Inter-Active Display, installing upgraded motherboards with the most recent firmware as well as upgrading the bezel for functional and visual usage. Use various types of hand tools, power tools, and specialized tools and meters to perform and complete the electronic, electrical, and mechanical tasks listed above.

(continued)

Figure 25.1: Sample Priority Placement Program resume.

(continued)

++ DUTIES AND ACCOMPLISHMENTS CONTINUED IN ADDITIONAL INFORMATION.
(Contact Supervisor: Yes, Supervisor's Name: Susan Matthews, Supervisor's Phone:
(410) 999-9999)

Naval Surface Warfare Center   4/1993 - 4/1997
Louisville, KY US
                                          Hours per week: 40

Electronics Technician
PERFORMED INSTALLATION, OPERATION, AND TESTING OF HARDWARE AND
ELECTRONICS: Worked as an Electronics Technician in the Electronics/Engineering,
Field Service, Test and Support Branch.

KEY ACCOMPLISHMENTS:
- Received Exceeds Fully Successful Award for multiple years.
- Outstanding Performance Award 1993.
- Received Exceeds Fully Successful for 1994, 1995, 1996, and 1997.

Naval Ordnance Station   9/1990 - 4/1993
Louisville, KY US
                                         Hours per week: 40

Electrical Equipment Worker
Served as an Electrical Equipment Worker with the Close-In Weapon Systems, Phalanx
Production. Disassembler, overhauler, reassembler, and tester of electromechanical,
electrical, and electronic equipment.

EDUCATION

R.E.T.S. Electronic Institute

Louisville, KY US
Associate Degree
Major: Electronic Engineering

**JOB RELATED
TRAINING**

Information Assurance Awareness (April 2010)
Fiber Optic Maintenance Technician Course, January 2008 (five-day course)
JCREW 2.1 FSR Training, August 2008 (four-day course)
AN/UYQ-70 Maintenance Course (M-32), 6/98, at Combat Systems Engineering
Development Site (CSEDS)
Hazardous Materials Coordinator (HAZMAT)
LightTech Fiber Optic FOT-SHIP-4 MIL-STD-2042A Certified, 1999

REFERENCES

William McCarthy	IBM Corporation	Program Manager
Phone Number:	(703) 333-3333	
Email Address:	wmmccarthy@ibm.com	
Reference Type:	Professional	

**ADDITIONAL
INFORMATION**

CONTINUED ... WORK EXPERIENCE .... MORE DUTIES AND ACCOMPLISHMENTS

April 1997 to Present
Electronics Technician
Naval Surface Warfare Center, Port Hueneme Louisville Detachment
Louisville, Kentucky

DEVELOP AND MAINTAIN PROBLEM TRACKING DATABASES AND INVENTORIES:
Responsible for developing and maintaining problem tracking and problem resolution
databases. Maintain inventories for test equipment and electronic/electrical parts using
several databases such as Macintosh Version 8.1 and a Dell PC. Responsible for
ordering and purchasing tools and supplies for the Engineering/Electronics lab.

ENSURE DATA AND QUALITY OF PRODUCT: Maintain confidentiality, integrity, and
availability of highly sensitive data. Ensure the application of information security
policies and procedures. Participated in a Lean workforce with emphasis on measuring,
evaluating, and communicating performance results. Metrics enable organizations
using Lean to identify and target the right problems during Lean and Six Sigma events

and projects; evaluate potential process improvements and select appropriate actions for implementation; establish baselines for process performance and track progress over time; understand and communicate the results (outcomes) of Lean; and monitor efforts to deploy Lean and Six Sigma throughout an organization. Yellow Belt in Lean.

EXHIBIT EXCELLENT CUSTOMER SERVICE: Diagnose and resolve problems in response to customer-reported incidents. Work well with both internal and external customers to assess needs, provide information, and resolve problems. Strong commitment toward customer satisfaction and providing quality products and services. Perform diagnosis and resolution of technical incidents and problems. Identify issues and independently determine course of action. Prepare and disseminate information and make recommendations to mitigate risk and maintain quality assurance.

EXCELLENT ORAL AND WRITTEN COMMUNICATION SKILLS: Interact with a wide range of internal and external customers to analyze and resolve a wide range of computer malfunctions and customer service issues. Provide advice and guidance. Provide representation in meetings. Work with management to improve existing procedures and prepare for future requirements. Interact with vendors daily and exchange information about current technology. Use tech manuals, drawings, wiring diagrams, and self-made work sketches to complete tasks.

STRONG PROBLEM-SOLVING SKILLS: Able to troubleshoot and identify equipment and component failures due to extensive knowledge of the various communication interfaces, fiber optics, and power distribution. Perform detailed research, analysis, evaluations, and tests. Very detail oriented—thorough and conscientious worker.

MAINTAINED TECHNICAL KNOWLEDGE FOR PRACTICES AND PROCEDURES: Extensive knowledge of Gun Computer Systems (GCS) and Electro-Optic Systems. Knowledge of emerging trends. Consistently strive to keep up to date on emerging technologies. Research new technologies and best practices; leverage knowledge to provide recommendations to take advantage of developments. Share developments and best practices with users. Currently providing direction and guidance to other technicians within the department.

EXPERIENCED TRAINER: Train Standard Operating Procedures (SOPs) to other technicians. Procedures included fabricating cables, setting dip switches, assembling/removing circuit cards, tech manual usage, meter skills, and connections using 400 Hertz (Hz) generators, and soldering techniques. In addition, provide training to vendors, engineers, and other technicians on the installation of Commercial Off-The-Shelf (COTS) equipment; serial port switch, backup batteries, UPS, power supplies, and how to connect portable chillers.

EXERCISE SOUND JUDGMENT: Handle unique issues not always covered in manuals and policy guidelines. Interpret and apply agency regulations, requirements, and practices to mitigate risk and promote quality assurance processes.

MAINTAIN SYSTEM CONFIGURATION AND RESOLVE HARDWARE/SOFTWARE INTEGRATION/INTEROPERABILITY PROBLEMS: Maintain configuration control of all software and hardware to ensure that the most current versions of software are available.

KEY ACCOMPLISHMENTS:

- Rework of Velocimeter resulted in significant cost savings for the navy and in developing a procedure to test units following repair.
- Developed watertight integrity procedures to protect against water intrusion aboard navy vessels for the Mark 5 Velocimeter.
- Received two On the Spot Awards.
- Recognized by management for the rapid completion of antenna repacking efforts at Tobyhanna, which made a positive difference in theater due to lack of antennas.
- Nominated for Employee of the Month, May 2008.

+++++++++

PROFESSIONAL LICENSES AND CERTIFICATES:

CompTIA Network Plus Certified N10-004 2009 Edition
Advanced Communications Continuing Education Certificate, Fiber Optic
Theory, 12/1999
Two Lean Rapid Improvement Events
Two 40-Hour Fiber Optic Training Certificates from KITCO

(continued)

(continued)

PERFORMANCE RATINGS, AWARDS, HONORS, AND RECOGNITIONS:
Exceeds Fully Successful, 1991, 1992, 1994, 1995, 1996, 1997, 1998, 1999
On the Spot Awards 5/98 and 12/98

OTHER INFORMATION: Secret Clearance

Summary

The PPP federal resume is even more complex to write than the competitive USAJOBS federal resume. You will have to really focus on two or three occupational series so that you can be flexible and so that the PPP human resources specialist can find positions for you within several series. This resume can be longer than the typical four- or five-page federal resume so that you can cover multiple skill sets. Good luck with the PPP federal application process. Be persevering and positive.

CHAPTER 26

Applying for a Federal Job with a Disability: Using the Schedule A Federal Hiring Authority

In Executive Order 12548 of July 26, 2010, President Obama established a hiring increase goal of 100,000 people with disabilities into the federal government over five years, including individuals with targeted disabilities.

"My administration is committed to ensuring people living with disabilities have fair access to jobs so they can contribute to our economy and realize their dreams," vowed President Barack Obama in his proclamation for October's special designation. "Individuals with disabilities are a vital and dynamic part of our Nation."

Schedule A is an excepted service hiring authority available to federal agencies to hire and/or to promote individuals with disabilities without competing for the job. Utilizing the Schedule A hiring authority to fill a vacancy allows federal agencies to avoid using the traditional, and sometimes lengthy, competitive hiring process.

Have positions been filled under Schedule A? Yes. EEOC's FY 2009 Annual Report states that as of September 30, 2009, the government employed 24,663 (0.88%) individuals with Targeted Disabilities (IWTD). This represents an increase of 236 employees over FY 2008 and a decrease of 479 employees since FY 2005. The participation rate for FY 2008 was 0.88% and for FY 2005 was 0.96%. Over the five-year period, the government had a net decrease of 0.08% in employees with targeted disabilities.

Which Agencies Employ People with Disabilities?

Following are the top 10 federal agencies using Schedule A over the period 2000–2009 (source: OPM's Central Personnel Data File [CPDF]). The numbers are the total new hires using Schedule A for the nine-year period. The breakdown is too small to mention per year—with the exception of SSA and Treasury, which both hired about 200 in 2009.

1. SSA: 791
2. Treasury: 696
3. VA: 579
4. Defense: 196

5. Air Force: 189
6. Army: 168
7. Navy: 129
8. USDA: 124
9. Interior: 117
10. HHS: 109

Applying Under Schedule A

Many job seekers with disabilities have heard about the hiring authority of Schedule A and wonder how they can take advantage of this hiring program. The person with a Schedule A letter can apply for jobs two ways or more:

- Applying through USAJOBS as a competitive candidate and putting your resume in the USAJOBS builder. Complete the application as directed in the announcement.

- Writing an e-mail directly to the Selective Placement Program Officer with your resume, a cover letter, and your Schedule A letter, to request a position in a certain occupation and grade. This request will be forwarded to managers who have positions that will be effective for a person with some accommodations.

Four Ways to Apply for a Federal Job as a Schedule A Applicant

You have several options as to how to apply using Schedule A. You can use any and all of the options to manage your federal job search campaign:

- Submit your application competitively for a position through USAJOBS (www.usajobs.gov), where approximately 20,000 federal jobs are posted daily. Identify yourself as disabled by checking off that you are authorized to be hired as person with a disability. Be prepared to build your resume if you have not already done so.

- Submit your application to USAJOBS without identifying yourself as disabled and compete for positions on your own merits with other federal job seekers.

- Directly contact a hiring manager you have identified at an agency where you want to be employed.

- Contact the Selective Placement Program Coordinator (SPPC) about particular openings; these hiring officials are on the lookout for talented employees who have disabilities. For a list of the coordinators, go to www.opm.gov/disability/SSPCoord.asp. For more on hiring through USAJOBS, go to www.usajobs.gov/individualswithdisabilities.asp.

Why Do I Need a Schedule A Letter?

In order to apply with the disabled status under the special hiring authority, job seekers must provide proof of a disability, and the Schedule A letter satisfies that requirement. The Schedule A letter confirming the disability should be signed by a licensed medical professional, state or private vocational rehabilitation specialist, or any government agency that issues or provides disability benefits. The letter often also notes your job readiness for the work you're seeking. Schedule A letters are submitted through USAJOBS and are given to other federal hiring authorities. You can see a sample Schedule A letter at the end of this chapter, and also at www.usajobs.gov/ individualswithdisabilities.asp. The letter should be brief and to the point, and not go into details about the nature of your disability. Focus on your skills and experience that will be relevant for that agency's mission and services.

What Does a Schedule A Application Include?

Whether you are applying through USAJOBS or you are sending your application through e-mail to a Selective Placement Officer or hiring manager, the application will be made up of these documents:

- Your own cover letter
- Schedule A letter
- Federal resume
- Transcript (if you are applying for positions with your education as a qualification)

You can upload the Schedule A letter, cover letter, and transcripts into USAJOBS or another resume builder and submit the resume into the USAJOBS resume builder. Or you can e-mail these documents separately as attached files to the SPPC.

Schedule A Application Tips

Here are the top tips for applying under Schedule A:

- **Know and emphasize your strengths.** It's your job to help a potential employer see your strong points and all you have to offer. Highlight strengths and previous accomplishments (not disabilities) throughout your campaign—in the cover letter, in your resume, in e-mail or phone interactions, and at the interview.

- **Study the job announcement and tailor your response to it.** In working with a job seeker who was recently hired, resume writer Carla Waskiewicz expanded the applicant's resume to include more keywords from the announcement and wrote a strong qualifications summary incorporating the core competencies this individual could deliver.

- **Network, network, network.** "This is the most crucial part of the campaign," says a successful Schedule A federal employee who was hired this year at a division of the Department of Health and Human Services. "When I started, I didn't know anyone at the division I targeted. But then I got an advocate. It just takes one." Find someone within an agency to watch out for openings for you.

- **To find contacts, look online for a department's organizational chart.** Chad located and studied organizational charts and department descriptions in two agencies. Then he used this info to figure out which departments and managers to contact. He got in touch with two departments. He received no response from one, but heard back from about five managers from the other. Then it was a matter of waiting for openings to come up. He points out that you may find a name on the chart and then have to work with how the agency's e-mail addresses are formulated to get the e-mail address.

- **Collect references from key people familiar with your strengths and talents.** They may be able to describe your strengths in ways you hadn't thought of. Remember to include persons involved in your volunteer or internship activities. Dave Warner, a disabled man who just started a new job at the National Institutes of Health, found that his volunteer activities were instrumental in getting interviews and finally a job offer. In fact, the federal job he landed was a step up from what he had originally sought.

- **Stay cutting edge with your skills and training.** A recent study found that employers can pass over resumes from the long-term unemployed, believing their skills and training will be out-of-date. Especially if you're unemployed, staying current will be important. If you're between jobs or want to advance, keep taking courses that could be relevant for you in your field, whatever it is—HR or budget or contracts, and so on.

- **Be realistic about what you can and cannot do.** I recently worked on a job search for Judy Mills, who was excellent with data management but had poor phone skills due to her disability. I located a position for Judy where phone work wasn't needed, and she was hired. Applying to do things you cannot do won't be good for you or the agency. Still, know that the federal agencies are willing to make "reasonable accommodations." This might include widening aisles for wheelchair access or providing special equipment, readers, or interpreters. Find more on special accommodations at www.usajobs.gov/ei/individualswithdisabilities.asp.

- **Consider hiring professionals to strengthen your resume and cover letter.** "I was sending out resumes and not getting any nibbles from federal employers," says Dave, recalling the days when he was job hunting on his own. But after his resume was revamped by the Resume Place, he got a series of interviews and was hired for a desirable job.

- **Practice your interviewing skills.** "It's like playing a sport," says Dave. "If you play the sport once, it won't result in the same improvement as when you do it regularly." This successful job seeker reports that he found himself performing better after having opportunities to volley replies back to interviewers.

- **Have the Placement Program Coordinator work as an advisor to an interested manager.** A manager who is considering hiring you may not fully understand Schedule A, Chad points out. The manager who selected him worked closely with the Placement Program Coordinator, who walked her through the process.

A Tip from a Selective Placement Program Coordinator (SPPC)

The Schedule A Hiring Authority is not a guaranteed entry into the federal government. Individuals with disabilities must meet minimum qualifications in order to qualify for a position. Most SPPCs perform this job as collateral duty, meaning they work full time at another job while simultaneously being an SPPC. Usually the other job takes precedence. SPPCs also receive many e-mails from applicants including attachments each week that can clog their inboxes. So do your homework before sending them an e-mail to make your efforts in becoming a federal employee count.

Try this: Send the SPPC a personal e-mail introducing yourself and *briefly* describe your skills and work experience so the SPPC will know what type of job you're looking for and can quickly figure out what you qualify for without going to the human resources office.

More importantly, make sure the SPPC you contact has a location near where you live, unless you are willing to relocate—keeping in mind that most agencies do not pay relocation costs. Also, visit the agency's website to see whether its mission—the nature of work performed—is of interest to you. If not, find an agency that has a mission similar to your interests and experience (unless you don't have a preference). Note that engaged employees are successful partly because they enjoy the nature of their work.

Finally, if you forget all that was mentioned above, remember this: *Don't rely on spell-check to proof your resume; have a friend or colleague read it before you submit it.* SPPCs are relied upon heavily to send hiring officials good, solid candidates, and if your resume has typos, there's no way it's going any further. So make it easy for your SPPC to work for you!

Pros and Cons of the Schedule A Process

Using the Schedule A process can sometimes work to the advantage of disabled job seekers. Through the special hiring authority based on disability, the manager who eventually hired Chad was not required to post the actual job opening he filled. He also did not have to go through the scoring process that is part of the competitive process. This can save time.

Still, in other cases, a hiring manager may be more likely to consider you when you apply competitively with the other candidates. This is why it's good to use all the approaches outlined at the beginning of this chapter.

Whichever approach you choose to go after federal employment, you'll need to learn to be patient. Chad's phone interview took place in the beginning of November 2009, but he didn't receive the job-offer call until February 2010. He adds that you should also be "persistent and consistent." After his winning interview, Chad asked the manager if he could e-mail her once a month to stay in contact. She agreed. "Don't let things go for several months," he advises. "Your resume could get lost in the system. The more your name is in front of the hiring manager, the more likely that you'll be hired. Follow up, and stay in touch with your contacts," he says. That's good advice that can pay off.

Community College Counselor Alice Hanson's Tips

Alice Hanson's career changed when she had a stroke. She is now working for a college and is a major advocate for students and job seekers with disabilities. Here are her own federal job search strategies:

- Identify some agencies you want to work for.
- Identify the GS level that the agency is looking for.
- Go to your DVR office and get a Schedule A that talks about your being disabled but is vague and emphasizes that you want to work.
- Contact the agency EEO office and ask how to apply with a Schedule A via that agency's preferred website (the staff probably won't know and will refer you to a local source).
- Call the local source and make yourself known.
- Apply for the job via the website. Be careful to click that you are disabled and answer all radio buttons pertaining to preferred status for being disabled. This means you are applying noncompetitively.
- Apply competitively (through USAJOBS) and noncompetitively (directly through e-mail and job fairs).
- Upload, e-mail, or fax your college transcripts and Schedule A. Most agencies like to have these documents before the job closes, but if you don't get them in before, they will ask for them once your resume gets beyond the first cut.

Networking and Knowing Your Agency—Chad's Story

I knew I had transferable skills, and I had 20-plus years of experience (16 with state government and 4.5 years with federal). I tried to locate what department was the closest to my knowledge base. They had no openings at the time but they knew of some openings coming about. But they did not know when and had to wait until they got the green light from personnel and hiring managers.

They liked my personality and work ethics, even though I don't have Medicaid policy background but dealt with Medicaid beneficiaries in the Vocational Rehabilitation world. They knew I could learn the system and had other pertinent transferable skills and would be an easier transition with training and support. I was also already in the federals system and could adapt to the coordination and implementation of CMS's legislative policies and procedures.

I researched the whole organizational chart because I needed to rule out how many departments my experience and background were fitted for. So I educated myself and became more aware of the departments' roles and duties. This way, I could reach out to as many managers as possible to get the communication going—because the more, the better. I kinda knew RSA from the Department of Education, but when it came to CMS I had to really research and see what departments were the best fit for me. It showed the managers that I took the time to learn about their departments. And they appreciated my desire to make a difference for them and their staff as an agency.

On a side note, I contacted numerous managers at the Social Security Administration (SSA) while pursuing CMS at the same time and not one manager responded (go figure). But that's their loss and this shows you that networking takes a lot of time; research to know the departments' roles, mission, and vision; and of course hope that someone would respond. CMS responded and I delivered!

The one thing to keep in mind is that I knew I would land somewhere because it's somewhat easier to network when you're already employed. So I'm building up the "army brigade" as I go along and I continue to network. You never know where the next new opportunity will take you.

Tips for Federal Job Search Strategies by Sandra Keppley

Sandra Keppley is a retired human resources manager from a Department of Defense agency. She has experience in assisting people with disabilities in finding quality career positions in government. These are her tips for federal job search strategies with the Schedule A letter:

1. Educate yourself regarding federal career options available to people with disabilities. Visit the website for the Office of Personnel Management (www.opm.gov/disability/) as well as the Department of Labor, Office of Disability Employment (www.dol.gov/odep/).
2. Know and understand the federal hiring process (see www.opm.gov/job_seekers/).
3. Utilize the Resume Place's prescribed "Ten Steps to Federal Employment" as a roadmap to success:
   - Step 1: Network
   - Step 2: Become Familiar with the Hiring Process
   - Step 3: Look for Openings on USAJOBS.gov
   - Step 4: Assess Your Soft Skills (Core Competencies)

- Step 5: Analyze Keywords in Announcements
- Step 6: Create Your Federal Resume—Preferably in the Outline Format
- Step 7: Write Your KSA Accomplishments for Your Resume and Essays (if they are requested) for Questionnaires
- Step 8: Apply for Jobs
- Step 9: Follow Up on Your Application
- Step 10: Interview for the Job

4. Seek the assistance of a professional who can assess your options relative to your specific skills, education, and goals. The Resume Place's website is an excellent resource in this regard; i.e., services, training, free resources, books, blogs, etc. (see www.resume-place.com/resources/).

5. Have a career strategy and be focused, persistent, and patient.

Sample Documents

We have compiled samples of each of the documents you will write for a direct campaign to a Selective Placement Officer or through the USAJOBS builder for a competitive position.

Sample Schedule A Letter

Your physician, state vocational rehabilitation counselor, or other counselor can write a Schedule A letter that will state that you have a disability. Letter writers do not have to give details of the specific disability. They can mention something good about you, if they like. Most of the time, they just make a statement about the disability.

To Whom It May Concern:

     This letter serves as certification that [name of individual] is a person with a severe disability that qualifies him/her for consideration under the Schedule A hiring authority.

[Name of individual] also is job ready and [is likely to succeed in performing the duties of the position he is seeking/is qualified to work in office setting, food service, call center, or warehouse, etc.].

You may contact me at:

Signature: _____   Date: _____

Figure 26.1: Sample Schedule A letter.

Paper Federal Resume E-mailed as Attached File to Agency Selective Placement Program Coordinator

The federal resume sample in Figure 26.2 will be sent by e-mail. It should be a Word file and formatted nicely for readability. The resume should focus on your most important skills for positions that you believe are the best for you.

You can find a list of Agency Selective Placement Program Coordinators (SPPC) at www.opm.gov/disability/SSPCoord.asp. Some of the e-mail addresses may be out-of-date, but you can write to most of them with this list.

JOHN WHEELER
5212 Street Drive
Waldorf, MD 20748
Mobile: (301) 333-3333
Email: jwheeler@aol.com

SSN: XXX-XX-XXXX
CITIZENSHIP: United States
Veterans' Preference: N/A
Schedule A Certified

OBJECTIVES:
Loan Specialist (Realty)
Housing Management Assistant
Public Housing
GS-7/9 objective

SPECIALIZED KNOWLEDGE
- Experienced Property Manager with expertise in family housing sales and leasing, property management, and customer care.
- Fair Housing, Public Housing Authority Policies.
- Negotiate and enforce lease agreements, collect rent, and prepare paperwork for lease termination; Equal Housing Opportunity policies and procedures.
- Interview applicants for financial information for rentals, loans, or leasing applications.
- Knowledge of public and assisted housing programs, to include Section 8 requirements and Affordable Housing Dwelling Unit Programs.
- Proficiently conduct research and analysis of real estate and property management issues to include the identification of production costs, market adjustments, cost containment measures, and plan alterations.

WORK EXPERIENCE

CUSTOMER SERVICE SPECIALIST, Office of Taxpayer Services, Real Property Services
District of Columbia Government, 1 Capital St., Washington, DC
3/09–Present (1 year and 1 month)
Hours: 40 hours/week
Salary: $58,135/year
Supervisor: Juan Rodriguez. Permission to contact.

Owner Realty Tax Customer Care and Outreach Services: Have contact with customers whose situations are more complex. This may include matters relating to individual taxpayers as well as tax practitioners and various agents, e.g., tax preparers, attorneys, property managers, or any representatives from professional associations and employees of other government agencies. Establish initial telephone contact of all incoming telephone calls within 2 minutes. ANALYZE, DETERMINE, AND RESOLVE tax processing problems and respond to taxpayer inquires ranging from tax delinquency to providing general information related to the preparation of tax returns.

Realty Tax Processing Services: Interpret regulations and policies for taxpayers. Use technical knowledge and best judgment in interpreting and applying state, local, and federal regulations and

(continued)

Figure 26.2: Sample paper federal resume e-mailed as an attached file.

(continued)

guidelines. For homeowners, assess problems as they arise and identify resolution approaches and resolve accordingly. Gather and organize information for inquires, or resolve problems referred by others.

Evaluate Incomplete Files: Analyze for shortfalls and reconstruct based on accumulated data and knowledge of file information. For the City Tax Department, recommend tax liens and/or notice of levy actions against taxpayers, and initiate other actions to resolve and adjust taxpayers' accounts.

Improve Processing Procedures: Based on analysis of results of applying guidelines, recommend changes. These changes may include suggesting specific changes to the guidelines themselves, the development of control mechanisms, additional training for employees, or specific guidance related to the procedural handling of documents and information.

Devise More Efficient Methods for Tax File Processing: Focus on customer-oriented practices that reduce taxpayer volume, enhance program performance, increase productivity, and improve the organization's overall effectiveness.

Administer Correspondence: Close all correspondence, including triage responsibilities, business tax registrations, offset, stop payment, undelivered checks, and transmittals assigned to manager's unit within 30 days. Use CTS software. Submit the weekly productivity report to management.

Accomplishment
Recognized for diligence and efficiency in resolving technical problems. Expertly use operational knowledge and carefully manage communication with customers who are often frustrated.

NEW HOME SALES CONSULTANT, PUBLIC HOUSING PROGRAM SPECIALIST
6/05–3/09
New Homes Company, 4090 Center Drive, City, VA.
Hours: 40+ hours/week
Salary: $15,000 base salary plus $100,000 commission
Supervisor: John Smith, (703) 333-3333. Permission to contact.

Site Manager: Managed two communities simultaneously under development. Served as first point of contact for the customers, ensuring seamless provision of service. Wrote and secured contracts with customers for the purchase of new homes. Supervised sales assistant and prepared commission statements.

Certified Buyers for Public Housing Program Through Accessory Dwelling Units (ADU) Program: Managed sale of lower-priced housing units that were integrated into existing neighborhood dwellings. Certified buyers under program and promoted sale of discounted units when appropriate. Reviewed official paperwork. Assisted customers with attending a first-time buyers' or renters' orientation and certified attendance.

Oversee Housing Construction: Coordinated with architects, interior designers, and upper management. Guided customers during the design, finish selections, and inspection phases of home-building process. Elicited design-and-build opinions and perspectives from prospective and actual buyers and relayed this information to design-and-build teams. Responded to customer inquiries regarding construction techniques, materials, and procedures. Monitored construction schedules and reported milestone achievement to clients and upper management. Resolved construction problems with appropriate stakeholders.

Site Inspector: Assessed condition of premises and arranged for necessary maintenance. Scheduled and assisted with preconstruction and any frame-orientation site visits with home buyers.

Customer Care: Maximized and strengthened customer relationships through understanding the customer's expectations and perceptions in building a home. Integrated customer design plans into the construction process and recommended any changes. Actively supported the customer needs.

Assisted with Financing Plans for Buyers: Assisted with securing financing and selecting designs. Prepared and executed conforming purchase agreements, necessary addenda, changes, and contract cancellations. Explained legal documents to prospects and homeowners. Qualified buyers for mortgages through financing.

Developed Work Schedules: Established and maintained tracking system for all incoming work assignments. Developed database for tracking backlog assignments. Oversaw, organized, scheduled, and coordinated construction activities. Formulated evaluation proposals that included the goals and scope of proposed projects.

Accomplishments
- Received an Excellent Performance Award in New Home Sales: $3,865,012.
- Received annual award in recognition of exceptional sales effort in 2007.

COMPUTER SKILLS
Microsoft Office, Windows, LDX, PBX, Microtech, AMSI, E-Site, ITS, Siebel

EDUCATION
Bachelor of Science, Business, with a Minor in Finance, University of Maryland University College, College Park, MD. Expected completion date: May 2011

The Principle and Practices of Real Estate & D.C. Housing Laws, Weichert Real Estate School, Washington, DC, 2005.

TRAINING
K. Hovnanian Contract, 2006
Purchaser Maintenances Action Log/Loan Status Report, 2006
Pre-Construction, 2006
Quality Standards Inspection Procedures, 2006
Warranty Procedures, 2006
Pre-Settlement Procedures, 2006
Negotiating Skills, 2006
Warranty & Construction, 2006
Fundamentals of Blueprint Reading, 2006
Contract Training, 2005
Construction Contract & Law, 2005
Customer Selection Sheet
Customer Change Order

Introductory Cover Letter for Special Emphasis Program Officer

The introductory letter can be written in the e-mail text or attached. This letter is very important and must describe your best knowledge, skills, and abilities for certain positions in their office. It should be upbeat, clear, and focused toward one or two federal occupational series so that the coordinator will see that you are professional, skilled, and determined to get attention as a quality candidate for a federal position. Figure 26.3 shows an example.

JOHN WHEELER
5212 Street Drive
Waldorf, MD 20748
Mobile: (301) 333-3333
Email: jwheeler@aol.com

Office of Human Resources
Ms. Kay Davis
Branch Chief, Special Emphasis Programs and Recruitment
451 7th Street, SW
Washington, DC 20410

Dear Ms. Davis,

I am submitting my federal resume and Schedule A Letter for consideration for positions that you have identified for Schedule A applicants. Please forward my resume to supervisors who may have positions for my qualifications, or hold my resume and cover letter until you find positions that are in these job series and grade levels. I am currently working and would be available for an interview and to come to work within two weeks.

I am qualified for the following positions at the GS-7/9 grade level:
* Loan Specialist (Realty), GS-1165
* Housing Management Assistant or Housing Program Specialist, GS-1101
* Contract Specialist (my degree is complete), GS-1102
* Office of Public Housing or other Housing Departments

My relevant qualifications include
* One year of experience with District of Columbia Realty Taxpayer services. Interpreted rules and regulations for taxpaying for homeowners. Improved administrative processing, resolved homeowner problems, and analyzed case cases.
* Five years of experience in new home sales for Public Housing Program through Accessory Dwelling Units (ADU) Program. Interpreted policies and procedures, interviewed buyers, and assisted with applications.

I would be an asset to your organization because
* I have 5 years of experience in public housing and customer communications.
* My ability to improve efficiency in administrative operations will benefit housing administration offices.
* Excellent communications, negotiation, and problem-solving skills with customers.
* Able to interpret complex policies, helping customers understand public programs and policies.

I would like to apply my public housing knowledge and experience, as well as administrative and customer services skills, in a position with HUD to improve housing for Americans. Thank you for your time and consideration.

Sincerely,

John Wheeler

Enclosures: Federal Resume, transcript, Schedule A Certificate

---

Figure 26.3: Sample introductory cover letter.

Introductory Cover Letter for Human Resources Specialist

Figure 26.4 is another cover letter introducing specialized experience for a federal position. The letter is very detailed so that the coordinator can see the specialized experience and skills quickly.

Nicolas J. Jones
1100 Sixth Street, NE
Washington, DC 20011
202-444-4444
nickjj@gmail.com

Office of Human Resources
Ms. Mary Smith
Branch Chief, Special Emphasis Programs and Recruitment
Center for Medicare and Medicaid Services, DHHS
451 7th Street, SW
Washington, DC 20410

Dear Ms. Smith,

I am submitting my federal resume and Schedule A Letter for consideration for positions that you have identified for Schedule A applicants. Please forward my resume to supervisors who may have positions for my qualifications, or hold my resume and cover letter until you find positions that are in these job series and grade levels. I am currently working and would be available for an interview and to come to work within two weeks.

I am qualified for the following positions at the 5/7/9/11 grade level:
- Human Resources Specialist, GS-0201
- Human Resources Technician/Assistant, GS-203

My relevant qualifications include
- One-plus year of experience as a career consultant, Gallaudet University, designing, developing, and implementing training strategies. Routinely apply human resources development training principles and techniques. Outstanding communication, collaboration, and consultation skill demonstrated, in part, through presentation of formal training and workshops.
- Six months as a senior vocational rehabilitation counselor, Florida Department of Education, managing, training, and assisting clients.
- Seven years as fingerprint technician within both correctional and police institutions.
- 18 months as case manager for the deaf and hard of hearing within the Center for Behavioral Health. Responsible for behavioral health case management, training development and deployment, and office services support.
- Attained Master of Arts Degree, 5/2008. Major: Rehabilitation Counseling. GPA: 3.97 out of 4.0.

I would be an asset to your organization because of the following:
- Experienced professional within the fields of career counseling, special emphasis and diversity, and vocational rehabilitation.
- Extensive knowledge of employment and disability federal, state, and local laws. Innovative with projects and solutions.
- Proficient in identification of training needs, development of training, and deployment. Outstanding interpersonal skills, to include collaboration and networking to achieve optimum program and individual results.
- Proficient in computer software applications and databases, such as Microsoft Word, Outlook, PowerPoint, Access, and Excel.
- Skilled in utilizing automated tools to monitor, evaluate, and market training programs and projects.

I would like to apply my human resources and general administration knowledge and experience, as well as my education specializing in rehabilitation counseling, in a position within your agency to support your organizational goals and objectives.

Thank you for your time and consideration.

Sincerely,

Nick Pezzarosi

Enclosures: Federal Resume, transcript, Schedule A Certificate

---

Figure 26.4: Detailed introductory cover letter.

Summary

Job seekers with disabilities can land a federal job, but it takes perseverance, marketing, networking, and writing on-target resumes and cover letters. Multiple methods can result in interviews, referrals, and activities of interest toward a federal job. You can apply with or without using the Schedule A Hiring Authority. It might take time to get referred and set up interviews, but it can happen. Try contacting a hiring official or Selective Placement Program Coordinator in an agency that has a location near you.

Part 7

Interviewing for Federal Jobs

Chapter 27: Preparing for a Structured, Behavior-Based Interview

Preparing for a Structured, Behavior-Based Interview

Congratulations—you have been selected for an interview! This is the point in the process when managers and human resource professionals select their best candidate. To increase your chances of success, you'll first need to do some preparation, including understanding different interviewing styles and typical questions you might encounter. In this chapter, we focus on the most common type of interview—and the one that requires the most preparation—the structured, behavior-based interview.

Types of Interviews

Interviews may be conducted in person, over the phone, or via the Internet on Skype on some occasions. Any of these types of interviews may include an interview panel (more than one interviewer) in addition to, or in place of, one-on-one interviews.

Interview methods may fall into one of these two formats. The most common interviewing methods include

- Structured behavior-based interviews
- Preliminary screening interview

The federal job interview calls for serious preparation on your part because you are required to provide examples of your experience from your past performance. Examples aren't always easy to think of on the spot, so it's best not to go in cold and try to "wing it."

When you are contacted for the interview, the human resources specialist will likely tell you about the interview. The most typical interview scenario is a 45-minute interview with seven to ten structured questions that will be given to each interviewee. Usually you are given the questions at the interview, either read to you or given to you on paper. Sometimes, you will get the questions ten minutes before the interview starts. The job-related, behavior-based questions will be based on the top skills required in the position. (You can study the vacancy announcement to try to determine what questions could be asked during the interview.)

If the person contacting you about the interview does not say anything about how the interview will be conducted, it is appropriate for you to request information regarding the interview type and method.

Let's look at brief definitions of both interview formats that are typically used by federal human resources specialists and hiring managers.

Structured, Behavior-Based Interviews

In the report "The Federal Selection Interview: Unrealized Potential" (published in February 2003), researchers at the U.S. Merit Systems Protection Board defined structured interviews as "interviews that use multiple mechanisms, such as questions based on job analysis, detailed rating scales, and trained interviewers to make the interview more job-related and systematic."

The interview is structured in that the same questions are asked of each candidate. There is a rating scale for your answers, usually from 1 to 5, and your answers will be scored while you are speaking. There is usually no dialogue or prompting from the interviewers while you are talking. The 1.5- to 2-minute answer time will be all yours. You have the floor. Do not expect help from the interviewers if you are stuck on an answer. That's why you have to prepare your answers and practice before the interview, so you don't forget important details in your accomplishment, for example.

A behavioral interview involves questions that are specific and situational in nature. In other words, these questions attempt to determine how applicants will react to certain situations or how they have done so in the past. Behavioral interviews are designed to forecast your future behavior on the job based on your past behaviors.

A behavioral interview can also be competency based. Interviewers can ask questions about the top competencies that will be required in this position.

Preliminary Screening Interviews

A preliminary screening interview could carried out by the human resources specialist before you talk to the hiring manager. The screening interview is usually done to ensure that you are still interested in the position and still available. These screening interviews can come any time of day, so answer your cell phone or have a professional message on your cell so that you can call back. The HR specialist *will* leave a message. If the HR specialist calls at an inappropriate time, you can ask whether you can call right back or set up a time very soon to answer the preliminary questions. This format is usually short (15 minutes or less) and includes a few questions that may cover a variety of topics related to skills, competencies, experience, and credentials for the position. This format is informal and is usually by phone, and then can turn into a possible structured interview with a hiring manager. The preliminary screening interview by HR does not mean that you will be guaranteed to be invited to a job interview with the hiring manager. HR is screening and determining who to interview.

Screening interviews may also include many questions that could easily be answered with a "yes" or "no." Resist that temptation! If you are asked a seemingly "yes/no" question such as "Are you proficient in Excel?" follow your "yes" reply with the number of years you have used Excel and include a statement of your level of expertise.

Here are some examples of general questions you may be asked:

- **Why are you interested in this position?** A good answer would mention that you are interested in the mission of the office, or that you would like to contribute to services to the customers of this office—something that includes some passion for the office or program. Do not mention that you want a stable position with great benefits (even if you do).

- **What do you know about our organization?** A good answer would have something to do with the mission of the organization, which you should have memorized before the interview.

The more you know about the organization, the more impressed they will be with your genuine interest in the position.

- **What are your goals?** Where do you see yourself in five years? A good answer would be that you would like to be working in this agency, providing excellent services to its customers; that you would like to perform this first job to the best of your ability and work toward promotions and continued excellent service in the agency. Do not mention that this position is a stepping stone to career advancement in some other agency.

- **What are your strengths and weaknesses?** A good answer would be two or three major strengths, which should include customer services. A weakness would be one that is correctable in an office. If you do have a real weakness that is really bad, do not use this weakness. Think of one that is only slightly weak and is correctible.

- **Why would you like to work for this organization?** A good answer would reflect the valuable mission that this organization provides to its customers. Look up the mission and really reflect on why you would like to contribute to it. Be genuine.

- **What is your most significant achievement?** A good answer would be a sincere answer about your most significant achievement—preferably work related, but it could also be education related. Do not include vacations, sports, or politics here. Prepare this answer ahead of time.

- **How would your last boss and colleagues describe you?** You can ask your current or last boss and colleagues how they would describe you (favorably), and memorize those answers. You could quote them.

- **Why should we hire you?** A good answer would be a sincere list of three important reasons the agency should hire you. Be prepared to give your best skills that match the position. List them off clearly and with compassion and positive attitude. You are advocating for yourself here.

Open-Ended and Behavioral Questions

For insight into the reasons behind behavior-based questions, read the following excerpt about open-ended and behavioral questions from the U.S. Merit Systems Protection Board report titled "The Federal Selection Interview: Unrealized Potential," which was published in February 2003). You can read its other reports about federal hiring and assessment processes at www.mspb.gov.

FOR THE SUPERVISORS: Ask effective questions. As we've indicated, effective interview questions are based on job analysis to ensure that they are job-related. Effective interview questions are also usually open-ended and behavioral so that they will elicit useful responses.

APPLICANT INSIGHT: Open-ended questions are questions that require the candidate to provide details, and cannot be answered in one word (such as "yes" or "excellent"). Such questions are much more effective than closed-ended questions at developing insight into a candidate's experience and abilities.

For example, the closed-ended question "Can you write effectively?" can be answered with an uninformative "Yes"—a response that sheds little light on the candidate's level of performance in this area.

An open-ended question, such as "Describe the types of documents you have written, reviewed, or edited," requires the candidate to provide specifics and provides much more insight into the candidate's writing accomplishments.

There is a place for the closed-ended question. For example, to learn whether a candidate is willing to travel frequently or can start work on a given date, it is perfectly appropriate to ask a closed-ended question.

Behavioral questions are just that: questions that ask the candidate to describe behaviors—responses, actions, and accomplishments—in actual situations. The case for the behavioral question is more subtle than the case for open-ended questions. Although research indicates that both behavioral questions ("What did you do?") and hypothetical questions ("What would you do?") can be effective, many researchers and practitioners generally recommend the behavioral question for two reasons. First, behavioral questions can provide greater insight into how the candidate will perform on the job, because the best predictor of future behavior is past behavior. Second, behavioral questions may be more reliable than hypothetical questions. Because the response can be verified through reference checks or other means, it is more difficult to fabricate an inaccurate or untruthful answer to a behavioral question than to a hypothetical one.

Preparation for the Structured, Behavior-Based Interview

Behavior-based, or behavioral, interviewing is the structured, practical interviewing approach that many federal agencies have formally adopted as a best practice. In a behavior-based interview, you will be asked to describe past experiences that demonstrate your competencies as related to the available position(s).

Take some time to think of examples from your past experiences that demonstrate skills needed for the job you are seeking. You can get an idea of the competencies or skills being sought by looking at the keywords in the announcement or by going to the agency's website and searching for its organizational competencies.

For example, you might be asked for a past work situation in which you demonstrated such competencies as attention to detail, teamwork, effective communication skills, or problem solving. Making the logical link from demonstrated past competencies to skills needed on the new job is what behavior-based interviewing is all about.

Pull your examples primarily from paid work experience relevant to the positions you'll be interviewing for, but don't hesitate to look for examples from other areas of your background, such as education or volunteer experiences, as long as they demonstrate relevant competencies.

Formula for Behavior-Based Questions

Federal hiring managers use the JOBS formula for behavior-based interview questions:

J   Job-Related

O   Open-Ended

B   Behavioral-Based

S   Skill- and Competency-Based

Sample Competency-Based Interview Questions

Let's look at typical competencies federal hiring managers are seeking in the best candidate and some questions they might ask to explore those competencies. As you review these, think about your own experience and start compiling examples you have to demonstrate these skill sets.

- **Attention to Detail:** Describe a project you have worked on that required a high level of attention to detail.
- **Communication:** Tell me about a time when you had to communicate with others, such as coworkers or customers, under difficult circumstances.
- **Conflict Management:** Describe a situation in which you found yourself working with someone who didn't like you. How did you handle it?
- **Customer Service:** Discuss a situation in which you demonstrated highly effective customer service.
- **Decisiveness:** Tell me about a time when you had to stand up for a decision you made even though it made you unpopular.
- **Leadership:** Describe a time when you led a project that required establishing an agenda and plan of action. How did you lead this project?
- **Planning, Organizing, and Goal Setting:** Describe a time when you had to complete multiple tasks. How did you prioritize and manage your time?
- **Presentation:** Tell me about a time when you developed a lesson, training, or briefing and presented it to a group.
- **Problem Solving:** Describe a time when you analyzed data to determine multiple solutions to a problem. What steps did you take?
- **Resource Management:** Describe a situation in which you capitalized on an employee's skills.
- **Teamwork:** Tell me about a time when you had to deal with a team member who was not pulling his or her own weight.

More Examples of Behavior-Based Questions

Here are some more behavior–based questions to get you thinking:
- Describe a time when you led a change in your organization.
- Tell me how you work as a member or leader of a team.
- When have you had to be adaptable in your job and how did you do it?
- Describe a customer service situation that was challenging.
- Tell me about a time when you were under pressure to be more productive. How did you change your work methods?

A Step-by-Step Approach to Preparing for a Behavior-Based Interview

Now that you have an idea of how a behavioral interview sounds, you're ready to start preparing for your own. Generally, your preparation will involve reviewing the job announcement, preparing to answer typical questions, practicing, and more practicing.

Specifically, there are six steps to follow to prepare for your interview. These steps, as outlined below, are based on a curriculum taught at federal agencies throughout the United States to prepare employees for better interview performance. I also used this formula to coach individuals for interviews. Applicants frequently report that they were well prepared, confident, and felt like they "knew the job" as a result of following these steps.

Step 1: Analyze the Job Duties Line by Line

Locate the job announcement of the position for which you'll be interviewing, or any other job description you've been provided with, and analyze each sentence in the Duties section (see Chapter 12, "Understanding Vacancy Announcements," for more on finding and analyzing vacancy announcements). Be sure to save any announcement for which you apply! Job announcements are taken off the Internet after the open period has closed.

Note the bold text in the announcement sample that follows; this is an example of key language to pay special attention to for potential interview questions. Start thinking about how your experience and skills relate to these job criteria, and jot down examples from your background to provide evidence of experience in these areas. There will be a very strong chance that the interview questions would support the top-level skills needed in this position.

Job Title: Supply Systems Analyst

Agency: Defense Logistics Agency

Salary Range: $35,452.00—$81,747.00/year

Series & Grade: GS-2003-7/9/11 to 12/13

Location: Defense Energy Support Center, Facility & Distribution Commodity Business Unit, Optimization Division, (DESC-FL)/Fort Belvoir, VA

Duties: Continually performs **analysis of existing fuel storage and distribution systems** throughout **the world** from original acquisition to final shipment to customers in order to determine the total cost of the system as well as strengths and weaknesses.

Knowledge of and experience in working with various **DoD fuel-supply systems** (product refineries, fuel storage terminal, fuel distribution systems and procedures) and military customer locations and product requirements.

Performs detailed **economic and cost/benefits analyses** in order to conduct studies of DoD fuel logistics operations and programs.

Factors analyzed include, but are not limited to, transportation cost, customer consumption quantities, economic order quantities, inventory-level requirements, facilities costs (both recurring and those requiring amortization), and risk of system failure.

Evaluates potential alternatives to current fuel storage and distribution systems to determine whether they justify detailed analysis.

Alternatives may be provided by the senior supply systems analyst, but may also be developed by the incumbent.

Step 2: Be Prepared; Write and Give Examples of Skills and Competencies

Your behavior-based "stories" are essentially the same as the CCAR stories you develop for your resume accomplishment statements and questionnaire essay answers. (See Chapter 9, "KSAs in the

Application: Presenting Your Accomplishments," for more on developing CCAR stories.) Review these stories to prepare yourself for a behavior-based interview. As Chapter 9 describes, a bulleted list format is especially helpful in preparing for an interview. In the interview, talk about these examples with animation and enthusiasm, and they will demonstrate your past performance in a positive way.

Make sure that you have written at least five stories to prepare for your interview, using examples that are related to the criteria you have analyzed in the job announcement. Then turn each of your KSAs or interview stories into seven or eight talking points that make it easier to practice and memorize your stories. It is important to practice speaking your interview stories so that you will be fluent in and easily remember your best examples.

Be sure to give your story a title to make it easier to remember. Story names should be interesting and descriptive, such as these:

> Saved USACE $20 Million
>
> Discovered Missing Funds
>
> Designed New Database, Saving Time
>
> Led Team Under Tight Deadline
>
> Supervised Team During a Huge Transition

The following exercise helps you develop interview answers for behavior-based questions that could be asked during an interview.

Title of Your Story: _____

Your Interview Story:

_____

_____

_____

Context:

_____

_____

Challenge:

_____

Actions:

_____

_____

_____

Result:

_____

_____

_____

Review Chapter 8, "Researching the Agency's Core Competencies," to find two to three competencies that are demonstrated by this example. List them here:

_____

_____

_____

Step 3: Study the Structured Interview Scoring System Used by Interviewers

Nearly all federal interviews are structured interviews, meaning that the interviewers are trained, the questions are determined in advance (based on competencies), and each candidate is asked the same questions. A structured interview is used so it can be objective, enabling the interviewer to score each interview and compare the performance/response of one candidate to that of another.

The following interview scoring system is an example of what an interviewer will follow in order to grade your answers to interview questions. As you can see here, you will get a top score of five points if your example of interpersonal skills demonstrates that you can communicate controversial findings in a challenging situation. The more detailed and accomplishment-driven your examples are (as they relate to the competency), the better chance you have of receiving a higher score.

Competency: Interpersonal Skills

Definition: Shows understanding, courtesy, tact, empathy, concern; develops and maintains relationships; may deal with people who are difficult, hostile, distressed; relates well to people from varied backgrounds and situations; is sensitive to individual differences.

Lead question: Describe a situation in which you had to deal with people who were upset about a problem.

Probes:

- What events led up to this situation?
- Who was involved?
- What specific actions did you take?
- What was the outcome or result?

Benchmark Level	Level Definition	Level Examples
5	Establishes and maintains ongoing working relationships with management, other employees, internal or external stakeholders, or customers. Remains courteous when discussing information or eliciting highly sensitive or controversial information	Presents controversial findings tactfully to irate organization senior management officials regarding shortcomings of a newly installed computer system, software programs, and associated equipment.

(continued)

(continued)

Benchmark Level	Level Definition	Level Examples
	from people who are reluctant to give it. Effectively handles situations involving a high degree of tension or discomfort involving people who are demonstrating a high degree of hostility or distress.	
4		Mediates disputes concerning system design/architecture, the nature and capacity of data management systems, system resources allocations, or other equally controversial/sensitive matters.
3	Cooperates and works well with management, other employees, or customers on short-term assignments. Remains courteous when discussing information or eliciting moderately sensitive or controversial information from people who are hesitant to give it. Effectively handles situations involving a moderate degree of tension or discomfort involving people who are demonstrating a moderate degree of hostility or distress.	Courteously and tactfully delivers effective instruction to frustrated customers. Provides technical advice to customers and the public on various types of IT, such as communication or security systems, data management procedures or analysis, software engineering, or Web development.
2		Familiarizes new employees with administrative procedures and office systems.
1	Cooperates and works well with management, other employees, or customers during brief interactions. Remains courteous when discussing information or eliciting nonsensitive or noncontroversial information from people who are willing to give it. Effectively handles situations involving little or no tension, discomfort, hostility, or distress.	Responds courteously to customers' general inquiries. Greets and assists visitors attending a meeting within own organization.

Source: United States Office of Personnel Management

Step 4: Research the Agency and Office to Learn the Latest News and Challenges

Research the agency and office carefully. Print pages from their websites. Find and memorize their mission. Discover who their customers are. Try to research any new challenges or changes occurring in the office or agency.

Step 5: Plan and Practice

Don't cut corners! Take the time to prepare properly by following these guidelines:

- Try to find out which kind of interview to expect. Will it be a structured behavioral with a panel or one hiring manager? Ask the HR specialist who is scheduling the interview so that you can know before you get there.

- Remember that nothing will make you look worse than not knowing what you put on your own resume. Study your resume carefully and be able to speak about it knowledgably. Read the KSAs and Questionnaire before you begin the interview. Take a few copies of your resume to the meeting.

  If you found an awesome report online about the mission, strategic plan, program, or budget, you can print it and take it to the interview. The HR specialist will be impressed that you found the document online and are reading these documents ahead of the interview. It will also help you learn about the job.

- Check out the website of the agency you're interviewing with and conduct research on its size, services, products, key leadership, and more. This is mandatory and is usually one of the interview questions. If you don't know the mission, you probably will not get hired.

- It's okay to take a few notes during the interview. Since the interviewers will be asking questions, feel free to take notes so that you don't forget the questions. Stay focused and relevant with your answers. Frequently interviewees start rambling and don't answer the questions. This is an immediate zero, or close to it, on your score.

- If the interviewers yawn, slouch, look dazed, nod off to sleep, or start texting, begin to wrap up your answer or say something interesting that will get their attention back on your answer and you. You can change your voice, smile, or get their attention in some way. Be aware that you are probably giving too many details and they are truly bored.

- Study the job announcement duties and qualifications sections line by line to identify the keywords and competencies you will want to gear your examples toward. You can prepare your top list of seven questions that HR might ask. You don't know what they will ask; you can only study the announcement and make educated guesses.

- Prepare a one-minute response to the "tell me about yourself" question. They may or may not ask this question; but just in case, prepare your answer. Keep the one-minute speech relevant to the job, work experience, and education. Do not mention your health, children, anything negative at all about anything, or politics.

- Write at least five success stories to answer behavioral interview questions. Memorize your stories. You will definitely be talking about your accomplishments in the interview. Practice these and time your answers to under two minutes. Use variation in your voice to sound positive and enthusiastic. Practice.

- Be likeable. The federal agencies are interested in you for your knowledge and specialized expertise, but they also will be working with you for a long time. They need to like you and want to see you every day and work with you. So, smile and be friendly and likeable so that they will *want* to work with you and see you again.

- Have three questions prepared for you to ask the interviewer at the end. He or she will ask you if you have any questions. Good questions will have to do with the position, the mission, the customers, and the challenges of the job. Don't ask about salary, benefits, supervisor, your office, or travel at this time. You can ask these questions of the HR specialist later.

- Practice with a recorder or video camera if you can. Listen to your voice. Watch your body language. If recording is not an option, consider practicing in front of a mirror or with a friend who can offer constructive feedback. This is a critical step for success. The structured interview is very challenging, and you must practice to feel confident in the interview.

- Prepare a list of references that might consist of former managers, professors, major clients, or people who know you through community service. Contact these people to get their permission for inclusion on the list. You also want them to be aware of the types of positions you're seeking and provide them with a copy of your resume so that they'll be prepared to praise you in a way that's relevant to the employer.

Step 6: Be Confident

Here are tips to consider before the interview:

- As you prepare to leave for the interview, make sure to take a printed copy of your reference list, paper and pen for note taking, and directions to the interview site.

- Arrive an hour early for your interview. You should ask if there will be security to get through for the interview. Make sure you take your ID.

- Stand and greet your interviewer with a firm handshake, looking him or her in the eyes.

- During the interview, be conscious of your body language and eye contact. Crossed arms make you appear defensive, fidgeting may be construed as nervousness, and lack of eye contact may be interpreted as being untrustworthy. Instead, nod while listening to show you are attentive and alert. And most importantly, do not slouch. Lean forward toward the desk or table if you can.

- Do not complain about your last employer or anything else, not even the weather or the traffic.

- End the interview on a confident note, indicating that you feel you are a good fit for the position at hand and can make a contribution. Emphasize your interest in the position and ask about the next step, as most offers are not extended on the spot.

- Thank the interviewer and ask for a business card so that you'll have the necessary contact information for follow-up.

After all interviews, promptly and carefully write a short e-mail of thanks to the interviewers for their time and to remind them of the valuable qualifications you bring to the job. Either way, don't miss this last chance to market yourself and highlight your skills relevant to the position.

If you do not hear anything from the HR specialist within two to four weeks of the interview, you can contact the HR specialist and ask where he or she is in the interview/hiring process.

Summary

Congratulations! You are much closer to achieving your next career position with the federal government. If you have prepared for the interview by analyzing the job, mission, and agency carefully and by practicing your interview stories and answers, you just might find yourself receiving a job offer!

Epilogue

This book is a compilation of all the most recent federal job search knowledge, strategies, and lessons I've learned during my 30 years of training federal employees in getting promoted and advising federal job seekers on their searches. If you have success with your search and land a federal position, please write to me at kathryn@resume-place.com to share your success!

—Kathryn K. Troutman, author

Index

Your federal resume can look as good as the samples in this book!

FEDERAL RESUME WRITING SERVICES—Your federal resume is your most important federal career document. After you read this book and look at the samples, consider the professional services of expert federal career consultants and federal resume writers

CERTIFIED FEDERAL RESUME WRITERS AND THE OUTLINE FORMAT—Our signature Outline Format designed by Kathryn Troutman is preferred by federal human resources specialists, because they can easily find the information they are seeking.

FEDERAL CAREER CONSULTING—Advice and recommendations on federal positions and occupational standards to match your experience, education, and specialized knowledge. Get the latest up-to-date strategies how to market your past experience into new careers in government.

SENIOR EXECUTIVE SERVICES ECQs—Our expert SES writers and consultants can help not only make your decision about pursuing an SES position but also in developing the best possible ECQs for your application.

From the Foreword :

"So – what's the savvy job applicant to do? Clearly, they will need to do their homework and pay close attention to the relevant details about the job and the application process contained in the announcement for each federal job in which they are interested. Simply submitting the same boiler-plate resume and cover letter to every job one sees is not going to be nearly as successful as a carefully tailored response that speaks to the specifics of each job.

… **Kathryn Troutman** has literally made a career out of understanding and tracking the evolution of the federal hiring system and translating that understanding into practical advice for the job seeker."

John Palguta
Vice President of Policy
Partnership for Public Service

More Information: www.resume-place.com
(888) 480-8265

Free federal career info!   >> Visit www.resume-place.com/resources

- Free webinars about federal resume and federal career consulting services
- Free webinars on Hiring Reform and how it will affect your federal job search
- Free KSA, Federal Resume, and Cover Letter Builders
- Register for our informative newsletter to receive up-to-the minute federal job search info
- Federal job search news articles, updated daily

The
Resume Place

Brought to you by:

Kathryn Troutman
Author, Federal Resume Guidebook
President and Founder of The Resume Place, Inc.
The Leading Federal Career Consulting and
Federal Resume Writing Firm in America

Resume Place Federal Resume Sample Database™

From ten of Kathryn Troutman's federal resume writing books and CD-ROMs, review samples of the best federal resumes to develop your own first draft and federal resume. Includes samples for over 50 occupational series and grades.

Over 400 outstanding, successful samples of federal resumes and KSAs from the following publications:
- Federal Resume Guidebook, 4th & 5th Editions
- Ten Steps to a Federal Job, 2nd & 3rd Editions
- Student's Federal Career Guide
- Jobseeker Guide, 3rd & 4th Editions
- Electronic Federal Resume Guidebook, 1st Edition
- Military to Federal Career Guide, 1st & 2nd Editions

License fee: $45.00 for a one year individual license.
Multi-user licenses are also available for military bases, federal agencies, universities, and career centers.

www.resume-place.com/certification-programs/online-federal-resume-database/

Expert federal career training resources for every need: jobseekers, federal agencies, military bases, career counselors, and conferences.

TEN STEPS TO A FEDERAL JOB WORKSHOP—In-person class in Catonsville, MD and webinars throughout the world.
Visit www.resume-place.com/training

CERTIFIED FEDERAL JOB SEARCH TRAINER PROGRAM—The only train the trainer program in government on federal job search, human resources hiring practices and programs, and license to teach Ten Steps to a Federal Job to your employees and audiences.

GOVERNMENT FEDERAL CAREER TRAINING—Leading federal career trainers and federal resume training throughout the government in the US and Europe. We are on the GSA Schedule.

CONFERENCE AND KEYNOTE SPEAKER—Kathryn Troutman speaks to government and professional associations and conference each year on federal careers, leadership accomplishments and entrepreneurial skills.

More information:
Email us at straining@resume-place.com
or visit our website at www.resume-place.com

FEDERAL CAREER Training Institute

Kathryn Troutman President